Tan Ping

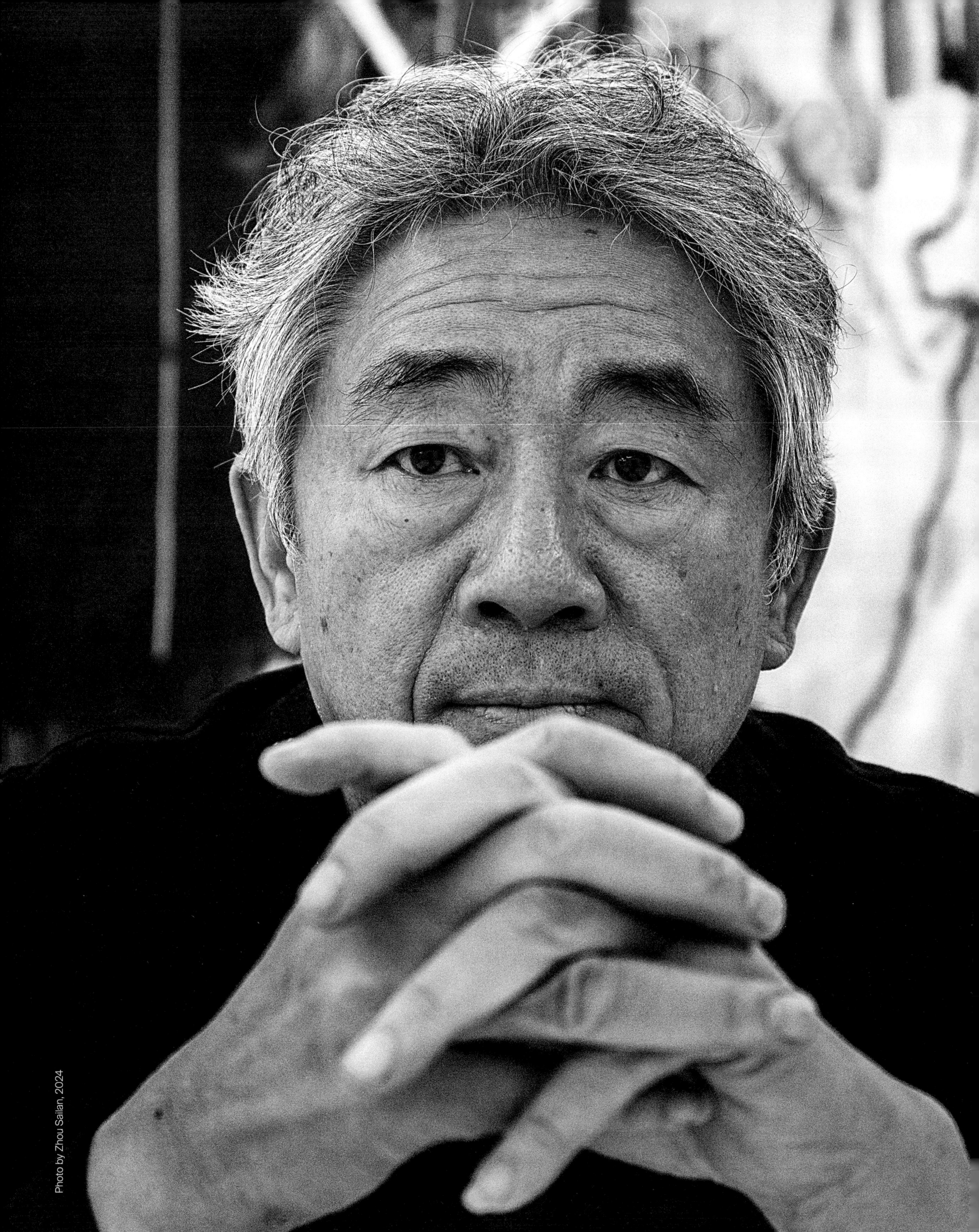
Photo by Zhou Sailan, 2024

Tan Ping
Body of Abstraction

Editor / **Herausgeber**
Beate Reifenscheid

SilvanaEditoriale

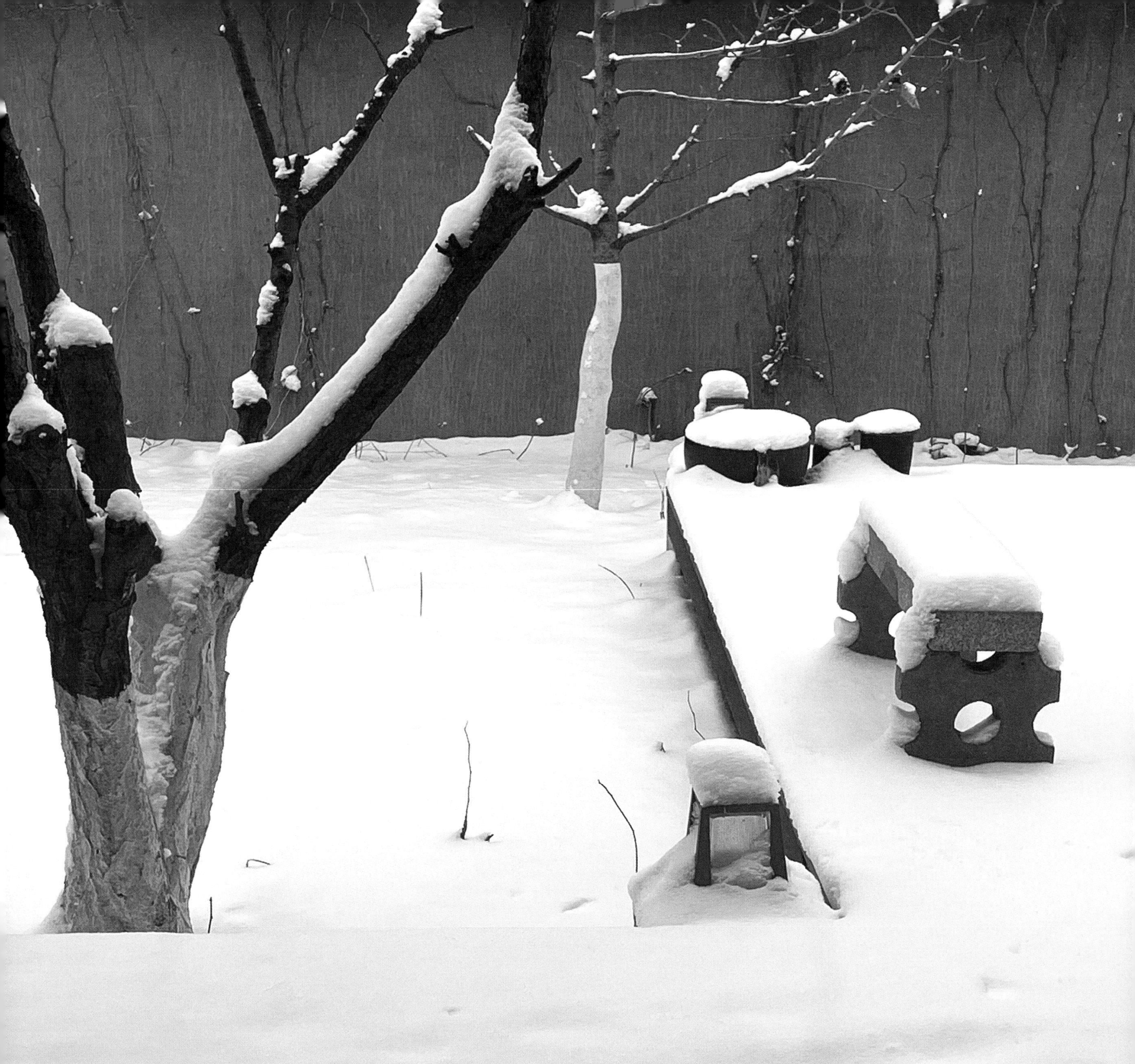

Contents
Inhalt

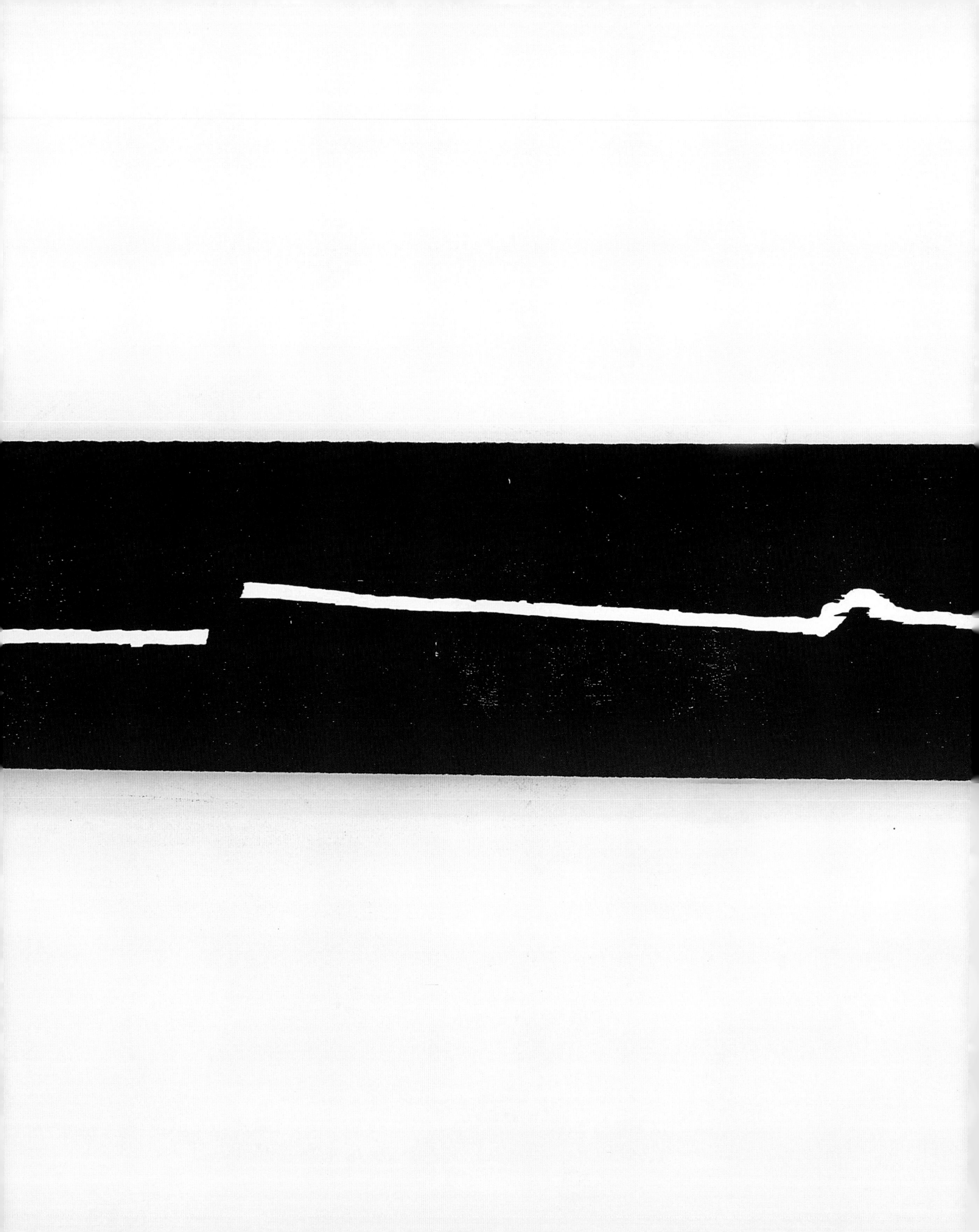

+40m (partial view / **Ausschnitt**),
2012
mixed media / **Mischtechnik**,
20×4000cm
Collection of National Art Museum
of China, Beijing, China

The line

Tan Ping's Multi-Perspective Concept

'My artistic development is closely linked to my experiences in Beijing and Berlin. The artistic education I received in China gave me a solid foundation and a deep understanding of Chinese culture and its dynamics within society. In contrast, the training in Germany broadened my artistic perspective and awakened a latent sense of freedom in me. For me, art is a process of self-realisation that requires constant exploration and personal discovery.'

Tan Ping[1]

There is no doubt that Tan Ping belongs to the generation of artists who played a decisive role in the reorientation of Chinese art after the opening of China in the 1980s. As one of the first to leave China to study abroad, a DAAD scholarship enabled him to come to Germany in 1989. His departure to Germany was also a significant date in political terms, as the wall between East and West Germany fell on 9 November 1989 and the Iron Curtain that had shielded many Eastern Bloc countries had already gradually collapsed. This gave millions of people a previously unknown feeling of freedom and new opportunities. The spirit of optimism and elation was enormous in the early years. Artists from China and other former Eastern Bloc countries, including the former USSR (now Russia), had to completely reorient themselves in two respects and leave the familiar behind. This was both a great challenge

and a special opportunity. Not all of them were able to really establish themselves in the other culture and develop their own linguistic canon. In Tan Ping's case, however, things seem to have changed quickly. His early works convey the classic style of academic training based on Russian and Chinese models: on the one hand, they are linked to socialist realism, although already interpreted much more freely, and on the other to the Chinese tradition, which is deeply rooted in ink painting. It was this academic 'armoury' with which he came to Germany, where he encountered a variety of styles and expressive possibilities that were largely unknown to him. It soon became clear that he was moving away from figurative painting – whether Russian or Western in character - and was clearly developing his turn towards abstraction from the tradition of Chinese calligraphy and ink painting. His daring reinterpretations were soon astonishing.

However, if we first look back and visualise what ink painting in China is all about, the comparison between composition and gesture, which asserts a very different attitude in Western culture, also becomes clear. While European art up to the end of the 19th century was based on the principles of compositional structures and a largely fixed iconographic canon, Chinese compositions were created from an approach based on a relatively rigid principle of tradition (the pupil copies the master until he surpasses him) and less emphasis on the individual gesture. This is already evident in calligraphy, which consistently plays a prominent role in Chinese art, as it is read and understood as both writing (text) and image (narrative context). The distinction between the two pictorial concepts (in the West and in Asia) is so important because they fundamentally contradict each other, even if the figurative compositions in both hemispheres appear to be more closely related.

Die Linie

Tan Pings multiperspektivisches Konzept

„Meine künstlerische Entwicklung ist eng mit meinen Erfahrungen in Peking und Berlin verbunden. Die künstlerische Ausbildung, die ich in China erhielt, vermittelte mir eine solide Grundlage und ein tiefes Verständnis der chinesischen Kultur und ihrer Dynamik innerhalb der Gesellschaft. Im Gegensatz dazu hat die Ausbildung in Deutschland meinen künstlerischen Blickwinkel erweitert und ein latentes Gefühl von Freiheit in mir geweckt. Kunst ist für mich ein Prozess der Selbstverwirklichung, der eine ständige Erforschung und persönliche Entdeckung erfordert.“

Tan Ping[1]

Ohne Zweifel gehört Tan Ping zu jener Künstlergeneration, die maßgeblich an einer Neuorientierung der chinesischen Kunst nach der Öffnung Chinas in den 1980er Jahren mitgewirkt hat. Als einer der Ersten, die China zum Auslandsstudium verlassen haben, ermöglichte ihm ein DAAD-Stipendium 1989 nach Deutschland zu kommen. Sein Aufbruch nach Deutschland war auch in politischer Hinsicht ein markantes Datum, da am 9. November 1989 die Mauer zwischen Ost- und Westdeutschland fiel und der Eiserne Vorhang, der viele Ostblockstaaten abgeschirmt hatte, bereits zuvor sukzessive zusammenbrach. Dies vermittelte Millionen von Menschen ein bis dato kaum gekanntes Gefühl der Freiheit und der neuen Möglichkeiten. Die Aufbruchstimmung und der Freudentaumel waren in den ersten Jahren riesig. Künstler aus China und anderen ehemaligen Ostblockstaaten, inklusive aus der ehemaligen UDSSR (heute Russland), mussten sich somit in doppelter Hinsicht völlig neu orientieren und Altvertrautes hinter sich lassen. Dies war eine große Herausforderung und eine besondere Chance zugleich. Nicht alle vermochten es, sich wirklich in der anderen Kultur zu etablieren und einen eigenen Sprachkanon zu entwickeln. Bei Tan Ping scheint dies jedoch rasch anders verlaufen zu sein. Seine frühen Arbeiten vermitteln den klassischen Duktus akademischer Ausbildung nach russischem und chinesischem Vorbild: zum einen dem sozialistischen Realismus verbunden, wenngleich bereits deutlich freier interpretiert, und zum anderen der chinesischen Tradition, die tief in der Tuschemalerei verwurzelt ist. Es ist dieses akademische „Rüstzeug“, mit dem er nach Deutschland kommt und hier auf eine für ihn weitgehend unbekannte Vielfalt der Stile und Ausdrucksmöglichkeiten trifft. Rasch wird deutlich, dass er sich von der figurativen Malerei – sei sie nun russischer oder westlicher Prägung – verabschiedet und die Hinwendung zur Abstraktion sichtlich aus der Tradition der chinesischen Kalligraphie und Tuschemalerei entwickelt. Erstaunlich sind sehr bald seine wagemutigen Neuinterpretationen.

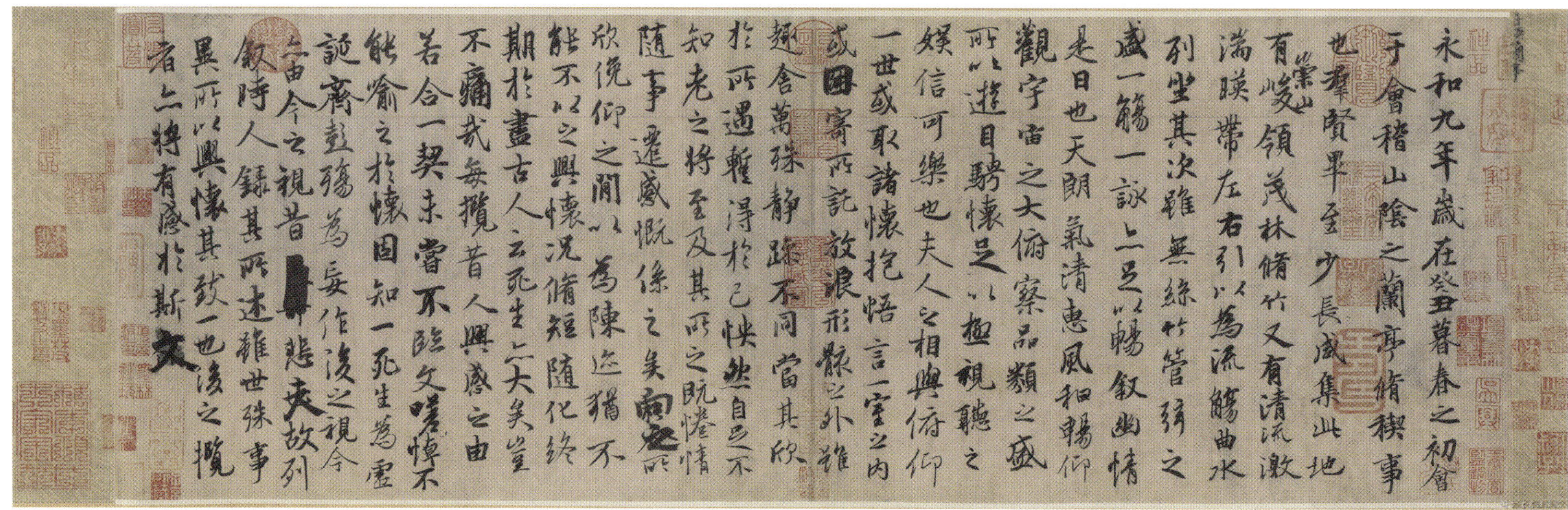

A few examples may serve to illustrate this.

Apart from the early decline of Roman civilisation, which had already produced magnificent figurative wall paintings, figurative painting only became visible again as a form of artistic expression in the Middle Ages. Initially in the context of book illumination, in which the text was more important than the ornament or the miniature. In architecture, alongside ornamental forms, figurative depictions only began to accompany the canon of images from the 10th century AD. From the 13th century, these were also created on wood, and increasingly on canvas from the early Renaissance onwards. In many cases, painting was initially dominated by the church and was based on an iconographic pictorial programme that became more and more in-depth and refined, helping to contextualise the narrative of the depiction, often because the majority of the population could not read. The narrative takes on increasingly complex forms in the iconographic representation. From the Renaissance onwards, secular motifs were also added, but these were no less intensely iconographically charged. In order to 'read' and understand these images, a corresponding codex of knowledge is required, through which the canon of pictorial elements can be deciphered. Only through this can the deeper meaning of the pictorial idea, its pictorial structure and the master's skill be understood by the viewer.

However, it is particularly interesting to note that it is always about narratives and that these are made up of individual components. In the Western pictorial tradition, these are – to put it simply – very consciously focussed on the human figure, even when it comes to spiritual and religious contexts. The motif of the landscape, especially nature, only appears much later. The spatial structure between the human figure and landscape only became relevant in the early Dutch and Italian Renaissance. Landscape as a topos in its own right, on the other hand, emerged much later. The reflective, reciprocal relationship between people and nature, whose emotional reflection in each other becomes clear, finally reaches its peak in Romanticism. Here, the outside and inside worlds, the individual and nature, are harmonised for the viewer.

Chinese painting, however, takes a completely different approach. Its pictorial invention is fundamentally based on the written language, whereby the respective calligraphic character already represents a complex pictorial unit in itself. As each character represents a pictorial unit, a word already contains a complex pictorial structure and at the same time a verbalised message. The culture of writing – as word content as well as pictorial sign – finds a special aesthetic and literary form here.[2] For a long time, writing dominated the pictorial culture in China, precisely because writing not only depicts language, but is also treated and understood as a compositional pictorial unit. The mastery of calligraphy has played a prominent role throughout the centuries. In addition, it is not only the text message itself that is important here, but above all the gestural execution of the stroke, the use of ink – sometimes deeply saturated, then again delicately liquefying, self-confidently and with controlled energy, at the same time executed with the appropriate emotion – as well as the

Blickt man jedoch zunächst zurück und vergegenwärtigt sich, was es mit der Tuschemalerei in China auf sich hat, wird auch der Vergleich zwischen Komposition und Gestus deutlich, der in der westlichen Kultur eine sehr verschiedene Haltung behauptet. Während die europäische Kunst bis zum Ende des 19. Jahrhunderts auf den Prinzipien kompositioneller Strukturen und einem weitgehend festgeschriebenen ikonographischen Kanon beruhte, entstanden chinesische Kompositionen aus einem Ansatz heraus, der auf einem relativ starren Prinzip der Tradierung (der Schüler kopiert den Meister bis er diesen überflügelt) und weniger auf der Betonung des individuellen Gestus beruht. Deutlich wird dies bereits in der Kalligraphie, die durchgängig in der chinesischen Kunst eine herausragende Rolle einnimmt, da sie sowohl als Schrift (Text) als auch als Bild (narrativer Kontext) gelesen und verstanden wird. Die Unterscheidung der beiden Bildkonzepte (im Westen sowie im asiatischen Raum) ist deshalb so bedeutsam, weil sie sich bereits im Kern grundlegend widersprechen, selbst wenn die figurativen Kompositionen in beiden Hemisphären scheinbar näher verwandt erscheinen.

Um dies zu veranschaulichen seien einige Beispiele erlaubt.

Abgesehen von der früh untergegangenen römischen Kultur, die bereits großartige figurative Wandmalerei hervorgebracht hatte, wird figurative Malerei erst wieder im Mittelalter als künstlerische Ausdrucksform sichtbar. Zunächst im Kontext der Buchmalerei, in der vor allem der Text wichtiger als das Ornament oder die Miniatur war. In der Architektur begleiten neben ornamentalen Formen erst ab dem 10. Jahrhundert n. Chr. auch figurative Darstellungen den Bilderkanon. Ab dem 13. Jahrhundert entstehen diese auch auf Holz, ab der Frührenaissance zunehmend auf Leinwand. Vielfach steht die Malerei zunächst ganz im Zeichen der Kirche und beruht auf einem sich mehr und mehr vertiefenden und verfeinernden ikonografischen Bildprogramm, das dazu beiträgt, das Narrativ der Darstellung zu kontextualisieren, oftmals auch deshalb, weil der Großteil der Bevölkerung nicht lesen kann. Das Narrativ nimmt in der ikonographischen Darstellung immer komplexere Formen an. Ab

der Renaissance kommen dann auch weltliche Motive hinzu, die jedoch nicht weniger intensiv ikonografisch aufgeladen werden. Diese Bilder zu „lesen"und zu verstehen, bedarf es eines entsprechenden Kodex des Wissens, durch den der Kanon an Bildelementen entschlüsselt werden kann. Nur durch diesen sind die Bildidee, deren Bildstruktur sowie die Fertigkeit des Meisters in ihrer tieferen Bedeutung für den Betrachtenden verständlich.

Interessant hierbei ist jedoch auch, dass es immer um Narrative geht und diese sich aus einzelnen Komponenten zusammensetzen. In der westlichen Bildtradition sind diese - vereinfacht gesagt - sehr bewusst auf die menschliche Figur ausgerichtet, und zwar auch dann, wenn es um spirituelle und religiöse Kontexte geht. Das Motiv der Landschaft, insbesondere der Natur, tritt erst viel später hinzu. Das Raumgefüge zwischen menschlicher Figur und Landschaft wird erst in der niederländischen und italienischen Frührenaissance relevant. Landschaft als eigener Topos hingegen taucht weitaus später auf. Die reflektive, wechselseitige Beziehung zwischen Menschen und Natur, deren emotionale Spiegelung im jeweils anderen, findet in der Romantik schließlich ihren Höhepunkt. Hier treten für den Betrachtenden Außen- und Innenwelt, Individuum und Natur, in einen Gleichklang.

relationship between the writing and the ground left free, which are in constant interaction. The effect of calligraphy is based not only on the complexity of its content (language), but also on the sum of multi-layered factors and nuances. Dawn Delbanco rightly remarks: 'And so, despite its abstract appearance, calligraphy is not an abstract form. Chinese characters are dynamic, closely bound to the forces of nature and the kinaesthetic energies of the human body. But these energies are contained within a balanced framework-supported by a strong skeletal structure-whose equilibrium suggests moral rectitude, indeed, that of the writer himself.'[3] It is precisely this notion that writing and the artist's kinetic energy enter into a correlation and that this decisively determines the expression of the form that will also crystallise as a defining characteristic in Tan Ping's work.

The narrative-figurative representation also initially played a subordinate role in the Chinese tradition and only became visible from the Han dynasty onwards.[4] Unlike in European landscape painting, the Chinese masters sought to depict nature as an almost immense, ultimately incomprehensible continuum in which the depiction of people hardly plays a role. With the development of shan shui painting (mountain-water painting), landscape depictions can be found from the 5th century onwards in the Liu Song dynasty which, although they appear to depict nature, essentially consist of additive elements. In contrast to the endeavour in Western art to reproduce nature as faithfully as possible, Chinese painting treats nature as a vision of originality, harmony and as the ultimate ideal in which man appears unimportant. What is significant here is that the painting does not fill the entire surface of the sheet right up to the edge, but rather leaves it blank, which makes the depicted landscape appear to float and thus reinforces the impression of the visionary ideal image. Much remains suggestive without being consciously formulated to the end.[5] The connection between landscape painting and calligraphy therefore remains clearly recognisable in the Chinese tradition for a long time. The cultural context, which for its part prescribes the most precise possible transmission of the canon and the virtuosity of the technique adopted by the master, only allows for gradual changes in the form of expression. These developments take a completely different course in European culture, which since the Renaissance has been fuelling intensive research into nature and reflecting this in painting. Techniques and styles changed in line with scientific findings.

In China, ink painting remained predominant until well into the 19th century and only various journeys by artists at the end of the 19th century and the beginning of the 20th century allowed oil painting, which played such a prominent role in Western art, to be taught at Chinese art academies.[6] Despite the study visits of various artists to Paris and Berlin, the appropriation of the new art form is visibly laborious and hardly leads to a deeper understanding of the composition and contextualisation of the depiction. A noticeable change in cultural penetration only occurred after 1989, when the Iron Curtain fell and the former Eastern Bloc states became independent.

Almost at the same time as Tan Ping, Wang Xiaosong (professor at Zheijiang University in Hangzhou since 2003), Xu Jiang (long-time president of the Hangzhou Academy of Fine Arts) and Miao Xiaochun (professor of photography at the Central Academy of Fine Arts in Beijing since 2002) were among those who arrived to study in Germany between 1986 and 1990. During their studies, many of these artists dedicated themselves to abstraction, a form of expression that was previously unknown in China. This is where the Western influences can be felt most clearly - from Informalism and the Abstract Expressionism of the New York School to Conceptual and Minimal Art. Tan Ping decided in favour of abstraction shortly after his arrival, but deliberately chose not to paint, instead intensively exploring drawing and the line as a form of artistic expression. To this day, it is the defining element of his works, significantly characterising the style of his works.

These early works, exhibited towards the end of his studies in 1993, prove to be completely abstract and yet reconcile two cultures: the Chinese (duration and progression) and the European (space, conceptual, discontinuity). Initially emphasised in the affinity to the ink drawing, which is determined by the free style and whose virtuosity proves itself for Chinese viewers above all in the drawn line, in its various courses of determining, broadly tapering or elegantly pointed, and above all in a stream of energy perceived as lively, which discharges itself in the line. Tan Ping limits this flow - marginally, but noticeably - by running the line across different sides of the sheet, creating

Die chinesische Malerei geht hier jedoch ganz anders vor. Ihre Bildfindung entsteht grundlegend über die Schriftsprache, wobei das jeweilige kalligraphische Zeichen bereits in sich eine komplexe Bildeinheit darstellt. Da jedes Zeichen eine Bildeinheit bedeutet, beinhaltet ein Wort bereits eine komplexe bildnerische Struktur und zugleich eine verbalisierte Mitteilung. Die Kultur der Schrift - als Wortinhalt sowie als Bildzeichen - findet hier zu einer besonderen ästhetischen und literarischen Form.[2] Lange Zeit dominiert die Schrift die abbildende Bildkultur in China, eben weil Schrift nicht nur Sprache veranschaulicht, sondern als kompositionelle Bildeinheit behandelt und verstanden wird. Dabei spielt die Meisterschaft der Kalligrafie durch die Jahrhunderte eine herausragende Rolle. Hinzukommt, dass es hier nicht nur die Textbotschaft an sich ist, sondern vor allem die gestische Ausführung des Striches, der Einsatz der Tusche - mal tief gesättigt, dann wiederum zart verflüssigend, selbstbewusst und mit kontrollierter Energie, zugleich mit der passenden Emotion ausgeführt - sowie das Verhältnis von Schrift und frei belassenem Blattgrund, welche in beständiger Wechselwirkung stehen. Die Wirkung der Kalligraphie beruht eben nicht nur in ihrer inhaltlichen Komplexität (Sprache), sondern in der Summe vielschichtiger Faktoren und Nuancen. Richtigerweise bemerkt Dawn Delbanco hierzu: „And so, despite its abstract appearance, calligraphy is not an abstract form. Chinese characters are dynamic, closely bound to the forces of nature and the kinesthetic energies of the human body. But these energies are contained within a balanced framework— supported by a strong skeletal structure— whose equilibrium suggests moral rectitude, indeed, that of the writer himself."[3] Gerade diese Vorstellung, dass Schrift und kinetische Energie des Künstlers eine Korrelation eingehen und dies maßgeblich den Ausdruck der Form bestimmt, wird sich auch bei Tan Ping noch als bestimmendes Merkmal herauskristallisieren.

Die narrativ-figürliche Darstellung spielt auch in der chinesischen Tradition zunächst eine untergeordnete Rolle und wird erst ab der Han-Dynastie sichtbar.[4] Anders als in der europäischen Landschaftsmalerei, suchten die chinesischen Meister die Natur als ein nahezu gewaltiges, letztlich nicht fassliches Kontinuum darzustellen, in dem auch die Darstellung der Menschen kaum eine Rolle spielt. Mit der Entwicklung der Shan-Shui-Malerei (Berge-Wasser-Malerei) finden sich ab dem 5. Jahrhundert in der Liu Song Dynastie Landschaftsdarstellungen, die ihrerseits zwar abbildend erscheinen, jedoch im Wesentlichen auf additiven Elementen bestehen. Anders als das Bestreben in der westlichen Kunst, die Natur möglichst naturgetreu wiederzugeben, behandelt die chinesische Malerei die Natur wie eine Vision von Ursprünglichkeit, Harmonie und als ultimatives Ideal, in dem der Mensch unwichtig erscheint. Bedeutsam ist hier, dass die Malerei nicht die gesamte Blattfläche bis zum Rand ausfüllt, sondern diese vielmehr frei bleibt, wodurch die dargestellte Landschaft zu schweben scheint und sich damit auch der Eindruck des visionären Idealbildes verstärkt. Vieles bleibt Andeutung, ohne bewusst bis zum Schluss ausformuliert zu sein.[5] Die Verbindung von Landschaftsbild und Kalligrafie bleibt deshalb lange Zeit in der chinesischen Tradition deutlich erkennbar. Der kulturelle Kontext, der seinerseits eine möglichst genaue Überlieferung des Kanons und die Virtuosität der Technik, übernommen vom Meister, vorschreibt, lässt nur allmähliche Änderungen in der Ausdrucksform zu. Ganz anders verlaufen diese Entwicklungen in der europäischen Kultur, die seit der Renaissance eine intensive Erforschung der Natur vorantreibt und dies auch in der Malerei widerspiegelt. Mit den wissenschaftlichen Erkenntnissen wechseln Techniken und Stile.

In China bleibt die Tuschemalerei bis weit ins 19. Jahrhundert vorherrschend und nur verschiedene Reisen von Künstlern lassen es Ende des 19. Jahrhunderts und zu Beginn des 20. Jahrhunderts zu, dass die Ölmalerei, die in der westlichen Kunst eine solche herausragende Rolle beherrscht, auch an den chinesischen Kunstakademien gelehrt wird.[6] Trotz der Studienaufenthalte verschiedener Künstler*innen in Paris und Berlin, erfolgt die Aneignung der neuen Kunstform sichtlich mühsam und führt kaum zu einem tieferen Verständnis von Bildaufbau und Kontextualisierung der Darstellung. Eine spürbare Änderung in der kulturellen Durchdringung erfolgt erst nach 1989, zu dem Zeitpunkt, als der Eiserner Vorhang fällt und die ehemaligen Ostblockstaaten unabhängig werden.

minimal interruptions and at the same time giving the drawing a minimal haptic quality. He anchors both free-floating in front of the pillars and, setting a sheet left in white as the end point, allows them to reach out mentally onto the floor. In this way, he emphasises the anchoring of time in space, not as a one-dimensional continuum, but in ruptures.

One of his first works documented here already shows the core of his conceptual approach. It is a work conceived as a spatial installation in which he affixes strips of paper, each with a single line of black ink, at various points in the foyer of the UDK Berlin. While one work stretches along the historical wall pillars, the other forms a kind of barrier in the room. A black line runs from top to bottom along each of the wall pillars, not as a single line but rather as a combination of several sheets of paper strung together. This is an essential element, as addition and sequencing emerge as striking, recurring aspects in Tan Ping's work. As determined as the individual line appears, it appears less unique in the interplay of the many individual sheets. The individual, it seems, can only be absorbed into the whole. This may well be a philosophical idea from Chinese culture, but it also applies to Western principles. With the structural elements of addition and sequencing through the juxtaposition of individual components, those elements characterised by Western art emerge in which structure, repetition and even the mechanical can be applied while avoiding the individual. There is also the aspect of movement. The continuation of a line over longer or shorter distances, depicted not in a single form, but interrupted several times, emphasised almost as a gradual, tentative progression, makes it clear that Tan Ping is concerned with the act of progression, with the momentum of the processual. Tan Ping conveys the line progressing in space, the emphasis on space and physicality, combined with the physicality and emotionality of the artist, in this sequential addition of individual lines running across different lengths of paper, which he joins together into a whole. Line and seam also interact in the process. He never thinks of the line in a singular way, it never remains just a line, but is a concept with which he emphasises traces of lines in architectural space and interprets them as time and movement.

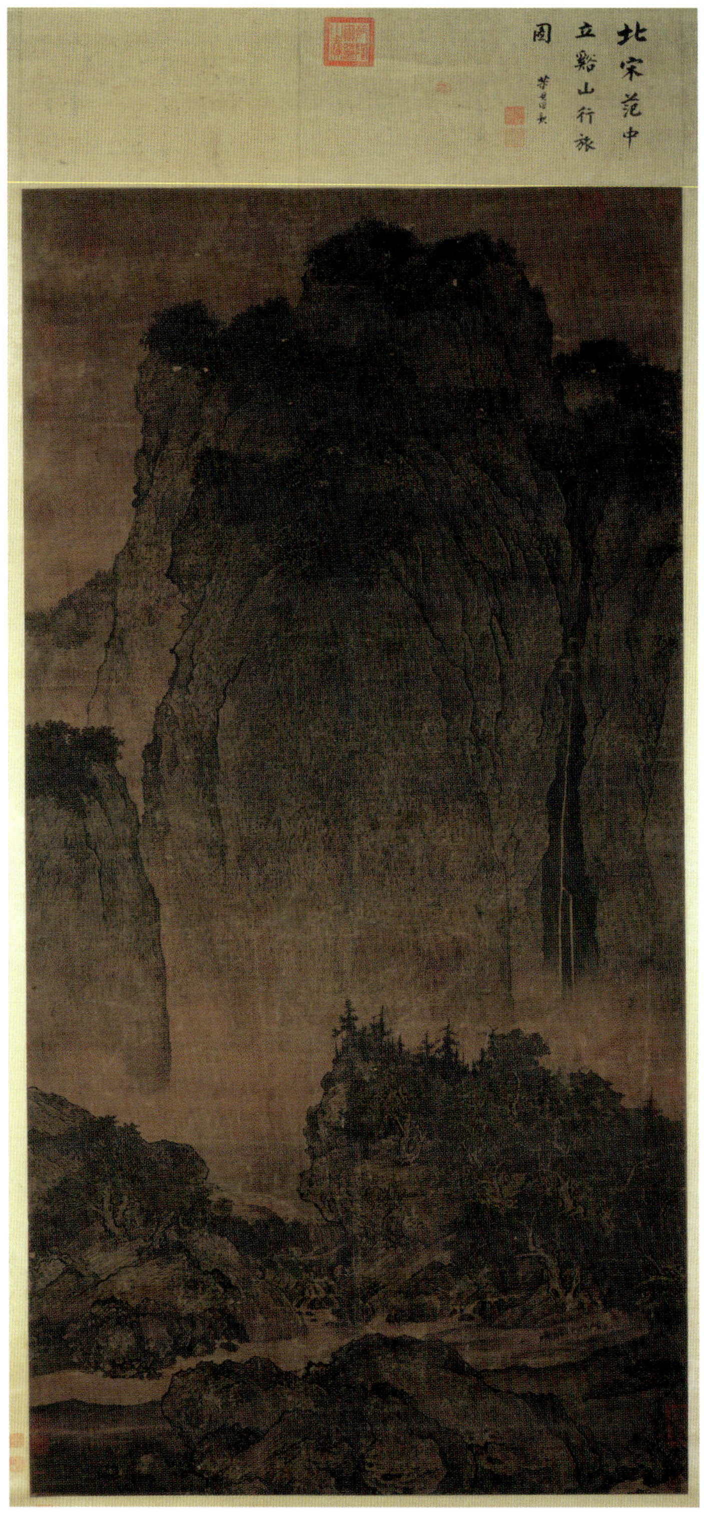

Fast zeitgleich zu Tan Ping kamen u.a. auch Wang Xiaosong (seit 2003 Professor an der Zheijiang University in Hangzhou), Xu Jiang (langähriger Präsident der Kunstakademie in Hangzhou), Miao Xiaochun (seit 2002 Professor für Fotografie an der Central Academy of Fine Arts in Beijing) zwischen 1986 und 1990 zum Studium nach Deutschland. Viele dieser Künstler haben sich während ihres Studiums der Abstraktion verschrieben, eine Ausdrucksform, die in China bis dato unbekannt war. Hier spürt man am deutlichsten die westlichen Einflüsse – angefangen vom Informell, dem Abstrakten Expressionismus der New York School bis hin zur Konzept und Minimal Art. Tan Ping entscheidet sich bereits kurz nach seiner Ankunft für die Abstraktion, wählt jedoch bewusst nicht die Malerei, sondern setzt sich intensiv mit der Zeichnung, der Linie, als künstlerische Ausdrucksform auseinander. Bis heute ist sie das bestimmende Element seiner Werke, prägt sie maßgeblich den Duktus seiner Arbeiten.

Eine seiner ersten hier dokumentierten Arbeiten zeigt bereits im Kern den konzeptionellen Ansatz seines Denkens. Es ist eine als Rauminstallation angelegte Arbeit, in der er an verschiedenen Stellen im Foyer der UDK Berlin Papierbahnen mit einer jeweils einzelnen Linie, bestehend aus schwarzer Tusche, anbringt. Während eine Arbeit sich entlang der historischen Wandpfeiler erstreckt, formiert sich die andere als eine Art Barriere im Raum. Entlang der Wandpfeiler verläuft jeweils eine schwarze Linie von oben nach unten, auch nicht als einzelner Strich, sondern zusammengesetzt über mehrere, additiv aneinandergereihter Blätter. Dies ist ein wesentliches Element, denn Addition und Reihung zeichnen sich als markante, wiederkehrende Stilmittel in Tan Pings Werk ab. So bestimmt die einzelne Linie auftritt, so wenig einzigartig erscheint sie im Zusammenspiel der vielen Einzelblätter. Das Einzelne geht - so scheint es - nur auf im Ganzen. Dies mag ein durchaus philosophischer Gedanke aus der der chinesischen Kultur sein, trifft aber auch auf westliche Prinzipien. Mit den strukturellen Elementen der Addition und der Sequenzierung durch die Aneinanderreihung einzelner Bestandteile tauchen jene von der westlichen Kunst geprägten Elemente auf, in denen Struktur, Repetition bis hin zum Mechanischen und unter Vermeidung des Individuellen angelegt sein können. Hinzu kommt der Aspekt der Bewegtheit. Die Fortsetzung einer Linie über längere oder kürzere Strecken, dargestellt nicht in einer einzelnen Form, sondern mehrfach unterbrochen, fast als sich allmählich vortastend betont, macht deutlich, dass es Tan

Ping um den Akt des Fortschreibens, um das Momentum des Prozessualen geht. Die sich im Raum fortschreibende Linie, das Betonen von Raum und Körperlichkeit, verbunden mit der Körperlichkeit und Emotionalität des Künstlers, vermittelt Tan Ping in diesem sequenziellen Addieren von einzelnen, über verschiedene Papierbahnen verlaufenden Linien, die er in ein Ganzen zusammenfügt. Linie und Nahtstelle interagieren dabei ebenfalls. Die Linie wird bei ihm nie singulär gedacht, bleibt nie nur Strich, sondern ist ein Konzept, mit dem er Linienspuren im architektonischen Raum verdeutlicht und diese als Zeit und Bewegung interpretiert.

Diese frühen, gegen Ende seiner Studienzeit 1993 ausgestellten Werke erweisen sich als vollkommen abstrakt und versöhnen dennoch zwei Kulturen miteinander: die chinesische (Kontinuität und Verlauf) und die europäische (Raum, konzeptuell, Diskontinuität). Zunächst betont in der Affinität zur Tuschezeichnung, die vom freien Duktus bestimmt ist und deren Virtuosität sich für chinesische Betrachter vor allem in der gezogenen Linie erweist, in ihren verschiedenartigen Verläufen von bestimmend, breit auslaufend oder elegant zugespitzt, und vor allem in einem als lebendig empfundenem Strom der Energien, der sich in der Linie entlädt. Tan Ping setzt diesem Fluss jedoch - zwar marginal, aber doch merklich - Grenzen, indem er die Linie über verschiedene Blattseiten ausführt, wodurch minimale Unterbrechungen entstehen und zugleich die Zeichnung marginal an Haptik gewinnt. Beides verankert er freischwebend vor den Pfeilern und lässt sie, ein in Weiß belassenes Blatt als Endpunkt setzend, gedanklich auf den Fußboden ausgreifen. Damit betont er die Verankerung von Zeit im Raum, jedoch nicht als eindimensionales Kontinuum, sondern in Rupturen.

Die zweite Arbeit, mit der Tan Ping den großen Saal unterteilt, suggeriert erneut das Motiv einer körperlich angelegten Zeichnung als Linie im Raum. Beide Arbeiten betitelt er „Time" und verknüpft dadurch nicht nur die sichtbare Spur der Zeichnung im Raum, sondern auch das Momentum ihrer Entstehung und damit die Prozessualität des künstlerischen Schaffens. Raum und Zeit verschränken sich für ihn im künstlerischen Akt.

The second work, with which Tan Ping divides the large hall, again suggests the motif of a physically created drawing as a line in space. He titles both works *Time*, thereby linking not only the visible trace of the drawing in space, but also the momentum of its creation and thus the processuality of artistic creation. For him, space and time are intertwined in the artistic act.

The *Time* installation is being created at a time when conceptual art is already established in the Western world, but no comparable art is even conceivable in China. During his time in Berlin, Tan Ping will have engaged with artistic positions such as those of
On Kawara (date paintings), Roman Opalka (1965/1-∞), Hanne Darboven, Nam June Paik and Marina Abramović.[7] In contrast to many artists, whose work focuses primarily on time as a factor influencing life and is sometimes broken down into very rational numbers, Tan Ping has been concerned from the outset with the interlinking of time and space, whereby both are perceived and characterised as movements that encounter and condition each other. For him, nothing is static, not even the architectural space, which he interprets through lines, traces on the walls, drawings on light boxes or performatively in collaboration with the dancer Huo Ying in 2023 at the Art Museum in Xiamen both as a three-dimensional and temporal movement (multidimensional, since time is not a single linear movement) and ultimately brings to perception through emotionality (individual time). The performance in Xiamen in particular shows in a moving way how strongly tradition is still integrated into the interpretation of the space-line-time composite. Tan Ping describes it – still as a reflection of the pandemic – as follows: "'The split scroll 'A thousand miles of rivers and mountains' symbolises the fragmented reality of the world after the pandemic. 'Tear' stands for the action, while 'split' refers to the result. The images painted on the long wall scroll are torn into two parts: One part remains blank and represents rivers, while the remaining ink on the wall symbolises mountains and serves as evidence of the divide between mountains and bodies of water.'"[8] The abstract nature of the ink brush drawing and its expansion into the space allow all the individual aspects of the conceptual approach to become visible. Tan Ping thus transcends all boundaries between tradition and modernity, simultaneously reconciling Eastern philosophy and spirituality with Western notions of individuality, rationality and freedom and formulating a new construct of time and space.

"'Time' is the medium in which my work is created, while 'space' is the field in which my creativity unfolds." (...) "Art has given me the opportunity to use 'time' as a tool. For me, time can be frozen, banished or fleeting. 'Time' has led me to concentrate on the void, to penetrate the space, and to give meaning to the emptiness inside and outside the canvas. Time is not only continuous, it is also fragmented and fleeting. Space is not only constructed, it is also empty and fluid. I constantly anticipate the chance encounter of time and space in their fluidity - these encounters are random and unrepeatable"[9]

Some of Tan Ping's works, which particularly emphasise the line as an ink line on paper, prove to be expressive. One could almost assume that he develops them in a free gesture like Jackson Pollock before him or artists after him who explored the free body-emphasised swing in painting and drawing – e.g. K.O. Götz, Franz Kline, Georges Matthieu or Marc Tobey. But with Tan Ping, the moving line always remains controlled, always controlled and reflected. It is not an unrestrained excess of drawing or painting, but consciously controlled at every moment. He is not primarily concerned with expression, but with the expansion of the line in space and this is linked to the individual motivation of the person himself. The line is the tool of an equally meticulous exploration of the space-time continuum, which in this particular context, however, is consciously orientated towards the individual himself. For him, it becomes field research, an exploration and questioning of the outside and the inside.

He does not exclude coincidences and some of the traces and gestures are reminiscent of John Cage, who for his part consciously engaged with the principle of coincidence after reading the book *I Ying - Book of Changes* in the English translation of the German edition by Richard Wilhelm from 1924. For his part, Cage was interested in space, in the reflection of the self under the conditions of life. The *I Ying* 'redeemed' him in a certain way from the Western idea that everything could be

Die Time-Installation entsteht in einer Zeit, in der in der westlichen Welt die Konzept-Kunst bereits etabliert ist, in China jedoch keine vergleichbare Kunst überhaupt denkbar ist. Tan Ping wird sich in seiner Berliner Zeit mit künstlerischen Positionen wie denen von On Kawara (date paintings), Roman Opalka (1965/1-∞), bis hin zu Hanne Darboven, Nam June Paik und Marina Abramović auseinandergesetzt haben.[7] Anders als bei vielen, in deren Werk vor allem die Zeit als ein das Leben beeinflussender Faktor thematisiert und mitunter auf ganz rationale Zahlen runtergebrochen wird, befasst sich Tan Ping von Anfang an mit der Verklammerung von Zeit und Raum, wobei beide als sich begegnende und bedingende Bewegungen empfunden und charakterisiert werden. Bei ihm ist nichts statisch, auch nicht der architektonische Raum, den er durch Linien, Spuren auf den Wänden, Zeichnungen auf Lichtkästen oder performativ in der Zusammenarbeit mit der Tänzerin Huo Ying 2023 im Kunstmuseum in Xiamen sowohl als einen dreidimensionalen als auch zeitlich als Bewegung (mehrdimensional, da Zeit nicht eine einzelne lineare Bewegung ist) interpretiert und schließlich durch Emotionalität (individuelle Zeit) zur Wahrnehmung bringt. Gerade die Performance in Xiamen zeigt auf bewegende Weise, wie stark auch noch die Tradition sich in die Interpretation des Raum-Linie-Zeit-Kompositums einfügt. Tan Ping beschreibt es – noch als Reflex auf die Pandemie – folgendermaßen: „Die gespaltene Schriftrolle ‚Tausend Meilen von Flüssen und Bergen' symbolisiert hier die fragmentierte Realität der Welt nach der Pandemie. ‚Tear' steht für die Handlung, während ‚split' das Ergebnis bezeichnet. Die auf die lange Wandrolle gemalten Bilder sind in zwei Teile gerissen: Ein Teil bleibt leer und stellt Flüsse dar, während die verbleibende Tinte an der Wand Berge symbolisiert und als Beweis für die Kluft zwischen Bergen und Gewässern dient."[8] Die Abstraktheit des Tuschpinselzeichnung und ihre Ausbreitung in den Raum lassen alle einzelnen Aspekte des konzeptionellen Ansatzes sichtbar werden. Tan Ping überschreitet damit alle Grenzen zwischen Tradition und Moderne, versöhnt zugleich östliche Philosophie und Spiritualität mit westlichem Vorstellungen von Individualität, Rationalität und Freiheit und formuliert ein neues Konstrukt von Zeit und Raum.

„Die ‚Zeit' ist das Medium, in dem meine Arbeit entsteht, während der ‚Raum' das Feld ist, in dem sich meine Kreativität entfaltet" (...) „Die Kunst hat mir die Möglichkeit gegeben, ‚Zeit' als Werkzeug zu benutzen. Für mich kann Zeit eingefroren, verbannt oder flüchtig sein. Die ‚Zeit' hat mich dazu gebracht, mich auf die Leere zu konzentrieren in den Raum einzudringen, und der Leere innerhalb und außerhalb der Leinwand einen Sinn zu geben. Die Zeit ist nicht nur kontinuierlich, sie ist auch fragmentiert und flüchtig. Der Raum ist nicht nur konstruiert, er ist auch leer und fließend. Ich erwarte ständig das zufällige Zusammentreffen von Zeit und Raum in ihrer Fluidität - diese Begegnungen sind zufällig und unwiederholbar."[9]

Einiges in Tan Pings Arbeiten, die insbesondere die Linie als Tuschebahn auf Papier akzentuieren, erweist sich als expressiv. Fast könnte man annehmen, er entwickelt sie im freien Gestus wie zuvor bereits Jackson Pollock oder Künstler nach ihm, die den freien, körperbetonten Schwung in Malerei und Zeichnung ausgelotet haben – z.B. K.O. Götz, Franz Kline, Georges Matthieu oder Marc Tobey. Aber bei Tan Ping bleibt die bewegte Linie immer kontrolliert, immer gesteuert und reflektiert. Kein unbändiges Ausufern von Zeichnung oder Malerei, sondern in jedem Moment bewusst gesteuert. Es geht ihm dabei auch nicht in erster Linie um die Expression, sondern um die Expansion der Linie im Raum und diese gekoppelt an die individuelle Motivation des Menschen selbst. Die Linie ist dabei Werkzeug einer ebenso akribischen Auslotung des Raum-Zeit-Kontinuums, das sich in diesem besonderen Kontext jedoch bewusst am Individuum selbst ausrichtet. Sie wird ihm zur Feldforschung, zur Erkundung und Befragung des Außen und des Innen. Zufälle schließt er dabei nicht aus und mitunter erinnern manche Spuren und Gesten an John Cage, der sich seinerseits bewusst auf das Prinzip Zufall eingelassen hatte, nachdem er das Buch „I Ying – Buch der Wandlungen" in der englischen Übersetzung der deutschen Ausgabe von Richard Wilhelm von 1924 gelesen hatte. Cage interessierte sich seinerseits für den Raum, für die Reflexion des Selbst unter den Bedingungen des Lebens. Das "I Ying" „erlöste" ihn in bestimmter Weise von der westlichen Vorstellung, dass alles vom Menschen kontrollierbar sein könne, indem es die Kategorie Zufall (Unberechenbarkeit) als Möglichkeitsmodell einführte. Es bezieht sich auf die Lebensphilosophie der Chinesischen Kaiser, die ab dem 3. Jahrtausend vor Chr. sich den Vorhersagen anpassten und dem Orakel Folge leisteten. Die chinesischen Kaiser ließen

controlled by man by introducing the category of chance (unpredictability) as a model of possibility. It refers to the philosophy of life of the Chinese emperors who, from the 3rd millennium BC onwards, adapted to the predictions and followed the oracle. For thousands of years, the Chinese emperors had their state strategies prophesied on the basis of the I Ying and followed the resulting advice, although this meant a purely speculative sounding out of very ambiguous suggestions. Cage introduced this world of ideas characterised by Eastern philosophy into Western culture and significantly changed music and art as well as their reception. Tan Ping repeatedly draws on chance as an extended constant in his work, not least to allow a one-dimensional perception of time and space to be experienced.

It may seem far-fetched, but the installation work *A Line*, a forty-meter-long single line (presented at NAMOC, Beijing, 2012) that Tan Ping drew or carved deeply into the paper, is particularly reminiscent of the culture of scroll paintings. In ancient China, they were often "travel luggage" – the painting and its owner went on a journey: the transitory nature of the movement and the – as Heidegger put it – the "readiness" of the work of art whenever it was to be viewed reinforce this aspect of movement, especially at the moment the picture carrier is unrolled.

One final thought is permitted: in Tan Ping's paintings, too, he repeatedly moves in the space of the drawing and interweaves painting with drawing. Sometimes it is visibly prominent, but sometimes it appears completely covered up. In his work *Overlay*, Tan Ping again works under the premise of exploring space and time. Drawing and painting, in a reciprocal process, often covering and then scraping and scratching, are for him ongoing processes of exploration similar to that of the palimpsest - historical stratification like in sediment deposits that archaeologists encounter. He himself sees this as a process of destruction in which the perfect image is questioned and found not to be "correct" and, due to its lack of reflection on personal fractures, "untrue". For Tan Ping, questioning the image as "this and not otherwise" is just as imperfect a construct as the idea that time and space must be thought of in a one-dimensional, stringently consistent continuum. The openness of his space-time questioning and the artist's direct involvement (as an individual, not purely logical component) proves to be a highly complex, never-ending process in which he consistently includes those who confront his art in amazement. It is a bridge between the two cultures and at the same time a permanent, never-ending questioning of their truth. Then as well as now.

1   Tan Ping, *Body of Abstraction*, ed. Beate Reifenscheid, Milan: Silvana Editoriale, 2024, p. 33.

2   Anett Dippner, Thorsten Benkel, "Zeichen der Ästhetik: Kunst, Kultur und Kalligraphie zwischen Tradition und Bedeutungsvielfalt". In: *Schriftenreihe: Schriften zur Kulturwissenschaft*. Band 78. Dr. Kovač, 2009.

3   Dawn Delbanco, *Chinese Calligraphy, In Heilbrunn Timeline of Art History*. New York: The Metropolitan Museum of Art, 2000–. http://www.metmuseum.org/toah/hd/chcl/hd_chcl.htm (April 2008).

4   "Artists from the Han (206 BC – 220 AD) to the Tang (618–906) dynasties mainly painted the human figure. Much of what we know of early Chinese figure painting comes from burial sites, where paintings were preserved on silk banners, lacquered objects, and tomb walls. Many early tomb paintings were meant to protect the dead or help their souls to get to paradise. Others illustrated the teachings of the Chinese philosopher Confucius or showed scenes of daily life." In: https://en.wikipedia.org/wiki/Chinese_painting; siehe auch Barnhart, Richard, et al., ed. Three Thousand Years of Chinese Painting. New Haven: Yale University Press, 2002.

5   "These landscape paintings usually centered on mountains. Mountains had long been seen as sacred places in China, which were viewed as the homes of immortals and thus, close to the heavens. Philosophical interest in nature, or in mystical connotations of naturalism, could also have contributed to the rise of landscape painting. The art of shan shui, like many other styles of Chinese painting has a strong reference to Taoism/Daoism imagery and motifs, as symbolisms of Taoism strongly influenced 'Chinese landscape painting'. Some authors have suggested that Daoist stress on how minor the human presence is in the vastness of the cosmos, or Neo-Confucian interest in the patterns or principles that underlie all phenomena, natural and social lead to the highly structuralized nature of shan shui." In: Robert J. Maeda; et al., *Two Twelfth Century Texts on Chinese Painting*. University of Michigan, Center for Chinese Studies, 1970, p. 16.

6   The Hangzhou Art Academy is the first in China to introduce this technique..

7   Kate Bretkelly-Chalmers, *Time, Duration and Change in Contemporary Art*, Chicago, 2018.

8   Tan Ping, Shan Shui Ying, in this catalogue, p. 125.

9   Tan Ping, 2024. p. 37.

sich über Jahrtausende ihre Staatsstrategien anhand des I Ying prophezeien und befolgten die daraus resultierenden Ratschläge, obwohl diese ein rein spekulatives Ausloten sehr uneindeutiger Vorschläge bedeuteten. Cage führte diese durch die östliche Philosophie geprägte Vorstellungswelt in die westliche Kultur ein und veränderte die Musik und Kunst sowie deren Rezeption maßgeblich. Tan Ping greift immer wieder auf den Zufall als erweitere Konstante in seinem Werk zurück, nicht zuletzt um eine eindimensionale Wahrnehmung von Zeit und Raum zu verhindern und vielmehr die Komplexität ihrer Lesarten zu spiegeln.

Es mag weit hergeholt erscheinen, aber insbesondere die als installative Arbeit „A Line", eine vierzig Meter lange einzelne Linie (präsentiert im NAMOC, Beijing, 2012), die Tan Ping gezogen bzw. tief ins Papier einritzt hatte, erinnert ihrerseits an die Kultur der Rollbilder. Im alten China waren sie oftmals „Reisegepäck" – Bild und Besitzer begaben sich gemeinsam auf Reise: Das Transitorische der Bewegung und die - wie Heidegger es formulierte – die „Zuhandenheit" des Kunstwerks, wann immer es betrachtet werden sollte, verstärken diesen Aspekt von multipler Bewegung, noch dazu im Moment des Ausrollens des Bildträgers, durch das sich die Bildgegebenheit fortlaufend verändert.

Ein letzter Gedanke sei noch erlaubt: Auch in der Malerei von Tan Ping bewegt er sich immer wieder im Raum der Zeichnung und verwebt Malerei mit Zeichnung. Mal tritt sie sichtbar hervor, mal jedoch erscheint sie völlig überdeckt. In seiner Arbeit „Overlay" arbeitet Tan Ping erneut unter der Prämisse, dass er Raum und Zeit erforscht. Zeichnen und Malen, im wechselseitigen Prozess, oftmals überdeckend und wieder schabend und kratzend hervorholend, sind für ihn fortlaufende Erkundungsprozesse, die dem des Palimpsests – historische Schichtung wie in Sedimentablagerungen, denen Archäologen begegnen – gleicht. Er selbst betrachtet dies als Prozess der Zerstörung, in dem das vollkommene Bild dadurch hinterfragt und es als für „unwahr" und aufgrund mangelnder Reflexion hinsichtlich persönlicher Brüche befunden wird. Die Befragung des Bildes als ein „so und nicht anders" ist für Tan Ping ein ebenso unvollkommenes Konstrukt wie die Idee, das Zeit und Raum in einem eindimensionalen, stringent konsequenten Kontinuum gedacht werden müssen. Die Offenheit seiner Raum-Zeit-Befragungen und das unmittelbare Einlassen des Künstlers (als individuelle, nicht rein logische Komponente) erweist sich als ein hoch komplexer, nie abgeschlossener Prozess, in den er mit aller Konsequenz auch jene mit einbezieht, die sich seiner Kunst staunend stellen. Es ist ein Brückenschlag zwischen den beiden Kulturen und zugleich eine permanente, nie nachlassende Befragung deren Wahrheit. Damals wie gegenwärtig.

1   Tan Ping, Body of Abstraction, hg. von Beate Reifenscheid, Silvana Editoriale, Mailand, 2024, Seite 33.

2   Anett Dippner, Thorsten Benkel: Zeichen der Ästhetik: Kunst, Kultur und Kalligraphie zwischen Tradition und Bedeutungsvielfalt. In: Schriftenreihe: Schriften zur Kulturwissenschaft. Band 78. Dr. Kovač, 2009.

3   Dawn Delbanco, Chinese Calligraphy, In: Heilbrunn Timeline of Art History. New York: The Metropolitan Museum of Art, 2000–. http://www.metmuseum.org/toah/hd/chcl/hd_chcl.htm (April 2008).

4   „Artists from the Han (206 BC – 220 AD) to the Tang (618–906) dynasties mainly painted the human figure. Much of what we know of early Chinese figure painting comes from burial sites, where paintings were preserved on silk banners, lacquered objects, and tomb walls. Many early tomb paintings were meant to protect the dead or help their souls to get to paradise. Others illustrated the teachings of the Chinese philosopher Confucius or showed scenes of daily life." In: https://en.wikipedia.org/wiki/Chinese_painting; siehe auch Barnhart, Richard, et al., ed. Three Thousand Years of Chinese Painting. New Haven: Yale University Press, 2002.

5   „These landscape paintings usually centered on mountains. Mountains had long been seen as sacred places in China, which were viewed as the homes of immortals and thus, close to the heavens. Philosophical interest in nature, or in mystical connotations of naturalism, could also have contributed to the rise of landscape painting. The art of shan shui, like many other styles of Chinese painting has a strong reference to Taoism/Daoism imagery and motifs, as symbolisms of Taoism strongly influenced ‚Chinese landscape painting.' Some authors have suggested that Daoist stress on how minor the human presence is in the vastness of the cosmos, or Neo-Confucian interest in the patterns or principles that underlie all phenomena, natural and social lead to the highly structuralized nature of shan shui." In: Robert J. Maeda; et al. (1970). Two Twelfth Century Texts on Chinese Painting. University of Michigan, Center for Chinese Studies. S. 16.

6   Die Kunstakademie in Hangzhou ist die erste in China, die diese Technik einführt.

7   Kate Bretkelly-Chalmers, Time, Duration and Change in Contemporary Art, Chicago, 2018.

8   Tan Ping, Shan Shui Ying, in diesem Katalog, S. 125.

9   Tan Ping, 2024, S. 37.

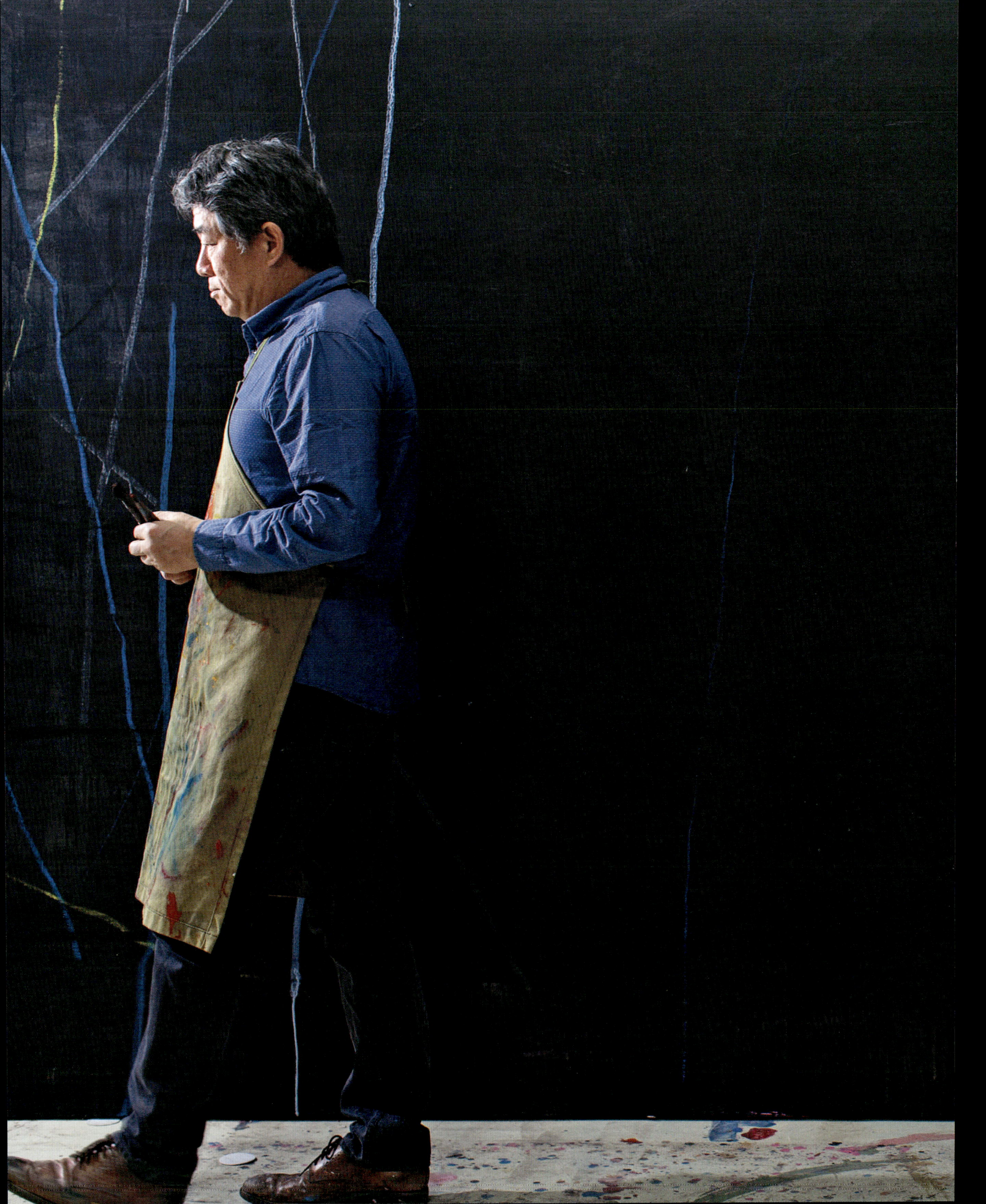

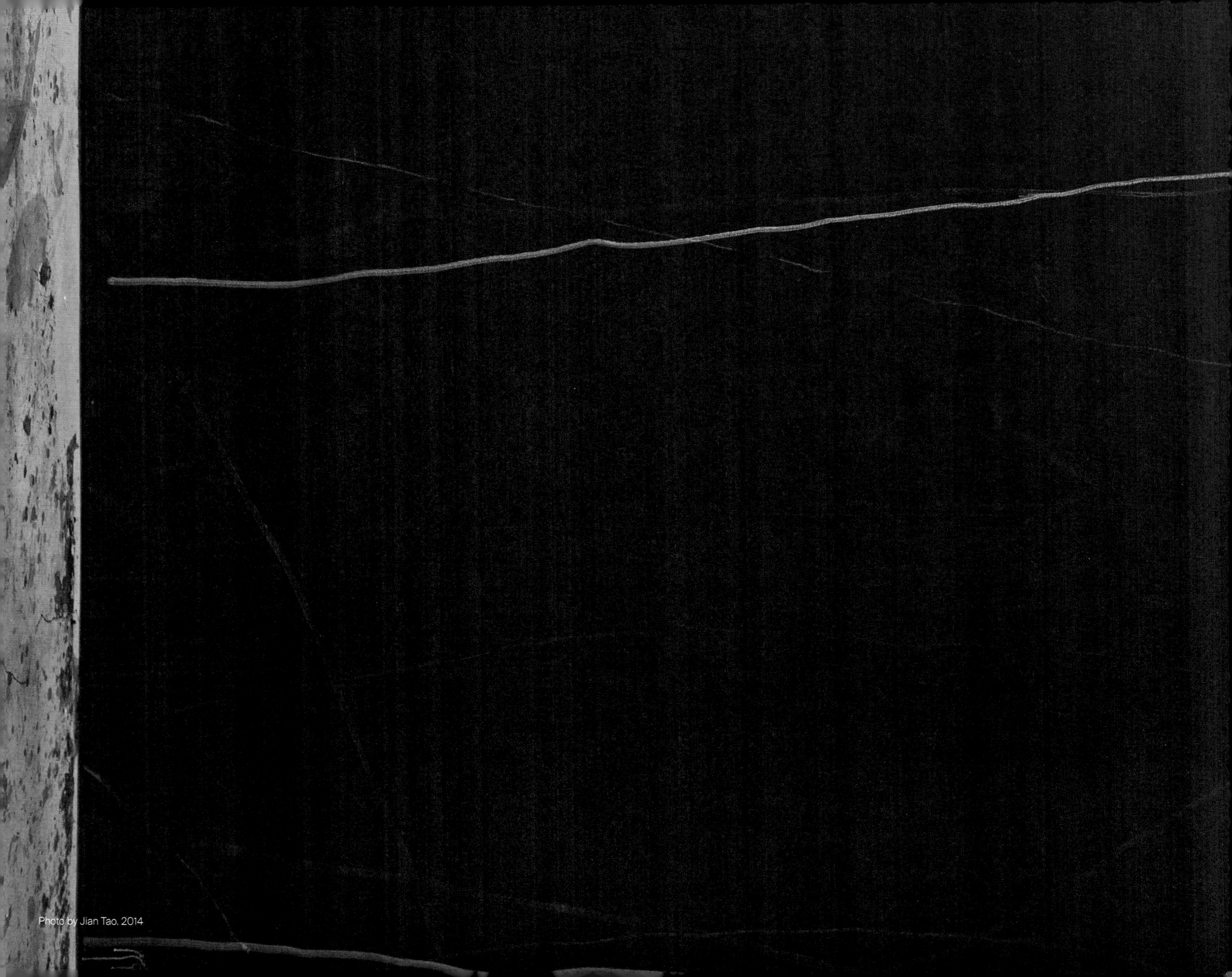

Photo by Jian Tao. 2014

How to Be "One"?

LaoZhu (Zhu Qingsheng)

A Philosophical Reflection on "One" from Nothing—Tan Ping and "the Third Abstraction"

Professor at Beijing University and Director of the WAI World Art History Institute and the Shanghai International Studies University. This text was translated from the Chinese by Eckhard Schneider, WAI World Art History Institute.

Professor an der Peking Universität und Direktor des WAI World Art History Institute und der Shanghai International Studies University. Dieser Text wurde aus dem Chinesischen von Eckhard Schneider, WAI World Art History Institute, übersetzt.

Tan Ping is a Chinese artist who received his education in Germany, underwent a significant artistic transformation there and developed his own distinct style in Berlin. Despite having been thoroughly immersed in Western abstract art, he resolutely continued his journey, returning to the profound roots of Eastern philosophy that transcends phenomenology. He came back to China, where he has continuously advanced the development of abstract art.

His work evolves from emphasizing structure, namely form and material (Form-Stoffe), to highlighting a singular line that, in the Chinese context, aligns with the concept of Taiyi (Einhait, "One", or the Great Unity), synonymous with Taiyi. According to Chinese philosophy, Taiyi generates two opposing forces, whose dialectical balance and interplay lead to the myriad complexities of our world and human experiences. From this perspective, it seems that "One" encompasses everything—the ultimate, absolute unity.

Thus, in his major exhibition at the National Art Museum of China in 2012, Tan Ping presented a work that consisted of a single line, "A Line". At that time, we discussed how this single line stands at the crossroads of unresolved contemporary art from both Eastern and Western roots. With the dawn breaking in the East and the Western sky tinged with twilight, nearly a century of history and uncertainty has unfolded. How could one single "line" possibly encapsulate all of this for Tan Ping? With this challenge in mind, Tan Ping diligently carried out his administrative duties—at the time, he was the Vice President responsible for teaching affairs at the Central Academy of Fine Arts. He was a dedicated professor at the School of Design, yet he never forgot his commitment to advancing abstract art. He seamlessly connected his cultural roots as a Chinese intellectual with the experiences he gained during his studies in Germany, all through that single line. This line was carved with a woodcut tool on a wooden board, leaving behind traces of the technique inherited from German Expressionist printmaking. Influenced by the Blue Rider and Die Brücke movements in Germany, this technique allowed for the direct expression of intense inner passion. However, it does not directly engage with the phenomena of reality, instead evoking the sensuous and melancholic lines of the Vienna Secession. This tempered the explosive potentials of Expressionism with a kind of surreal, latent human emotions—an emotion tinged with a physiological sense of Eros. While the technique is rooted in Western, particularly German, traditions, the abstraction, devoid of concrete imagery, reflects the legacy of abstract art developed in Germany. It traces back to early Kandinsky and later Hans Hartung, but with an added layer of Eastern spiritual essence. This combination elevates it to a third form of abstraction, gently flowing toward ever-distant horizons.

What kind of abstraction can be properly termed "Third Abstraction"?

Wozu das Eine?

Tan Ping und die Dritte Abstraktion
- eine philosophische Reflexion über das Entstehen
des Einen aus dem Nicht-Existenten

Tan Ping ist ein chinesischer Künstler, der seine Ausbildung in Deutschland erfuhr, dort eine entscheidende künstlerische Transformation vollzog und seinen eigenen Stil in Berlin entwickelte. Nach dieser umfassenden Erziehung und Prägung durch die westliche abstrakte Kunst machte er entschlossen weiter und kehrte sich wieder den Grundlagen des chinesischen Denkens zu, die über das Phänomenologische hinausgehen. Er selbst kehrte auch nach China zurück, um sich ununterbrochen der Entwicklung der abstrakten Kunst zu widmen.

Seine Arbeiten betonten ursprünglich eine Struktur aus Form und Stoff, gingen dann allmählich zu nur „einem Strich" über, mit dem im Chinesischen das Höchste Eine taiyi ausgedrückt wird. Das Höchste Eine generiert zwei sich widersprechende Kräfte, die sich in dialektischer Weise im Gleichgewicht halten, sich auf millionenfache Weise verändern und so die Dinge der Welt und die menschlichen Emotionen hervorbringen. Aus dieser Sicht scheint es, dass das Eine das Allumfassende ist, das heißt, die absolut höchste Einheit der Existenz.

Deshalb gab es 2012 im Nationalen Kunstmuseum China eine große Ausstellung mit einer Arbeit, die nur aus einer Linie, aus nur „einem Strich" bestanden. Damals wurde diskutiert, wie diese einzelne Linie an der noch ungelösten Schnittstelle zwischen den beiden zeitgenössischen Kunstrichtungen, in Ost und West, wurzelt. Mit der hellen Morgendämmerung im Osten und dem abendlichen Zwielicht im Westen konnte auf eine wechselvolle, fast hundertjährige Geschichte zurückgeblickt werden. Wie konnte es da angehen, dass Tan Ping mit einem einzigen „Strich" auskam? Tan Ping arbeitete danach verantwortungsbewusst als Vizepräsident der Zentralen Kunstakademie, verantwortlich für Lehre und Ausbildung und als Professor in der Fakultät für Design. Er vergaß aber niemals, die abstrakte Kunst weiter zu entwickeln, eine Verbindung seiner kulturellen Herkunft als chinesischer Intellektueller und seiner persönlichen Erfahrung in Deutschland herzustellen, und dies eben nur mit „einem Strich". Diesen einen Strich schnitzte er mit einem Holzschnittmesser auf einen Holzdruckstock, die Spuren des Messers aus der Technik des Holzschnittes im deutschen Expressionismus weiterführend, angespornt von den Künstlern des Blauen Reiters und der Brücke als direkter Ausdruck innerer Emotionen und intensiver Leidenschaften. Gleichzeitig hingen diese Spuren nun nicht mit den Erscheinungen der realen Welt zusammen, sondern glichen eher den Linien der Wiener Secessionisten in ihrer Bedeutung von Sanftheit und Dekadenz. Tan Ping schuf darin einen Ausdruck, der die intensiven Gefühlsausbrüche des Expressionismus ausglich, und aus dem ein unendliches Potenzial surrealer Emotionen entstand, Emotionen aller Art körperlicher Leidenschaften. Diese seine Arbeit war ein Bild, ein Holzschnitt mit nur einem einzigen Schnitt des Holzschnittmessers. Dies ist eine Art von Kultur, die Art des Schnittes ist eine westliche, insbesondere deutsche Technik. Da es sich um ein Bild handelt, das nichts Konkretes abbildet, sondern eine Abstraktion darstellt, trägt es das Erbe der in Deutschland entwickelten Abstraktion. Sie lässt sich auf Kandinsky in der Frühzeit und Hans Hartung in der Spätzeit zurückführen. Sie hat etwas mehr von ostasiatischer Spiritualität, bringt eine dritte Abstraktion hervor und fließt langsam in Richtung noch weiterer Entfernungen.

Welcher Art von Abstraktion ist diese dritte Abstraktion?

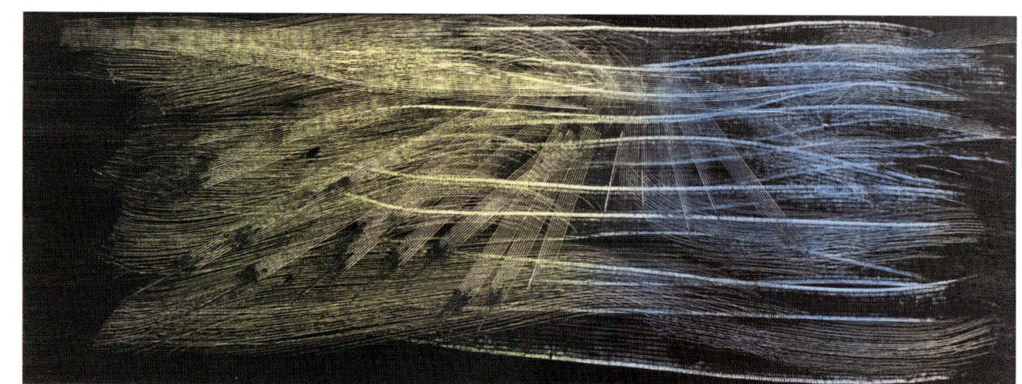

Abstraction is an inherent method by which humans grasp both human nature and the world within art. It is a path that has been singled out for artistic exploration, serving as a direction for conceptual breakthroughs. When observed through the lens of art sociology, especially as exemplified by the Bauhaus movement, abstraction also reflects an internationalist artistic strategy rooted in ideals of communism and universal human brotherhood. This approach advocates that art should serve the broadest spectrum of people, particularly the working class and the underprivileged. However, in this service, the artist is not required to play the role of a propagandist or advertiser, and those being served are not subjected to uniformity or control. Abstract art provides a space where presence—or the lack thereof—depends on an individual's independent attitude and their encounter with freedom of choice or refusal. The concept of internationalism seeks to eliminate social traditions and habits that distinguish people based on nationality, race, gender, class, and other demographic categories. Along with this, it aims to dissolve fixed norms in worldviews, ontology, ideologies, and religions. Instead, it advances and explores through the shared experiences and mutual understanding found in the cultural exchange that transcends conflicts. The question then arises: Can the experimentation with abstract art, through its ability to tap into shared human experiences and mutual understanding, contribute to the advancement of a global human community and promote world peace?

When Kandinsky viewed abstraction as a form of language, or when Mondrian considered abstract painting as a way to express the fundamental structure of the world and the basic forms of things, they were, in fact, still operating within a predetermined and definitive philosophical ontology. They believed that the world exists as a concrete reality, possessing both material and form, which can be understood and expressed by the subject.

Given this belief that objects exist and that the world serves as the dwelling place and foundation for humanity, abstraction is merely an extraction of a cognitive mechanism from the process of understanding things and the world, treated as a medium. Thus, Kandinsky viewed abstract painting as a language, even going so far as to design a "grammar" of "points, lines, and planes" as a symbolic system to convey his understanding of the world and his expression of spirit (human consciousness). This method aimed to return to the concept of linguistic uniformity mentioned earlier, wherein he believed that humanity "necessarily" shares a commonality in using the symbols of abstract painting as a medium. Therefore, as long as one uses this language, one essentially enters the framework of this unique linguistic system. We refer to this earliest form of abstract painting (as represented by Kandinsky and Mondrian) as "First Abstraction."

In 1929, when Hans Hartung visited Kandinsky[1], he quickly realized that the art Kandinsky spoke of was not what he himself understood as art. Rather, it was a new language and symbolic system that Kandinsky had defined for the international art community—a new set of rules for spiritual expression. As a result, Hartung chose not to follow Kandinsky's footsteps. Instead, he embarked on a different path, transforming his abstract paintings into direct expressions of his emotions and actions. This method later found experimental expansion in the works of American Abstract Expressionist artists such as Pollock and Motherwell. In other words, art ceased to be merely a system of symbols and became traces of human actions and emotional states. Correspondingly, Minimal Art later emerged in the United States, aiming to reveal the essence of objects (matter) directly without interpretation or definition. Instead, it allowed objects—especially everyday and industrial materials—to be exposed directly to the viewer, becoming a form of abstraction. This form of art is referred to as "Second Abstraction."

Hans Hartung,
Rayonnement, 1962
oil on canvas / Öl auf
Leinwand, 65 x 177cm
Musei Vaticani,
Città del Vaticano

Die Abstraktion war ursprünglich eine in der Kunst veranlagte Methode zur Erfassung der menschlichen Natur und der Welt. Sie wurde im Prozess der Formalisierung gesondert herausgearbeitet, um einen Weg für künstlerische Erkundung und auch die Richtung für einen konzeptionellen Durchbruch zu finden. Nimmt man als Beispiel das Bauhaus und betrachtet es aus der Perspektive der Kunstsoziologie, so war dies tatsächlich in hohem Maße eine internationalistische Kunststrategie, die auf dem Kommunismus und der Vorstellung von der Menschheit als Gemeinwesen basierte. Die Kunst diente der großen Mehrheit der Menschen, insbesondere der werktätigen Mehrheit. Und in diesem Dienst muss der Künstler weder die Rolle der Propaganda und der Werbung übernehmen, noch müssen diejenigen, für die der Dienst geleistet wird, vereinheitlicht und kontrolliert werden. Abstrakte Kunst ermöglicht einen Ort. Sogar ob man an diesem Ort präsent ist oder nicht, hängt vom Individuum ab, ob es mit seiner autonomen Einstellung und seinem Schicksal diesen Ort freiwillig akzeptiert oder ablehnt. Unter Internationalismus verstehen wir die Abschaffung jeglicher gesellschaftlicher Traditionen und Gebräuche, die nach Land, Ethnie, Geschlecht, Klasse und anderen demographischen Konzepten differenzieren, und damit auch die Abschaffung fester Normen von Weltanschauung bzw. von Ontologie, Ideologie und Religion. Wir verstehen darunter vielmehr Weiterentwicklung und Erprobung in gemeinsamer Kunsterfahrung und in gegenseitigem Austausch über eine Kunst, die kulturelle Konflikte überwindet. Können also Experimente in der abstrakten Kunst für ein Gefühl der Gemeinsamkeit und für gegenseitiges Verständnis, können sie bei der Förderung der menschlichen Gemeinschaft und des Weltfriedens eine Rolle spielen?

Aber wenn auch Kandinsky diese Abstraktion als Sprache verstand oder Mondrian die abstrakte Malerei wiederum als Darstellung der grundlegenden Struktur der Welt und der Grundformen der Dinge ansah, trugen sie in der Tat noch eine vorherbestimmte und explizite philosophische Ontologie in sich, die die Welt als existentiell und real ansah, aus Stoffen und Formen bestehend, die vom Subjekt erkannt und ausgedrückt werden können. Da man davon ausgeht, dass die Dinge existieren und die Welt der Ort ist, den die Menschen bewohnen und in der sie stehen, ist die Abstraktion nur ein Teil des kognitiven Mechanismus im Prozess der Erkenntnis von den Dingen und der Welt, die separat als Medium extrahiert wurde. Kandinsky betrachtete demnach die abstrakte Malerei als eine Art Sprache, ging sogar noch weiter und entwarf eine „Grammatik" von „Punkt, Linie und Fläche" als ein System von Symbolen, als Ausdruck seiner Erkenntnis der Welt und Ausdruck des Geistes (des menschlichen subjektiven Bewusstseins). Dieser Ansatz versuchte, zu dem oben beschriebenen Konzept einer homogenen Normierung zurückzukehren. Seiner Ansicht nach habe die Menschheit „notwendigerweise" die Gemeinsamkeit, die Symbole der abstrakten Malerei als Medium zu verwenden, so dass, sobald man diese Sprache verwendete, man tatsächlich schon in den Normenbereich dieser besonderen Sprache eingetreten sei. Wir nennen die Kunst dieser am frühesten entstandenen abstrakten Malerei (vertreten durch Kandinsky und Mondrian) „Erste Abstraktion".

1929 besuchte Hans Hartung Kandinsky, und unmittelbar nach dem Gespräch stellte er fest, dass das, was Kandinsky Kunst nannte, in Wirklichkeit nicht die Kunst war, wie er sie verstand, sondern eine neue Art der Sprache und ein Symbolsystem, das Kandinsky für die internationale Kunstwelt (die Basis der Kunst) festgelegt hatte.[1] Das war eine neue Norm für den geistigen Ausdruck. Aus diesem Grund lehnte er es ab, seine Kunst weiterhin nach den Methoden Kandinskys zu praktizieren, und schlug einen anderen Weg ein, indem er die abstrakte Malerei zu einem direkten Ausdruck seiner eigenen Emotionen und Bewegungen machte. Dieser Ansatz wurde später von amerikanischen Künstlern des Abstrakten Expressionismus wie Pollock und Motherwell fortgesetzt und experimentell erweitert. Das implizierte, dass Kunst nicht länger ein System sprachlicher Symbole war, sondern die Spur menschlichen Handelns und emotionaler Zustände. Entsprechend dazu entstand später in Amerika die Minimal Art, die unter anderem bedeutet, das Wesen der Dinge (ihres Materials) direkt zu offenbaren, weder zu erklären noch zu reglementieren, sondern das Objekt, vor allem als alltägliches, industriell hergestelltes Material, direkt vor den Augen des Menschen zu exponieren und zu einer Art Abstraktion werden zu lassen. Diese Kunst nennen wir die „zweite Abstraktion".

their own philosophical traditions. As Lee Ufan, a representative figure of Mono-ha (of Korean descent), stated, he sought to reveal the essence of objects in the Heideggerian sense. Although Japan, where Mono-ha emerged, is part of the East, they fully embraced Western philosophical thought to articulate their understanding of the world, particularly through the concepts of "object" and "place" [2] as discussed by philosophers like Nishida Kitaro (1870–1945). From their perspective, placing "place" above both the existence of objects and the subject's "mind" and dissolving the duality of subject and object represented an Eastern artistic transcendence over Western philosophical thought. The theorists and artists influenced by Mono-ha slightly retreated from this transcendental approach, settling into a state where they "encounter existence" within a specific place—a state that, in essence, continues Heidegger's notion that existence is not simply a being.

During the same period, Zen Buddhism was also gaining popularity worldwide. The Westernized version of Zen (distinct from traditional Zen and its underlying philosophies of Madhyamaka and Yogacara) was indeed a unique form of thought introduced to the West by the Japanese. D.T. Suzuki and Erich Fromm co-authored a book titled Zen Buddhism and Psychoanalysis, which presented Zen not in its true essence, but rather through historical anecdotes and seemingly paradoxical actions (known within Zen as "koans"). For Western readers, this kind of presentation could easily lead to misunderstandings and misinterpretations, much like how artists such as Pollock and John Cage referenced Zen. Today, it's difficult to ascertain how Heidegger and the Western academic community understood Zen, but the Zen they discussed was a version specifically presented to the West by the Japanese using English (or other Western languages). This is why, in Western languages, "Zen" follows the Japanese pronunciation rather than the Chinese pronunciation "Chan." This linguistic shift made dialogue possible, but it also resulted in the emergence of something new—what we now refer to as "Western Zen."

In the realm of "Second Abstraction," whether it is Hartung's European "lyrical" abstraction or Pollock's American "action" abstraction, there is a strong presence of human actions and subjectivity. The difference lies in whether these actions are controlled and whether they are intended to express a specific meaning. Although their abstractions can be classified as "expressionism," what they express has no fixed meaning. In fact, their work often transcends conscious thought, making it indescribable and instead relying on imagery (painting, sculpture, or what might be called two-dimensional, three-dimensional, or even dynamic images) to convey human emotions and spiritual intentions, evolving into practices like automatism [as seen in the works of Roberto Matta]. When it comes to Minimal Art, while human subjectivity is removed, the material, the essence of objects, and the existence of "things" can still be perceived. In this direction, Japan's Mono-ha (School of Things) explored further by combining the Eastern concept of "emptiness" as a fundamental ontology. By this time, Mono-ha had been significantly influenced by Western phenomenology and existentialism. Essentially, it was the Eastern artists (primarily Japanese and Korean at the time) who, inspired by Western modernism, developed phenomenological concepts in their art as a continuation of Zen and

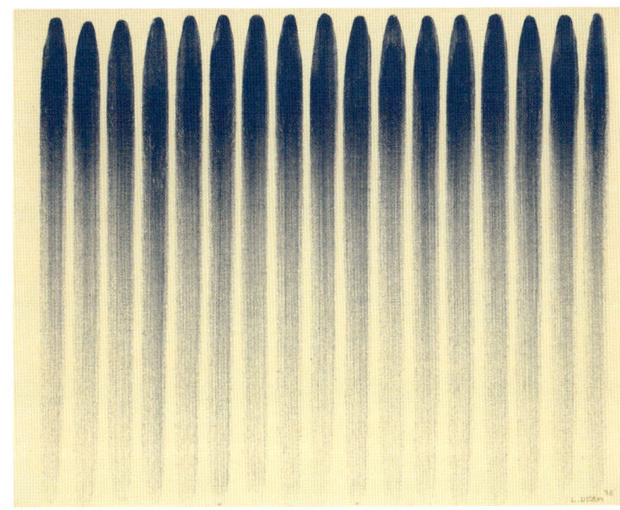

In der zweiten Abstraktion, sei es nun eine europäische „lyrische" Abstraktion wie die von Hartung oder eine amerikanische, zufällige „Aktions"-Abstraktion, wie die von Pollock, sind menschliche Verhaltensweisen und Subjektivität stark präsent. Der Unterschied besteht nur darin, ob man dabei kontrolliert vorgeht oder nicht und ob der Ausdruck einer exakten Bedeutung beabsichtigt ist oder nicht. Durch ihre Abstraktion ist es zwar möglich, solche Künstler als „Expressionisten" zu definieren und zu bezeichnen, aber es gibt keine Aussage über eine bestimmte Bedeutung dessen, was ausgedrückt wird, ja es kann nicht einmal bewußt und damit sprachlich nicht beschrieben werden. Um menschliche Emotionen und spirituelle Richtungen auszudrücken, musste man auf die äußere Gestalt zurückgreifen (Malerei und Skulptur, zwei-, dreidimensional oder animiert), ja entwickelte sogar die automatische Malerei (Roberto Matta).

In der Minimal Art ist es trotz der Eliminierung der Subjektivität des Menschen immer noch möglich, die Materie, das Wesen des Objektes und die Existenz der „Dinge" zu sehen. In dieser Richtung erforschte die japanische „Schule der Dinge" (Mono-ha) ihrerseits umgekehrt das Sein des „Nichts" (Bereich des Nichtexistenten) im ostasiatischen Denken. Die „Schule der Dinge" war zu diesem Zeitpunkt bereits stark von der westlichen Phänomenologie und vom Existenzialismus beeinflusst, und es waren tatsächlich damals ostasiatische Länder wie vor allem Japan und Korea, die sich in ihrer Absicht, den Chan-Buddhismus / Zen-Buddhismus und die Idee des Selbst zu entwickeln, von der westlichen Moderne inspirieren ließen und Kunst mit phänomenologischen Konzepten direkt aus der Minimal Art ableiteten.

Wie der koreanische Künstler Lee Ufan, ein Vertreter der „Schule der Dinge", sagte, brachte die Natur das Wesen der Dinge im Sinne Heideggers zum Ausdruck. Auch wenn Japan, wo die „Schule der Dinge" entstand, im Osten liegt, hatten sich die Japaner hier das westliche philosophische Denken vollständig zu eigen gemacht, um ihr Verständnis der Welt auf der Grundlage der Begriffe Ding und Ort auszudrücken, wie es in der von Nishida Kitaro (1870-1945) vertretenen Philosophie zum Ausdruck kam. Ihrer Ansicht nach sei der „Ort" auf einer Ebene oberhalb der „Dinge" und des subjektiven „Geistes" zu verorten, wo die Subjekt-Objekt-Dichotomie aufgehoben sei, und damit überträfe die ostasiatische Kunst das westliche Denken und führe es weiter. Die von der „Schule der Dinge" beeinflussten Theoretiker und Künstler machten einen kleinen gedanklichen Schritt rückwärts und fielen damit in einen Bereich, wo im „Ort" eine „Begegnung mit dem Sein" stattfindet, und dieser Bereich im Grunde eine Fortsetzung von Heideggers Aussage ist, dass das Sein nicht das Seiende sei. Zur gleichen Zeit wurde auch der Chan-Buddhismus in der Welt populär. Der verwestlichte Chan (und nicht der Chan-Buddhismus mit seinen philosophischen Grundlagen der Madhyamaka, einer Schule des Mahayana-Buddhismus, und der Yogachara-Schule) war in der Tat eine besondere Art des Denkens, die von den Japanern in den Westen eingeführt wurde. Daisetsu Teitaro Suzuki und Erich Fromm schrieben das Buch mit dem Titel Zen-Buddhismus und Psychoanalyse, in dem Zen nicht als Essenz des Chan-Buddhismus beschrieben wird, sondern als historische Anekdoten und scheinbar paradoxe Aktionen für Zen in der Praxis aufgeführt werden (im Chan-Buddhismus Koan genannt). So etwas kann bei westlichen Lesern zu allen möglichen Missverständnissen und Fehlinterpretationen führen, wenn etwa Künstler wie Jackson Pollock oder John Cage über Zen sprechen. Nun ist es schwer vorstellbar, wie Heidegger und die westliche akademische Welt Zen verstanden haben, aber das Zen, von dem sie sprachen, war eine Art von Zen, das die Japaner dem Westen in Englisch, also in einer westlichen Sprache vorstellten, so dass bis heute „Zen" in den westlichen Sprachen nach der japanischen Aussprache (zen) und nicht nach der chinesischen (chan) geläufig ist. Erst durch diese Sprachverschiebung wurde der Dialog möglich, und so entstand etwas Neues, etwas, das man westliches Zen nennt.

This issue is not a novel realization emerging from modern critiques of Eurocentrism but rather one that has deep roots distinct from Western traditions. It is grounded in the ancient artistic traditions of China and East Asia, which developed a different kind of art based on a non-Western ontology, drawing from the ancient Chinese philosophy of Daoism and the ancient Indian Buddhist traditions. Although Daoist and Buddhist thought diverge significantly, both center on the concepts of "Wu" (Non-being) and "Kong" (Emptiness) as their ontological foundations, contrasting with traditional Western ontology. In China, Laozi's philosophy posits that "all things are born from being, and being is born from non-being." Around the time of Emperor Ming of the Han Dynasty (57-75 AD), China absorbed the complex and multifaceted early Indian Buddhist thought, which eventually crystallized in Chan Buddhism with the notion that "there is nothing from the beginning; where does the dust alight?" This discussion of "Wu" and "Kong" as ontological concepts laid the theoretical foundation for traditional Chinese and East Asian art, particularly in explaining the nature of calligraphy and expressive painting. In this art history, calligraphy was once the most fundamental form, representing a synthesis of Chinese and Indian philosophical thought in art (a convergence that occurred primarily during the Eastern Jin Dynasty, 312-420 AD). A significant later development was the replacement of depiction with calligraphy, which effectively severed the direct connection between artworks and the physical objects, as well as the material aspects of space, perspective, color, and texture (a transformation that took place primarily during the Yuan Dynasty, 1271-1368 AD). This divergence led to a fundamental split between Eastern thought and Western philosophy in their respective arguments about the nature of objects and existence.

Calligraphy once represented a significant "leap" in the fusion of Chinese and Indian philosophical traditions within Eastern thought, manifesting in a unique art form achieved through the act of writing. This art form, referred to as "brush and ink", does not specifically link to or depict any particular object or concept, nor does it directly express a fixed intention or immediate emotion. Instead, it reveals a state that is both present and absent, embodying the concepts of "Wu" (Non-being) and "Kong" (Emptiness). Thus, Tan Ping's work cannot be fully explained through the lens of Western interpretations of Zen. To understand his work, we must return to the fundamentals. To realize the full potentials of this art form, Tan Ping seeks to explore the nuances of the concepts and their relationship to the void within changes. Since "Wuji generates Taiyi," beyond the concept

of Taiyi ("One", or the Great Unity) lies an even more fundamental source, which is "Wu" (Non-being). During the Axial Age, Laozi's concept of "Wu" accurately reflects a notion that is distinct from the Indian Buddhist concept of "Shunyata" (Emptiness). While, as mentioned earlier, Buddhism—especially Mahayana Buddhism—merged with Chinese thought after it was introduced to China, the Buddhist notion of "Kong" was assimilated into the Chinese notion of "Wu", leading to the development of Sinicized Zen Buddhism and the Neo-Confucianism of the Song and Ming dynasties, including the Yangming School of Mind, which marked a new phase in Confucianism known as the "Second Epoch of Confucianism" (as described by Tu Weiming).

Recent archaeological discoveries, such as the Guodian Chu Slips, further underscore these ancient ideas. These bamboo slips, dating back to approximately the 4th century BCE and discovered in Guodian, Hubei Province, clearly inscribe the concept that "all things are born of being, and being is born of non-being." In contemporary discourse, this is often expressed as "the existence of non-being," though this modern interpretation reflects the ongoing development of the concept of "Wu" within the context of modernity.

The Guodian Chu Slips (郭店楚简) were found in a Chu tomb dating from the mid-4th century BCE to the early 3rd century BCE. The transcription of the Laozi (老子) text found in the tomb is estimated to have been made around 300 BCE or slightly earlier. This predates the previously known oldest versions of the Laozi, the Mawangdui Silk Manuscripts (Laozi versions A and B), which were transcribed around the late Qin to early Han periods, by approximately 100 years.

Bambustexte aus Guodian aus der Zeit des Staates Chu (Mitte 4. bis frühes 3. Jh. v. Chr.) Das Chu-zeitliche Grab Nr. 1 in Guodian wird auf die Mitte des 4. Jh. v. Chr. bis zum frühen 3. Jh. v. Chr. datiert, die darin gefundenen Bambusstreifen mit den Abschriften von Texten des Philosophen Laozi stammen also ungefähr aus dem Jahr 300 v. Chr. Damit datieren sie noch ungefähr 100 Jahre früher ist als die bislang bekannten ältesten Abschriften, nämlich die der Mawangdui-Seidentexte aus der Zeit des Übergangs von der Qin- zur Han-Dynastie.

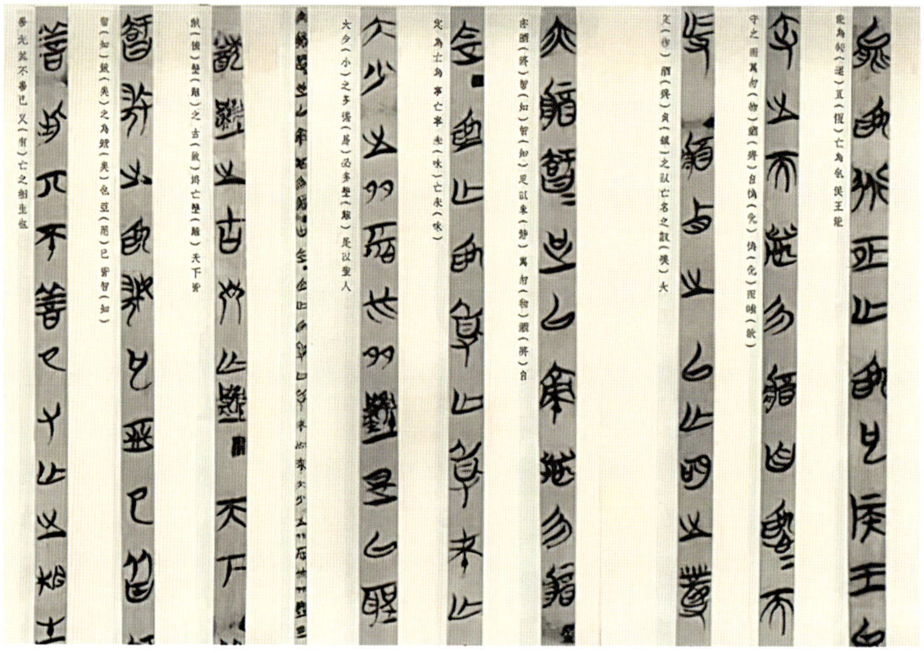

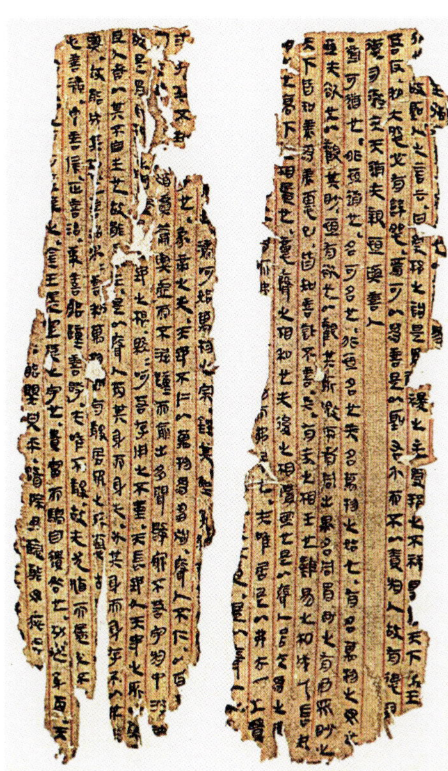

Mawangdui Silk Manuscripts
(Laozi versions A and B).

Mawangdui-Seiden-
manuskripte (Laozi-
Versionen A und B).

Dieses Problem ist indes kein völlig neues, das erst durch die Kritik am Eurozentrismus in der Moderne erkannt worden wäre, sondern hat Ursprünge, die sich von denen des Westens unterscheiden und die beispielsweise in der chinesischen bzw. in der ostasiatischen Kunst wurzeln - eine andere Art von Kunst, die ebenfalls in der ewig langen Geschichte der Kunst aufgekommen ist. Sie ist in einer „nicht-westlichen" Ontologie verwurzelt, richtet sich nach der Tradition des Daoismus aus dem chinesischen und nach der Tradition des Buddhismus aus dem indischen Altertum. Obwohl es einen großen Unterschied zwischen daoistischem und buddhistischem Denken gibt, gehen beide vom „Nichts" (Bereich des Nichtexistenten) und der „Leere" (im Unterschied zu der Welt der Erscheinungen) als ihrer Ontologie aus, die sich von der traditionellen westlichen Ontologie unterscheidet. In China formuliert Laozi: „Die zehntausend Dinge entstehen im (Bereich des) Existenten, das Existente (an sich) entsteht im (Bereich des) Nichtexistenten." Und zur Zeit des Kaisers Ming der Han-Dynastie (57-75 n. Chr.) gelangte das frühe buddhistische Denken Indiens nach China. Dies war in seinen Schulen vielfältig, in seinen Praktiken und Lehren komplex und verwoben. Im Chan-Buddhismus wurde schließlich resümiert: „Im Ursprung existiert kein einziges Ding, worauf sollte also Staub fallen?". Diese Diskussion über das ontologische Nichts und die Leere bildet das theoretische Fundament der traditionellen chinesischen und ostasiatischen

Kunst und kann zur Erklärung der Kalligraphie und der spontan-expressiven xieyi-Malerei in der orientalischen Kunst herangezogen werden. In der Geschichte dieser Kunst war die grundlegendste Arbeitsweise die Kalligraphie gewesen, die den künstlerischen Höhepunkt im Zusammenfließen des chinesischen und indischen Denkens darstellte, was hauptsächlich während der Östlichen Jin-Dynastie (312-420 n. Chr.) geschah; in der Folge bestand vornehmlich während der Yuan-Dynastie (1271-1368 n. Chr.) die überaus wichtige Entwicklung darin, dass die Kalligraphie wiederum die abbildende Malerei ersetzte und so die Verbindung zwischen Werk und Gegenstand grundlegende trennte, Ding und Stoff (Raum, Perspektive, Farbe, Textur) nicht mehr mimetisch abbildete. Auf diese Weise gibt es in der Auslegung der Dinge und des Seins einen grundlegenden Unterschied zwischen dem östlichen Denken und der westlichen Philosophie.

Nachdem sich chinesische und indische Denkquellen verbunden hatten, manifestierte sich mit der Kalligraphie als künstlerischem Ausdruck ein „Entwicklungssprung" im orientalischen Denken. Sie ist eine besondere Form der Kunst, die mit Hilfe der Schrift ausgeführt wird. Diese Art der künstlerischen Methode wird „bimo" („Pinsel und Tusche") genannt, deren Form sich weder auf bestimmte Objekte und Konzepte bezieht noch diese direkt erklärt und ausdrückt. Es ist die Sichtbarmachung des Zustands des „Nichts" (Bereich des Nichtexistenten) und der „Leere" (Bereich ohne Erscheinungen), halb seiend und halb nichtseiend.

Das Werk von Tan Ping lässt sich also nicht durch das westliche Zen erklären, wir müssen uns auf das grundlegende Wesen seiner Arbeit besinnen. Tan Ping tut an dieser Stelle sein Bestes, um die Möglichkeiten von Variationen in ihren Feinheiten von Veränderungen und deren Wechselbeziehungen zur Leere zu ergründen, denn da „Wuji" aus „Taiyi" hervorgeht und über das Konzept von „Taiyi" (Eins, oder die große Einheit) hinausgeht, und über diesem die noch fundamentalere Quelle, das „Wu" (Nicht-Sein), liegt. Über dem höchsten Einen „Taiyi" gibt es eine fundamentalere Quelle, nämlich den Bereich des Nichtexistenten, des „Nichts". In den Beschreibungen des Achsenzeitalters wird sehr genau und richtig verstanden, dass das „Nichts" des chinesischen Philosophen Laozi, welches der höchsten Stufe der Leere entspricht, aus der der Höchste Pol „Taiyi" bzw. das Eine „yi" entstehen, und die „Leere" des indischen Shakyamuni-Buddhismus aus zwei

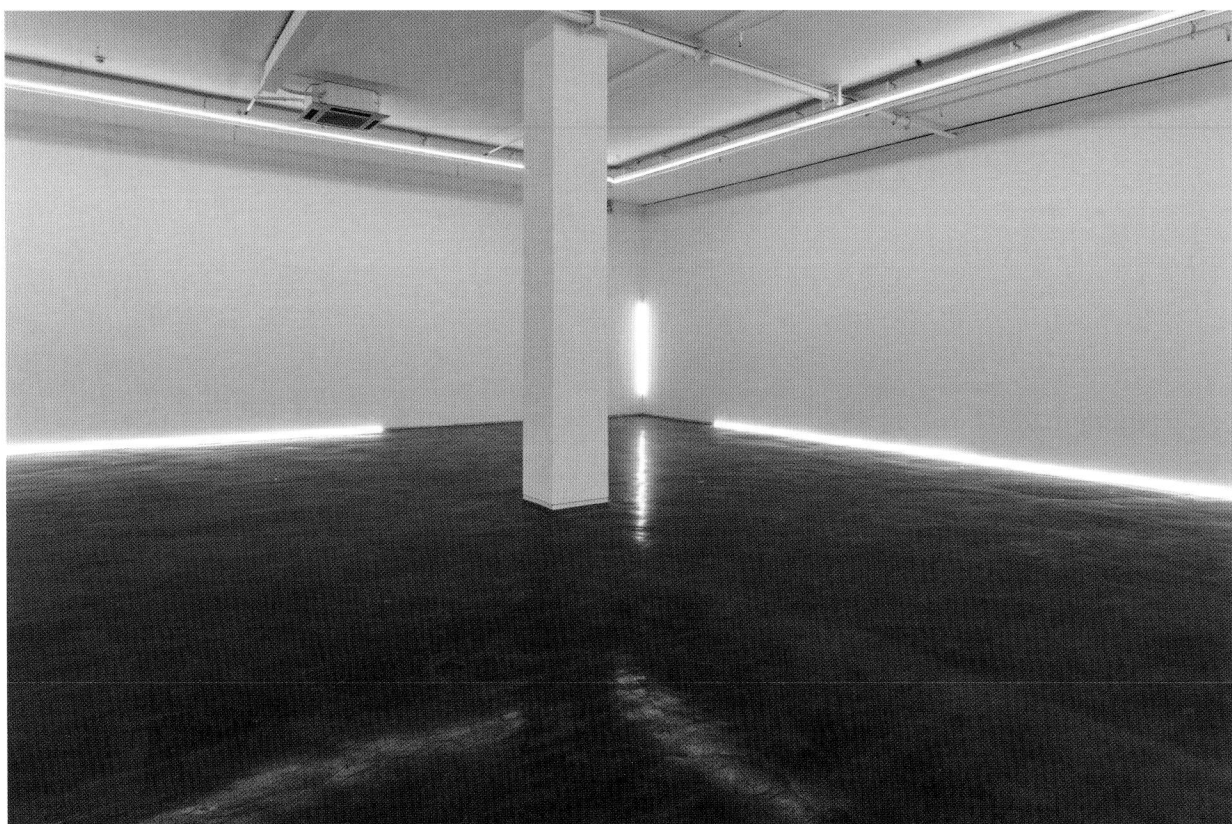

In 2017, Tan Ping held an exhibition at the Yuan Art Museum. Upon entering the gallery, one found a space that, apart from a few glowing light tubes, was largely empty. The lighting, interacting with sunlight reflecting from the windows at various angles, created a seemingly ambiguous space. Originally, this space was entirely devoid of anything, but the arrangement of the lights and the resulting shifts in illumination created subtle, ineffable meanings. The exhibition was intriguingly titled "......." This title referenced the Chinese art scene of the 1980s, specifically the so-called "85 Art Movement," during which Chinese artists embraced Western modernist art to further their own artistic exploration. This movement represented a shift toward investigating the ontological question of "being emerging from non-being". During this period, both Tan Ping and I were students at the Central Academy of Fine Arts, where we later stayed on as faculty members. This theme resonates with a discussion we had at the Academy in the 1980s, where Professor Chang Youming posed a question to the group: "What is art?" The diverse answers from over 20 students were published in a student-edited wall journal, capturing a wide range of perspectives. My own response at the time was a simple but profound "......". Throughout his career, Tan Ping has consistently and consciously explored and presented this concept in his work. This exhibition, in a sense, marked the culmination of his exploration of the void.

The previous text discusses how Japanese Zen Buddhism evolved into a form of Western Zen that is articulated in English (or Western languages), which led to a specific way of expressing the concept of emptiness. Yves Klein, a notable figure, represented a realm of emptiness through his work, showcasing the void and exploring the concept of Nichts as Heidegger described it – a "nothingness" that holds the same existential significance as any other entity (Etwas). Klein used a non-materialistic approach to define and express a universe that transcends the physical realm, maintaining that this void is, in its own way, a form of material existence akin to the earth, sky, and sea. He even held an exhibition featuring nothing as the exhibit itself, where the absence of objects was the artwork, and emptiness was his creation. Similarly, Robert Rauschenberg's early *White Paintings* featured blank canvases, presenting a void. However, the "Wu" explored by Pan Ping in his space is not the same as the previously mentioned "void". In simple terms, Pan Ping's exhibition focuses on the concept of "non-being" rather than "emptiness." The distinction between "non-being" and "emptiness" is that emptiness refers to the state of having or not having something—it represents the difference between Etwas and Nichts. Regardless of whether something exists or not, it is a form of existence. As Jean-Paul Sartre

verschiedenen Quellen stammen. Wie oben erwähnt, wurde der Buddhismus später als Mahayana-Buddhismus in China eingeführt, und die buddhistische Leere verband sich mit dem chinesischen „Nichts". Daraus entstanden ein sogenannter sinisierter Chan-Buddhismus und später die Denkschulen des Neokonfuzianismus in der Song- und mit Wang Yangming in der Ming-Zeit, für die Du Weiming die historische Bezeichnung „der zweite Konfuzianismus" prägte.

Inzwischen gibt es jüngere archäologische Funde, wie die sogenannten Guodian-Bambustexte aus der Zeit des Staates Chu (Mitte 4. bis frühes 3. Jh. v. Chr.) In der heutigen Provinz Hubei liegt ein Ort namens Guodian, dort fand man beschriebene Bambusstreifen des Staates Chu, auf denen eindeutig zu lesen ist: Die zehntausend Dinge entstehen aus dem Sein, und das Sein entsteht aus dem Nichts. In modernen Erläuterungen heißt es dann, das Nichts sei seiend, habe eine Existenz, aber dies ist dann schon eine moderne Weiterentwicklung der Frage nach dem Nichts.

Im Jahr 2017 hatte Tan Ping eine Ausstellung im Yuan Art Museum in Peking mit einer Installation: nachdem man die Ausstellungshalle betreten hatte, sah man außer dem Licht einiger Leuchtröhren auch Spiegel, die durch Fenster einfallendes Tageslicht in unterschiedlichen Winkeln reflektierten. So wurde ein gleichzeitig wirklicher und unwirklicher Raum hervorgebracht, ein Raum in dem eigentlich kein einziges Ding vorhanden war, ein Raum des Nichts, aber sobald dieser Raum durch die Anordnung der Lichter entstanden war und sich veränderte, erhielt er eine unbeschreibliche Bedeutung, wie auch der vielsagende Titel der Ausstellung „……".

Nachdem die chinesische Kunstwelt in den 80er Jahren, in der Zeit der sogenannten Kunstbewegung 85, sich mit der westlichen Moderne auseinandersetzte und auf der Grundlage derer Errungenschaften eine Weiterentwicklung anstrebte, war Tan Pings Ausstellung „ … " bei der Frage nach der Existenz, die aus dem Bereich des Nichtexistenten entsteht, bereits eine Weiterentwicklung hin zum grundlegenden Wesen des Seins, der Ontologie. Damals waren sowohl Tan Ping als auch ich Studenten an der Zentralen Kunstakademie in Peking, an die wir beide später als Lehrer berufen wurden. Beim letzten einer Reihe von Seminaren an der Akademie in den 1980er Jahren stellte Professor Chang Youming eine Frage, die alle beantworten sollten: Was ist Kunst? Das Ergebnis wurde

in einer von Studenten herausgegebenen Wandzeitung veröffentlicht. Die etwa 20 Studenten, die an dem Kurs teilnahmen, gaben Dutzende von verschiedenen Antworten, und meine damalige Antwort war wirklich „ … " gewesen. Tan Ping hat sich damals und später in einer Reihe von künstlerischen Praktiken sehr bewusst und deutlich in diese Richtung bewegt und gezeigt. Endlich wurde diese Ausstellung über das Leere verwirklicht.

Es wurde oben bereits erwähnt, dass sich das japanische Zen später zu einem westlichen Zen entwickelte, das in Englisch (einer westlichen Sprache) speziell für den Westen ausgedrückt wurde, was auch zu einer bestimmten Art des Darstellung der Leere führte. Es gab einmal einen Bereich der Leere, der von Yves Klein (1928-1962) repräsentiert wurde, eine Ausstellung der Leere, in der man das Nichts verwenden konnte, das, wie Heidegger betonte, dieselbe existentielle Bedeutung hat wie jede Art des Seienden. Klein verwendete eine immaterielle Bildsprache, um eine kosmische Welt zu definieren und auszudrücken, die das Materielle übersteigt, wobei er dieses Nichts immer als „materielle Existenz" wie die Erde, den Himmel und das Meer betrachtete. Er machte einmal eine Ausstellung, in der kein einziges Exponat ausgestellt wurde, das Exponat war das Nichts gewesen, sein Werk war die Leere. Auch die White Paintings des frühen Robert Rauschenberg am Black Mountain College sind als Gemälde bekannt, auf denen nichts zu sehen ist, eben nur eine leere Fläche.

Der von Tan Ping geschaffene Raum des „Nichts" und diese Art von Kunst sind in Wirklichkeit nicht dieselbe Art von „Leere". Um es einfach auszudrücken, geht es in Tan Pings Ausstellung „ … " um „Nichts" im Sinne von Nichtexistenz und nicht um „Leere", die frei von Erscheinungen ist. Der Unterschied zwischen Nichts und Leere besteht darin, dass die Leere der Unterschied zwischen dem Haben von etwas und dem Nicht-Haben von etwas ist, der Unterschied zwischen Etwas und Nichts. Ob dieses Etwas nun anwesend ist oder nicht, es ist eine Art der Existenz, und

posited, negation is a form of nothingness, and nothingness is a necessary form of existence, even an indispensable one. In contrast, the "non-being" in Pan Ping's work does not address the nature of existence (Sein), whether it is present or absent. Instead, it directly negates the verb "to be" itself. "Non-being" is seen as a primordial evolutionary force before existence. It can transform into "being", into "One," moving from nothing to something, from a state of "having or not having" to a state of "having." From utter nothingness to the initial unity of "One," then evolving from "One" to "Two," from "Two" to "Three," and from "Three" to the myriad of all things. This progression illustrates the idea that "being arises from non-being," where "non-being" is a regenerative, birth-giving, and creative form of nothingness.

In a space completely devoid of people, the question of "presence or absence" has not arisen; thus, this state is "non-being." It is only when a subject enters that "being" becomes possible. The act of human intervention, or the subject's entry into the world, marks the process from "non-being" to "being," because it is through the presence of "people" that the world comes into existence. The world is neither an objective material entity nor a subjective human perception; rather, it is the encounter between humans and everything else, and it is fundamentally a human issue. "Being" only has significance in relation to humans; it is a form of existence, consciousness, and judgment pertinent to the subject. Any attempt to define "being" outside the subject is an effort to place humans in a higher position, where they believe they can perceive something beyond themselves. However, such a viewpoint fails to recognize that this concept itself is a product of human consciousness and self-delusion.

A person initially feels a sensation and recognizes it as "basic human consciousness." This is the most crucial boundary that distinguishes humans from animals or other life forms, marking the essence of being human. The fundamental human sensation and conscious behavior itself, and its recognition and definition, constitute the concept of "One" (or Taiyi). In Pan Ping's exhibition, what is presented is not the absence of things, but rather a reenactment of human (in this case, the audience's) actions in a space of nothingness, where these actions leave a trace, symbolizing "One" due to their intervention. This intervention might leave a mark or not, but once a person engages with the exhibition, "being" is created from "non-being." If someone translates their sensations and awareness into a tangible trace and creates an artwork from these sensations and actions, they are essentially reenacting this original

process. For a visual artist, this might manifest as a painting or a brushstroke, as exemplified by Pan Ping's 2012 piece titled *A Line* exhibited at the National Art Museum of China and shown repeatedly in various exhibitions. For a musician, it would be a note; for a poet, it would be a moment of epiphany.

Theoretically, all living beings, throughout their existence, continuously leave marks on other mediums. However, it is only humans who, when creating marks through their actions, not only notice that a mark has appeared in the world but also recognize that this mark exists because of their own actions. This represents the transformation from nothing to something— the manifestation of "being" emerging from "non-being", where "being" reflects human understanding of the world.

This absolute leap from "non-being" to "being" is traditionally expressed in ancient Chinese thought as "Wuji generates Taiyi," forming its most fundamental philosophical principle. However, the path from Wuji to Taiyi does not stop at "One"; it is not singular. The emergence of humanity is a process of the evolution of a species. Once humans possess their essential nature, it is not merely a matter of individual humans forming and then replicating different individuals. Rather, it is a collective, synchronized, or jointly evolving process that constitutes humanity. Within species, human nature not only becomes aware of its own existence but also develops uniquely across different individuals. This variation in self-perception and consciousness means that when a mark evolves into a powerful force representing the unity and coherence of all humanity, it simultaneously transforms into the unique self-expression of each individual within the larger group. This unity and the individual's unique expression of "One" could be seen as a mutual paradox[3]: the consistency of the unified "One" and the distinctiveness of its discrete, individual expressions.[4]

wie Jean-Paul Sartre sagt, ist die verneinte Existenz eine Art von Leere, und die Leere ist eine notwendige Form der Existenz, oder sogar eine unverzichtbare Form der Existenz. Im „Nichts" gibt es keine Diskussion darüber, was für ein Ding das Sein als Existenz ist, ob es anwesend oder abwesend ist. Und im „Nichts" gibt es keine Diskussion darüber, was das Sein als Wesen ist, ob es anwesend ist oder nicht. Eigentlich ist das Nichts eine direkte Negation des Verbes „vorhandensein", das Nichts ist eine evolutionäre Kraft, die der Existenz vorausgeht. Aus dem Nichts kann Vorhandensein entstehen, es kann das „Eine" entstehen. Es ist der Übergang von einem Zustand, in dem es die Frage nach Existenz oder Nicht-Existenz nicht gibt, in einen Zustand, in dem es Existenz gibt, und erst dann ist der Zustand gegeben, dass etwas vorhanden ist oder etwas nicht vorhanden ist. Aus einem Zustand, in dem es keine Existenz gibt, entsteht zu Beginn das Eine, nämlich das Höchste Eine. Dieses „Eine" verwandelt sich dann zu „Zwei", „Zwei" zu „Drei" und „Drei" zu den zehntausend Dingen. Dies ist die Bedeutung des Satzes „etwas entsteht im Nichtexistenten", und diese Art von Nichts ist ein Nichts, aus dem Geburt, Wiedergeburt und Schöpfung entstehen kann!

Solange der leere Ausstellungsraum noch von niemandem betreten wurde, stellt sich die Frage nach Existenz und Nichtexistenz noch nicht. Dieser Zustand entspricht dem des „Nichts". Erst wenn der Mensch als Subjekt eintritt, wird „Existenz" möglich. Deswegen ist also das Eingreifen des Menschen in die Welt, d.h. der Eintritt des Subjekts in die Welt, ein Prozess der Erzeugung von „Existenz" aus dem „Nichts". Durch den „Menschen" „existiert" die Welt. Die Welt ist weder objektive Materie noch subjektive menschliche Natur, sondern sie ist die Begegnung des Menschen mit Jedwedem. Die Welt an sich ist eine Frage des Menschen. „Existenz" kann nur in Bezug auf den Menschen gesagt werden, sie kann nur als auf ein Subjekt bezogen vorhanden sein, sie ist für das Subjekt Bewußtsein und Urteil. Jegliches Unterfangen, Existenz außerhalb des Subjektes als Existenz anzunehmen, bedeutet, dass der Mensch sich selbst auf einen anderen, einen noch höheren Standpunkt stellt und annimmt, von Teilen außerhalb des eigenen Subjektes noch Bewusstsein haben zu können. Aber eine solches Konzept übersieht, dass eine solche Annahme immer noch eine Art des

menschlichen Bewusstseins ist und aus Selbstgerechtigkeit herrührt. Was der Mensch zunächst als erste Empfindung wahrnimmt, wovon er zuerst Bewusstsein erlangt, ist das „Lebensverhalten der menschlichen Natur", so wird der Mensch zu dem, was er ist, und das ist die wichtigste Grenze für den Menschen zur Unterscheidung im Lebensverhalten von Tieren oder anderer Lebewesen. Dass die menschliche Natur wahrnimmt und Bewußtsein von etwas erlangt, begründet sich im Konzept des „Taiyi", des höchsten Einen. Was Tan Ping in seiner Ausstellung „ ... " zeigt, ist nicht ein „Nichtvorhandensein", sondern die nochmalige Wiedergabe dessen, dass der Mensch (in diesem Falle der Betrachter) mit seiner Aktion des Eintretens in den existenzfreien Raum eben durch seine Aktion des Eintretens zum ersten Mal die Spur des „Einen" hinterlässt. Sein diesmaliges Eintreten mag eine Spur hinterlassen oder auch nicht, aber in dem Moment, wenn er den Ausstellungsraum betritt, ist aus dem „Nichts" bereits „Existenz" entstanden. Wenn jemand sein Fühlen und sein Bewusstsein in eine Spur verwandelt und aus dem Akt des Fühlens und des Bewusstseins ein Kunstwerk erschafft, muss es sich unbedingt um die Wiederholung der erstmaligen Wandlung am Urananfang handeln. Wenn ein bildender Künstler sich dieser Aufgabe annimmt, dann malt er einen Strich oder schnitzt ihn mit dem Messer, wie es Tan Ping in seiner 2012 im Nationalen Kunstmuseum Chinas und an vielen anderen Orten ausgestellten Arbeit „Ein Strich" tat. Ein Musiker würde daraus einen Ton machen, beim Dichter wäre es die erste Eingebung. In der Theorie hinterlassen alle lebenden Wesen im Laufe ihres Lebens auch Spuren auf anderen Trägern, aber nur der Mensch, und nur der Mensch bemerkt, wenn er mit seinen Handlungen Spuren hinterlässt, dass in der Welt eine Spur erzeugt wurde, und erkennt auch, dass diese Spur nur aufgrund seiner eigenen Handlung entstanden ist. Dies ist der Prozess des Übergangs vom Nichts zu Etwas. Im Prozess der Wandlung von Nichts zu Etwas ist das Etwas das Bewusstsein des Menschen von der Welt.

When humans encounter and interact with the world, they first confront the "I-I" problem within themselves. In the process of opposing the conscious self and the physical self as a living entity, individuals discover their desires, wishes, and hopes. All of these elements drive and stimulate behavior, becoming motives. Before such behavior is consciously recognized and thus transformed into (life) will, it remains merely life itself. Once recognized by the individual, alienation occurs. In an independent subjectivity, alienation manifests as the differentiation of motives where desires, wishes, and hopes split human behavior into reactions to actual situations and responses not directly tied to current reality but rather influenced by a priori, empirical, and transcendental (memory and imagination) factors. The distance between a priori, empirical, and transcendental factors and actual reflection and response represents the original intention of human nature. This distance generates feelings and consciousness of achievement or failure, glory and shame, ideals and regrets, happiness and anxiety within the individual, continuously and without cessation. Perhaps, as religious expressions suggest, humanity has lost paradise as a result. There is a thin thread between motive and purpose; when it becomes manifested as "a line", being is created from non-being.

As a species, human alienation is characterized by the differences in alienation formed between individuals, which in turn creates unique connections between the motives and purposes of each individual within humanity. Alienation does not become singular because of this; rather, it consists of an infinite plurality of unique elements that make up everything. Therefore, individuals consistently perceive themselves and others as "others," making the relationship between "I" and "other" a fundamental human issue.

The "I-Other" relationship represents how humans navigate their existence within the world. Among humans, not only do differences exist, but these differences also create distinctions between people. To highlight, preserve, and perpetuate these distinctions, humanity has constructed social order, driven by individual desires, wishes, and hopes. Before the formation of order, the "I-Other" relationship in human society was directly manifested as the survival of the fittest.

+40m (partial view /
Ausschnitt), 2012
mixed media /
Mischtechnik,
20 × 4000cm
Collection of National Art
Museum of China, Beijing,
China

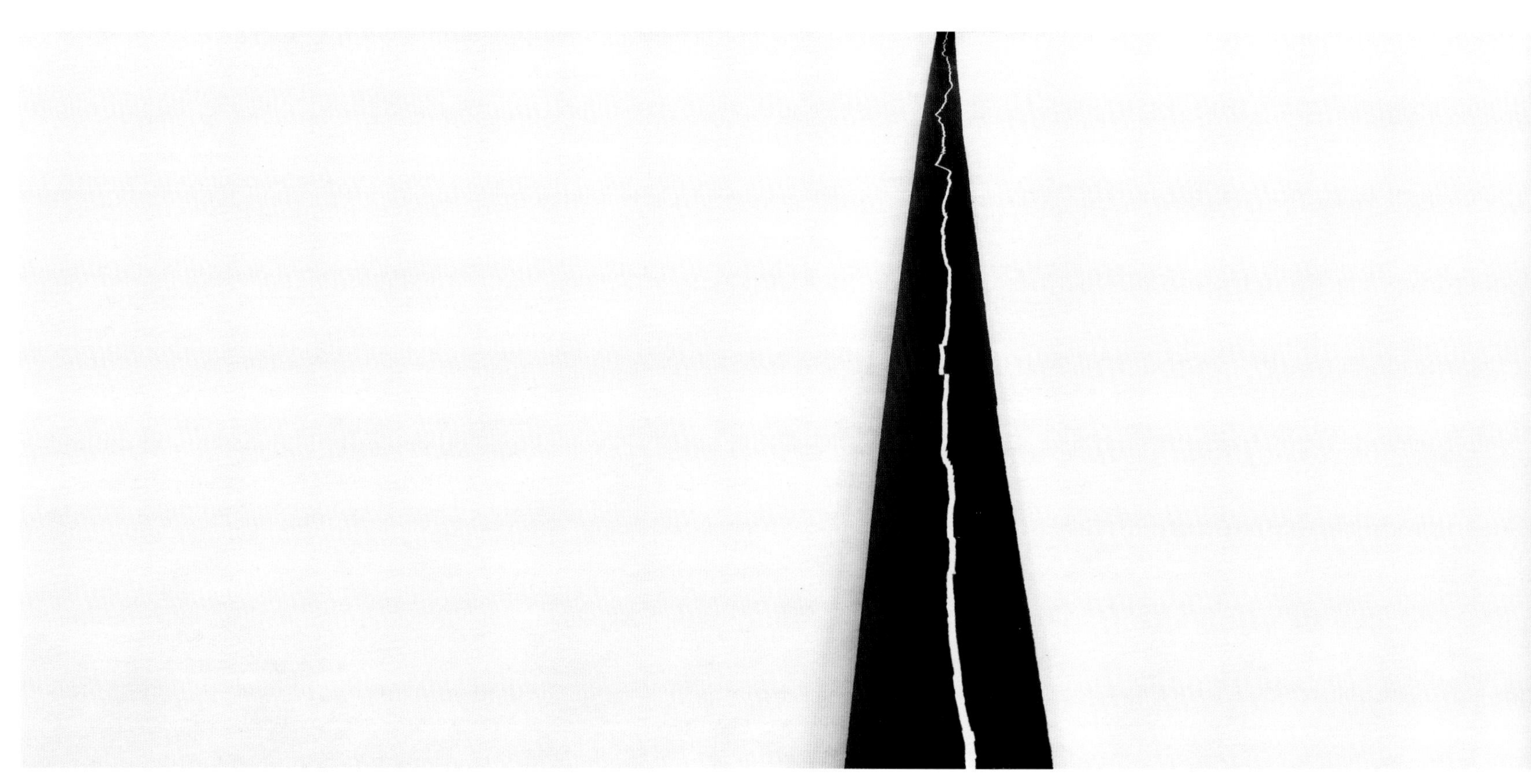

Dieser absolute Sprung von Nichts zu Etwas wurde im alten China beschrieben als „die Höchste Leere erzeugt den Höchsten Pol" und entspricht dem grundlegendsten Urteil im Denken. Aber der Weg von Nichts zum Höchsten Pol hört nicht bei „Eins" auf, ist nicht nur etwas Einziges, denn die Entstehung des Menschen ist die Entstehung seiner Spezies. Sobald diese Spezies das Menschliche hat, ist es nicht ein einzelnes Individuum, das zum Menschen wird und dann verschiedene Menschen reproduziert, sondern eine Spezies, die gemeinsam, synchron und koevolutionär zu Menschen wird. Innerhalb dieser Spezies wird sich die menschliche Natur nicht nur ihrer selbst bewusst, sondern auch dessen, dass Gefühl und Bewusstsein von sich selbst von Mensch zu Mensch unterschiedlich sind, weil sich die Bedeutung des Lebens bei verschiedenen Individuen unabhängig voneinander entwickelt.

Genau aus diesem Grund verwandelt sich der eine Strich zu einer starken Kraft der Einheit und Kohärenz aller Menschen, aber auch in den Selbstausdruck jedes Individuums in der Menge der Menschen und stellt ein einzigartiges „Eines" dar. Die Einheitlichkeit des gemeinsamen „Einen" und die diskrete Form des freien Einen können ein „Paradoxon mit zwei Richtungen" sein.[2+3]

Indem der Mensch auf der Welt ist und der Welt gegenüber steht, entsteht in ihm selbst zunächst die Frage nach der Beziehung zwischen dem Ich und dem Selbst, dem „Ich-Ich". Im Prozess der Opposition zwischen dem Ich eines bewussten Subjekts und dem Ich als physischem Objekt des Lebens entdeckt der Mensch sein eigenes Begehren, seine Bestrebungen und Hoffnungen. All diese Dinge treiben und inspirieren sein Handeln und dient ihm zur Motivation. Bevor sich der Mensch dieses Vorganges bewusst wird, aus dem ein (Lebens-) Willen entsteht, ist es das Leben an sich. Sobald es dem Menschen bewusst wird, ist eine Dissimilation, eine größere Ausdifferenzierung eingetreten. Die Dissimilation im unabhängigen Subjekt des Individuums und die Motivierung durch den Willen spalten seine Wünsche, Bestrebungen und Hoffnungen auf und unterteilen sein Verhalten in Reflexe und Reaktionen des Lebens auf die tatsächliche (äußere) Situation und auf die unmittelbare, davon unabhängige Wirklichkeit. Das alles geschieht im Apriorischen, Empirischen und Transzendentalen (im Gedächtnis und in der Vorstellung). Der Abstand zwischen dem Apriorischen, Empirischen und Transzendentalen einerseits und den tatsächlichen Reflexen und Reaktionen andererseits ist der Abstand zwischen der ursprünglichen Absicht der menschlichen Natur, dem Gefühl und dem Bewusstsein der Verwirklichung oder Nichtverwirklichung der Motive und Ziele des Menschen, die im Menschen selbst Ruhm und Schande, Ideal und Mangel, Glück und Angst hervorrufen, und dies unentwegt und unaufhörlich. Vielleicht hat der Mensch in religiöser Hinsicht hier das Paradies verloren. Zwischen Motivierung und Ziel gibt es eine Verbindungslinie, und wollte man sie visualisieren, wäre sie „ein Strich", ein Strich von Nichts zu Etwas. Die gesamte (kollektive) Dissimilation des Menschen als Gattung ist diejenige Dissimilation, die sich zwischen den Individuen herausbildet und so unterschiedliche Verbindungen zwischen den Motiven und Zwecken herstellt, die für jedes Individuum einzigartig sind. Die Dissimilation ist also nicht eine einzig alleinige, sondern es gibt eine unendliche Vielfalt von ausdifferenzierten Einzigartigkeiten, aus denen sich alles zusammensetzt. So sieht der Mensch sich selbst und die anderen seiner Art immer als eine Art Anderer. Es entsteht die Frage „Ich-Andere", d.h. die Frage nach der Beziehung zwischen den Menschen untereinander.

However, thanks to the a priori, empirical, and transcendental aspects (memory and imagination) of human nature, people have come to realize that coexistence among their kind (at least initially within the same family, tribe, or nation, and ultimately within all of humanity) is not only necessary but may also concern the survival and safety of each individual. Countless efforts have been made to construct, overturn (what already exists), revive (what once existed), and develop (what has yet to exist) a self-centered collective order (family, nation, world)—which we call politics— the endless extension and extreme manifestation of this order is "universal harmony," a unified world order. This process involves continuous self-development and transcending other human individuals and collectives, incorporating them into a unified order centered on the self and dominated by those in higher ruling positions. However, the distinctions between individual members and groups within humanity are always in flux, constantly growing and diminishing. As the saying goes, "Unity follows division, and division follows unity." In this infinite cycle of rise and fall, "world peace" is a temporary state wherein all individuals delineate their boundaries and limits through struggle and negotiation, defining these limits with a line or mark.

A line continues to delineate the boundaries between "I" and "other," and among individuals. By using a single line to define boundaries, one creates a separation from unity, which is a manifestation of "One becoming Two" in human relationships and it forms the fundamental method by which humans engage in everyday economic and political activities. In ancient Egyptian murals, for example, officials are depicted measuring land in the fields. The boundaries of lands were generally clear in ancient China or other early agricultural societies where land systems and distribution were well-defined. However, in Egypt, the annual flooding of the Nile would erase all such demarcations, making land measurement a routine task each year. Land, as an object of cultivation, initially lacks boundaries—it is "nothing." However, because it is necessary for people to establish boundaries between themselves and others to create "something," human relationships and distinctions are defined through this line. This process of differentiation gives rise to the notion of the "other". "One becomes Two", marking the beginning of society. Hence, society begins from this initial line of division.

The medium of the line is the "object" that contrasts with humans, bringing us into the realm of the "I-It" problem. In reality, material objects are part of the environment essential for human survival. For humans, anything that does not possess equal human rights is considered an object. These objects are considered in three levels: pure objects, objects that serve as tools or products, and objects that are observed and depicted. Historically, societies that have viewed certain individuals as tools or slaves (human beings treated as livestock or labor) are regarded as unjust and barbaric. Conversely, recognizing all sentient (animal) and inanimate (organic and inorganic) entities as having equal rights reflects a form of human conscience and religious belief. Since the emergence of life, human existence has coexisted with the material world. Thus, the medium that the line represents is the perception of the material and the world as the essence of reality, intertwined with human nature, where both are simultaneously One and Two. Objects, in essence, are what humans require and intervene with—whether by following, transforming, utilizing, or protecting them. The relationship between humans and objects is, therefore, one of utility and knowledge (science), and it involves both practical use and understanding. However, the relationship between humans and material is not all-encompassing; it is specifically about how objects as external entities nurture or challenge humanity. This interaction involves a dialectical unity between nurture and constraint: humans cannot exist without the material world, yet it is because of humanity that we recognize material existence as a fundamental premise of our being. This belief is reflected in the saying, "Humans die for wealth just as birds die for food." It becomes a basic human conviction. Humans and the world are unified in a sense, but the "I-It" question introduces a division, rendering the relationship between humans and the world as "Two." This "Two" then evolves into "Three," representing the multitude that encompasses all of humanity in historical context since the advent of human civilization.

Im „Ich-Andere" vollendet der Mensch seine eigene Existenz unter den Menschen. Unter den Menschen gibt nicht nur Unterschiede, sondern die Unterschiede in der Existenz treten auch sichtbar zu Tage. In der zwischenmenschlichen Ordnung sind individuelle Wünsche, Bestrebungen und Hoffnungen verpackt, eine Ordnung, die man aufzeigt, bewahrt und vererbt. Solange noch keine solche Ordnung entstanden ist, gilt unter den Menschen hinsichtlich der Frage „Ich-Andere" das Gesetz des Dschungels, der Starke frisst den Schwachen. Gleichermaßen aus dem Apriorischen, Empirischen und Transzendentalen (Gedächtnis und Vorstellung) wird sich der Mensch dessen bewußt, dass ein Zusammenleben mit seinesgleichen (mindestens zu Beginn in derselben Familie, Ethnie, Land und zuletzt mit allen Menschen) eine Notwendigkeit ist, die Überleben und Sicherheit eines jeden Einzelnen selbst berührt. Der Einzelne tut sein Bestes für eine Ordnung mit ihm selbst als Zentrum durch Subversion von Bestehendem, durch Wiederbelebung von Früherem, durch Weiterentwicklung von Zukünftigem in einem kollektiven Akt (Familie, Land, Welt), also durch Politik. Die unendliche Ausdehnung und extreme und vollständige Manifestation dieser Ordnung ist die „universelle Einheit der Welt". Ihr Prozess ist die kontinuierliche Selbstentwicklung und das individuelle oder kollektive Übertreffen anderer Menschen. Kollektive werden dadurch in eine einheitliche Ordnung mit dem „Ich" als Zentrum und einer übergeordneten Dominanz- und Herrschaftsposition gebracht. Die Unterschiede zwischen einzelnen und kollektiven Mitgliedern werden jedoch immer größer und verändern sich, lange Vereintes wird getrennt, lange Getrenntes wird vereint. In diesem Prozess des unendlichen Wachstums und Verfalls ist der „Weltfrieden" ein vorübergehender Zustand, in dem alle Menschen ihre Grenzen und Bereiche auf der Grundlage der Ergebnisse bestimmter Kämpfe und Verhandlungen aufteilen. Grenzen und Bereiche werden mit einem Strich definiert.

Ein Strich, der in der Folge die Grenze zwischen mir und anderen zieht. In der Markierung einer Grenze mit einem Strich manifestiert sich unter den Menschen, dass aus dem Einen Zwei entsteht. Es ist auch die grundlegende Verhaltensmethode der Menschen, um alltägliche wirtschaftliche und politische Aktivitäten auszuführen. Auf altägyptischen Wandgemälden sind Beamte des Pharaos in einem Weizenfeld zu sehen, wie sie mit anderen Menschen das Land vermessen. Ursprünglich waren die Flurgrenzen eindeutig. Im alten China oder in anderen frühen landwirtschaftlichen Gesellschaften waren die Grenzen nie unklar, unabhängig davon, welches Landsystem und Verteilungssystem herrschte. Da in Ägypten die jährlichen Nilfluten alle Flurgrenzen überschwemmten, war ihre erneute Markierung eine normale und jährlich wiederkehrende Maßnahme. Land als Gegenstand ohne Grenze ist „Nichts", und da Abgrenzungen zwischen Menschen gezogen werden müssen, entsteht daraus „Etwas". Unter den Menschen wird also mit einem Strich die Beziehung zwischen einem selbst und den anderen definiert, daraus entsteht der Andere, aus Eins wird Zwei. Das ist der Beginn der Gesellschaft, und die Gesellschaft beginnt mit einem Strich.

Das Trägermedium eines Striches ist das dem Menschen gegenüberliegende „Ding", und das bringt den Menschen auf die Ebene des „Ich-Es". Tatsächlich sind die materiellen Gegenstände die Dinge, auf die die Menschen ihre Existenz gründen. Für Menschen werden Objekte, die nicht gleichermaßen Menschenrechte haben, als Dinge betrachtet und in die drei Kategorien reine Dinge, Werkzeuge und Produkte und anzuschauende bzw. gemalte Dinge unterteilt. Natürlich betrachten wir hier Gesellschaften in der Geschichte der Menschheit, die andere Menschen als Werkzeuge oder Sklaven (Menschen als Vieh und Arbeitskräfte) ansahen, als ungerecht und barbarisch. Alle fühlenden Wesen (Tiere), emotionslose, organische und anorganische Wesen und Dinge als gleichberechtigt mit Menschen zu betrachten, ist eine Art menschlichen Gewissens und religiöser Glaube. Nach der Entstehung menschlichen Lebens ist die menschliche Existenz und die Existenz der Materie gleichermaßen existent. Das Medium der Darstellung des einen Strichs besteht also darin, die Dinge und die Materie als das Wesen der Welt zu betrachten, welche mit dem Wesen des Menschen, aus zwei zu einem werden,

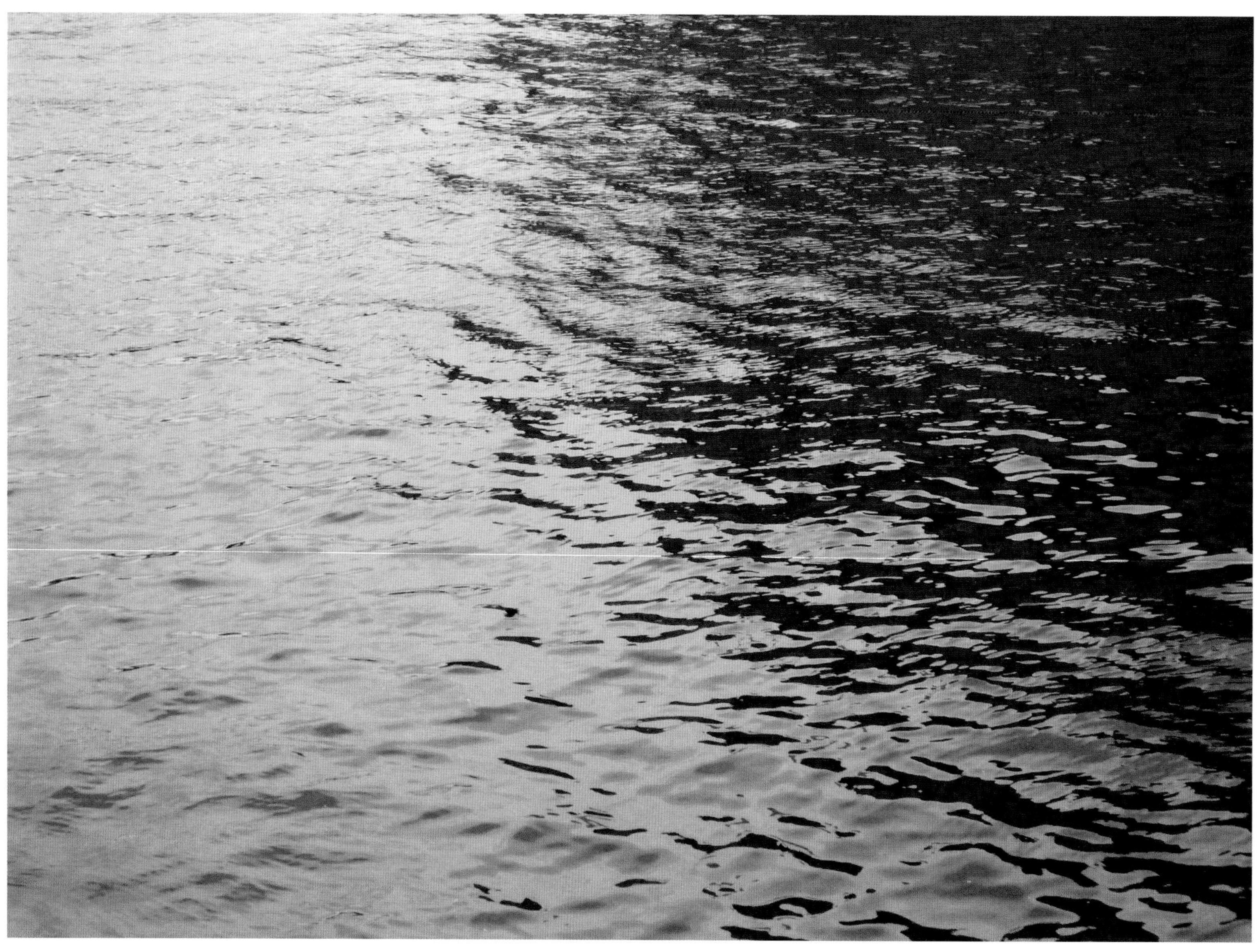

Photo by Tan Ping, 2022

When confronting one's own existence, human contemplation leads to the pursuit of an infinite scope and the ultimate goal. The thoughts generated within human nature drive individuals to transcend the limitations imposed by reality and everyday life, aspiring towards the divine and the mysterious. This aspiration reflects human divinity, demanding a fundamental resolution of existence itself, which ultimately returns to the concept of "One." Therefore, the representation of "one line" embodies all meanings and also transcends and negates all meanings.

Returning now to Tan Ping's latest exhibition, he once again addresses the Germany that nurtured and educated him, sharing his reflections on the world and his thoughts on life accumulated over the years. The "single line" this time differs from the one that appeared in 2012. It is no longer a conclusion encompassing everything, but rather an expression of his boundless and ineffable entirety. This "line" now begins to reveal a more fundamental origin that comes from nothingness.

Any "One" is a collection of countless "Many," and conversely, any "One" can be dispersed into an infinite "Many." Whether in addressing any part of the world or delving into the deepest recesses of our individual inner selves, this process can produce a new, indistinguishable, solitary figure, as if temporarily "reuniting into one form"—this temporary "reuniting into one form" exists only to scatter the "One" once more into infinite "Many," or perhaps it perpetually exists as both "One" and "Many".

aber zwei verschiedene Verwendungen haben. Objekte sind das, was Menschen brauchen und in die sie interferieren, sei es, um sich ihnen unterzuordnen, sie umzuwandeln, zu benutzen oder zu bewahren. Die Beziehung zwischen Menschen und Objekten ist natürlich die von Nutzung und Erkenntnis. Erkenntnis bedeutet sowohl Gebrauch als auch Wissen bzw. Wissenschaft. Wie dem auch sei, die Beziehung zwischen Mensch und Materie bedeutet nicht die Beziehung zur gesamten Materie, sondern zu der Materie, die sich außerhalb des Menschen befindet, die für den Menschen ein Objekt ist, welches für ihn zum Ernährer oder zur Bedrohung wird, zur widersprüchlichen Einheit im Verlauf des Ernährens und Bedrohens. Wenn es für den Menschen keine Materie in der äußeren Welt gibt, kann er nicht selbst zu dem Mensch werden, der er eigentlich ist, aber da er über Talente verfügt, hält er die Voraussetzungen und Grundlagen seiner Existenz für Materie. Das bin ich selbst, wagt er zu sagen. Ach und die Existenz des Vogels? Der Mensch stirbt für den Reichtum, der Vogel verendet für sein Futter, das wurde zu einer Grundüberzeugung der Menschen. Mensch und Welt sind ein einheitliches Eines, aufgrund der Frage „Ich-Es" sind Mensch und Welt aber auch „Zwei". Dieses Zwei bezieht sich auf das menschliche Haben, und dieses Haben kann sich zu einem „Drei" und zu einer Vielheit entwickeln, bis hin zum relativen Besitztum der gesamten Menschheit in der Geschichte (seit Menschen zu Menschen wurden).

Mit dem Begriff Ich-Gott wird die unbegrenzte Kategorie und das ultimative Ziel zusammengefasst, über dessen Erreichung der Mensch nachdenkt, wenn er seiner eigenen Existenz gegenübersteht. Die in der menschlichen Natur entstandene Idee ist, sich von der Realität zu lösen und die Grenzen des Endlichkeit des Lebens zu überwinden, zum Heiligen und Mysteriösen zu schreiten, die Göttlichkeit im Menschsein zu erfahren. Es fordert eine Art grundlegender Zusammenfassung der endgültigen Existenz, eine vollständige und grundlegende Zusammenfassung, nur um schließlich wieder zum „Einen" zurückzukehren. Gerade deshalb liegen in der Darstellung des „einen Striches" alle Bedeutungen und alles, was diese Bedeutungen transzendiert oder negiert.

Nun kommen wir zu Tan Pings diesmaliger Ausstellung zurück. Er erzählt noch einmal für Deutschland, den Nährboden seiner künstlerischen Ausbildung, wie er seit Jahren die Welt wahrnimmt und von seinen Gedanken über das Leben. „Ein Strich" hier unterscheidet sich von dem „Einen Strich", der 2012 erschien. Damals war der „Eine Strich" eine Zusammenfassung von allem, nun ist er dessen unendliche Ausdehnung und unbeschreibliche Totalität. Der „Eine Strich" dieser Ausstellung hat begonnen, einen grundlegenderen Ursprung zu offenbaren, der aus dem Nichts kommt.

Jedes „Eine" ist eine Ansammlung unzähliger „Vieler", und umgekehrt kann jedes „Eine" in unendliche „Viele" geteilt werden. In jedem Teil der Welt, in den inneren Tiefen eines jeden von uns Menschen ist es möglich, ein neues, ununterscheidbares, einsames und stilles Wesen zu erschaffen, als wäre es ein momentanes „wieder gemeinsam in einer Form". Dieses „wieder gemeinsam in einer Form" auch deswegen, damit sich dieses „Eine" wiederum in einer unendliche Anzahl von „Vielen" manifestiert, oder eben von Anfang bis Ende immer sowohl das „Eine" als auch das „Viele" ist.

Die dritte Abstraktion entspricht dem Sein der zehntausend Dinge. Dieses Sein meint aber nicht dasjenige der westlichen Philosophie, ein Sein der bereits existierenden Dinge, sondern bezieht sich auf den ontogenetischen Zustand des „Nicht-Seins", des „existenzlosen" Seins der östlichen Philosophie. Die dritte Abstraktion ist Ausdruck und die Manifestation eines Prozesses, der von dem Zustand, „seinslos" zu sein, zu dem „seiend" zu sein führt, was der Entstehung von Etwas aus dem Nichts entspricht.

1 From Hans Hartung's *Autobiography*, cited in the exhibition catalog Hartung, 2003, National Art Museum of China.

2 Nishida divides "Place" into three stages: the "place of being," the "place of relative nothingness," and the "place of absolute nothingness," believing that the "place of absolute nothingness" is the true "place of nothingness." "Absolute nothingness" is neither "being" nor "nothing"; its fundamental function is like that of a mirror, reflecting "objects as they are." "Place" is also referred to as the "field of consciousness," where intellect, emotion, and will come together, and all phenomena of both the subjective and objective realms are established within it.

3 The concept of a "mutual paradox" is introduced here as a methodology. A mutual paradox is based on the fundamental understanding that any factor can develop in opposite or contrasting directions. Alongside (Greek) logic and (Indian) Nyaya, it constitutes one of the primary perspectives of human thinking, known as "dialectics" (in the Chinese sense). This dialectical thinking, which seeks a middle ground, is somewhat different from dialectics in Western philosophy. In the West, dialectics refers to debates between language, stemming from the Greek word dialektos (speech, dialogue, discourse, and, of course, also a regional dialect), and from dialegesthai [to engage in discussion or debate between two parties, derived from the roots dia (between) and the Proto-Indo-European root leg (to speak)], thus focusing on "debate" in a linguistic sense. In contrast, "mutual paradox" holds that all things are in a state of contradictory unity (a point shared with Western dialectics), but emphasizes that each opportunity for movement and change can develop in any direction. The direction of development depends on the conditions and position in which it occurs, yet this direction does not define the entirety of its nature or characteristics. Rather, it contains within it a paradox that points towards its opposite direction. (*Theoretical Studies on Art*, pp. 48-49, annotation)

4 In Chapter 11 of *The Commentaries on the Book of Changes* (Yizhuan, Xici Shangzhuan), it is stated: "Thus, the Yi contains the Supreme Ultimate (Taiyi), which generates two opposing forces (Liangyi)." Since ancient times, there have been at least seven interpretations of how the Supreme Ultimate gives rise to Two: one interpretation sees it as yin and yang; another as heaven and earth; one as odd and even; one as firmness and gentleness; one as black and yellow; another as Qian and Kun (active and receptive); and another as spring and autumn. In truth, any opposing factors can be understood as binary oppositions, though the process of their generation may differ.

1   Zitiert nach Hans Hartungs „Autobiographie", Ausstellungskatalog Hans Hartung, Nationales Kunstmuseum China, 2003.

2   Das hier dargestellte „Paradoxon mit zwei Richtungen" ist eine Denkmethode. Sie entspricht einem grundlegenden Verständnis dafür, dass jedweder Faktor die Tendenz hat, sich in entgegengesetzte, relativ unterschiedliche Richtungen zu entwickeln. Zusammen mit der griechischen Logik und der indischen Lehre der Kausalität bildet sie eine der wichtigsten Methoden des menschlichen Denkens, nämlich die chinesische Dialektik. Sie bedient sich einer von der westlichen Dialektik verschiedenen Art des Denkens. Diese entstammt einerseits dem griechisch-lateinischen dialectos (Unterredung, Rede, Diskussion, natürlich auch Dialekt im Sinne von Mundart), andererseits von dialégesthai [Gespräch, Diskussion, Streitgespräch zweier Seiten, mit dem Präfix dia- (durch, über) und dem ursprünglich indogermanischen leg (sprechen)]. Deswegen ist es eine Dialektik im Sinne der Sprache. Das Paradoxon mit zwei Richtungen geht davon aus, dass alles eine Einheit von Gegensätzen im Widerspruch ist (wie bei der westlichen Dialektik), betont aber, dass für einen Faktor jede Bewegungs- und Veränderungsmöglichkeit in die eine oder andere Richtung geht, abhängig von den Bedingungen, unter denen sie stattfindet, und vom jeweiligen Standort des Faktoren. Eine eingeschlagene Entwicklungsrichtung bestimmt nicht in Gänze seine Natur und Eigenschaften, sondern enthält das Paradoxon seiner entgegengesetzten Richtung in sich. Siehe meine Theorie der Kunstwissenschaft, S. 48f.

3   Im 11. Kapitel der Kommentare zum „Buch der Wandlungen" heißt es: „Daher gibt es den Höchsten Pol, der die beiden Werkzeuge hervorbringt". Seit alters her gibt es mindestens sieben Erklärungen für diese beiden Werkzeuge: Yin und Yang, Himmel und Erde, gerade und ungerade, hart und weich, geheimnisvoll und gelb (als Farben des Himmels resp. der Erde), Qian und Kun (etwa Himmel und Erde) und Frühling und Herbst. Tatsächlich können alle gegensätzlichen Faktoren als binäre Gegensätze interpretiert werden, ihr Entstehungsprozess ist unterschiedlich.

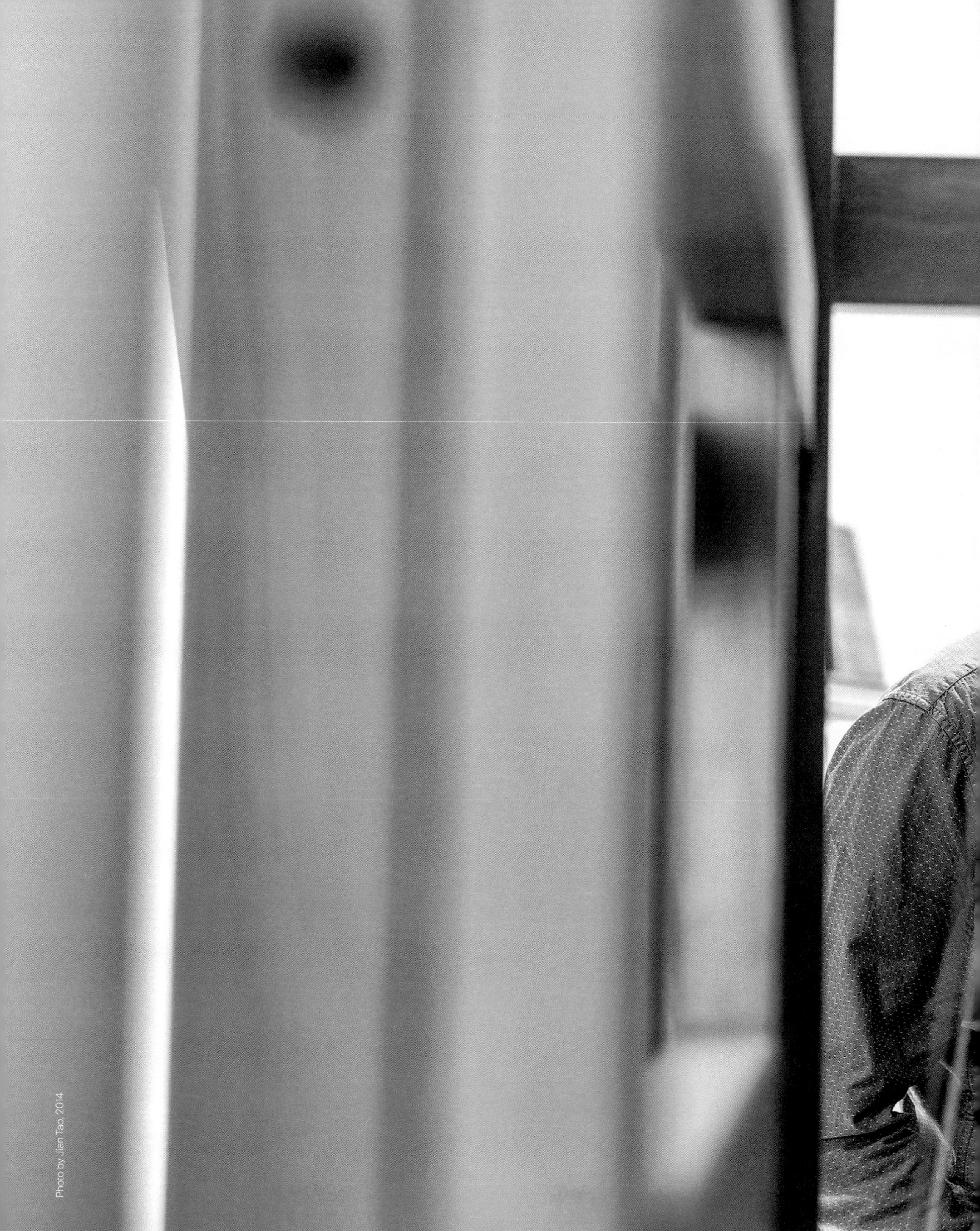

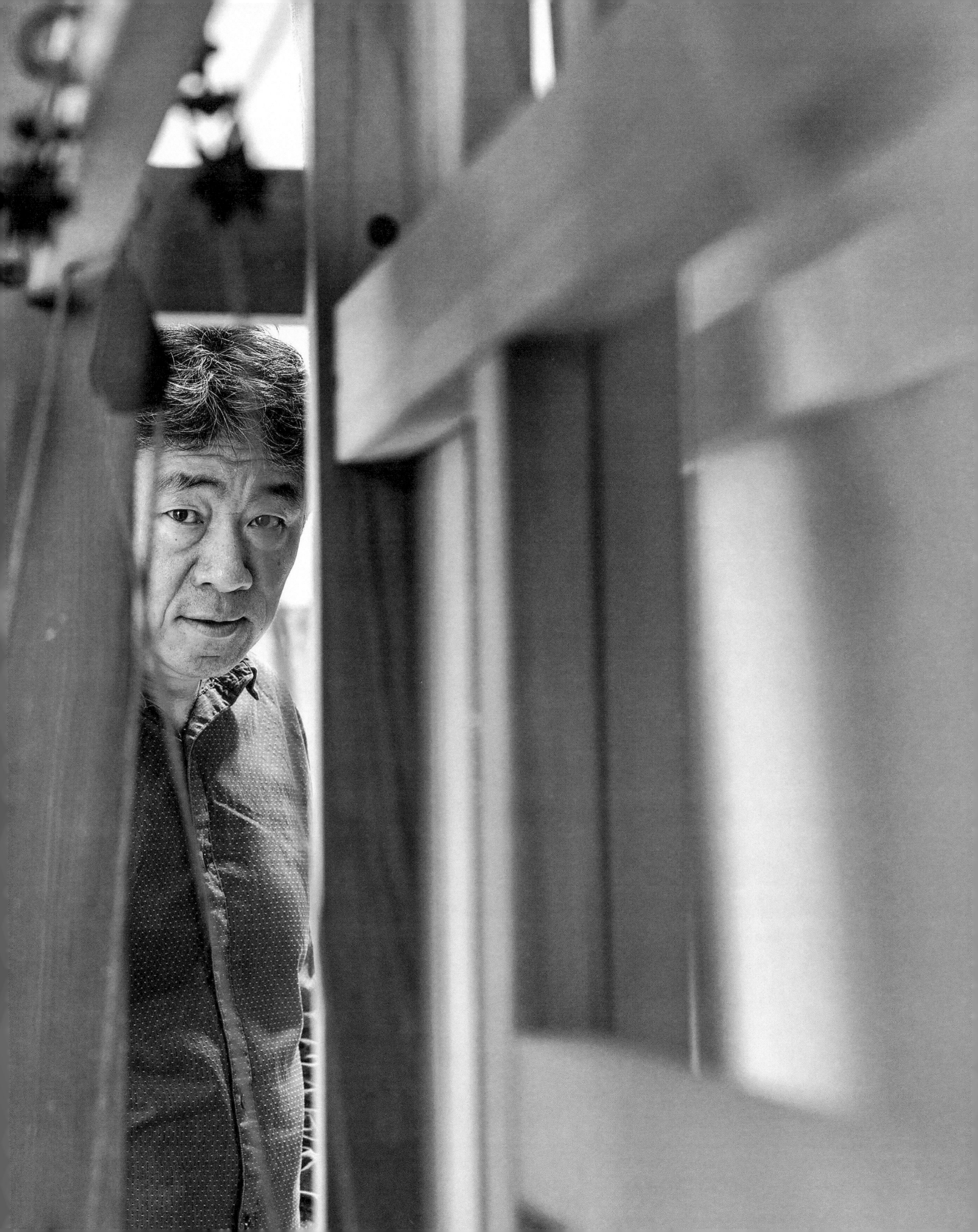

Self-Statement

Tan Ping

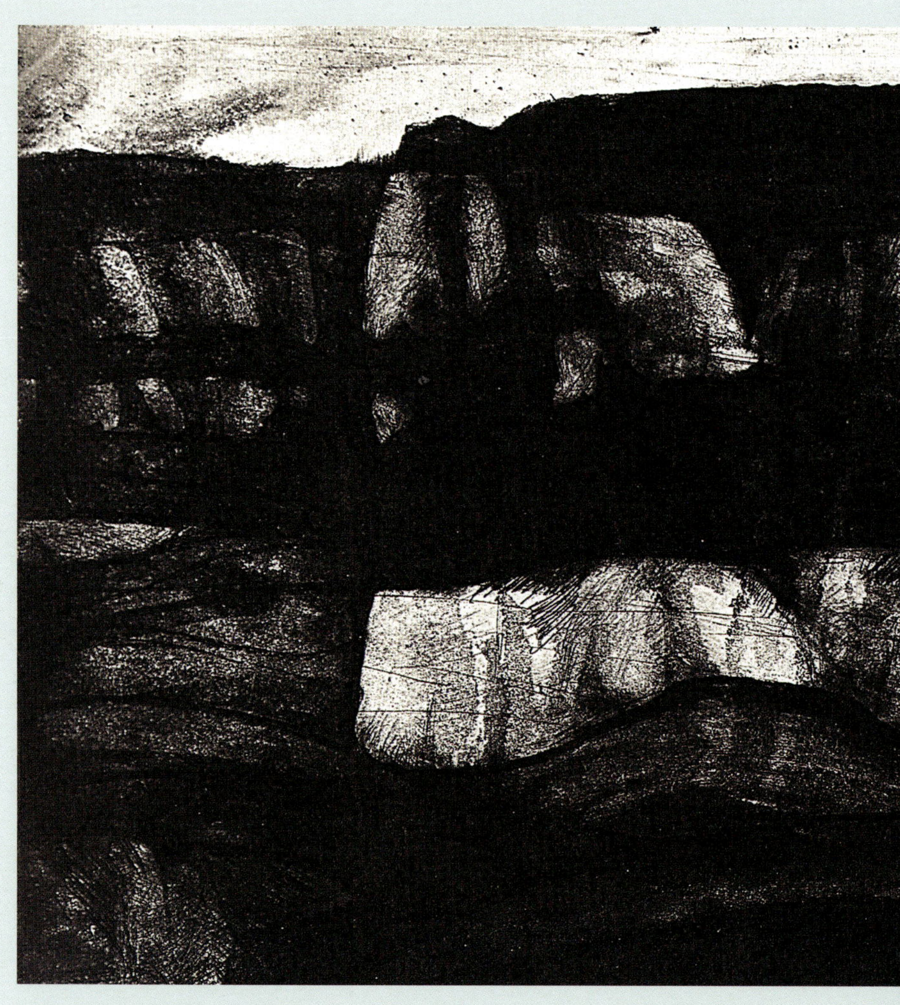

Taihang Mountain, 1982
etching / **Radierung**,
20 × 50.6cm
Beijing, China

I was born in 1960 in Chengde, China. In 1980, I began my studies in printmaking at the Central Academy of Fine Arts in Beijing, where I earned my bachelor's degree. In 1989, I was awarded the Federal German Cultural Exchange Scholarship (DAAD) and went on to study in the Free Painting Department at the Berlin University of the Arts, where I obtained my master's degree. From the early stages of technical learning to expressing my own feelings and thoughts through art, my journey has been profoundly shaped by significant historical events, such as China's Reform and Opening Up in the 1980s and the fall of the Berlin Wall in 1989. These experiences, coupled with the diverse cultural influences I encountered, have had a tremendous impact on my artistic development.

My artistic growth is closely tied to my experiences in both Beijing and Berlin. The art education I received in China provided me with a solid foundation and a deep understanding of Chinese culture and its dynamism within society. In contrast, the education I received in Germany broadened my artistic perspective and awakened a latent sense of freedom within me. Art, as I see it, is a process of self-realization—one that requires continuous exploration and personal discovery.

Selbstauskunft

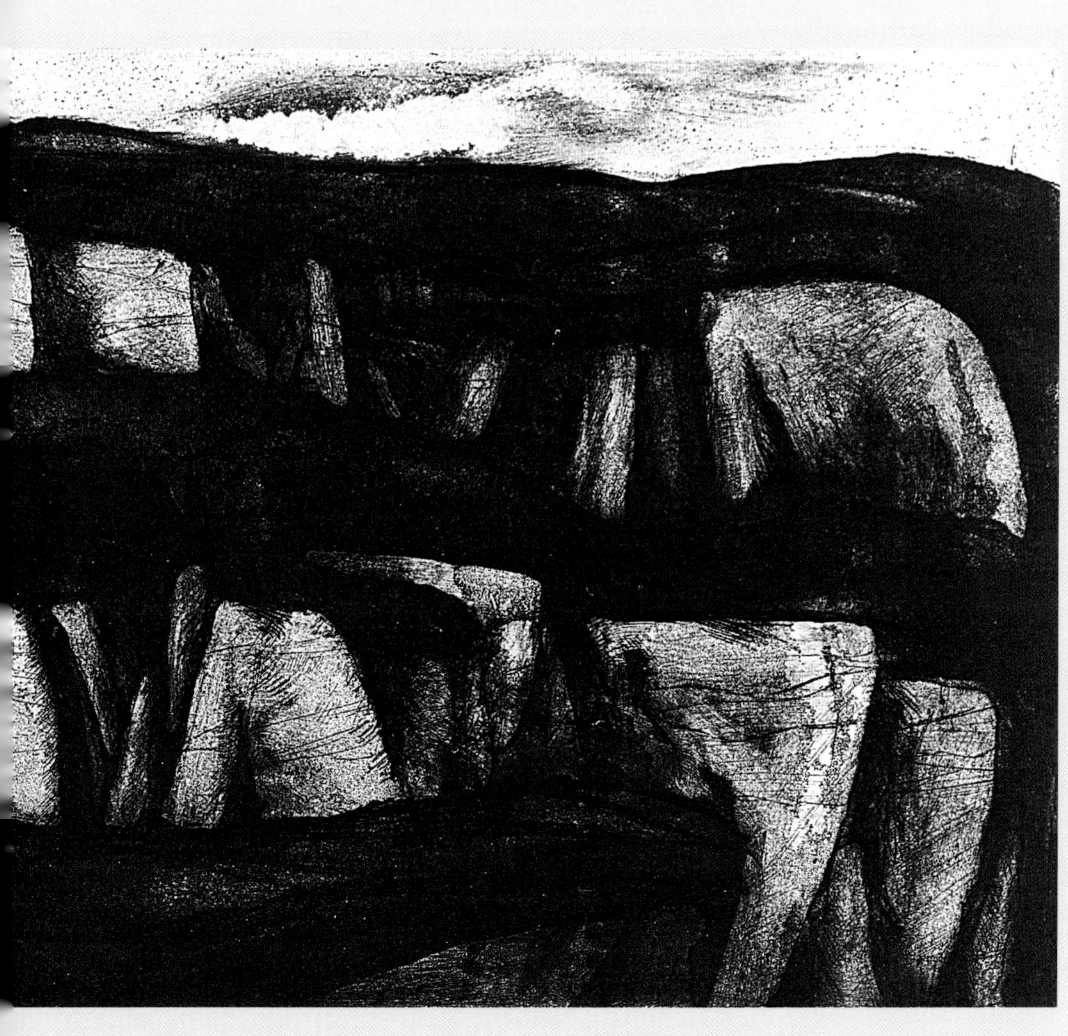

Ich wurde 1960 in Chengde, China, geboren. Im Jahr 1980 begann ich ein Studium der Druckgrafik an der Zentralen Akademie der Schönen Künste in Peking, das ich mit dem Bachelor abschloss. 1989 erhielt ich ein DAAD-Stipendium und studierte an der Universität der Künste Berlin im Fachbereich Freie Malerei, wo ich meinen Master machte. Von den Anfängen des technischen Lernens bis hin zum Ausdruck meiner eigenen Gefühle und Gedanken durch die Kunst wurde mein Weg von bedeutenden historischen Ereignissen wie der Reform und Öffnung Chinas in den 1980er Jahren und dem Fall der Berliner Mauer in 1989 tiefgreifend geprägt. Diese Erfahrungen und die vielfältigen kulturellen Einflüsse, denen ich begegnet bin, haben meine künstlerische Entwicklung enorm beeinflusst.

Meine künstlerische Entwicklung ist eng mit meinen Erfahrungen in Peking und Berlin verbunden. Die künstlerische Ausbildung, die ich in China erhielt, vermittelte mir eine solide Grundlage und ein tiefes Verständnis der chinesischen Kultur und ihrer Dynamik innerhalb der Gesellschaft. Im Gegensatz dazu hat die Ausbildung in Deutschland meinen künstlerischen Blickwinkel erweitert und ein latentes Gefühl von Freiheit in mir geweckt. Kunst ist für mich ein Prozess der Selbstverwirklichung, der eine ständige Erforschung und persönliche Entdeckung erfordert.

Drawing / **Zeichnung**, 2021
charcoal pencil /
Kohlestift, 110 × 79cm
Collection of ZiWU, Beijing,
China

[**Art is the perfect synthesis of body and mind, as well as the anticipation that follows a playful act of "destruction."**

My work often begins with free, spontaneous line drawing and smudging. At predetermined points in time, I employ a destructive technique to "cover" the artwork, regardless of how perfect the image may appear. Every time I apply this destructive "overlaying" method on a seemingly flawless image, I am challenging the limits of my inner self, making the experience of continual "destruction" the very core of my art. On a material level, the overlaid images still exist beneath layers of color, much like human history, where traces and imprints remain despite natural decay or human destruction. The act of "overlaying" creates a slice of time, while history is an accumulation of these slices. On a spiritual level, overlay is akin to a form of mind-cultivating practice. I strive to keep my work in a perpetually unfinished state, allowing it to be continuously overlaid, which keeps it closely connected to my inner self. In art, the excitement of thought and inner emotions always emerged through the process of "destruction."

[**Kunst ist die perfekte Synthese von Körper und Geist sowie die Vorfreude auf einen spielerischen Akt der „Zerstörung".**

Meine Arbeit beginnt oft mit freien, spontanen Strichzeichnungen und Verwischungen. Zu vorbestimmten Zeitpunkten wende ich eine zerstörerische Technik an, um das Kunstwerk zu „überdecken", unabhängig davon, wie perfekt das Bild erscheinen mag. Jedes Mal, wenn ich diese zerstörerische „Überlagerungs"-Methode auf ein scheinbar makelloses Bild anwende, fordere ich die Grenzen meines inneren Selbst heraus und mache die Erfahrung der ständigen „Zerstörung" zum Kern meiner Kunst. Auf einer materiellen Ebene existieren die überlagerten Bilder immer noch unter den Farbschichten, ähnlich wie in der menschlichen Geschichte, wo Spuren und Abdrücke trotz natürlichen Verfalls oder menschlicher Zerstörung bestehen bleiben. Der Akt des „Überlagerns" schafft einen Zeitabschnitt, während die Geschichte eine Ansammlung dieser Abschnitte ist. Auf einer spirituellen Ebene ist die Überlagerung mit einer Art geistiger Kultivierungspraxis vergleichbar. Ich bemühe mich, meine Arbeit in einem immerwährenden unvollendeten Zustand zu halten, so dass sie ständig überlagert werden kann, wodurch sie eng mit meinem inneren Selbst verbunden bleibt. In der Kunst ist die Erregung des Denkens und der inneren Gefühle immer durch den Prozess der „Zerstörung" entstanden.

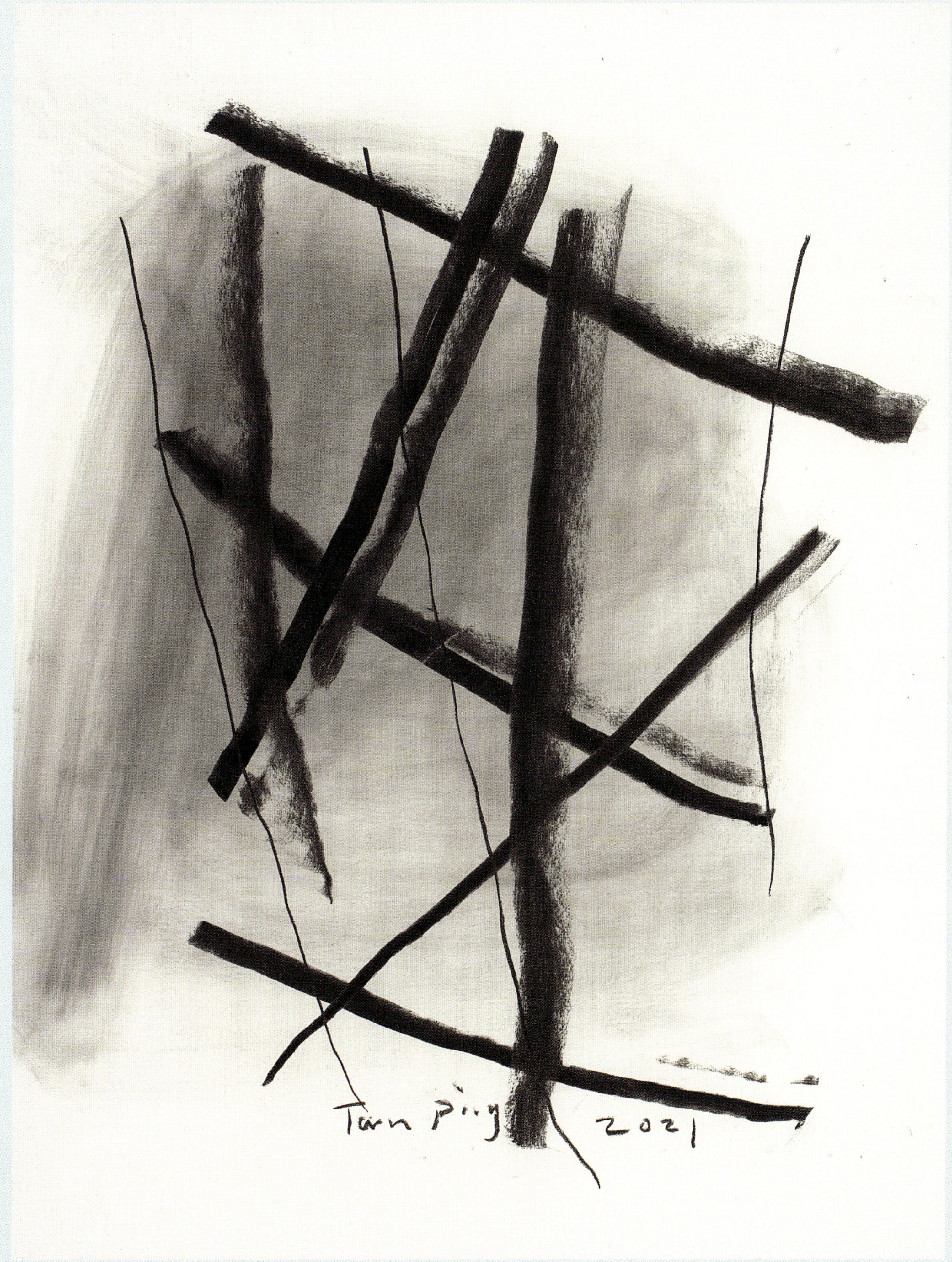

Tan Ping 2021

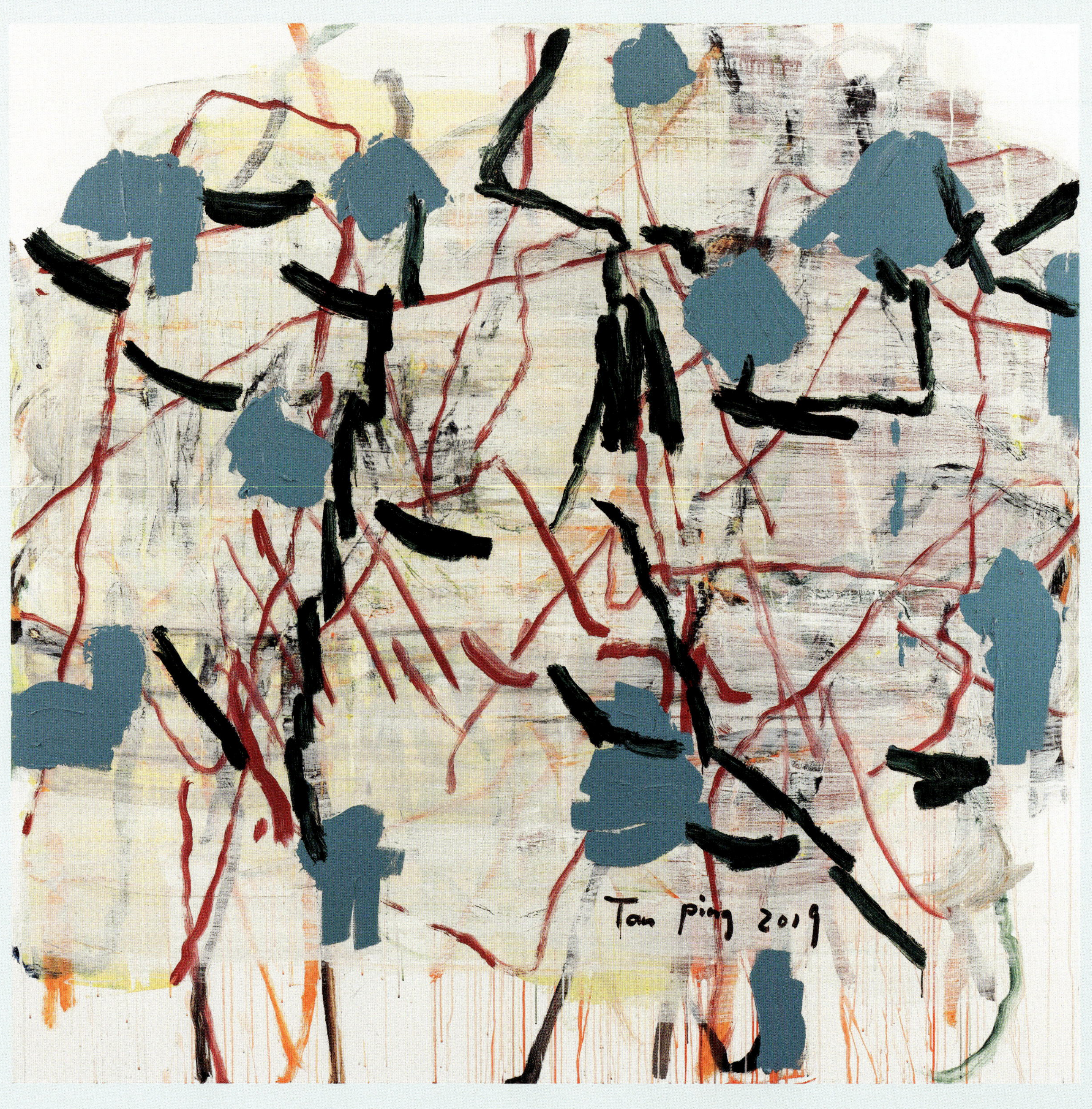

Die „Zeit" ist das Medium, in dem meine Arbeit entsteht, während der "Raum" das Feld ist, in dem sich meine Kreativität entfaltet.

Ein Kunstwerk mag dem Betrachter statisch und augenblicklich erscheinen, aber für mich ist es dynamisch und ständig im Wandel begriffen – eine kontinuierliche Schichtung von Zeitfragmenten, die das wahre Wesen der Dinge zum Vorschein bringt. Die Kunst hat mir die Möglichkeit gegeben, „Zeit" als Werkzeug zu benutzen. Für mich kann Zeit eingefroren, verbannt oder flüchtig sein. Die „Zeit" hat mich dazu gebracht, mich auf die Leere zu konzentrieren, in den Raum einzudringen, und der Leere innerhalb und außerhalb der Leinwand einen Sinn zu geben. Die Zeit ist nicht nur kontinuierlich, sie ist auch fragmentiert und flüchtig. Der Raum ist nicht nur konstruiert, er ist auch leer und fließend. Ich erwarte ständig das zufällige Zusammentreffen von Zeit und Raum in ihrer Fluidität - diese Begegnungen sind zufällig und unwiederholbar. Dennoch kann die Anhäufung von Fragmenten und sich überschneidenden Momenten in einem Künstler unendliche Vitalität und Kreativität auslösen. Vor allem aber entdeckt der Künstler die veränderlichen und unveränderlichen Aspekte seines Selbst, indem er die abstrakten Konzepte von Zeit und Raum in die Ebbe und Flut der Zeit stellt.

"Time" is the medium through which my work is created, while "space" is the field in which my creativity unfolds.

A work of art may appear static and momentary to the viewer, but for me, it is dynamic and ever-changing—a continuous layering of fragments of time that allows the true nature of things to emerge. Art has granted me the opportunity to use "time" as a tool. To me, time can be frozen, exiled, or fleetingly ephemeral. "Time" has led me to focus on the void, to enter space, giving meaning to the emptiness both within and outside the canvas. Time is not just continuous; it is also fragmented and momentary. Space is not just constructed; it is also empty and flowing. I constantly anticipate the chance encounter between time and space in their fluidity—these encounters are random and unrepeatable. Yet, the accumulation of fragments and overlapping moments can spark infinite vitality and creativity in an artist. Most importantly, by placing the abstract concepts of time and space within the ebb and flow of the era, an artist discovers the mutable and immutable aspects of the self.

Tan Ping

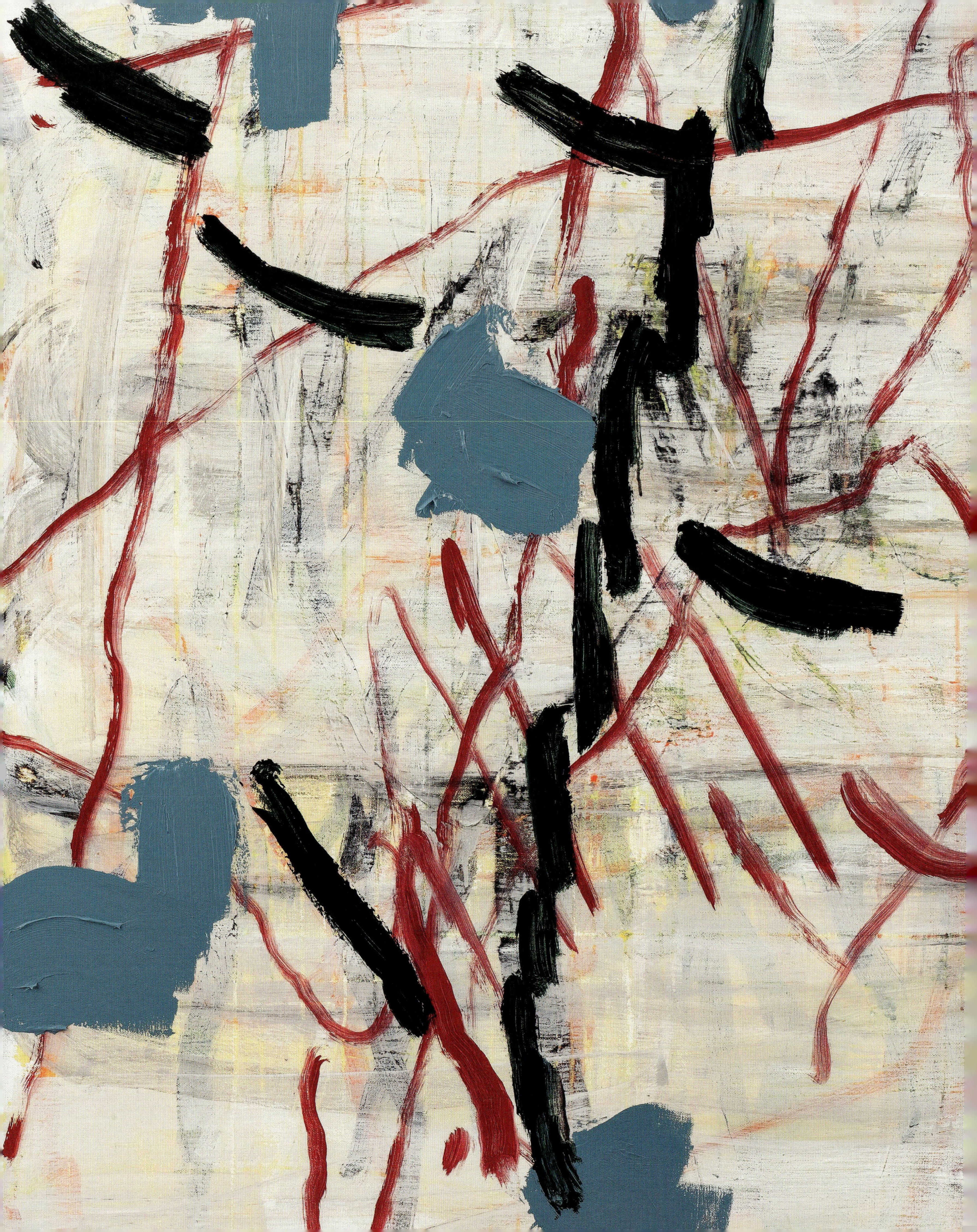

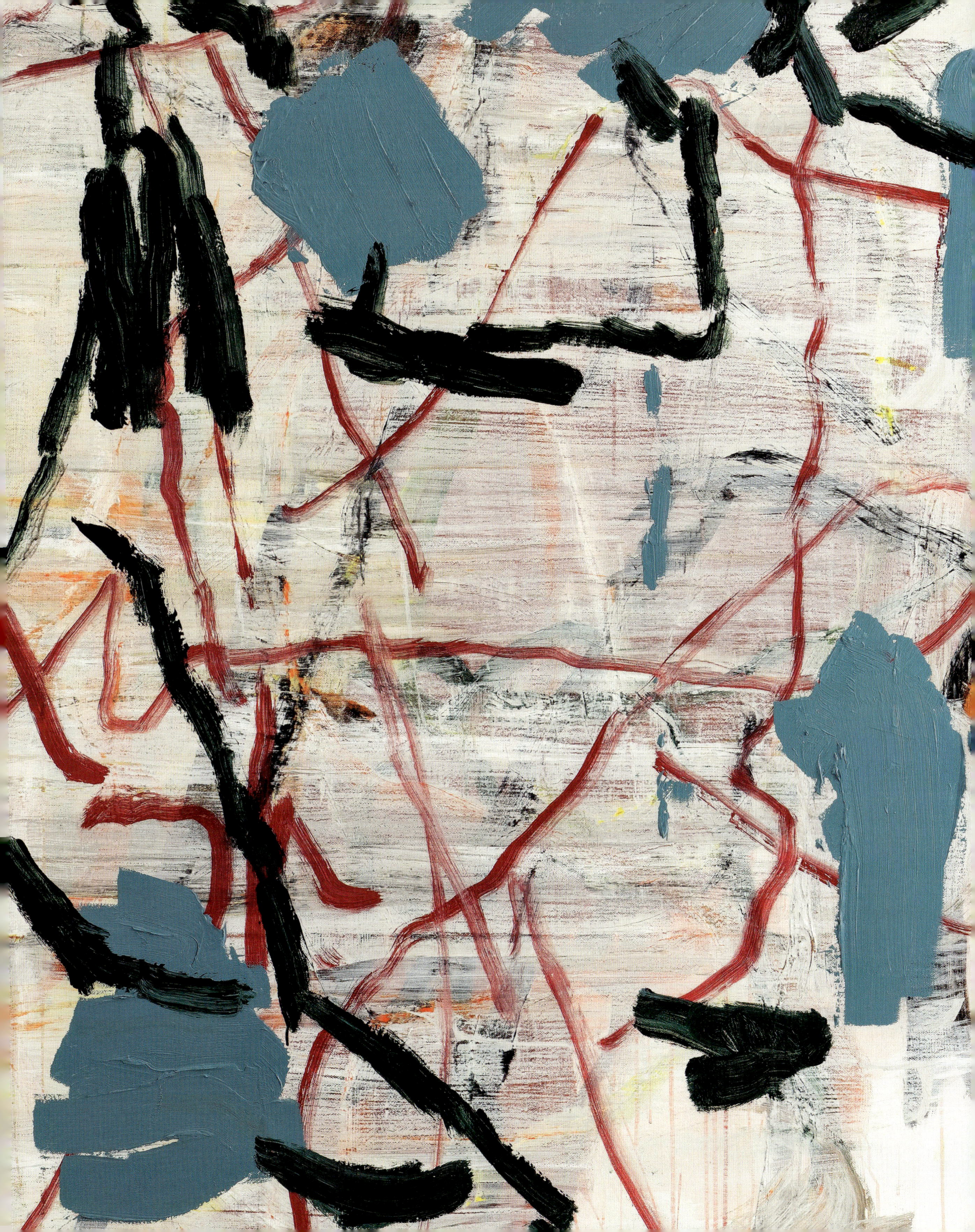

Art is the remembrance of "pain".

Today's world is engulfed in profound uncertainty, a chaotic state where control seems lost. The constant clashes of global political, economic, cultural, and ideological forces leave us with little time to reflect on the past, and even less to dream of a brighter future. Our bodies and souls have lost their foothold, as if the future and the past have become two towering walls slowly closing in, compressing the "beautiful reality" into a lifeless specimen trapped within a narrow crevice. As an artist, I find myself in this perpetual state of uncertainty, seeking a spiritual home. Perhaps the "beauty" in an image must be underpinned by "pain" to possess true substance. My numbed senses can only be awakened through "wounds." It is through his/her own "pain" that an artist can bring certainty to the uncertain. In the space between past and future, life and death, art becomes the means through which life is liberated from the turmoil, confusion, fear, and self-conflict of existence. By manifesting these experiences through art, the artist achieves spiritual transcendence, leaving imprints in every fleeting moment of our era.

In the darkest of times, art is the light that pierces through darkness.

Kunst ist die Erinnerung an den „Schmerz".

Die heutige Welt ist von tiefgreifender Unsicherheit geprägt, einem chaotischen Zustand, in dem die Kontrolle verloren zu gehen scheint. Das ständige Aufeinanderprallen globaler politischer, wirtschaftlicher, kultureller und ideologischer Kräfte lässt uns wenig Zeit, über die Vergangenheit nachzudenken, und noch weniger, von einer besseren Zukunft zu träumen. Unser Körper und unsere Seele haben den Halt verloren, als wären die Zukunft und die Vergangenheit zu zwei hohen Mauern geworden, die sich langsam schließen und die „schöne Wirklichkeit" zu einem leblosen Exemplar in einem engen Spalt zusammenpressen. Als Künstler befinde ich mich in diesem ständigen Zustand der Ungewissheit, auf der Suche nach einer geistigen Heimat. Vielleicht muss die „Schönheit" eines Bildes durch „Schmerz" untermauert werden, um wahre Substanz zu besitzen. Meine betäubten Sinne können nur durch „Wunden" geweckt werden. Durch seinen eigenen „Schmerz" kann ein Künstler dem Ungewissen Gewissheit geben. Im Raum zwischen Vergangenheit und Zukunft, Leben und Tod wird die Kunst zum Mittel, das das Leben aus dem Aufruhr, der Verwirrung, der Angst und dem Selbstkonflikt der Existenz befreit. Indem er diese Erfahrungen durch die Kunst manifestiert, erreicht der Künstler eine spirituelle Transzendenz, die in jedem flüchtigen Moment unserer Zeit Spuren hinterlässt.

In den dunkelsten Zeiten ist die Kunst das Licht, das die Finsternis durchdringt.

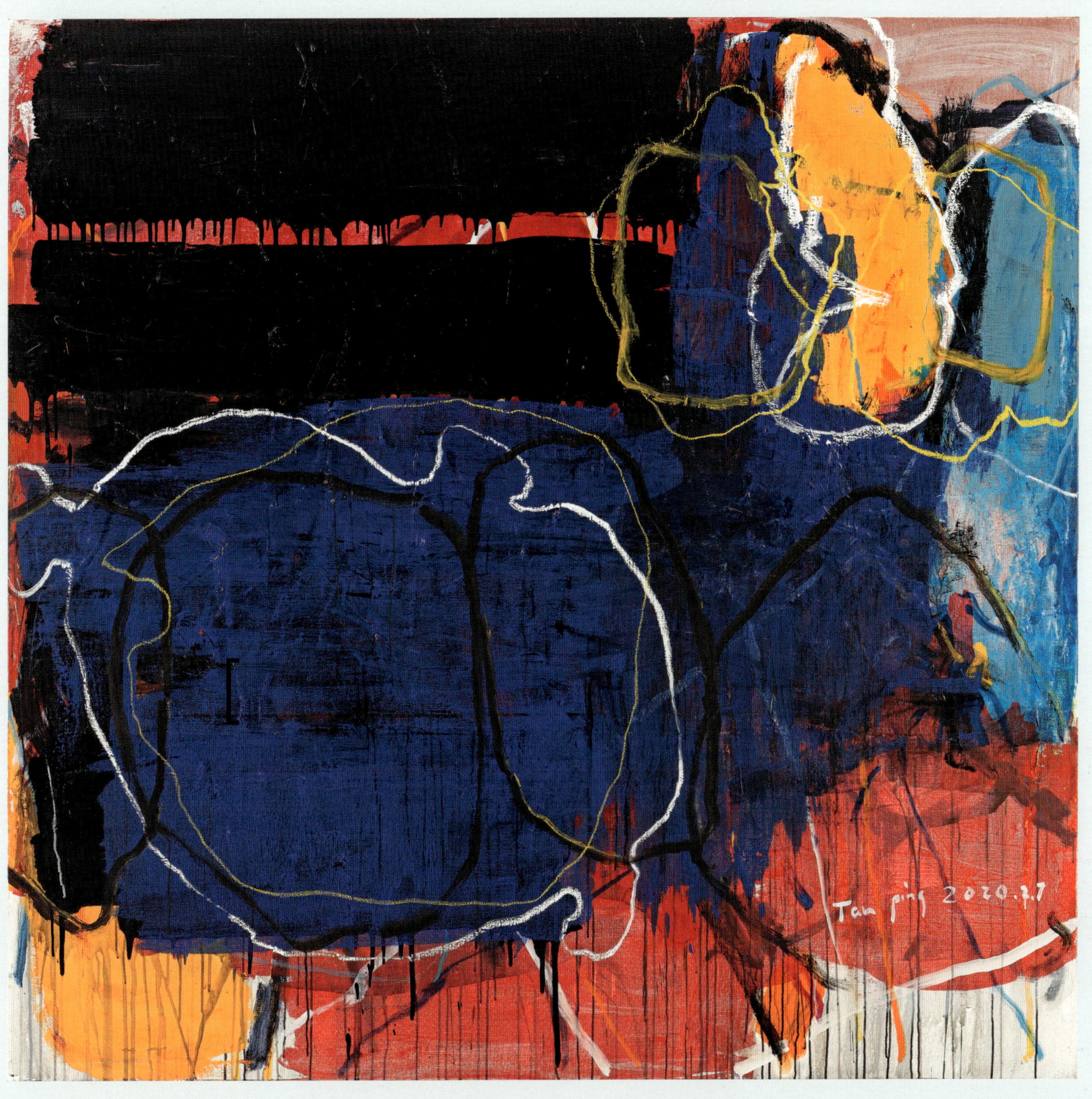

Tan ping 2020.7.7

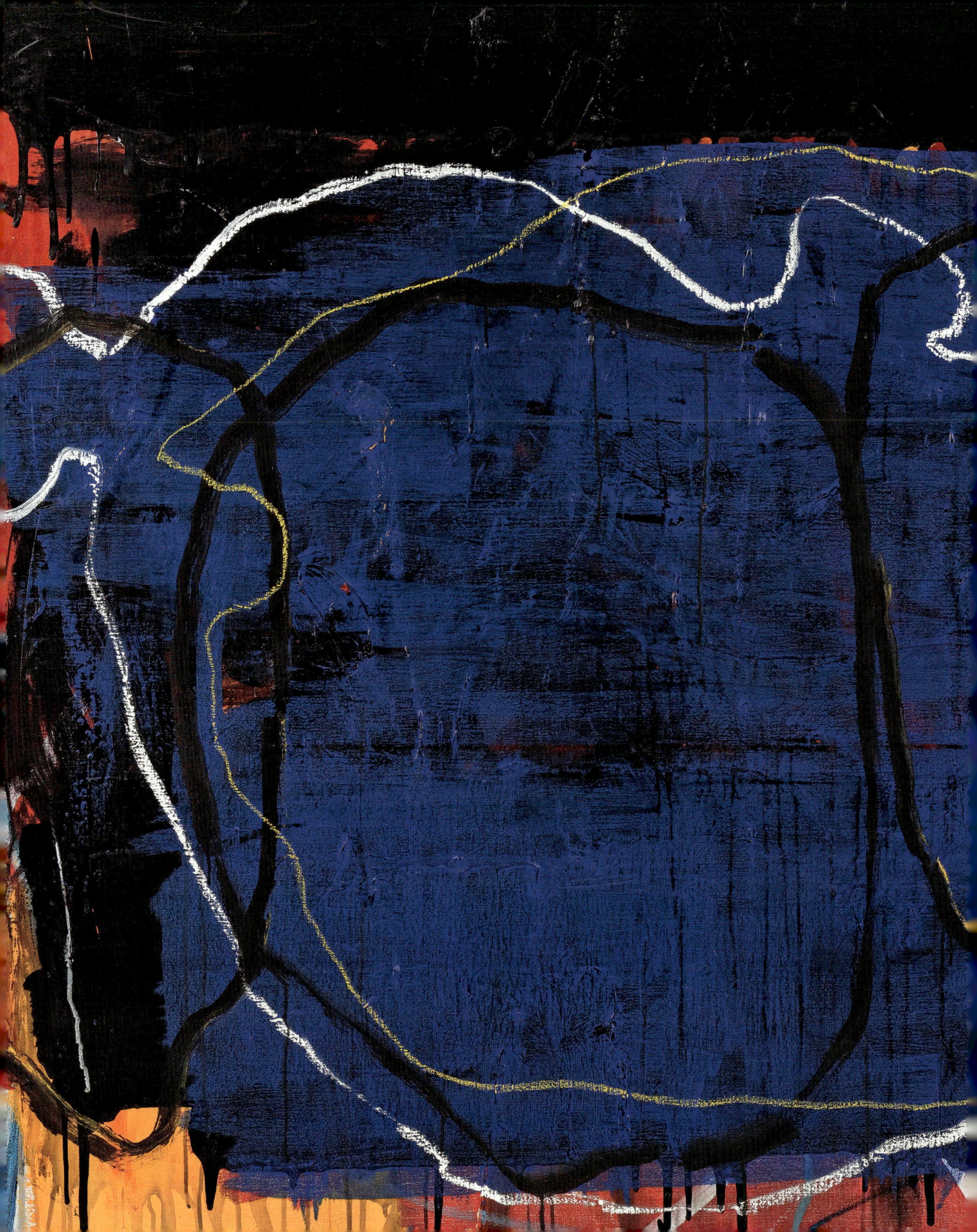

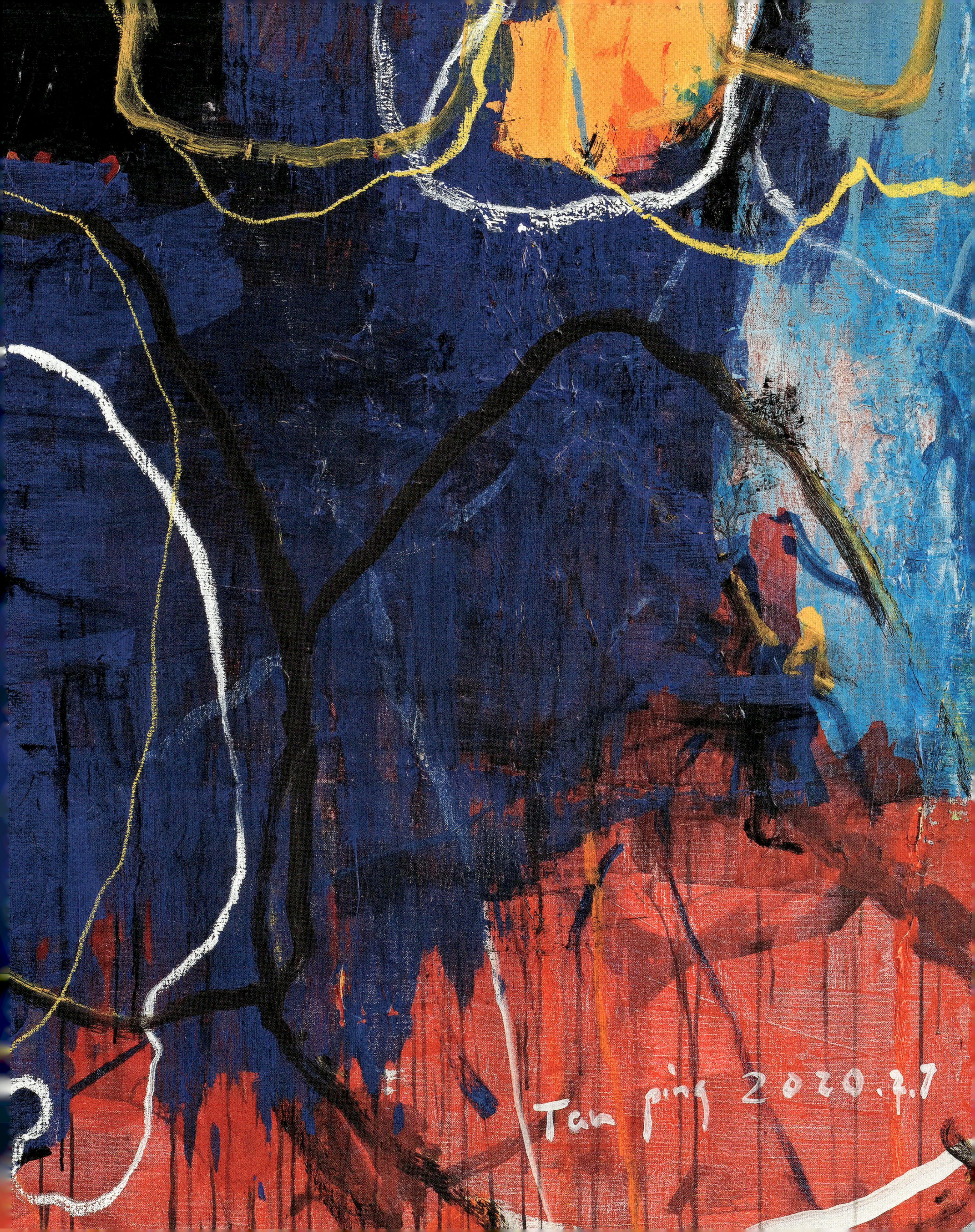
Tan ping 2020.7.7

A Line

Transcending Time

Conceptual art has played a crucial role in my artistic trajectory. It marked a shift in my work from focusing on meaningful formal expression to addressing deeper themes. This shift also allowed my originality to stem not from art itself, but from a broader range of fields.

Tan Ping

During his time in Germany, despite experimenting extensively with different media and styles, Tan Ping rarely created non-canvas works. The piece Time from 1993 is likely his first formal installation. The initial inspiration for Time still stems from his experience with copperplate etching. However, the work no longer confines itself to the two-dimensional plane; it enters space and engages with time. In this piece, the artist explores the concept of "time" from various perspectives. In the creation of Book, a complete copperplate is corroded according to a set timeline, with the visual effects of each stage being recorded.

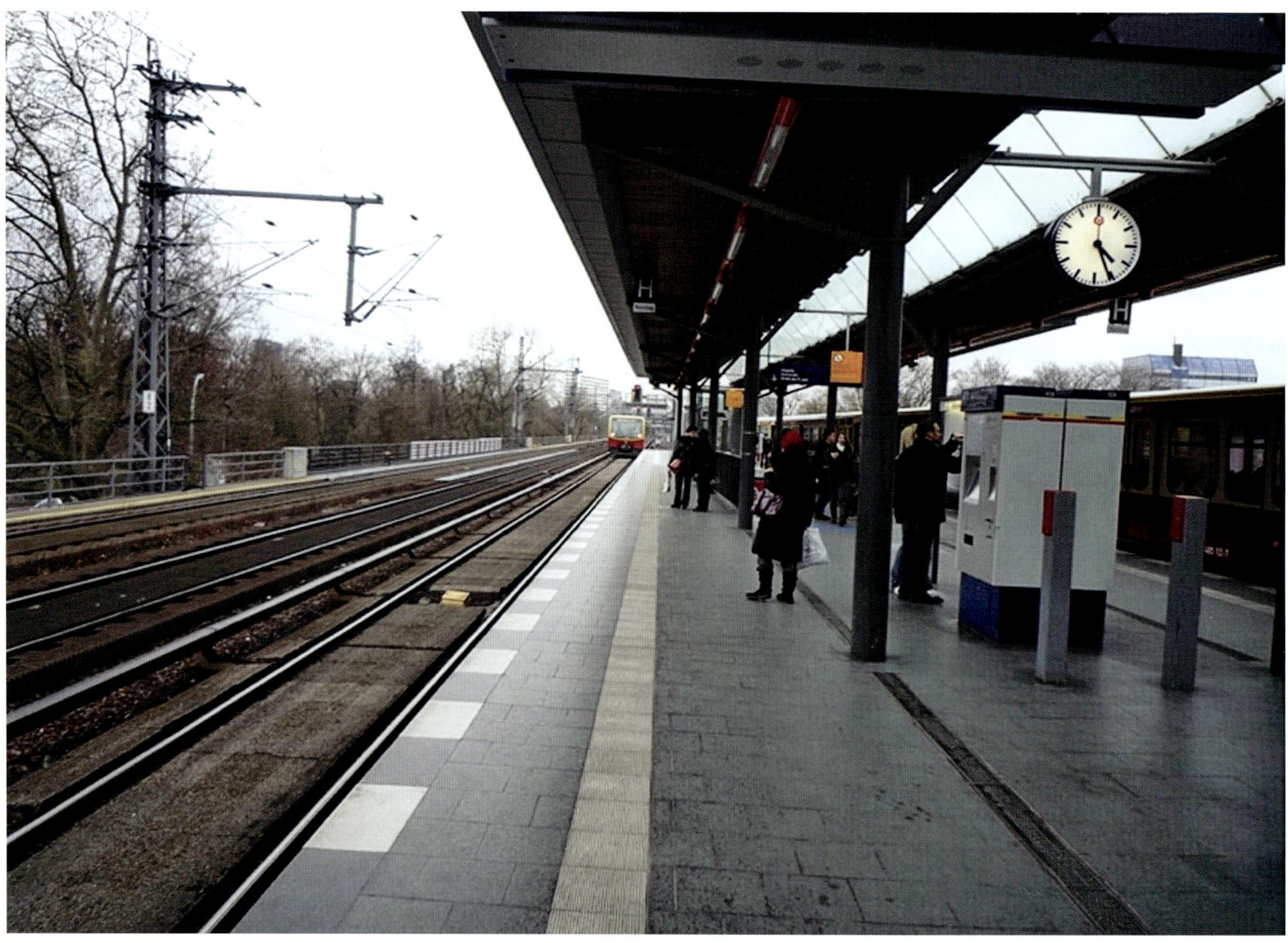

Photo by Tan Ping, station, 2023

Eine Linie

Transzendieren der Zeit

Die Konzeptkunst hat in meinem künstlerischen Werdegang eine entscheidende Rolle gespielt. Sie markierte eine Verschiebung in meiner Arbeit von der Konzentration auf einen bedeutungsvollen formalen Ausdruck hin zur Auseinandersetzung mit tieferen Themen. Dieser Wandel ermöglichte es mir auch, meine Originalität nicht aus der Kunst selbst, sondern aus einem breiteren Spektrum von Bereichen zu beziehen.

Tan Ping

Während seiner Zeit in Deutschland experimentierte Tan Ping zwar ausgiebig mit verschiedenen Medien und Stilen, schuf aber nur selten Werke, die nicht auf Leinwand entstanden. Die Arbeit Time/ Zeit von 1993 ist wahrscheinlich seine erste formale Installation. Die ursprüngliche Inspiration für Time stammt noch von seinen Erfahrungen mit Kupferstichen. Das Werk beschränkt sich jedoch nicht mehr auf die zweidimensionale Ebene, sondern betritt den Raum und setzt sich mit der Zeit auseinander. In diesem Werk erforscht der Künstler das Konzept der „Zeit" aus verschiedenen Perspektiven.

Time, 1993
installation,
100 × 1000 cm
Universität der Künste,
Berlin, Germany /
Deutschland

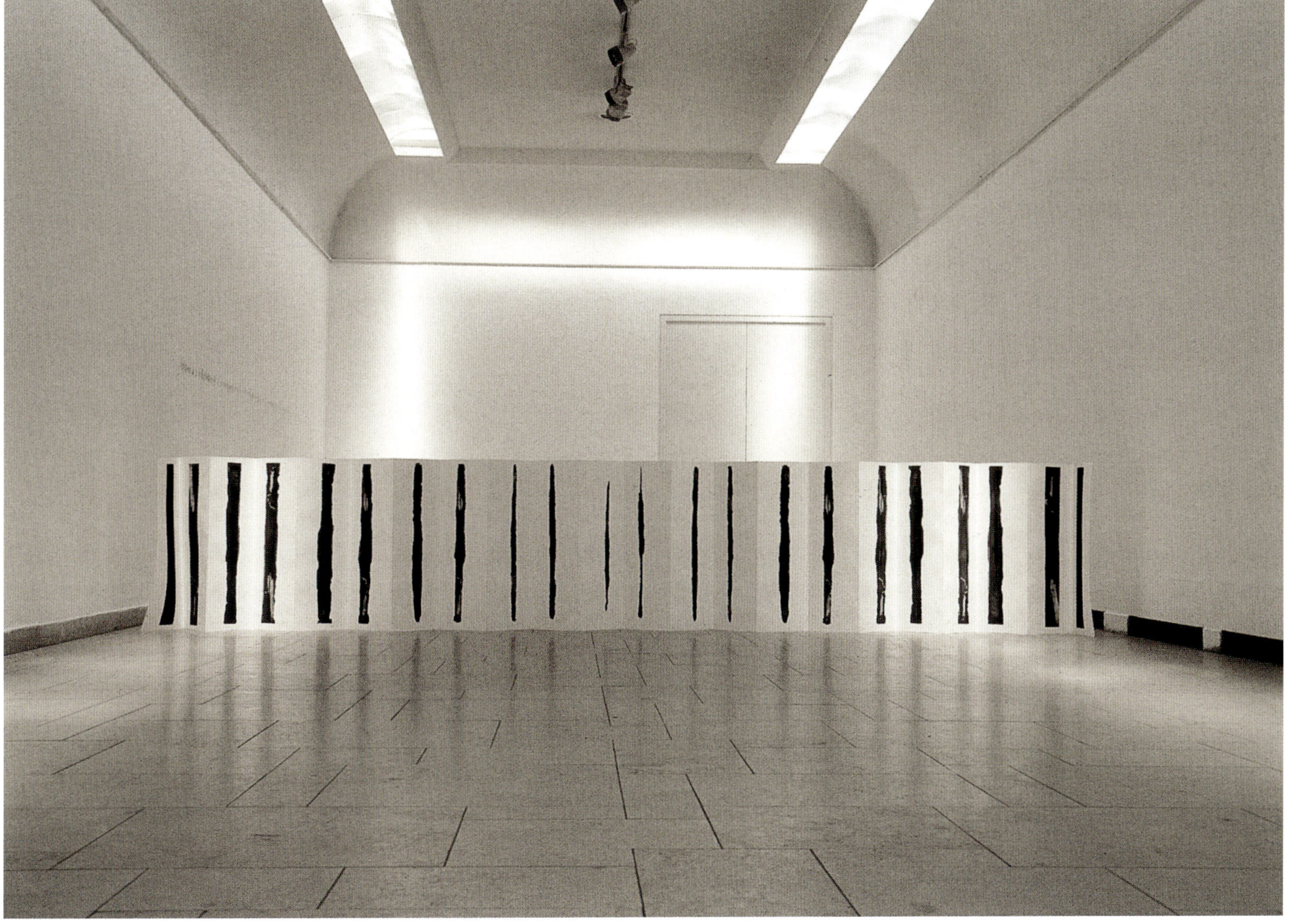

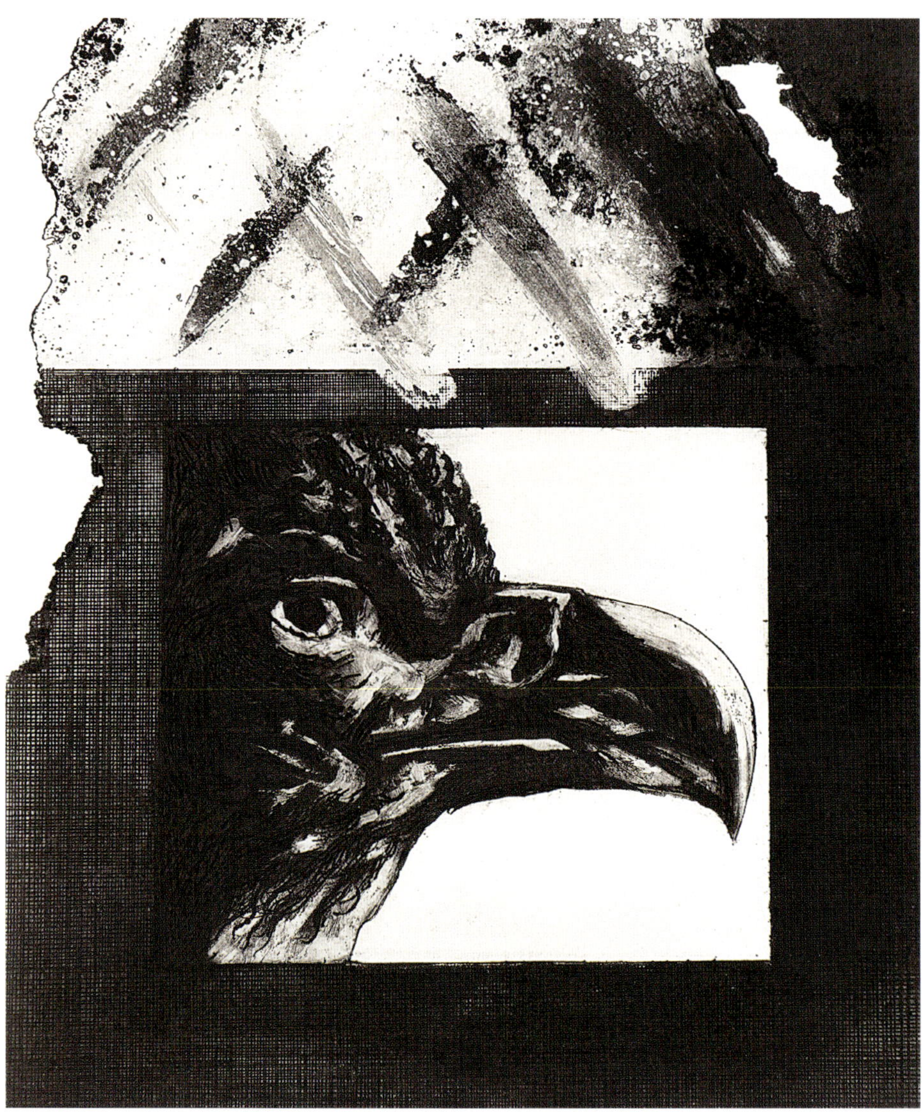

In Tan Ping's personal creative trajectory, the concept of "time" first emerged as a result of his copperplate work in 1987. From that point onward, Tan Ping consciously integrated the concept of "time" into his works. Due to the copperplate being placed in the nitric acid bath for an extended period, its edges became damaged, and the image on it blurred. However, an abstract "significant form" was thus created. At this stage, the work was no longer about form, image, or even the creator; the only thing that existed between the copperplate and the nitric acid was a manifestation of time. "Time" became the true creator, shaping the meaning of the work. Those abstract forms and the uneven textures were merely visual manifestations of time in another state of existence. From another perspective, once "time" is positioned as the central element in the creation of a work, it transcends its mere physical existence. It becomes conceptualized, and can even evolve into an aesthetic principle.

He Guiyan

Professor at Sichuan Fine Arts Institute and Director of the Art Museum of Sichuan Fine Arts Institute

The goal was to present the process of "time" as a creative force to the viewer. Each stage is filled with randomness and uncertainty, making the outcome unpredictable and unimaginable. All the artist can control is the length of the corrosion period. If Book discusses how time, in a physical sense, enhances the creative process, then another form of installation reveals the cultural and spiritual depth accumulated behind time. The inspiration for the piece comes from Tan Ping's experience with an old building at the Berlin University of the Arts. "In that place, you could feel the elusive sense of time lingering in the air after the passage of years, a sense of change and transience. The architectural style imitated the Renaissance period, yet it was merely a reproduction of the 'classical' style. When I placed 22 marks on these columns, I was trying to seek out the true classical spirit that had faded with time. I wanted to bring to light the hidden sense of time embedded in this architectural space."

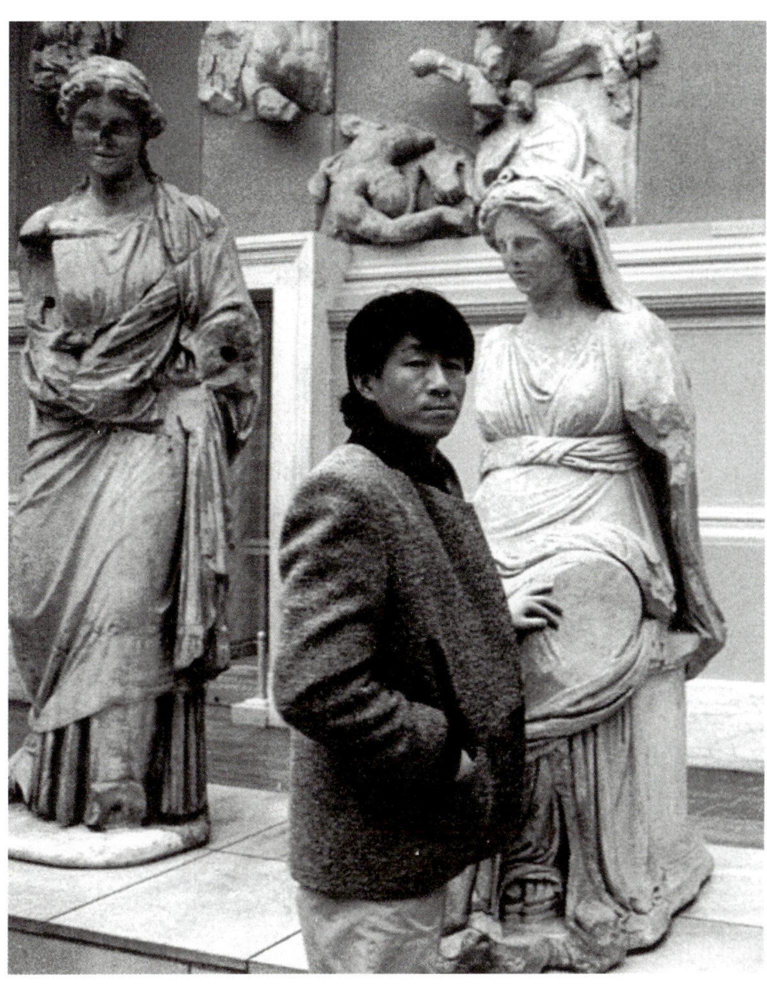

Bei der Entstehung von Book wird ein kompletter Kupferstich nach einem festgelegten Zeitplan korrodiert, wobei die visuellen Effekte jeder Phase aufgezeichnet werden. Ziel war es, dem Betrachter den Prozess der „Zeit" als kreative Kraft vor Augen zu führen. Jede Phase ist von Zufälligkeit und Ungewissheit geprägt, was das Ergebnis unvorhersehbar und unvorstellbar macht. Alles, was der Künstler kontrollieren kann, ist die Länge der Korrosionsperiode. Wenn Book erörtert, wie die Zeit im physischen Sinne den kreativen Prozess fördert, dann offenbart eine andere Form der Installation die kulturelle und geistige Tiefe, die hinter der Zeit steckt.

Die Inspiration für das Werk kam Tan Ping durch das alte Gebäude der Berliner Universität der Künste. „An diesem Ort konnte man das schwer fassbare Gefühl von Zeit spüren, das nach dem Vergehen von Jahren in der Luft lag, ein Gefühl von Veränderung und Vergänglichkeit. Der architektonische Stil ahmte die Renaissance nach, war aber lediglich eine Reproduktion des ‚klassischen' Stils. Als ich 22 Zeichen auf diesen Säulen anbrachte, versuchte ich, den wahren klassischen Geist zu finden, der mit der Zeit verblasst war. Ich wollte den verborgenen Sinn der Zeit, der in diesem architektonischen Raum steckte, ans Licht bringen."

In Tan Pings persönlichem Schaffensprozess taucht der Begriff „Zeit" erstmals 1987 in seinen Kupfersticharbeiten auf. Von diesem Zeitpunkt an hat Tan Ping den Begriff „Zeit" bewusst in seine Werke integriert. Da der Kupferstich über einen längeren Zeitraum im Salpetersäurebad lag, wurden die Ränder beschädigt, und das Bild auf dem Kupferstich verschwamm. Dennoch entstand so eine abstrakte „signifikante Form". In diesem Stadium geht es nicht mehr um die Form, das Bild oder gar den Schöpfer; das Einzige, was zwischen dem Kupferstich und der Salpetersäure existiert, ist eine Manifestation der Zeit. Die „Zeit" wurde zum wahren Schöpfer, der die Bedeutung des Werks formte. Diese abstrakten Formen und die ungleichmäßigen Texturen waren lediglich visuelle Manifestationen der Zeit in einem anderen Zustand der Existenz. Aus einem anderen Blickwinkel betrachtet, geht die „Zeit", sobald sie als zentrales Element bei der Schaffung eines Werks eingesetzt wird, über ihre bloße physische Existenz hinaus. Sie wird begrifflich gefasst und kann sich sogar zu einem ästhetischen Prinzip entwickeln.

He Guiyan

Professor am Institut für Schöne Künste Sichuan und Direktor des Kunstmuseums des Instituts für Schöne Künste Sichuan

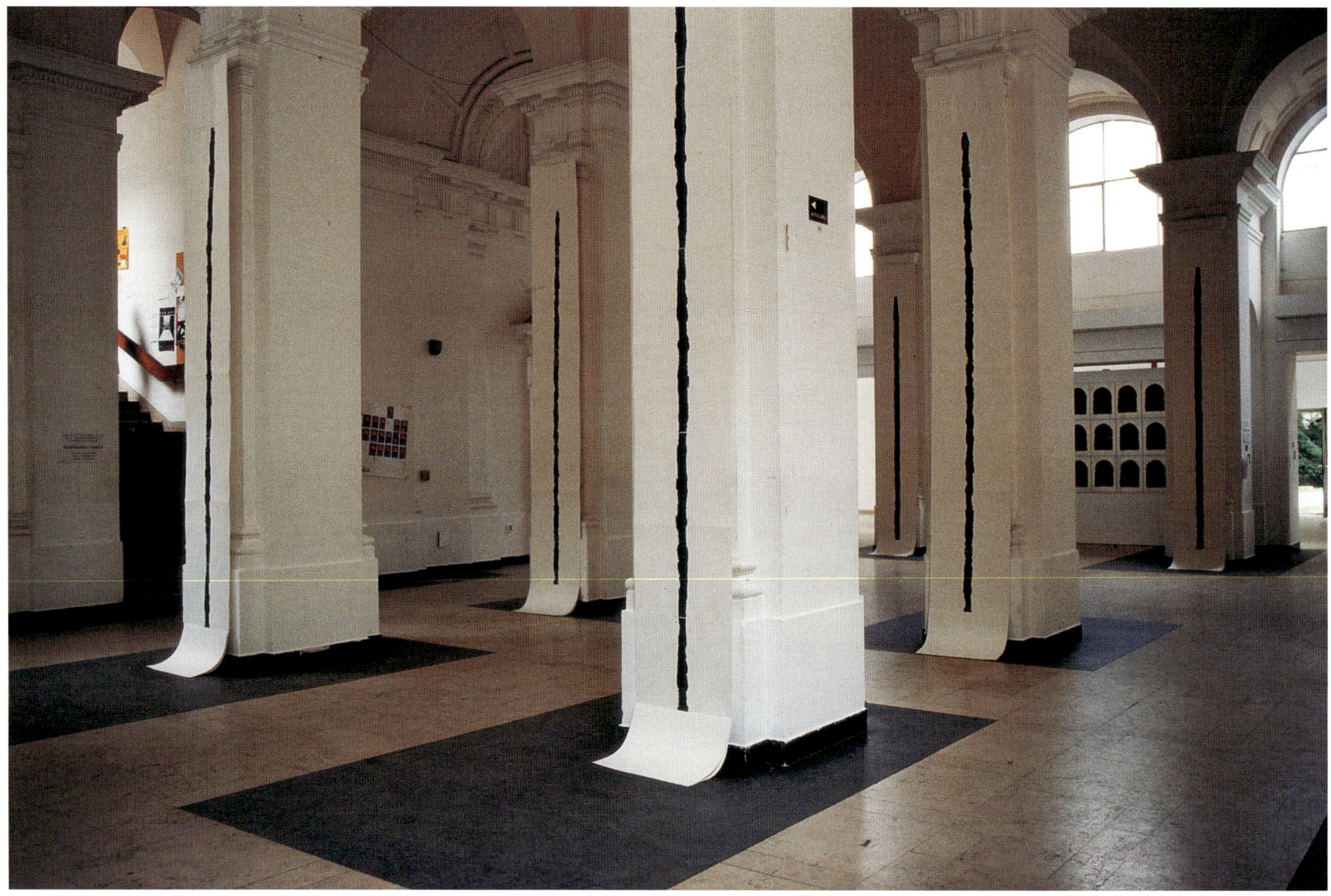

Time, 1993
installation,
1000cm × 40cm × 22
pieces / **Stücke**
Universität der Künste,
Berlin, Germany /
Deutschland

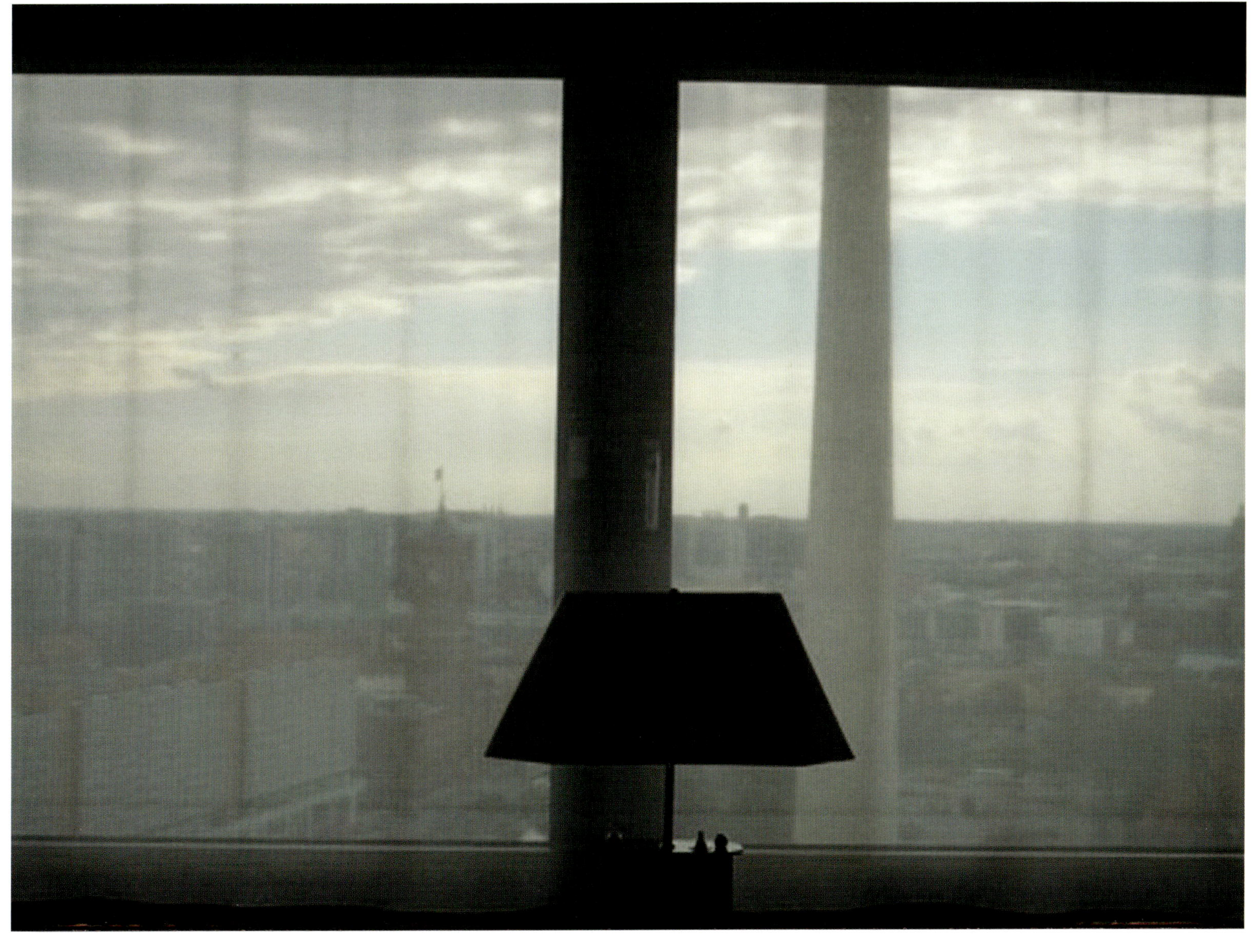

Eine Linie

"Calligraphy" series, 2000
etching / **Radierung**,
24 × 98cm
Beijing, China

Yin-Yang
(The "Calligraphy" Series)

In Tan Ping's prints, I sense a deep Eastern spirituality. This spirituality resonates with those who have studied traditional culture and art, or with anyone who can perceive the subtle nuances within his work. There is a shared understanding that these elements evoke.

Tan Ping's prints express a deep Chinese appreciation for ink. The black lines, due to the texture of the paper pulp, seem to diffuse like ink, evoking a distinct Eastern sensibility. This feeling seems inherent to Chinese artists—it requires no in-depth study, as it is something innate, something within the collective consciousness.

Printmaking must carry the "trace of the print" to feel satisfying. Unlike painting, which emphasizes the texture of brushstrokes, printmaking demands the sensation of an imprint. "Imprint" is itself a form of expression, possessing an inherent beauty. It's a mysterious quality, difficult to articulate. Tan Ping's prints are exhilarating to me because he places special emphasis on the "print," capturing the essence of the imprint in a deeply resonant way.

When I look at Tan Ping's prints, they exude a quiet, Eastern spirituality. This tranquility reveals what he is thinking, what he is striving for—a mind free of distractions, with no need for disguise or explanation. Anyone can see it.

It is beyond words, and that very quality of being "beyond" is what makes it indescribable.

Zhang Jing

Designer

Yin-Yang
(„Kalligraphie" Serie)

In den Drucken von Tan Ping spüre ich eine tiefe östliche Spiritualität. Diese Spiritualität schwingt bei denen mit, die traditionelle Kultur und Kunst studiert haben, oder bei jedem, der die subtilen Nuancen in seinem Werk wahrnehmen kann. Es gibt ein gemeinsames Verständnis, das diese Elemente hervorrufen.

Tan Pings Drucke sind Ausdruck einer tiefen chinesischen Wertschätzung für Tinte.
Die schwarzen Linien scheinen aufgrund der Textur des Papierbreis wie Tinte zu diffundieren und rufen eine ausgeprägte östliche Sensibilität hervor. Dieses Gefühl scheint den chinesischen Künstlern innezuwohnen - es bedarf keines eingehenden Studiums, da es etwas Angeborenes, etwas im kollektiven Bewusstsein ist.

Die Druckgrafik muss die „Spur des Drucks" tragen, damit sie befriedigend ist. Im Gegensatz zur Malerei, bei der die Textur der Pinselstriche im Vordergrund steht, verlangt die Druckgrafik das Gefühl eines Abdrucks. Das „Eingeprägte" ist selbst eine Ausdrucksform, die eine inhärente Schönheit besitzt. Es ist eine geheimnisvolle Qualität, die sich nur schwer in Worte fassen lässt. Tan Pings Drucke begeistern mich, weil er besonderen Wert auf den „Abdruck" legt und das Wesen des Abdrucks auf eine tiefgründige Weise einfängt.

Wenn ich mir Tan Pings Grafiken ansehe, strahlen sie eine ruhige, östliche Spiritualität aus. Diese Ruhe verrät, was er denkt, wonach er strebt – einen Geist, der frei von Ablenkungen ist und keine Verkleidung oder Erklärung braucht. Jeder kann es sehen.

Sie ist jenseits von Worten, und genau diese Eigenschaft, „jenseits" zu sein, macht sie unbeschreiblich.

Zhang Jing

Designer

"Calligraphy" series, 2000
etching / Radierung,
98 × 33cm
Beijing, China

Eine Linie

A Line +40m

A 40-meter long wood-cut line. It takes 10 minutes to proceed with one meter. The whole work takes more than six hours with uninterrupted efforts. The moment the knife touches the wooden panel it feels like slicing open the skin with a piercing blade. The knife thus proceeds deeply and steadily into the depth of this black plane.

A single chisel carves a spare, plain line 40 meters long, through a layered setting of various interwoven pictures. These two clashing images are what this exhibition presents to viewers in #1 Gallery, as it visually encapsulates the core curatorial conception. Both opposed and complementary, these two kinds of imagery distill 30 years of artistic exploration by Tan Ping…along a path filled with deepening interplay of lines and color, form and melody, action and cogitation, "enlightenment" and "gradual insight." On this path the ongoing "duet" between oil painting and woodcut printing has exerted a crucial effect. Tan Ping's combined explorations into these two artistic genres, whether in length of time or depth of excavation, are rarely seen in contemporary art. While oil painting and woodcuts are both two-dimensional representations, their special features in terms of material, technique and media lead to unceasing tensions between them. At the same time, their resonances and harmonies trigger new possibilities of visual expression. Such a "duet" has endowed Tan Ping's artistic quest with vivid personality and unique logic. At the same time, it can be taken as an important case study in the broader scope of formal and conceptual experimentation in contemporary art.

Wu Hung

Art Historian, Director of the Center for the Art of East Asia at the University of Chicago

Eine Linie   +40m

Eine 40 Meter lange Holzschnittlinie. Es dauert 10 Minuten, um mit einem Meter fortzufahren. Die gesamte Arbeit beansprucht mehr als sechs Stunden bei ununterbrochener Anstrengung. In dem Moment, in dem das Messer die Holzplatte berührt, fühlt es sich an, als würde man die Haut mit einer durchdringenden Klinge aufschneiden. Das Messer dringt tief und gleichmäßig in die Tiefe dieser schwarzen Fläche ein.

Ein einziger Meißel ritzt eine 40 Meter lange, schlichte Linie durch ein mehrschichtiges Setting aus verschiedenen, miteinander verwobenen Bildern. Diese gegensätzlichen Bilder sind es, die dem Betrachter in der Galerie # 1 präsentiert werden, da sie das Kernkonzept des Kurators visuell verkörpern. Diese Bildern sind sowohl gegensätzlich als auch komplementär und destillieren 30 Jahre künstlerischer Erkundung von Tan Ping… entlang eines Weges, der von einem sich vertiefenden Zusammenspiel von Linien und Farbe, Form und Melodie, Aktion und Nachdenken, „Erleuchtung" und „allmählicher Einsicht" geprägt ist. Auf diesem Weg hat das ständige „Duett" zwischen Ölmalerei und Holzschnitt einen entscheidenden Einfluss ausgeübt. Tan Pings kombinierte Erkundungen dieser beiden Kunstgattungen, sei es in Bezug auf die Dauer oder die Tiefe der Ausgrabungen, sind in der zeitgenössischen Kunst selten zu sehen. Ölmalerei und Holzschnitt sind zwar beide zweidimensionale Darstellungen, aber ihre Besonderheiten in Bezug auf Material, Technik und Medien führen zu ständigen Spannungen zwischen ihnen. Gleichzeitig ergeben sich aus ihren Resonanzen und Harmonien neue Möglichkeiten des visuellen Ausdrucks. Ein solches „Duett" hat Tan Pings künstlerische Suche mit einer lebendigen Persönlichkeit und einer einzigartigen Logik ausgestattet. Gleichzeitig kann es als eine wichtige Fallstudie im breiteren Rahmen der formalen und konzeptionellen Experimente in der zeitgenössischen Kunst betrachtet werden.

Wu Hung

Kunsthistoriker, Direktor des Zentrums für ostasiatische Kunst an der Universität von Chicago

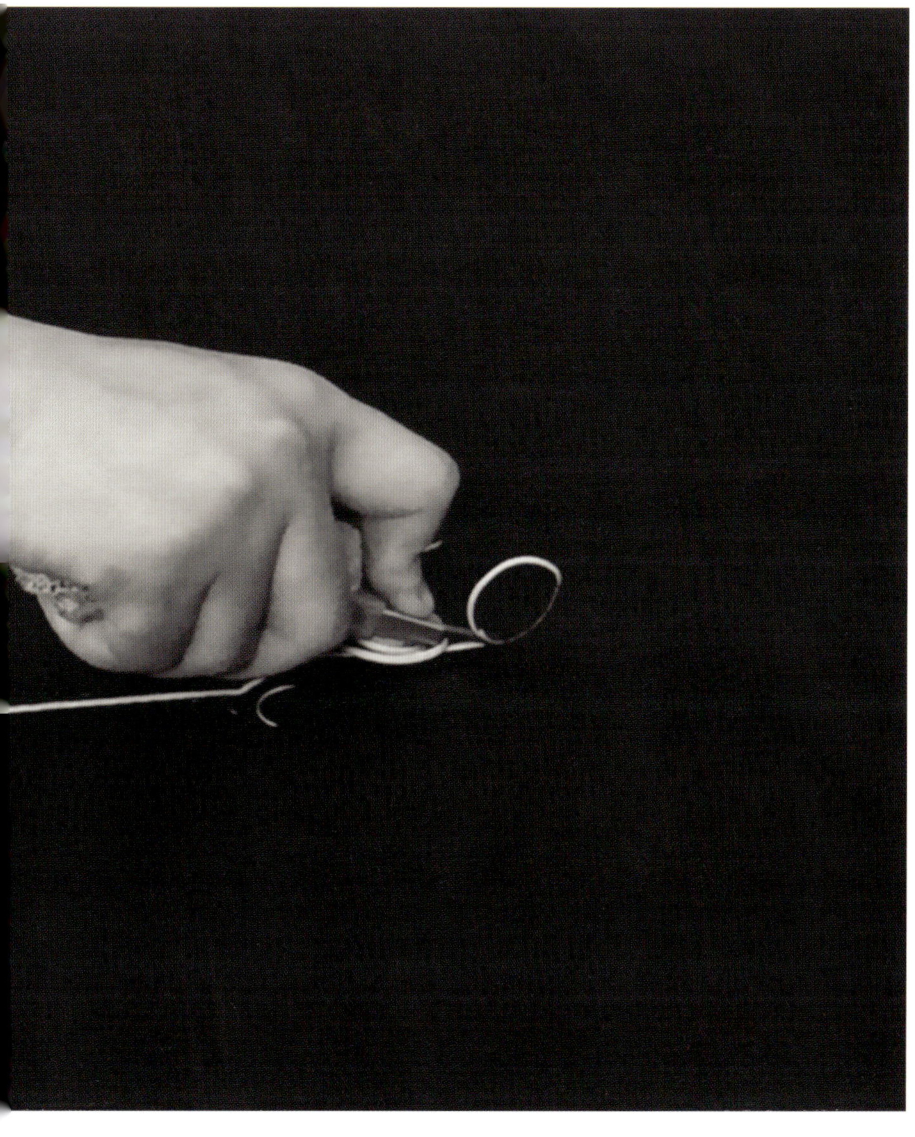

+40m, work process / Arbeitsprozess, 2012

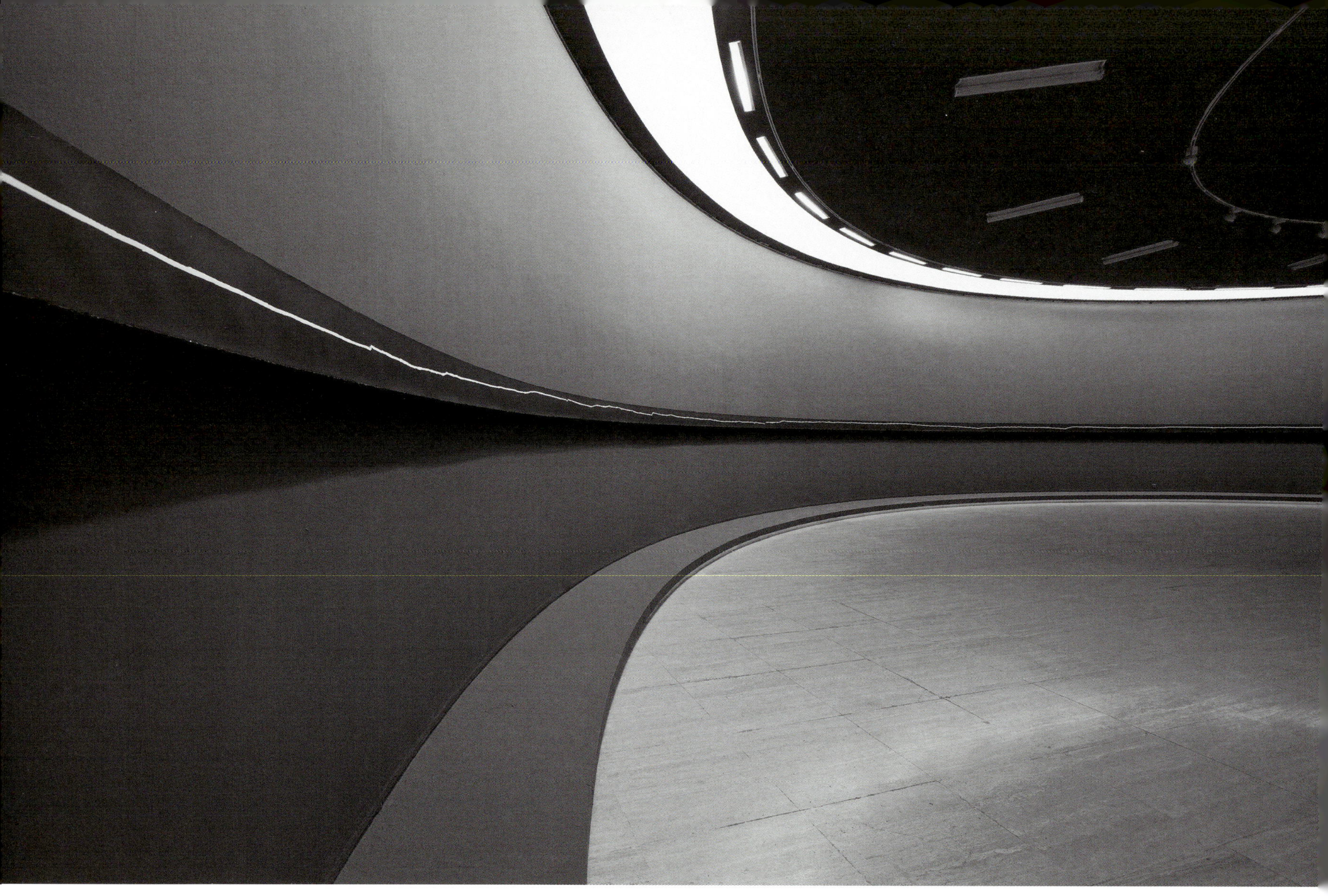

Geometry can be a means to create a spiritual inner place, in fact the 40-meter-long wood-cut scroll by Tan Ping exhibited in the National Art Museum of China seems to develop a space-time concept based on silence and concentration. Its chromatic values confirm the painter's desire to set a threshold between art and life: the first claims independence while the second imparts depth.

Achille Bonito Oliva

Art Critic, Art Historian

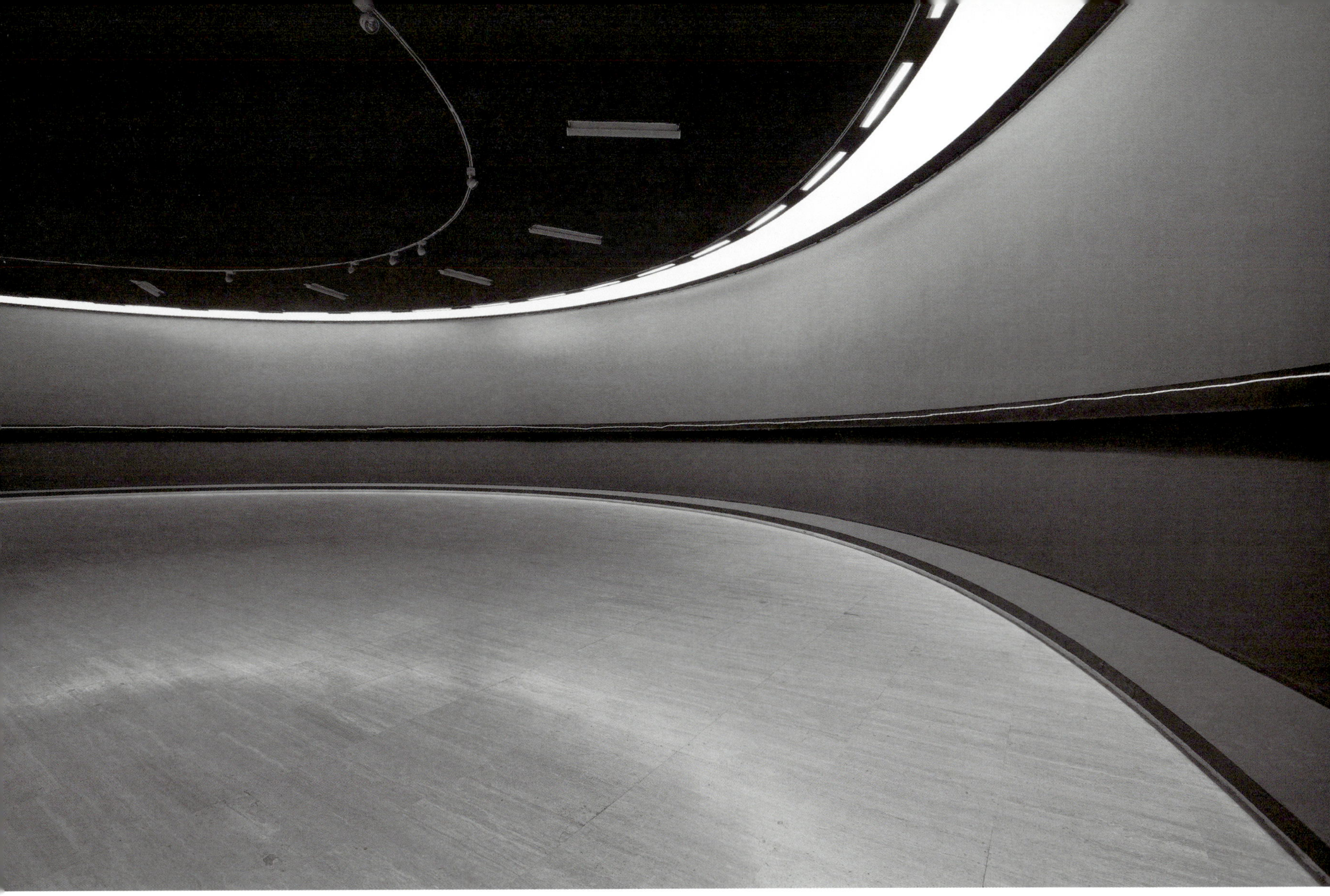

Geometrie kann ein Mittel sein, um einen
spirituellen inneren Ort zu schaffen. So scheint
die 40 Meter lange Holzschnittrolle von Tan
Ping, die im National Art Museum of China
ausgestellt ist, ein Raum-Zeit-Konzept zu
entwickeln, das auf Stille und Konzentration
beruht. Ihre Farbwerte bestätigen den Wunsch
des Malers, eine Schwelle zwischen Kunst
und Leben zu setzen: die erste beansprucht
Unabhängigkeit, während die zweite Tiefe
vermittelt.

Achille Bonito Oliva
Kunstkritiker, Kunsthistoriker

Eine Linie

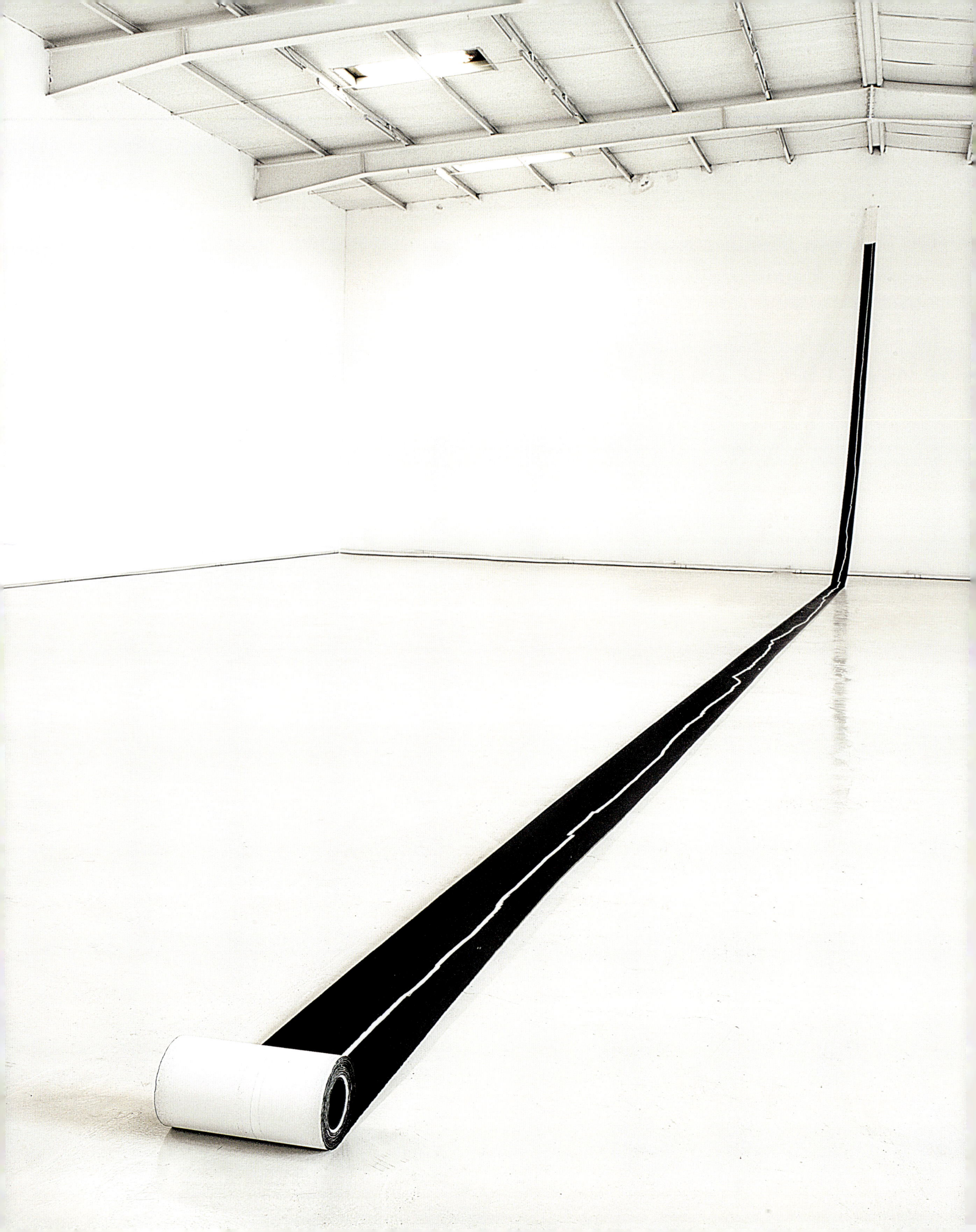

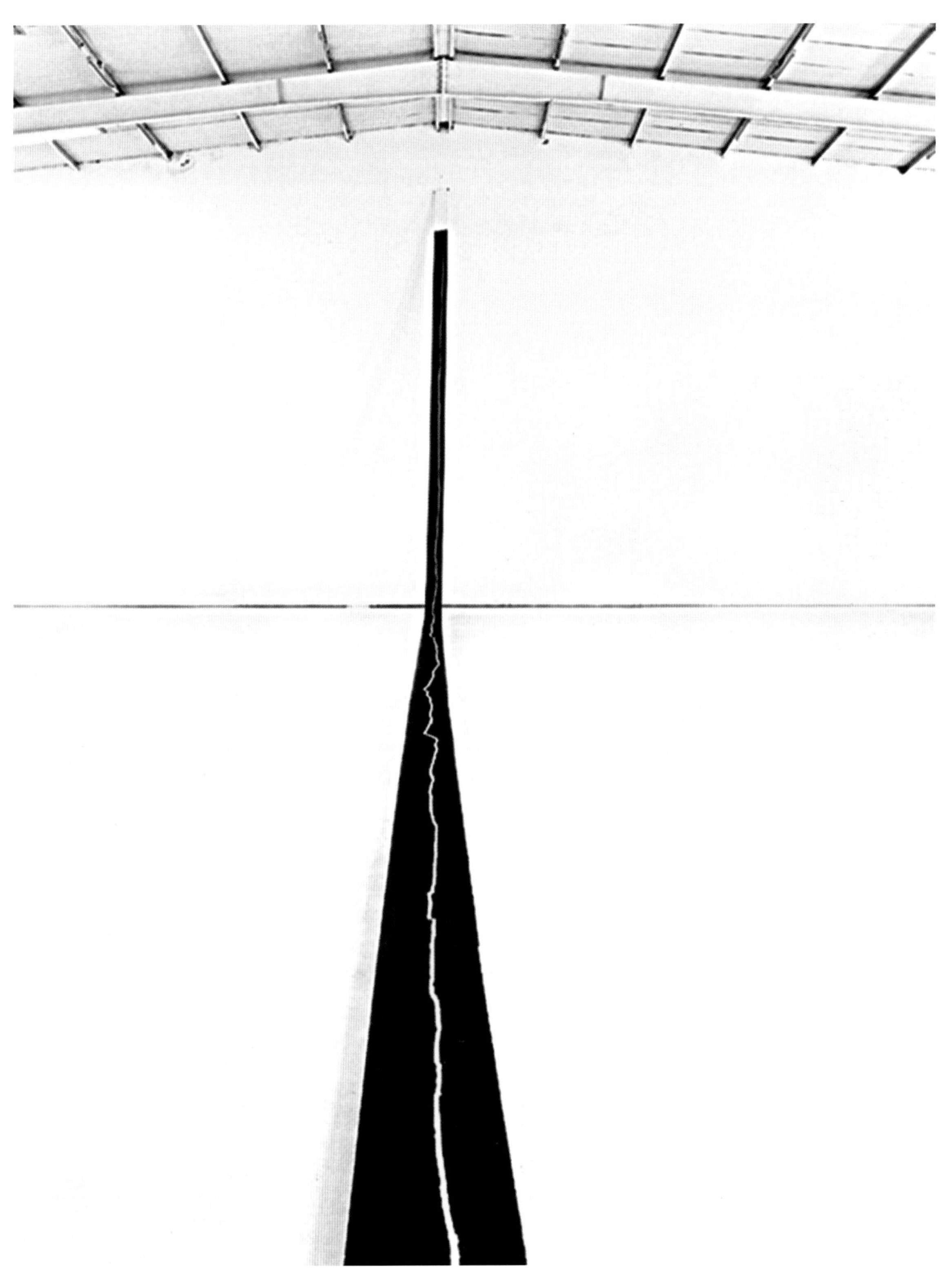

+40m (vertical installation /
vertikale Installation), 2012
mixed media / **Mischtechnik**,
20 × 4000cm
Collection of National Art Museum
of China, Beijing, China

+40m (partial view /
Ausschnitt), 2012
mixed media / **Mischtechnik**,
20 × 4000cm
Collection of National Art
Museum of China, Beijing,
China

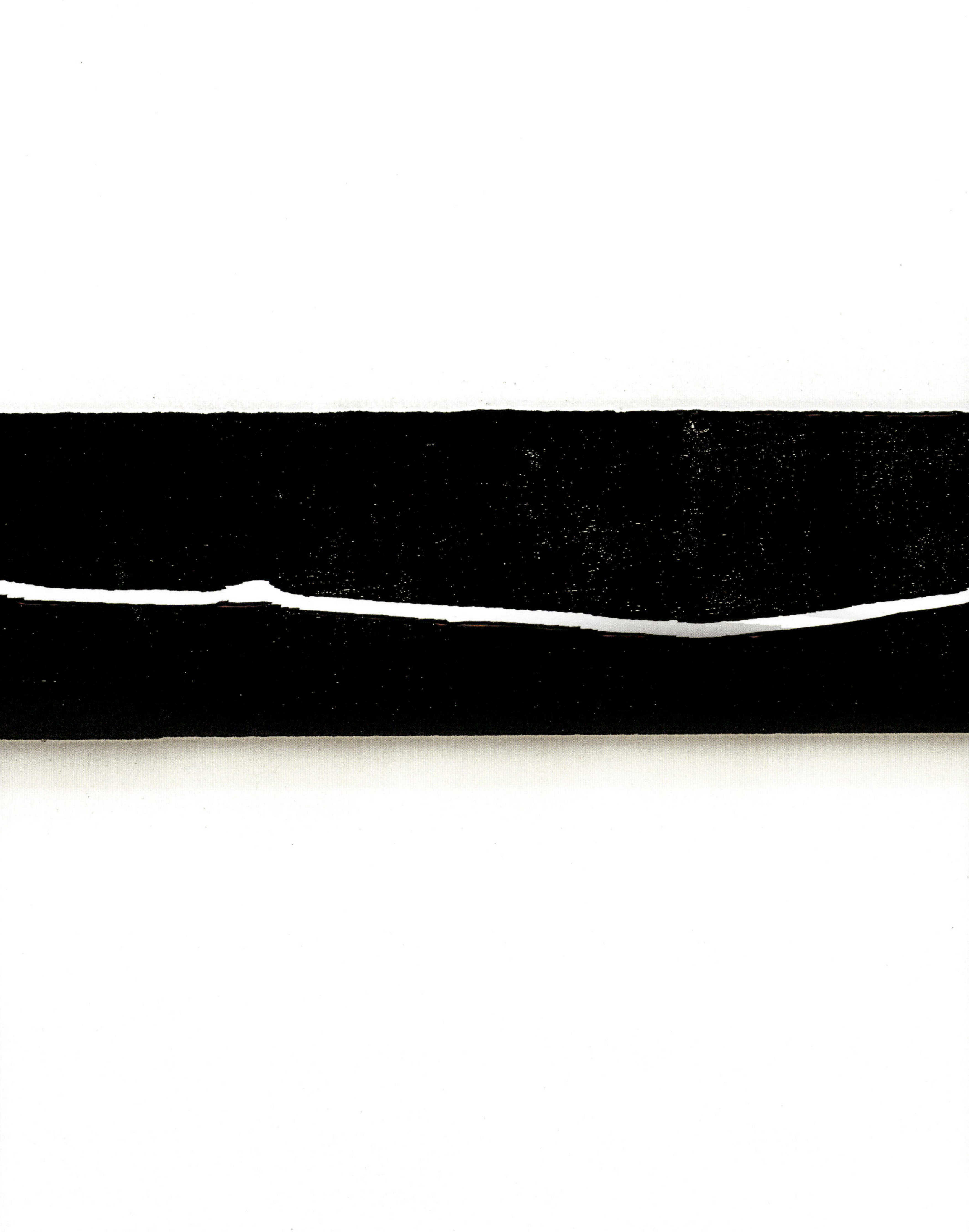

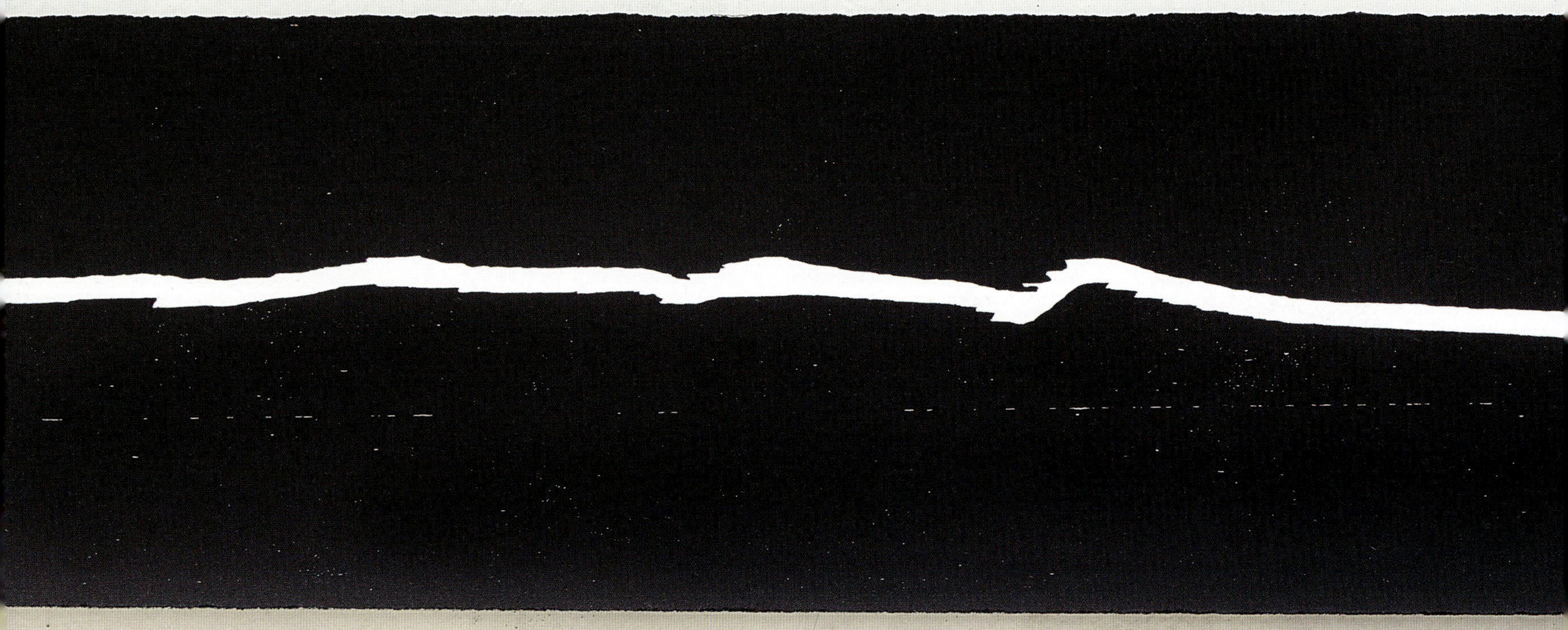

+40m (partial view / **Ausschnitt**), 2012
mixed media / **Mischtechnik**,
20 × 4000cm
Collection of National Art
Museum of China, Beijing,
China

A Line -40m

For his major solo exhibition at the National Art Museum of China in the end of 2012, Tan Ping tailored a new piece specifically for the Round Hall of the Museum. In this 40-metre-long dark grey woodprint, there is nothing except one single white line – carved from the left to the right in one go – like a beam of light swept through the center of the scroll. It is as if a child has run alongside the curved wall of the Round Hall, leaving a playful mark, highlighting the most authoritative art space in China.

During the process of making this 40-meter-long print, there simultaneously appeared two parallel lines of marks on the paper sheets originally placed underneath the actual work to prevent the excessive ink. To the artist, these sheets became another piece of work, -40m, which had been "achieved accidentally outside the proposed agenda, yet equally significant in terms of the subtle variety of visual presentation as well as the sense of rationality." The unexpected piece urges us to re-think the notion of 'artwork', whilst the real freedom of art always lies beyond the constructed framework. Together with the originally envisioned work, -40m shown at this Guangzhou Triennial is respectively independent, again in an abstract form. Being produced at the same time, these two pieces had removed the boundary between the 'original' and the 'attached'. They still have the kinship, but not to be shown at the same museum space; they are complementary not only visually, but also spiritually, when the 'present' can reflect the 'absent' in a distance. When one looks back at the image on those 'waste' sheets in the Museum, there becomes no distinction of the primary or the secondary, the positive or the negative and the authoritative or the non-authoritative, but only an even stronger and brighter beam of light between the ink marks.

Jiang Jiehong

Curator, Professor at Birmingham Institute of Art and Design, UK

-40m, 2012
mixed media / **Mischtechnik**
Beijing, China

Eine Linie -40m

Für seine große Einzelausstellung im National Art Museum of China Ende 2012 entwarf Tan Ping ein neues Werk speziell für den runden Saal des Museums. In diesem 40 Meter langen dunkelgrauen Holzdruck gibt es nichts außer einer einzigen weißen Linie, die in einem Zug von links nach rechts geschnitzt wurde - wie ein Lichtstrahl, der durch die Mitte der Schriftrolle fegt. Es ist, als ob ein Kind an der geschwungenen Wand des Runden Saals entlanggelaufen ist und eine spielerische Spur hinterlassen hat, die den bedeutendsten Kunstraum Chinas hervorhebt.
Während der Herstellung dieses 40 Meter langen Drucks erschienen gleichzeitig zwei parallele Markierungslinien auf den Papierblättern, die ursprünglich unter das eigentliche Werk gelegt wurden, um ein zu starkes Auslaufen der Tinte zu verhindern. Für den Künstler wurden diese Blätter zu einem weiteren Werk, -40m, das „zufällig außerhalb des geplanten Programms entstanden ist, aber ebenso bedeutsam ist, was die subtile Vielfalt der visuellen Darstellung und den Sinn für Rationalität angeht".

Das unerwartete Werk fordert uns auf, den Begriff „Kunstwerk" neu zu überdenken, denn die wahre Freiheit der Kunst liegt oft jenseits des konstruierten Rahmens. Zusammen mit dem ursprünglich geplanten Werk ist -40m, das auf dieser Guangzhou Triennale gezeigt wird, ebenfalls unabhängig und in abstrakter Form. Da diese beiden Werke zur gleichen Zeit entstanden sind, wurde die Grenze zwischen dem „Original" und dem „Anhängsel" aufgehoben. Sie sind immer noch verwandt, aber nicht im selben Museumsraum zu sehen; sie ergänzen sich nicht nur visuell, sondern auch geistig, wenn das „Anwesende" das „Abwesende" in der Ferne spiegeln kann. Wenn man im Museum auf das Bild auf diesen „Abfallblättern" zurückblickt, gibt es keine Unterscheidung mehr zwischen dem Primären und dem Sekundären, dem Positiven und dem Negativen, dem Autoritativen und dem Nicht-Autoritativen, sondern nur noch einen noch stärkeren und helleren Lichtstrahl zwischen den Tintenflecken.

Jiang Jiehong

Kurator, Professor am Birmingham Institute of Art and Design, UK

-40m, 2012
mixed media / **Mischtechnik**
Beijing, China

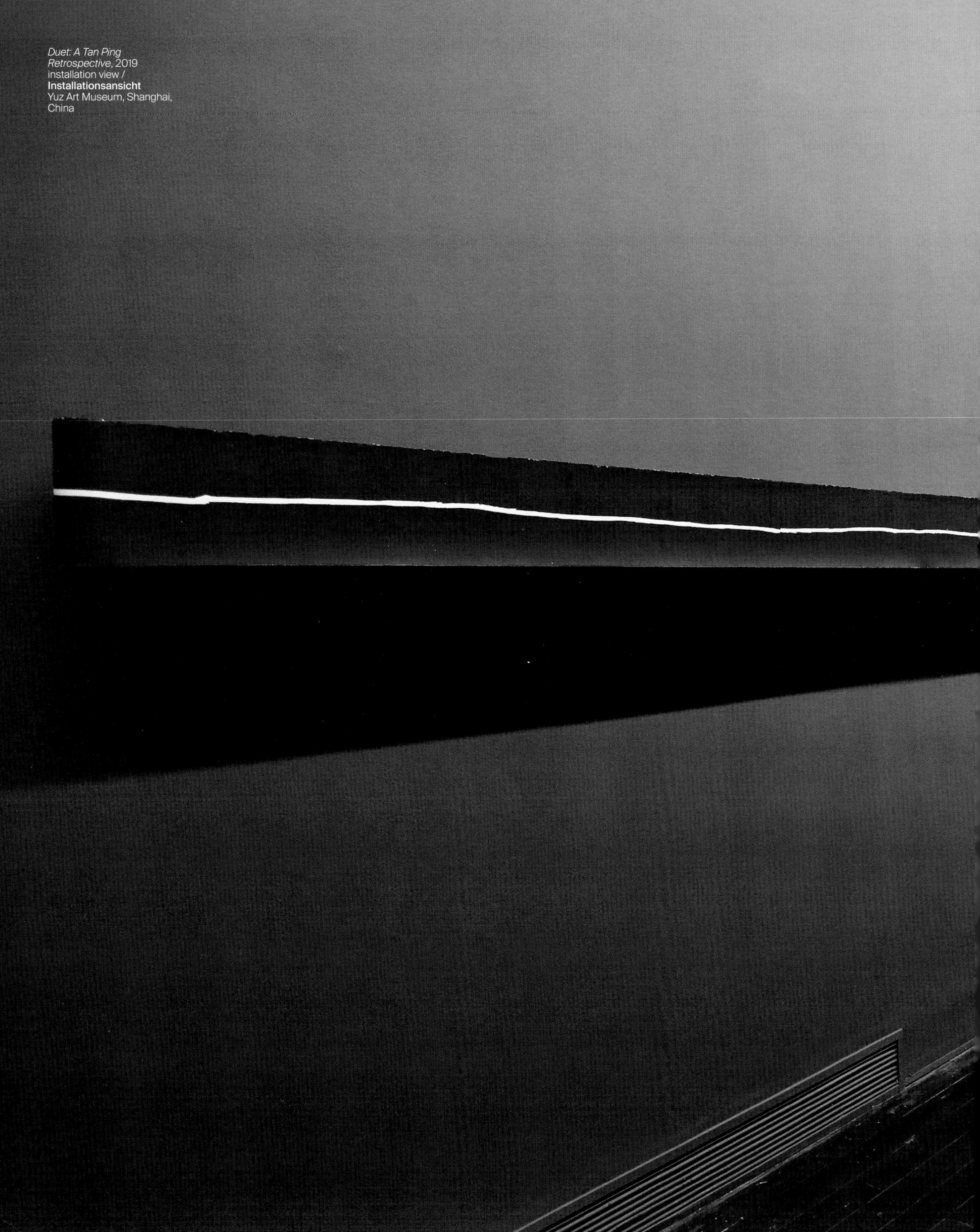

Duet: A Tan Ping Retrospective, 2019
installation view /
Installationsansicht
Yuz Art Museum, Shanghai,
China

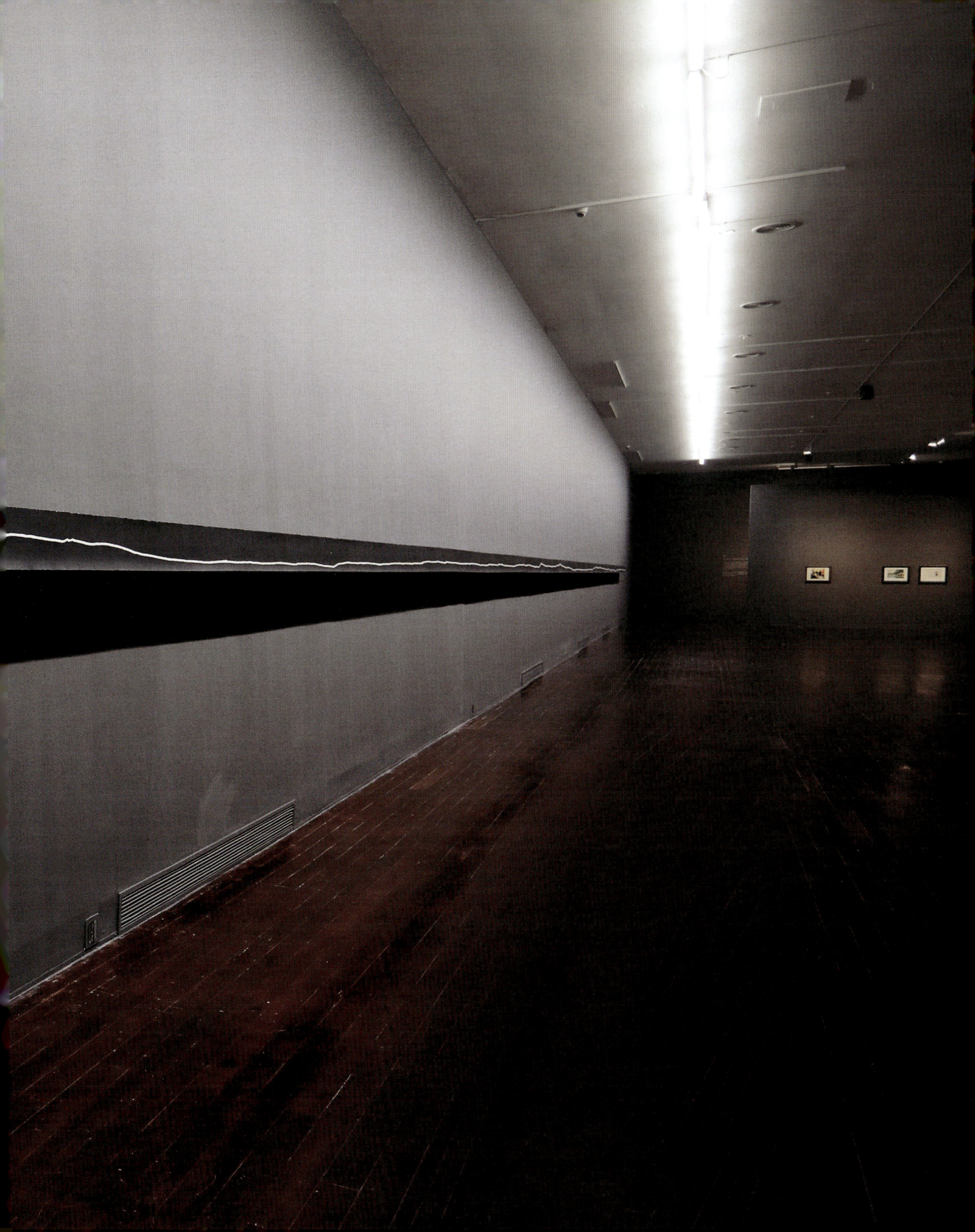

Point, Line, Plane

One Cup: There Are No Two Identical Leaves in the World

The worldview embedded in the work *One Cup* can be interpreted through the philosophical idea of the 17th-century German philosopher Leibniz, who posited that "there are no two identical leaves in the world." Even with the same cup of ink, it is impossible to pour out two identical circles. This is the origin of *One Cup*.

Tan Ping

Punkt, Linie, Ebene

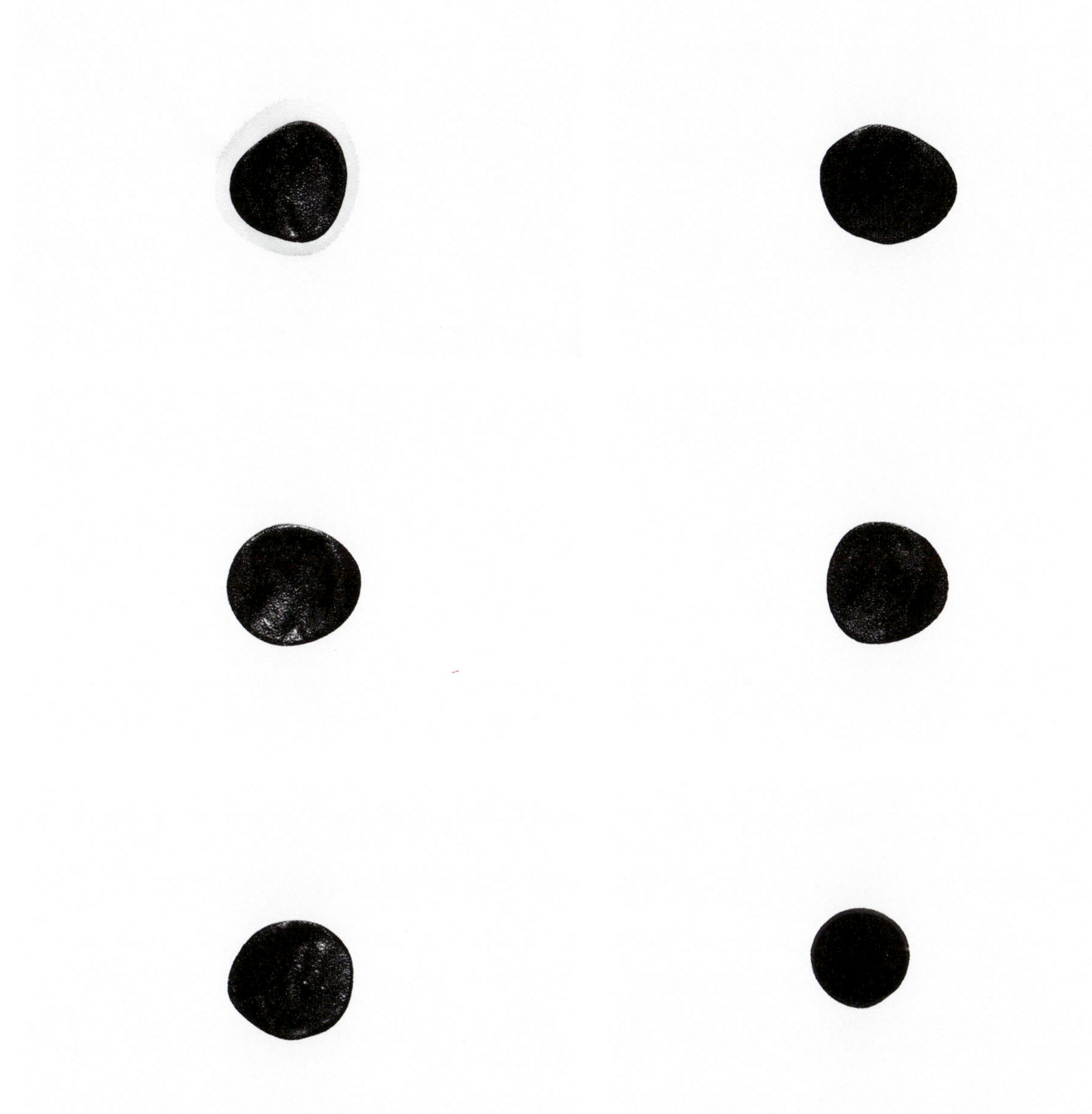

One Cup, 2011
mixed media / **Mischtechnik**,
26 × 38cm
Beijing, China

One Cup: Es gibt keine zwei identischen Blätter auf der Welt

Die in das Werk One Cup (Eine Tasse) eingebettete Weltanschauung lässt sich anhand der philosophische Idee des deutschen Philosophen Leibniz aus dem 17. Jahrhundert interpretieren, der postulierte, dass es „keine zwei gleichen Blätter in der Welt gibt". Selbst mit demselben Becher Tinte ist es unmöglich, zwei identische Kreise auszugießen. Dies ist der Ursprung von One Cup.

Tan Ping

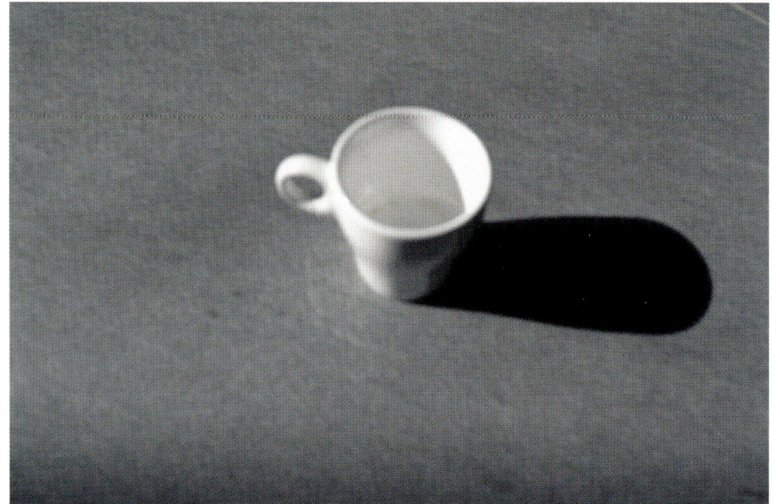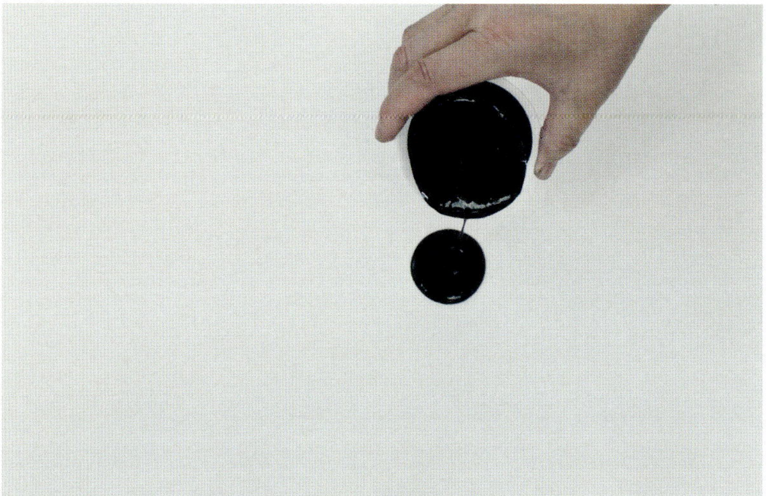

One Cup, work process /
Arbeitsprozess, 2011

In the 2011 multi-media piece *One Cup,* which blends print with video, installation and performance, the conceptual component has gotten even stronger. When Tan Ping carefully pours a bowlful of ink or acrylic paint onto rice paper or canvas, the act itself is pure and simple; especially upon continued repetition, it takes on the purity of a meditation, and has no meaning outside of itself. In various Chinese-style abstraction emerged in the past few years, we often find meditative practice behind as a spiritual support. Simple, constant repetition confers tremendous power upon these actions.

If we compare Tan Ping's ink pouring behavior with the ink and wash performance of some expressionist painters, we will see the conceptualized aspect of Tan Ping's performance. Ink and wash performance is mostly related to emotional release or catharsis. As for the act of ink pouring, it is a way of assessing the relation between mechanism and craft; it tests the tension between uniformity and multiformity. In the act of pouring ink, subjective emotions are controlled or held back; the repeated action embodies strong uniformity and mechanicalness. However, no matter how strongly controlled, the seemingly ultra-simple act cannot be repeated exactly. Here Tan Ping extends his accustomed theme of setting up tension. However, when Tan Ping lets many ink traces converge or overlap at one place, the situation changes. When ink traces in a critical quantity overlap in the same area, the resulting mark on the surface is a perfect circle. When they all converge on a single place, the differently shaped ink traces will be seen as a round region. As Tan Ping realizes, stars in space may have their own unique shapes, but in our eyes they all look like round spots twinkling with greater or lesser intensity. When we look at entities of a different order of magnitude, their unique features appear wavering and indefinite. The only definite thing is what we consider as the essence. This is nothing but common-sense observation. Tan Ping's installation *One Cup* expresses our common sense understanding of things. Such an understanding can be seen as a critique of collectivist thought, or it can be seen as endorsing essentialism. But essentialism, having been subverted by post-modernity, slinks along like a pest exposed to the light of day. To endorse essentialism in this era would seem anachronistic. However, philosophical trends go through ups and downs. Post-modernism was in its heyday for a time, but it is not so fashionable now. The anti-essentialism that was closely allied with post-modernism is now being opposed by new forms of essentialism. This new essentialism revealed in Tan Ping's artworks can be viewed as part of a nascent anti-post-modern trend.

Peng Feng

Dean and Professor at the School of Arts, Beijing University

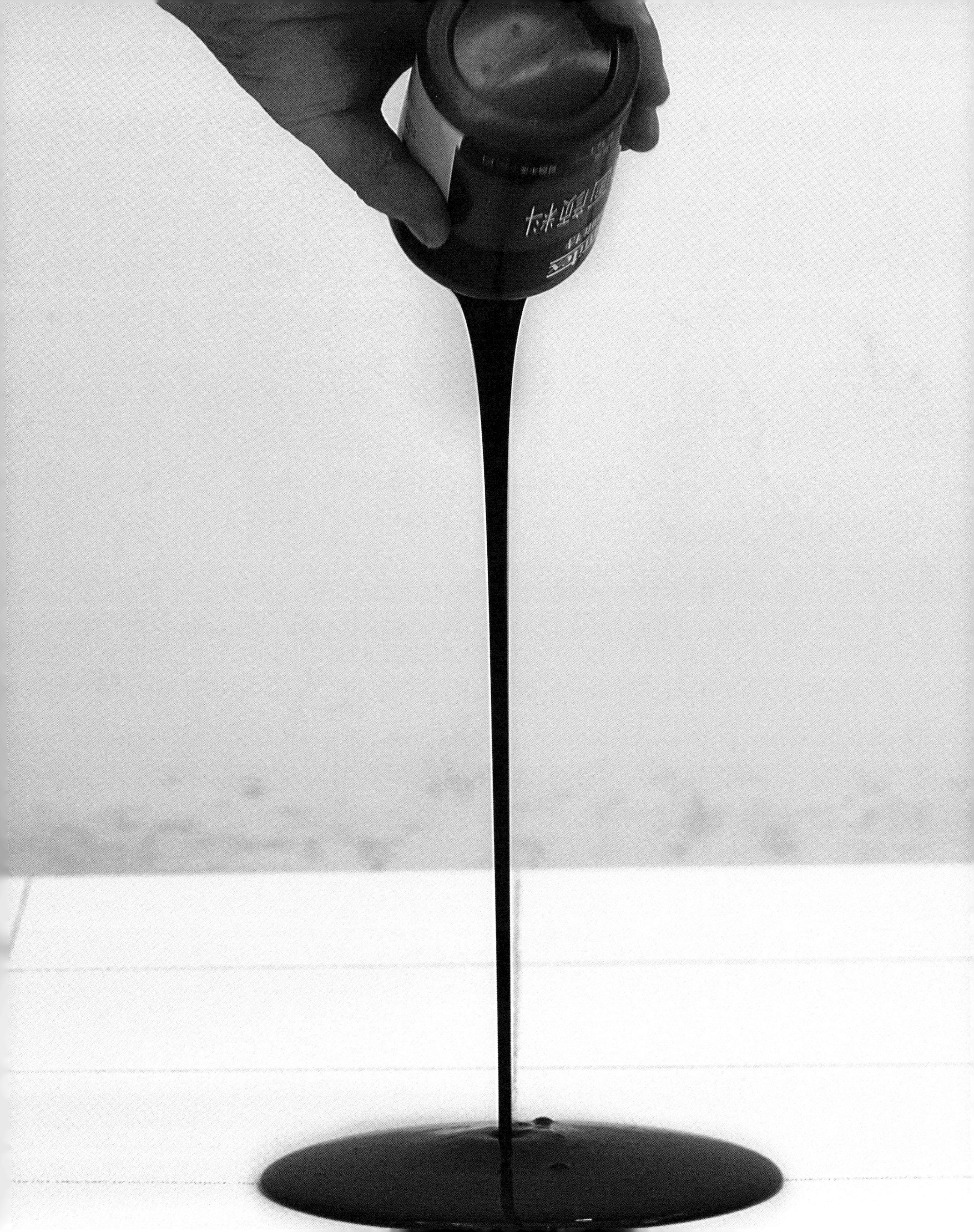

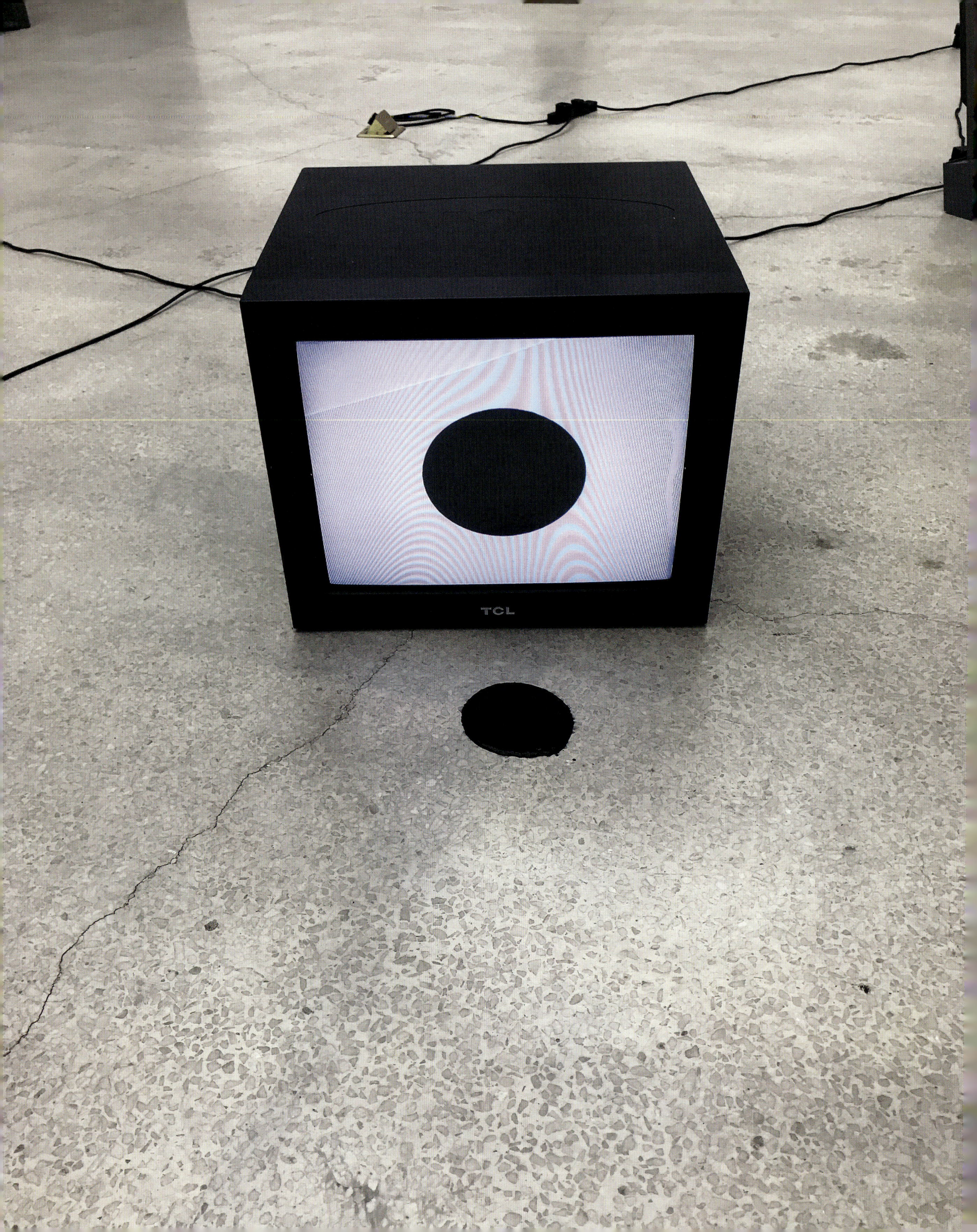

In der 2011 entstandenen multimedialen Arbeit One Cup, die Druck mit Video, Installation und Performance verbindet, ist die konzeptionelle Komponente noch stärker geworden. Wenn Tan Ping vorsichtig eine Schale mit Tinte oder Acrylfarbe auf Reispapier oder Leinwand gießt, ist der Akt selbst rein und einfach; besonders bei fortgesetzter Wiederholung nimmt er die Reinheit einer Meditation an und hat keine Bedeutung außerhalb seiner selbst. In verschiedenen chinesischen Abstraktionen, die in den letzten Jahren entstanden sind, finden wir oft eine meditative Praxis als spirituelle Stütze. Die einfache, ständige Wiederholung verleiht diesen Handlungen eine enorme Kraft.

Wenn wir Tan Pings Verhalten beim Tuscheguss mit der Tusche- und Waschtechnik einiger expressionistischer Maler vergleichen, erkennen wir den konzeptuellen Aspekt von Tan Pings Leistung. Tuschearbeiten stehen meist im Zusammenhang mit emotionaler Befreiung oder Katharsis. Der Akt des Tuschegießens ist eine Möglichkeit, die Beziehung zwischen Mechanismus und Handwerk zu bewerten; er testet die Spannung zwischen Einheitlichkeit und Vielgestaltigkeit. Beim Gießen von Tinte werden subjektive Emotionen kontrolliert oder zurückgehalten; die wiederholte Handlung verkörpert eine starke Gleichförmigkeit und Mechanik. Doch egal wie stark kontrolliert, der scheinbar so einfache Akt kann nicht exakt wiederholt werden. Hier erweitert Tan Ping sein gewohntes Thema des Spannungsaufbaus. Wenn Tan Ping jedoch viele Tuschespuren an einer Stelle zusammenlaufen oder sich überschneiden lässt, ändert sich die Situation. Wenn sich Tintenspuren in einer kritischen Menge im gleichen Bereich überschneiden, entsteht auf der Oberfläche ein perfekter Kreis. Wenn sie alle an einer einzigen Stelle zusammenlaufen, werden die unterschiedlich geformten Farbspuren als runder Bereich gesehen.

Wie Tan Ping feststellt, mögen die Sterne im Weltraum ihre eigenen, einzigartigen Formen haben, aber in unseren Augen sehen sie alle wie runde Flecken aus, die mit mehr oder weniger Intensität blinken. Wenn wir Wesenheiten einer anderen Größenordnung betrachten, erscheinen ihre einzigartigen Merkmale schwankend und unbestimmt. Das einzig Bestimmte ist das, was wir als die Essenz betrachten. Dies ist nichts anderes als eine Beobachtung des gesunden Menschenverstands. Tan Pings Installation One Cup drückt unser Verständnis der Dinge mit gesundem Menschenverstand aus. Ein solches Verständnis kann als Kritik am kollektivistischen Denken oder als Befürwortung des Essentialismus gesehen werden. Aber der Essenzialismus, der von der Postmoderne untergraben wurde, schleicht wie ein Ungeziefer, das dem Licht der Welt ausgesetzt ist. Die Befürwortung des Essenzialismus in dieser Zeit würde anachronistisch erscheinen. Philosophische Strömungen durchlaufen jedoch Höhen und Tiefen. Die Postmoderne hatte eine Zeit lang ihre Blütezeit, aber jetzt ist sie nicht mehr so in Mode. Dem Anti-Essentialismus, der eng mit der Postmoderne verbunden war, werden nun neue Formen des Essentialismus entgegengesetzt. Dieser neue Essenzialismus, der sich in Tan Pings Kunstwerken zeigt, kann als Teil eines aufkommenden anti-postmodernen Trends betrachtet werden.

Peng Feng

Dekan und Professor an der Hochschule der Künste, Universität Peking

Follow My Line:
"To Draw" Is a Verb

Each drawing is completed within two minutes.
Within this limited time, I slow down the movement
of my charcoal, allowing my hand to instinctively
control the pressure and intensity. The charcoal
moves steadily and rhythmically across the paper,
accurately and subtly reflecting my psychological
state.

"Draw" is a verb; while "drawing" is a state of
projection.

Tan Ping

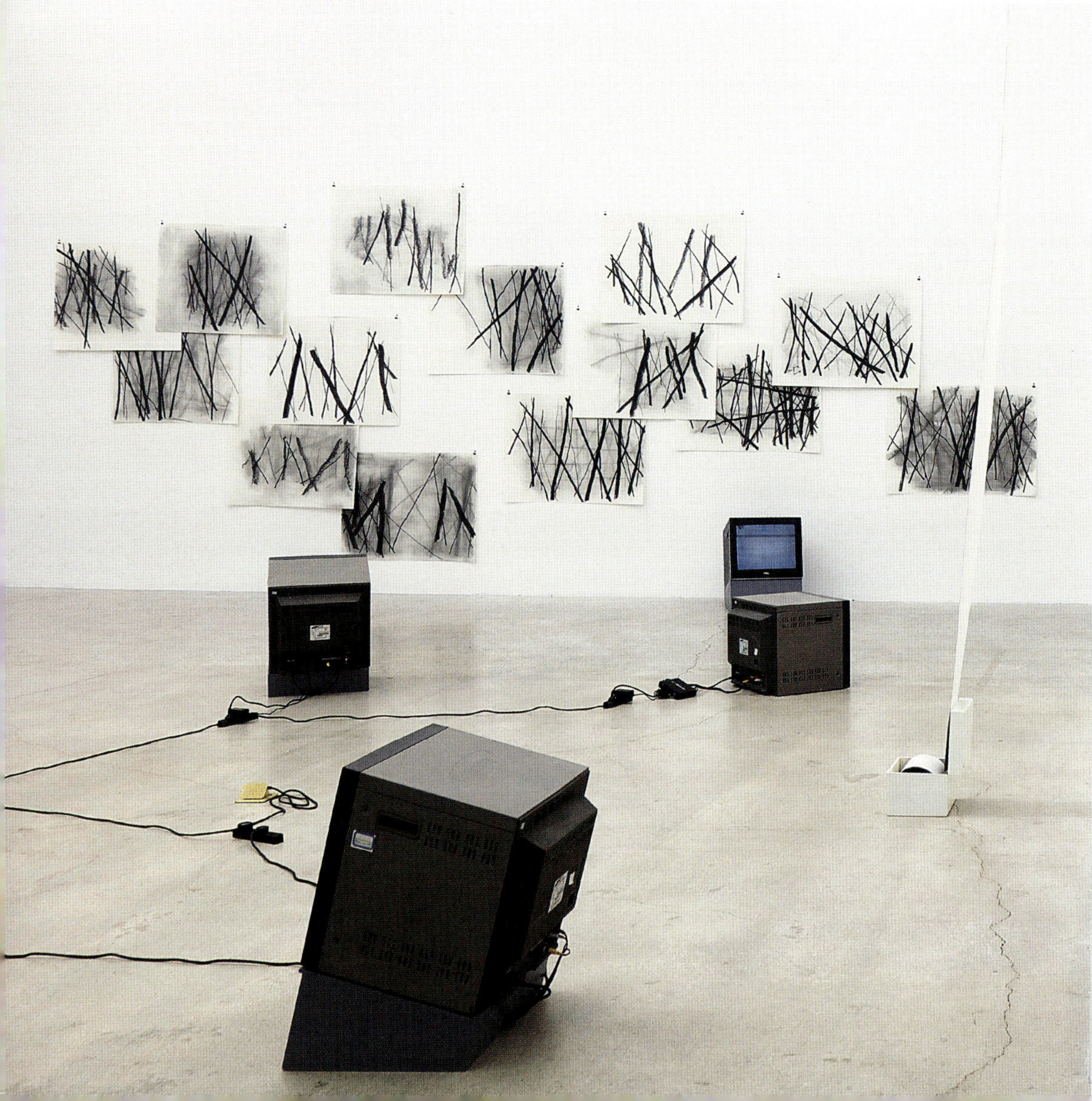

*Tan Ping 1993: The
Beginning of Two Modules*,
2018
installation view /
Installationsansicht
Platform China, Beijing,
China

Folge meiner Linie:
„Zeichnen" ist ein Verb

Jede Zeichnung wird innerhalb von zwei Minuten fertiggestellt. Innerhalb dieser begrenzten Zeit verlangsame ich die Bewegung meiner Kohle und erlaube meiner Hand, den Druck und die Intensität instinktiv zu kontrollieren. Die Kohle bewegt sich gleichmäßig und rhythmisch über das Papier und spiegelt so genau und subtil meinen psychologischen Zustand wider.

„Zeichnen" ist ein Verb, während „der Akt des Zeichnens" ein Zustand der Projektion ist.

Tan Ping

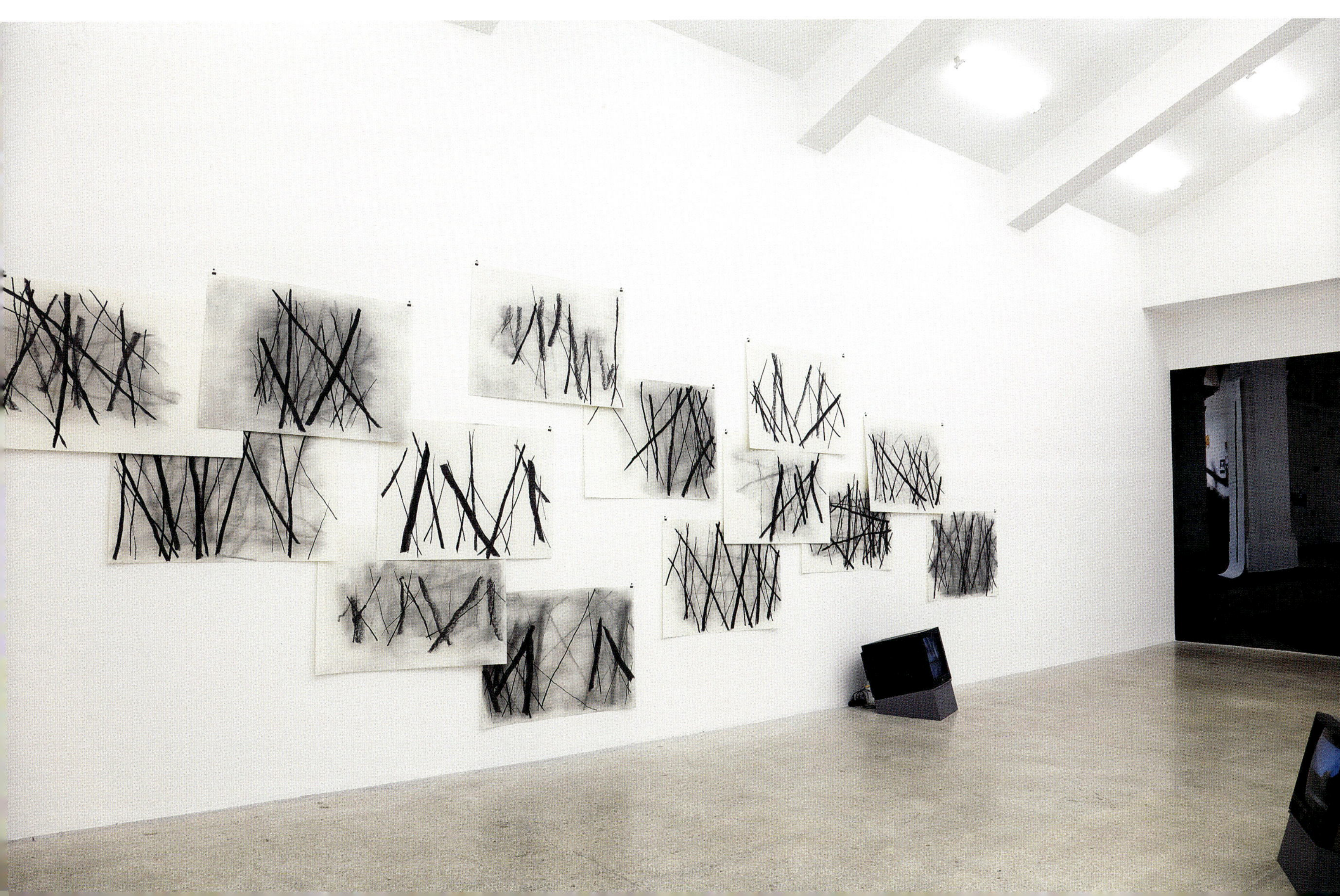

Tan Ping 1993: The Beginning of Two Modules, 2018
installation view /
Installationsansicht
Platform China, Beijing, China

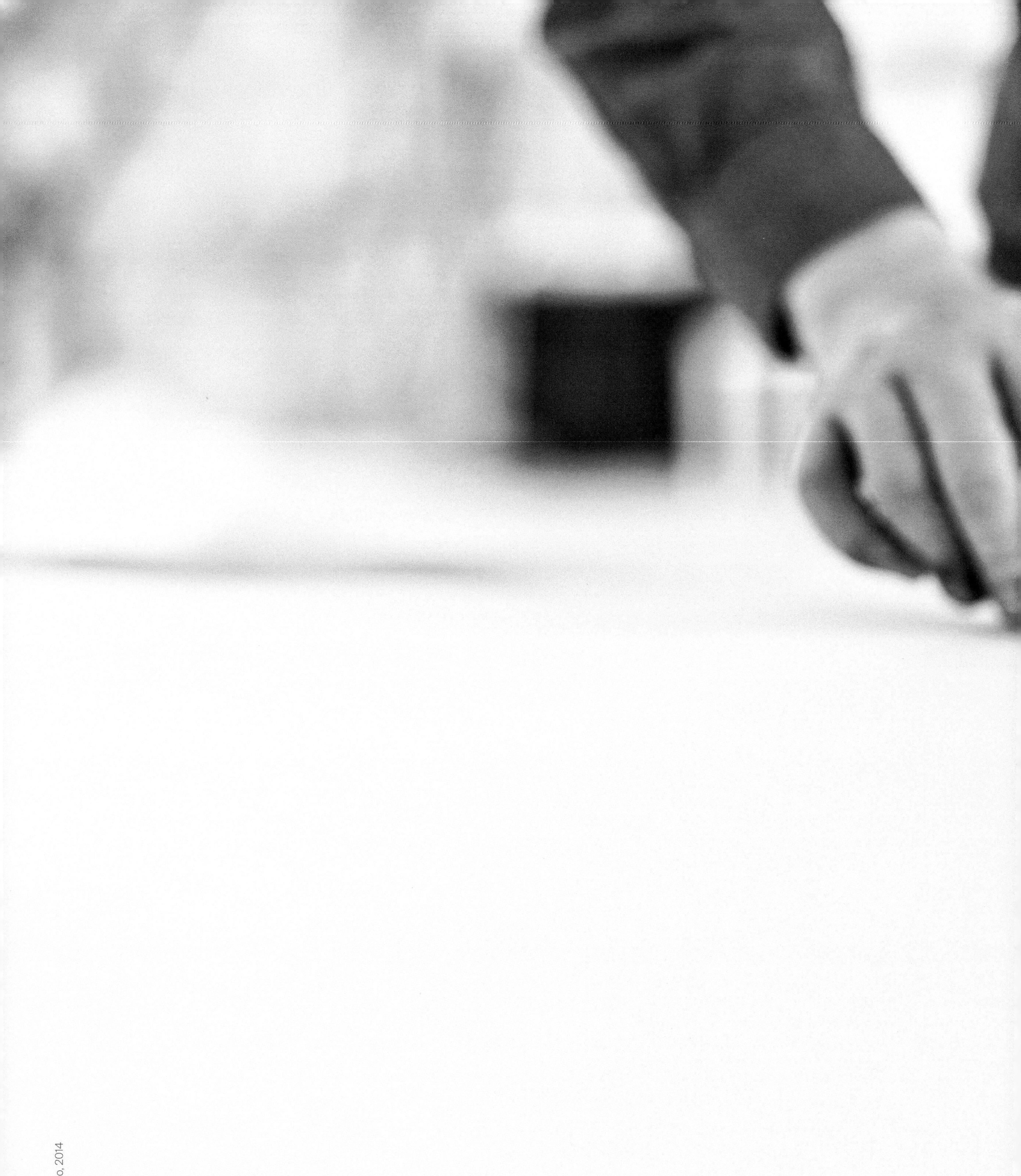

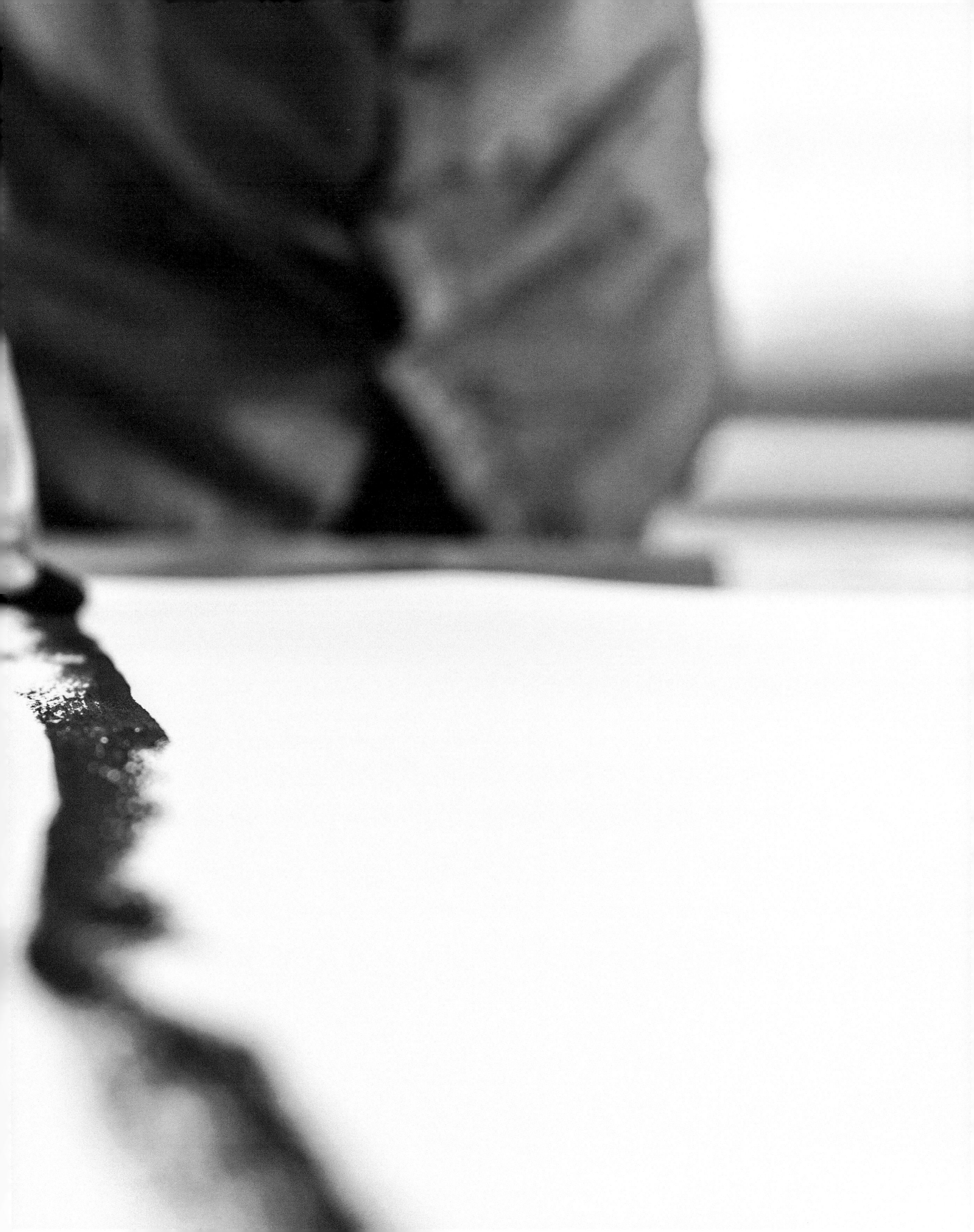

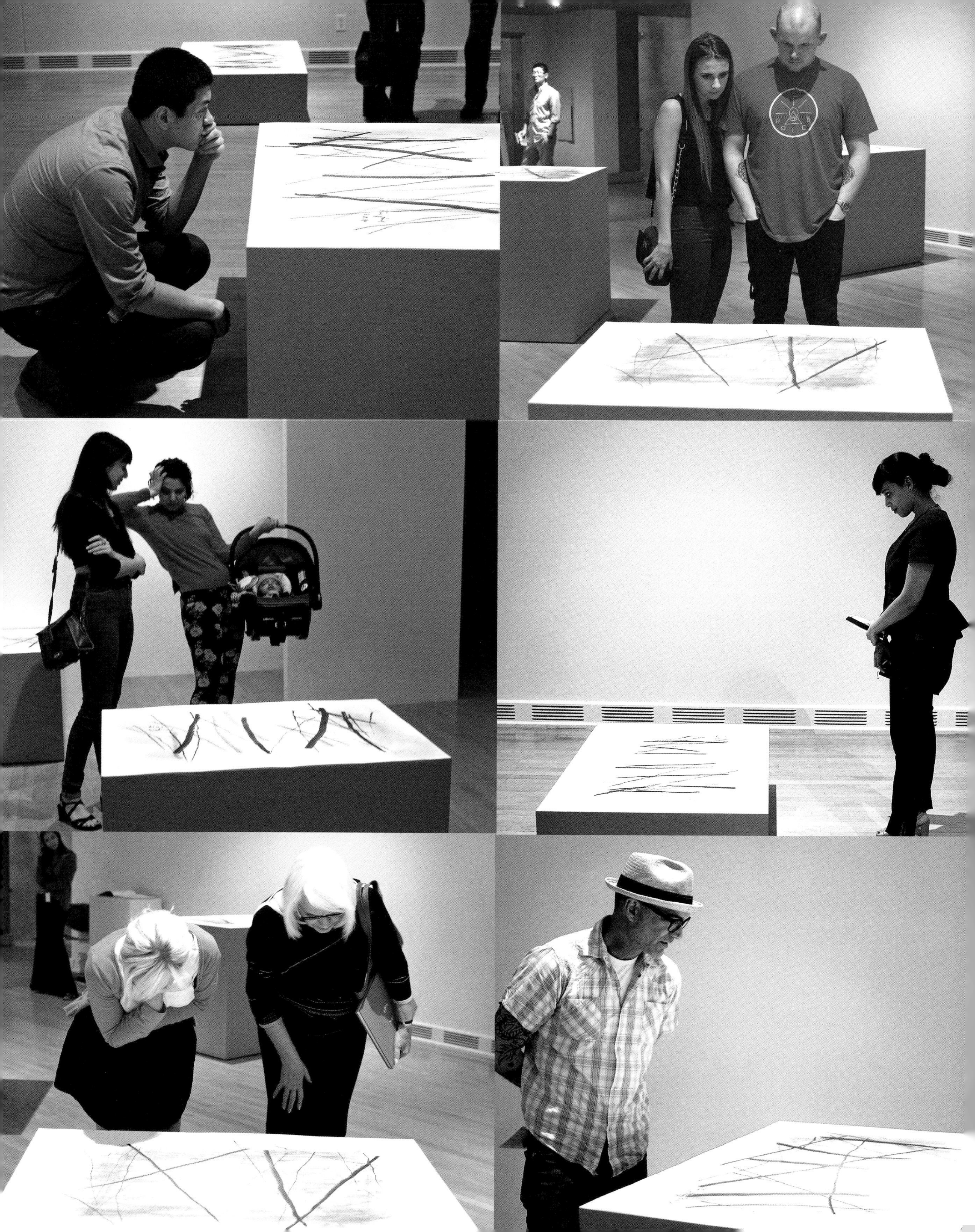

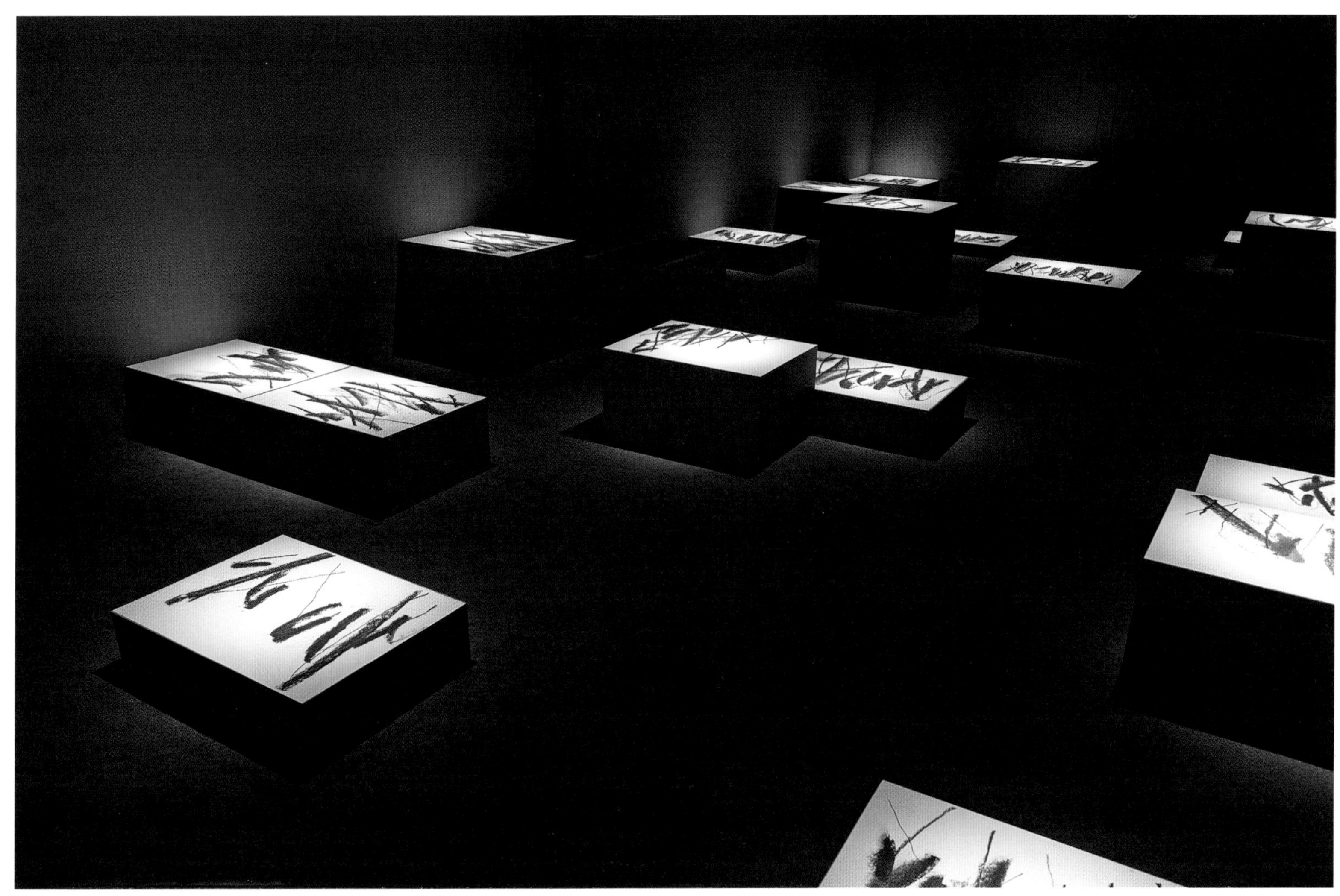

Punkt, Linie, Ebene

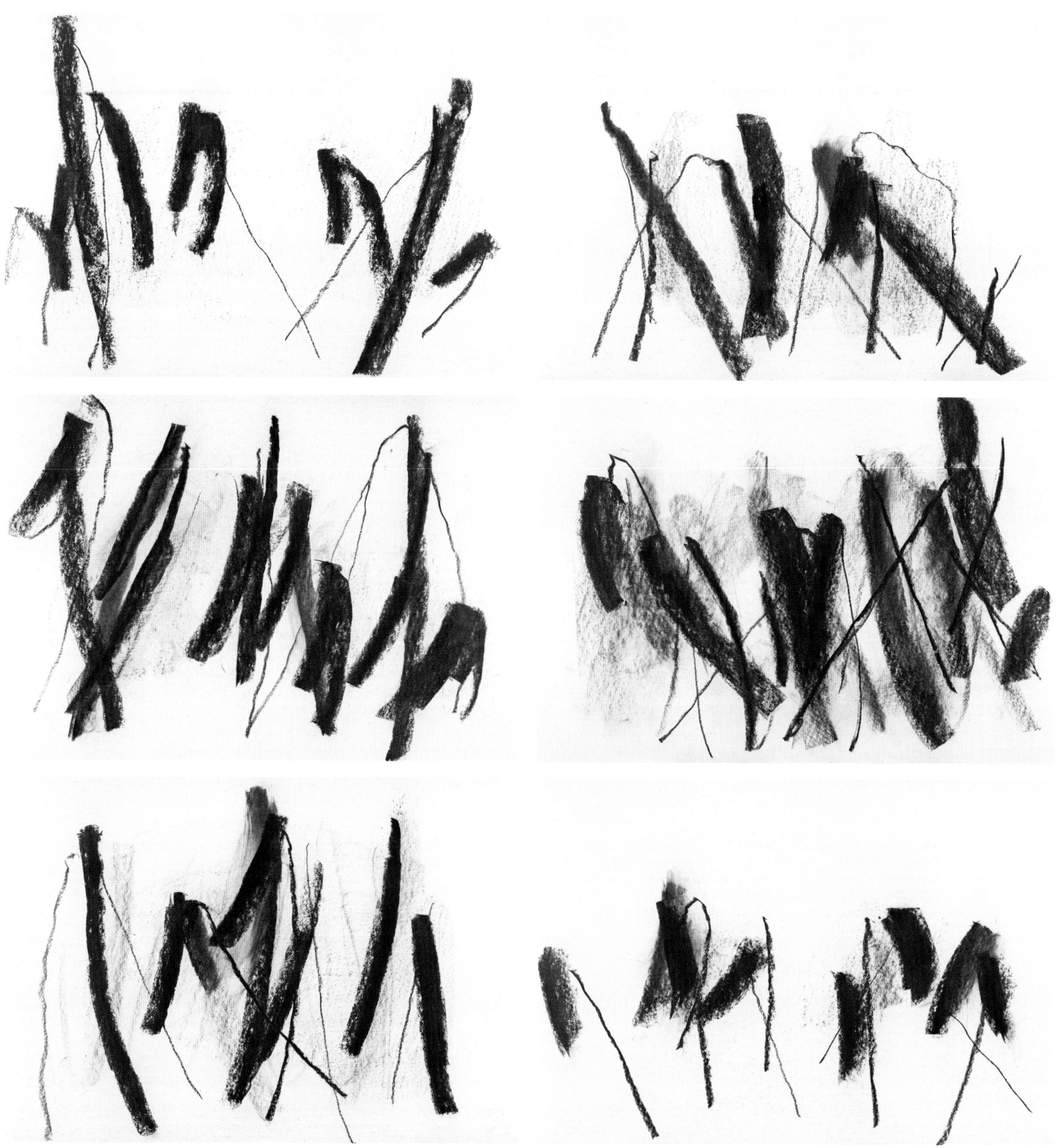

Drawing / **Zeichnung**, 2023
charcoal pencil / **Kohlestift**,
79 × 110cm
Beijing, China

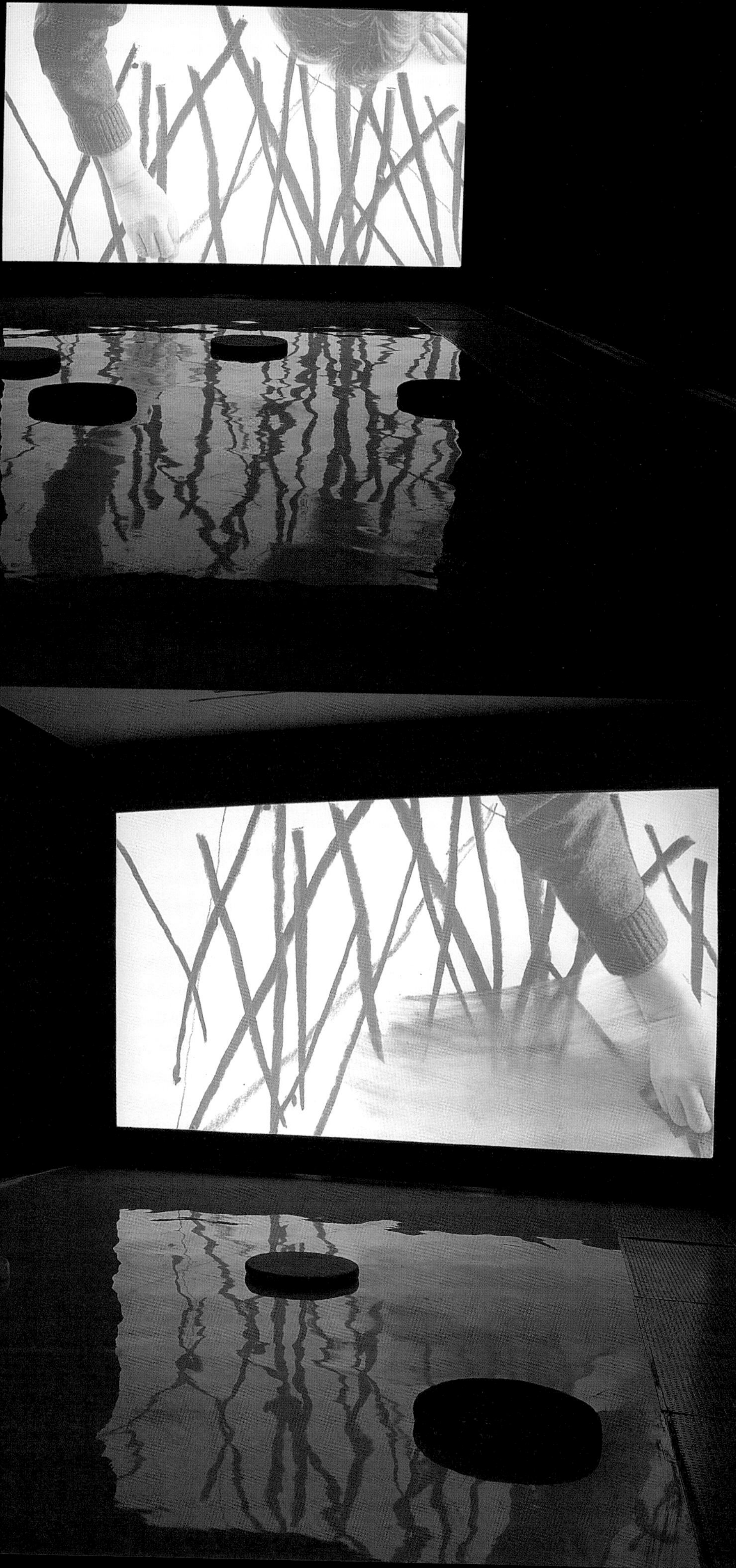

Clement Greenberg the American art critic saw
in Pollock's painting a new kind of painting that
was distinctly different from anything before
and he passionately promoted it as uniquely
American. Greenberg rebutted any reference
made to automatism from the surrealistic school of
painting as it was French not American in origin, for
Greenberg Pollock's style embodied the American
spirit of freedom of expression and individuality.
Marc Toby's paintings are probably the only works
of this period that had any reference made to
Chinese calligraphy, probably because he was
the only artist who spoke openly about it. As is
well known today, American abstract painting of
this time was used to support a strong nationalist
identity and consequently a political tool to support
the political agenda of this period (the cold war).
Jackson Pollock the wild individualistic cowboy
who was killed in a car crash while drunk and later
like the actor to follow in his footsteps and further
propagate the same American mythical image as
Pollock, James Dean the main actor in his most
celebrated film a 'Rebel Without a Cause' would
also die in his Porsche in a high-speed car crash.
The mythical image of these American artists as
rebel has become an ongoing theme all the way to
the Neo-expressionist Jean Michel Basquiat's drug
over dose.
This image does not correspond to the sensibility
of Tan Ping's work. Tan Ping as an artist and in his
work as they are not rooted in either the American
artist's myth or the polemics surrounding American
Abstract painting but is of a very different more
contemplative and reflexive manner than the later.
In Tan Ping's exhibition "Follow My Line", for the
first time his black and white paper drawings
are presented on pedestal giving the spectator
the same vantage point as the artist when the
drawings were made. The spectator can freely
walk through this maze of drawings, discovering
the shifting visual elevations in the drawings, with
each drawing's elevation reveals the process of
its making; lines drawn and then whipped away
to leave; traces, residue, phantom lines turned
into gray zones. Tan Ping's decision to present his
work in an innovative way is not new for this artist,
as he had presented a bold single line 40 meters

long print for his personal exhibition at the National
Museum. In choosing to mount his drawings on
the pedestals which are usually reserved to the
domain of sculpture, he has conceptually and
visually confirmed the physicality of the drawings.
Concurrently, presenting the works in this manner
strongly acknowledges the Chinese traditions of
drawing horizontally as it does with the tradition
of ink calligraphy drawing, a tradition where the
use of gravity and force played an important role.
In the documentary video of Tan Ping's drawing
we see charcoal sticks shattering off the fracture
and shards of the stick falling onto the paper as
he draws. We see the regularity and consistency
of movement, his hand moving at the same even
regular strong speed with his controlling the
pressure and force varying it as he desires. This
is not Jackson Pollock frenetically moving and
dancing in the middle of his canvas, neither is it
the mechanical movements of the Process Art of
Robert Ryman paintings where he tries to paint a
perfectly straight line.

Tony Brown

Artist, Professor at the École Nationale Supérieure
des Beaux-arts de Paris

Tan Ping
Drawing (partial view)
/ *Zeichnung* (Detail),
2014 charcoal pencil /
Kohlestift, 79 x 110cm
Beijing, China

Der amerikanische Kunstkritiker Clement Greenberg sah in Pollocks Malerei eine neue Art von Malerei, die sich deutlich von allen bisherigen unterschied, und er propagierte sie leidenschaftlich als einzigartig amerikanisch. Greenberg wies jede Bezugnahme auf den Automatismus der surrealistischen Malschule zurück, da dieser französischen und nicht amerikanischen Ursprungs sei. Für Greenberg verkörperte Pollocks Stil den amerikanischen Geist der Ausdrucksfreiheit und Individualität. Die Gemälde von Marc Toby sind wahrscheinlich die einzigen Werke dieser Periode, die sich auf die chinesische Kalligraphie beziehen, wahrscheinlich weil er der einzige Künstler war, der offen darüber sprach. Wie heute bekannt ist, wurde die abstrakte amerikanische Malerei dieser Zeit zur Unterstützung einer starken nationalistischen Identität und folglich als politisches Instrument zur Unterstützung der politischen Agenda dieser Zeit (des Kalten Krieges). Jackson Pollock, der wilde, individualistische Cowboy, kam bei einem Autounfall ums Leben, als er betrunken war, und später, wie der Schauspieler, der in seine Fußstapfen trat und das gleiche amerikanische mythische Bild wie Pollock propagierte, starb auch James Dean, der Hauptdarsteller in seinem berühmtesten Film „Rebel Without a Cause", in seinem Porsche bei einem Autounfall mit hoher Geschwindigkeit. Das mythische Bild dieser amerikanischen Künstler als Rebellen hat sich bis hin zur Drogenüberdosis des Neoexpressionisten Jean Michel Basquiat durchgesetzt.
Diese Vorstellung entspricht nicht der Sensibilität von Tan Pings Werk. Tan Ping ist als Künstler und in seinem Werk weder im amerikanischen Künstlermythos noch in der Polemik um die amerikanische abstrakte Malerei verwurzelt, sondern hat eine ganz andere, kontemplativere und reflexivere Art als letztere.

In Tan Pings Ausstellung „Follow My Line" werden seine Schwarz-Weiß-Papierzeichnungen zum ersten Mal auf einem Sockel präsentiert, der es dem Betrachter erlaubt, denselben Blickwinkel einzunehmen wie der Künstler bei der Entstehung der Zeichnungen. Der Betrachter kann frei durch dieses Labyrinth von Zeichnungen gehen und die sich verändernden visuellen Erhebungen in den Zeichnungen entdecken, wobei die Erhebung jeder Zeichnung den Prozess ihrer Entstehung offenbart; Linien, die gezeichnet und dann weggepeitscht werden, um Spuren, Rückstände und Phantomlinien zu hinterlassen, die sich in Grauzonen verwandeln. Tan Pings Entscheidung, sein Werk auf innovative Weise zu präsentieren, ist für diesen Künstler nicht neu, denn er hatte bereits für seine Soloausstellung im Nationalmuseum einen kühnen einzeiligen, 40 Meter langen Druck präsentiert. Mit der Entscheidung, seine Zeichnungen auf Sockeln zu montieren, die normalerweise der Bildhauerei vorbehalten sind, hat er die Körperlichkeit der Zeichnungen konzeptionell und visuell bestätigt. Gleichzeitig ist die Präsentation der Werke auf diese Weise ein starkes Bekenntnis zur chinesischen Tradition des horizontalen Zeichnens und zur Tradition der Tuschkalligraphie, einer Tradition, in der der Einsatz von Schwerkraft und Kraft eine wichtige Rolle spielt. In dem Dokumentarvideo von Tan Pings Zeichnung sehen wir, wie die Kohlestifte beim Zeichnen zerbrechen und Splitter auf das Papier fallen.
Wir sehen die Regelmäßigkeit und Beständigkeit der Bewegung, seine Hand bewegt sich mit der gleichen gleichmäßigen, starken Geschwindigkeit, wobei er den Druck und die Kraft kontrolliert und nach Belieben variiert. Das ist weder Jackson Pollock, der sich frenetisch bewegt und in der Mitte seiner Leinwand tanzt, noch sind es die mechanischen Bewegungen der Process Art von Robert Ryman, bei denen er versucht, eine perfekt gerade Linie zu malen.

Tony Brown

Künstler, Professor an der École Nationale Supérieure des Beaux-arts de Paris

"Overlay" series, 2019
acrylic on canvas /
Acryl auf Leinwand,
200 × 200cm
Beijing, China

Overlay:
Accumulated Slices of Time

"Overlay" is the counter action against conventional painting methods, with the aim to "destroy" rather than construct. The more perfect the "overlaid" image is, the more effectively this action conveys its underlying concept.

Tan Ping

"OVERLAY" AS A WORKING METHOD

In 2019, Tan Ping created a work almost entirely covered in a single shade of grey. It neither tells a moving "story" like classical painting or realism, nor offers an aesthetic "form" like modernism or abstract art. This was not a singular creation; he produced a large number of similar pieces. Although such works are not uncommon in art history, Tan Ping's pieces do not aim, like those of Malevich, Rauschenberg, Mark Rothko, or Reinhardt, to express a transcendent "spirit" through minimalist "form," nor do they pursue the "ultimate" in religious or philosophical terms.

"Overlay" series, 2018
oil on canvas /
Öl auf Leinwand,
200 × 200cm
installation view /
Installationsansicht
Beijing, China

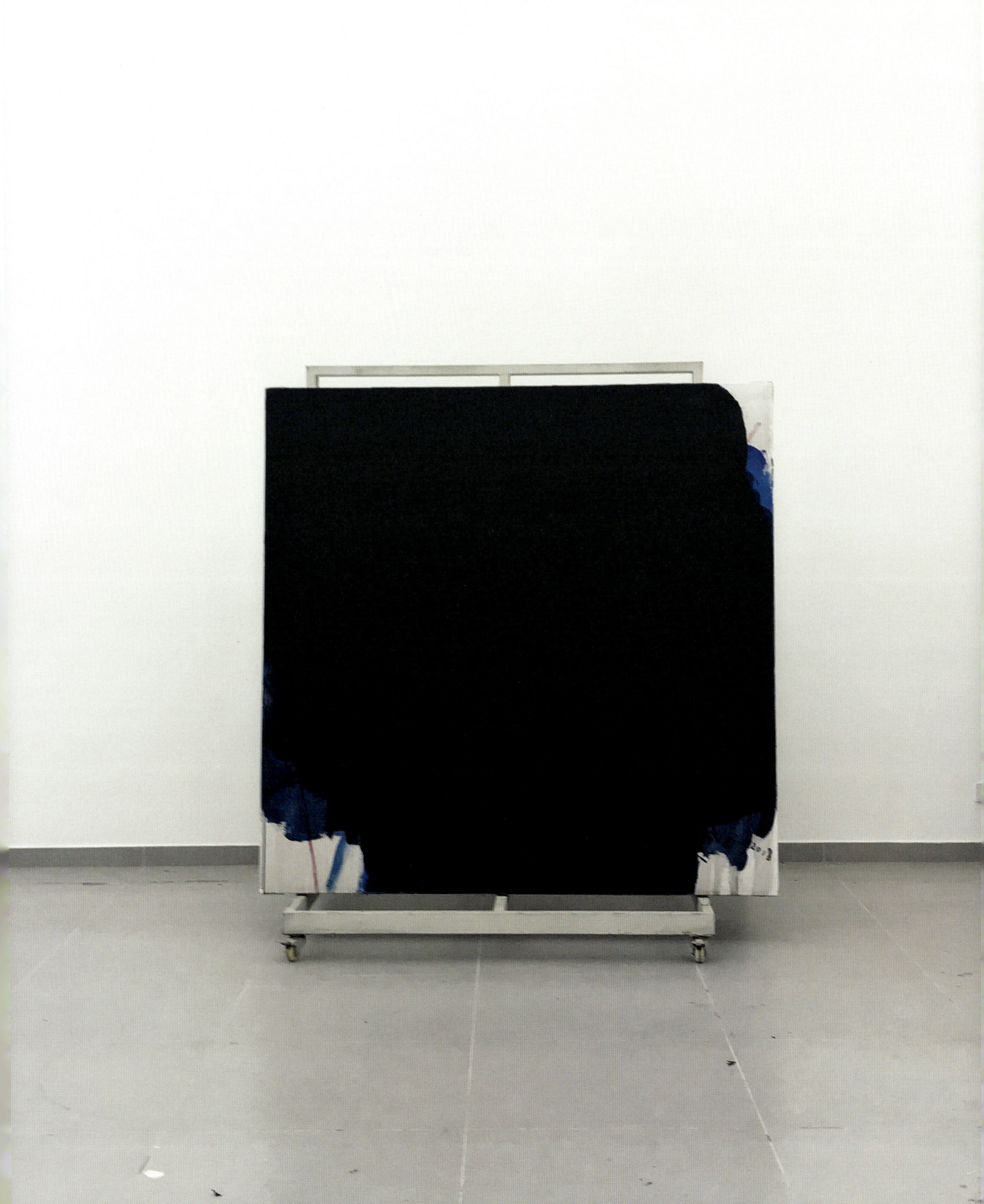

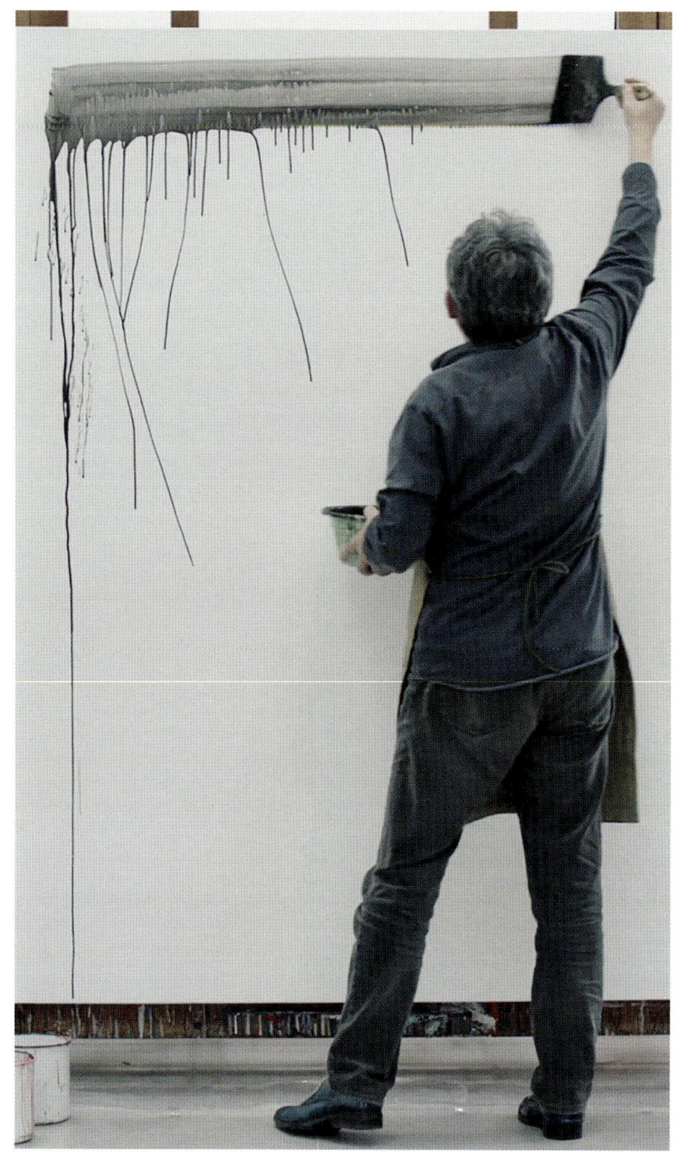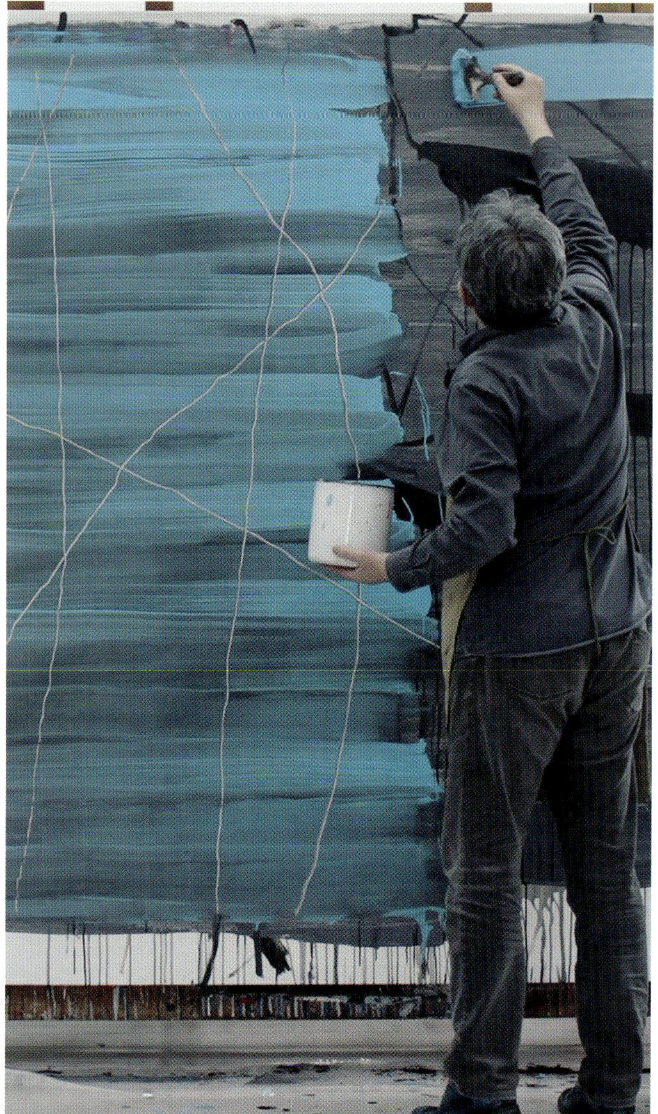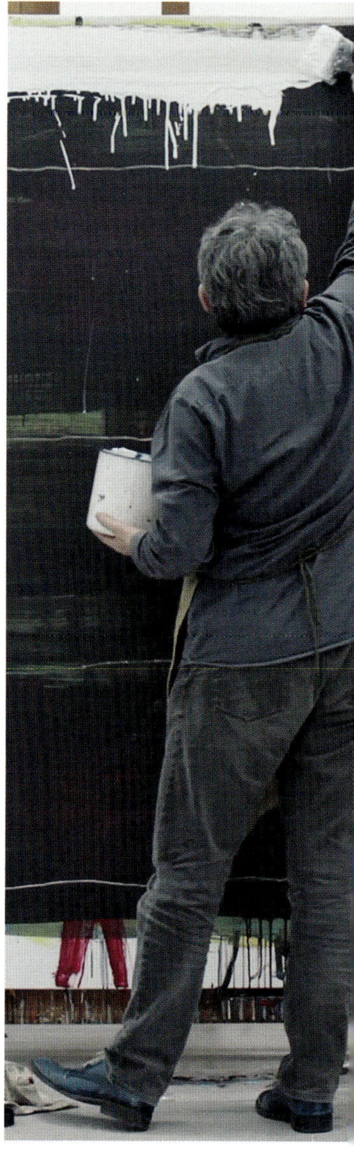

"Overlay" series, 2019
work process /
Arbeitsprozess, video clip

At first glance, Tan Ping's "gray paintings" appear strikingly similar to the works of the aforementioned artists. However, upon closer examination, one will notice significant differences, particularly in the fact that the single shade of gray in Tan Ping's work does not completely cover the canvas. The key lies in the barely noticeable spots of pure color at the four corners—often overlooked by viewers. These colors in the corners form a layered relationship, rather than a flat juxtaposition. In other words, the final visual effect is created by successive layers of color, with the last layer being gray. This is why it initially appears as a "gray painting." The artist has left us a clue for understanding his work. While other artists strive to fully express themselves on the canvas, Tan Ping hides himself. So, what exactly has the artist done?

Another of his video works reveals the answer to this mystery. Typically, the process begins with a blank canvas. Tan Ping, following his usual creative method, paints lines, dots, and circles onto the canvas. At various stages, the piece has already become what we recognize as a complete and remarkable "Tan Ping-style" abstract painting. But in a surprising turn, in the next moment, Tan Ping overlays "that piece" with another color, returning it to the blank canvas it once was. For the artist, this act means destroying a satisfying work, while simultaneously heralding the start of something new. He may then use a scraper to remove everything, turning the canvas into a perplexing state where past and present are interwoven. For the viewer, after witnessing the birth of a masterpiece, they are immediately confronted with its destruction, followed by its rebirth, and then its demise once more—a repeated cycle. The process is "heart-stopping," until it finally becomes a "gray painting."

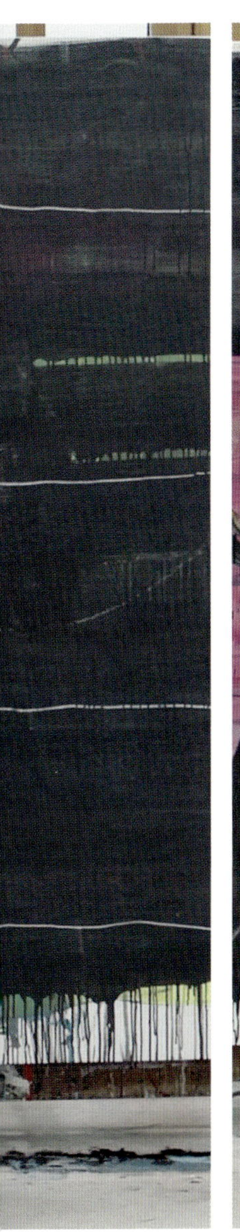
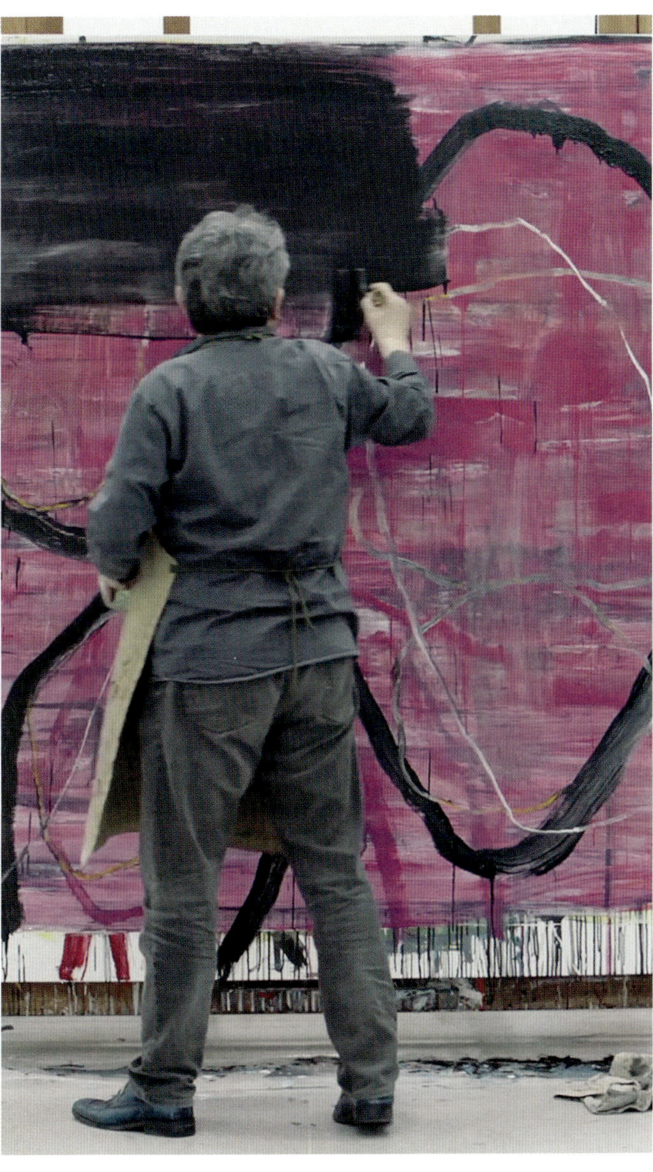

er schuf eine große Anzahl ähnlicher Werke. Obwohl solche Werke in der Kunstgeschichte nicht ungewöhnlich sind, zielen Tan Pings Werke nicht wie die von Malewitsch, Rauschenberg, Mark Rothko oder Reinhardt darauf ab, einen transzendenten „Geist" durch minimalistische „Form" auszudrücken, noch streben sie das „Letzte" in religiöser oder philosophischer Hinsicht an.

Auf den ersten Blick erscheinen Tan Pings „graue Gemälde" den Werken der oben genannten Künstler auffallend ähnlich. Bei näherer Betrachtung werden jedoch erhebliche Unterschiede festgestellt, insbesondere in der Tatsache, dass der einzelne Grauton in Tan Pings Werk die Leinwand nicht vollständig bedeckt. Der Schlüssel liegt in den kaum wahrnehmbaren Flecken reiner Farbe an den vier Ecken – die vom Betrachter oft übersehen werden. Diese Farben in den Ecken bilden eine geschichtete Beziehung, statt einer flachen Gegenüberstellung. Mit anderen Worten: Der endgültige visuelle Effekt wird durch aufeinanderfolgende Farbschichten erzeugt, wobei die letzte Schicht grau ist. Deshalb erscheint es zunächst als „graues Gemälde". Der Künstler hat uns einen Hinweis zum Verständnis seiner Arbeit hinterlassen. Während andere Künstler danach streben, sich auf der Leinwand voll auszudrücken, versteckt sich Tan Ping. Was also hat der Künstler genau getan? Eine andere seiner Videoarbeiten enthüllt die Antwort auf dieses Rätsel.

Normalerweise beginnt der Prozess mit einer leeren Leinwand. Tan Ping malt, seiner üblichen kreativen Methode folgend, Linien, Punkte und Kreise auf die Leinwand. In verschiedenen Stadien ist das Werk bereits zu dem geworden, was wir als vollständiges und bemerkenswertes abstraktes Gemälde im „Tan Ping-Stil" erkennen. Doch in einer überraschenden Wendung überzieht Tan Ping „dieses Werk" im nächsten Moment mit einer anderen Farbe und macht es wieder zu der leeren Leinwand, die es einmal war. Für den Künstler bedeutet dieser Akt die Zerstörung eines zufriedenstellenden Werks und gleichzeitig den Beginn von etwas Neuem. Er kann dann einen Schaber verwenden, um alles zu entfernen und die Leinwand in einen verwirrenden Zustand zu versetzen, in dem Vergangenheit und Gegenwart miteinander verwoben sind. Der Betrachter wird, nachdem er die Geburt eines Meisterwerks miterlebt hat, sofort mit seiner Zerstörung konfrontiert, gefolgt von seiner Wiedergeburt und dann erneut seinem Untergang – ein sich wiederholender Zyklus. Der Prozess ist „atemberaubend", bis schließlich ein „graues Gemälde" entsteht.

Overlay:
Angesammelte Zeitsequenzen

„Overlay" ist die Gegenmaßnahme zu herkömmlichen Malmethoden, mit dem Ziel, zu „zerstören", statt zu konstruieren. Je perfekter das „überlagerte" Bild ist, desto effektiver vermittelt diese Aktion das zugrunde liegende Konzept.

Tan Ping

„OVERLAY" ALS ARBEITSMETHODE

Im Jahr 2019 schuf Tan Ping ein Werk, das fast vollständig in einem einzigen Grauton gehalten ist. Es erzählt weder eine bewegende „Geschichte" wie die klassische Malerei oder der Realismus, noch bietet es eine ästhetische „Form" wie die Moderne oder die abstrakte Kunst. Dies war keine einmalige Schöpfung;

We can view this "gray painting" as a collective body of several of Tan Ping's works. Although we cannot fully detect them with our eyes, what is unseen does not mean it doesn't exist: "they" are right there, beneath the seemingly featureless layer of "gray." So why are already completed or nearly completed works "destroyed" by being covered, only to start again from scratch? In fact, "overlay" is one of Tan Ping's most frequently used methods in his creative process. His constant re-painting, covering, and re-painting is not due to dissatisfaction with the work or a desire to correct the existing image, but rather a deliberate act. Critics interpret this approach as "conceptual." This suggests that Tan Ping is not merely "painting," but creating a form of conceptual art, with the act of painting as the medium and the process of painting as the vessel for conveying the idea.

The "gray painting" represents an extreme case where viewers see nothing at all, yet they know it is not merely a featureless gray surface. Beneath the gray, there are many complete paintings— masterful creations of the "hand" that are not entirely governed by the mind. Under the gray lies a typical Tan Ping palette—pinks, bright yellows, and lake blues, along with his signature circles and diagonal lines. They are there, unmistakably present beneath the gray, much like the stratified "cultural layers" at an archaeological site or the ever-covered murals of Dunhuang. These are the accumulated results of time, and without human intervention to reveal them, we might never be able to see the layers beneath.

In the field of archaeological stratigraphy, archaeologists are able to determine and study chronological, geographical, and cultural features through the analysis of strata. For example, at the Gantangqing Paleolithic site in Jiangchuan, Yunnan,

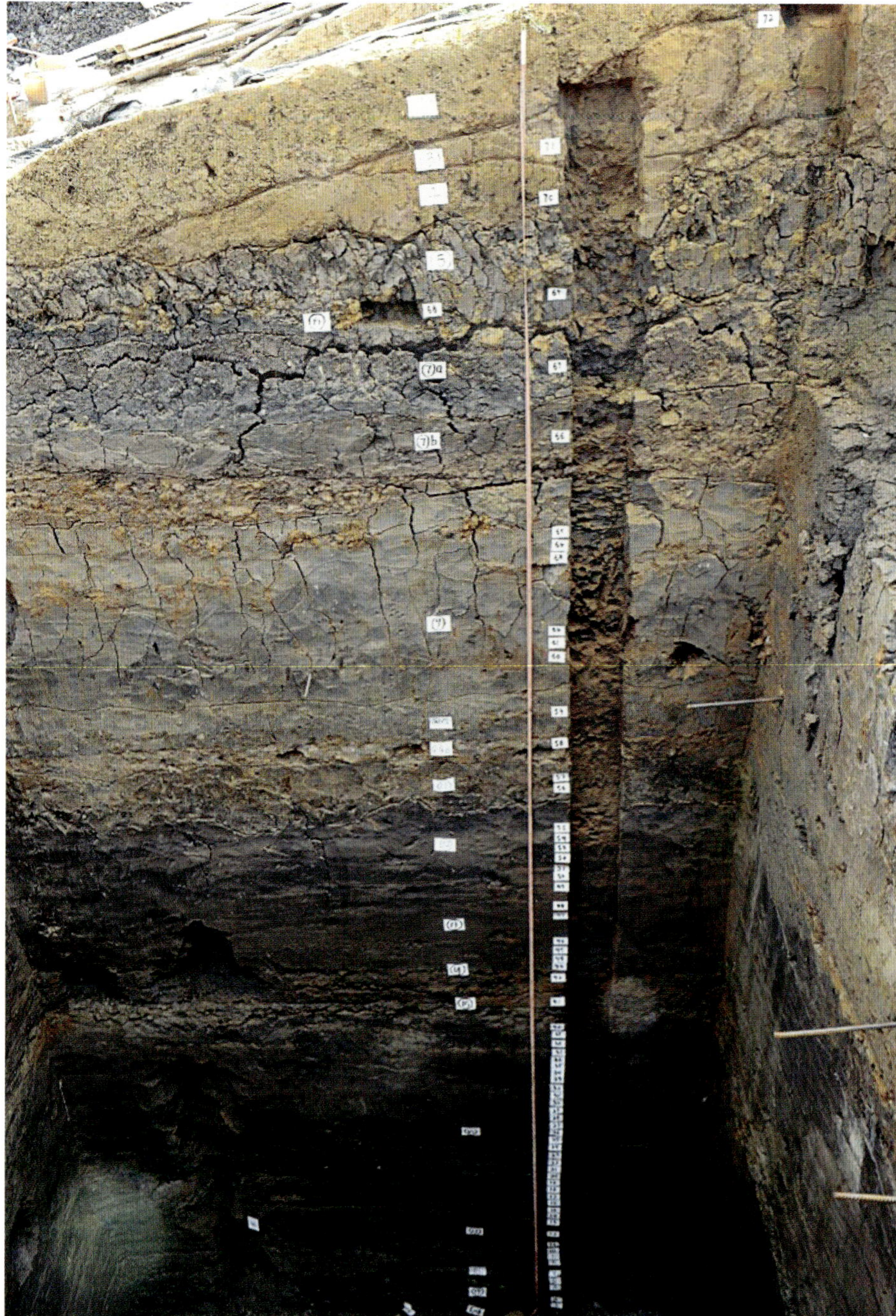

The Paleolithic Site of Gantangqing in Jiangchuan, Yunnan / **Die paläolithische Stätte von Gantangqing in Jiangchuan, Yunnan, China**

excavations have revealed a depth of approximately 6 meters, showcasing five sedimentary cycles and 20 stratigraphic layers. Layers 1-13, from the bottom upwards, contain no artifacts or signs of civilization, while layers 14-19 are cultural layers. Through the analysis of stone tools, bone implements, wooden artifacts, and evidence of fire use, we gain a clear understanding of the progression of human tool-making, usage, and civilization over time. Millions of years of sediment accumulation represent a natural covering, and uncovering the secrets behind this covering reveals the secrets of human civilization. Time is harsh; it ultimately reduces nature, people, and objects to layers of soil, which are then mercilessly buried by the soil of the next era.

Wir können dieses „graue Gemälde" als eine Sammlung mehrerer Werke von Tan Ping betrachten. Obwohl wir sie mit unseren Augen nicht vollständig erkennen können, bedeutet das Unsichtbare nicht, dass es nicht existiert: „Sie" sind genau dort, unter der scheinbar strukturlosen Schicht von „Grau". Warum also werden bereits fertiggestellte oder fast fertiggestellte Werke „zerstört", indem sie abgedeckt werden, nur um dann wieder von vorne zu beginnen? Tatsächlich ist „Überlagern" eine der am häufigsten verwendeten Methoden von Tan Ping in seinem kreativen Prozess. Sein ständiges Übermalen, Abdecken und Übermalen ist nicht auf Unzufriedenheit mit der Arbeit oder den Wunsch zurückzuführen, das vorhandene Bild zu korrigieren, sondern vielmehr eine absichtliche Handlung. Kritiker interpretieren diesen Ansatz als „konzeptionell". Dies deutet darauf hin, dass Tan Ping nicht nur „malt", sondern eine Form konzeptueller Kunst schafft, bei der der Akt des Malens das Medium und der Prozess des Malens das Gefäß zur Vermittlung der Idee ist. Das „graue Gemälde" stellt einen Extremfall dar, bei dem der Betrachter überhaupt nichts sieht, aber dennoch weiß, dass es sich nicht nur um eine gesichtslose graue Oberfläche handelt. Unter dem Grau befinden sich viele vollständige Gemälde – meisterhafte Schöpfungen der „Hand", die nicht ausschließlich vom Verstand gesteuert werden. Unter dem Grau liegt eine typische Palette von Tan Ping – Rosa, leuchtendes Gelb und Seeblau, zusammen mit seinen charakteristischen Kreisen und diagonalen Linien. Sie sind da, unverkennbar unter dem Grau vorhanden, ähnlich wie die geschichteten „Kulturschichten" an einer archäologischen Stätte oder die ewig bedeckten Wandmalereien von Dunhuang. Dies sind die angesammelten Ergebnisse der Zeit, und ohne menschliches Eingreifen, um sie freizulegen, könnten wir die darunter liegenden Schichten vielleicht nie sehen.

Im Bereich der archäologischen Stratigraphie können Archäologen durch die Analyse von Schichten chronologische, geografische und kulturelle Merkmale bestimmen und untersuchen. Beispielsweise haben Ausgrabungen an der paläolithischen Stätte Gantangqing in Jiangchuan, Yunnan, eine Tiefe von etwa 6 Metern freigelegt, die fünf Sedimentzyklen und 20 stratigraphische Schichten offenbart. Die Schichten 1-13 enthalten von unten nach oben keine Artefakte oder Zeichen der Zivilisation, während die Schichten 14-19 kulturelle Schichten sind. Durch die Analyse von Steinwerkzeugen, Knochengeräten, Holzartefakten und Hinweisen auf die Verwendung von Feuer erhalten wir ein klares Verständnis der Entwicklung der menschlichen Werkzeugherstellung, -verwendung und -zivilisation im Laufe der Zeit. Millionen von Jahren der Sedimentablagerung stellen eine natürliche Abdeckung dar, und die Aufdeckung der Geheimnisse hinter dieser Abdeckung enthüllt die Geheimnisse der menschlichen Zivilisation. Die Zeit ist gnadenlos; sie reduziert Natur, Menschen und Objekte letztendlich zu Erdschichten, die dann gnadenlos vom Boden der nächsten Ära begraben werden.

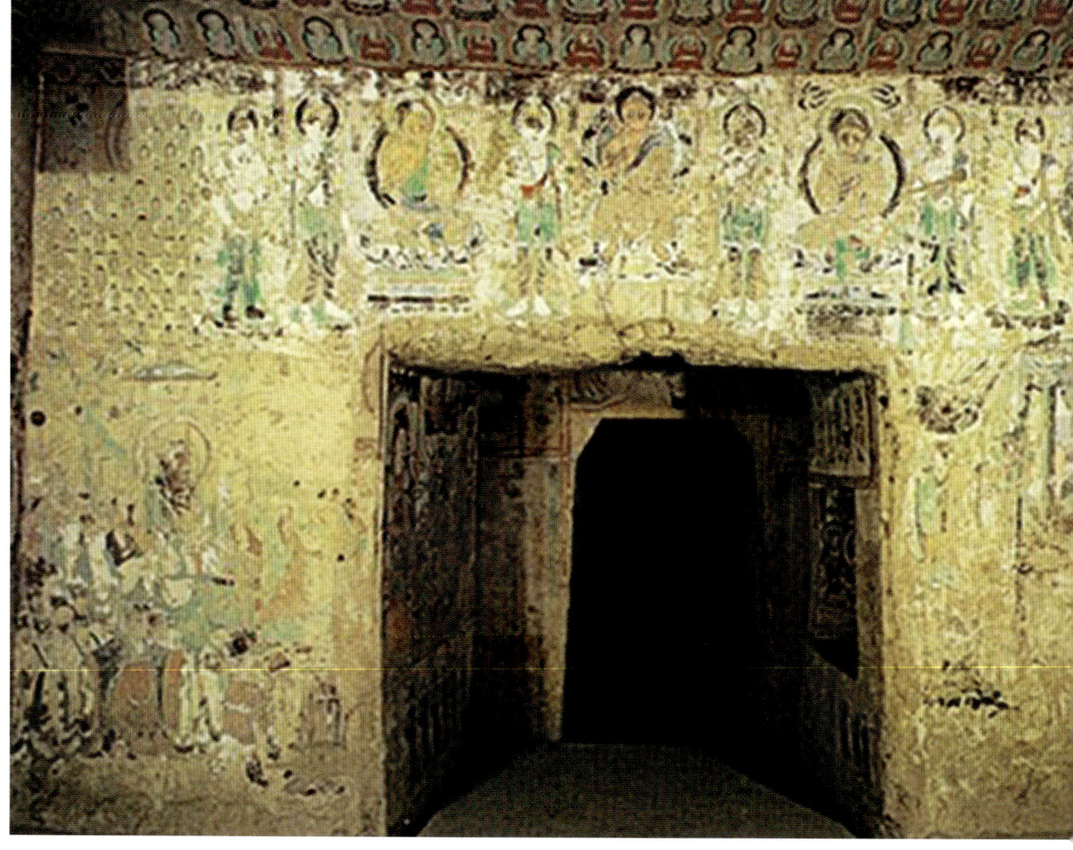

The history of the Dunhuang murals is much shorter than the accumulation of geological strata, yet they similarly reveal layers of time to the viewer. To uncover the "secrets" hidden beneath the painted layers, researchers at Dunhuang sometimes peel back the upper layers of paintings in certain corners of walls adorned with multiple layers of murals, allowing viewers to see the underlying works. Some mural walls even feature three or more layers of paintings. For instance, in the east wall of Cave 220 at the Mogao Caves, a square opening in the upper left corner allows viewers to see floral designs from the Western Xia and early Tang periods beneath the Song Dynasty's depiction of *The Thousand Buddhas*. The layers beneath Tan Ping's "gray paintings" are far more numerous than those in the Dunhuang murals, yet they also have similar revealing "corners." Here, attentive viewers can discern details beneath the gray surfaces—bright color layers hidden underneath, sparking interest and contemplation.

So, what exactly is the "overlay" shaped by "time"? In other words, what is the specific "concept" behind Tan Ping's art? In the examples of archaeological "cultural layers" and the layered Dunhuang murals, the passage of time signifies human "history," bearing witness to civilizations. In contrast, in Tan Ping's "gray paintings," the layering of time represents deeply personal experiences, which together form "life." A human life lasts only a few decades, and the creation of an artwork takes just a few hours or dozens of hours. When compared to the million-year-old archaeological strata or the thousand-year-old murals of Dunhuang, it is as fleeting as a blink. Yet, this fleeting moment becomes intensely real within the painting and the act of painting. The concept becomes materialized—it is there, layer upon layer.

During the creative process, Tan Ping places great emphasis on the "clash of emotions, their harmonious coexistence, and even the stillness of calm." These fleeting "experiences" cannot be simulated or replicated; they are the "truth" beneath the gray surface. Each stroke, line, and layer of paint is unique, not in terms of the "image" of the painting or the "concept" of the art, but in relation to the artist's own subjectivity. Tan Ping states, "The world is ever-changing, filled with drama and various uncertainties. Each day and every moment are irreplaceable and non-repeatable. However, accumulated fragments and overlapping moments can create an uncertain yet vivid reality." Tan Ping's "overlay" is an ongoing process. Beneath the monotone gray lies history, life, and existence.

Sheng Wei

Editor-in-Chief of *Fine Arts magazine*, Professor at Tsinghua University

Die Geschichte der Dunhuang-Wandmalereien ist viel kürzer als die Ansammlung geologischer Schichten, doch offenbaren sie dem Betrachter auf ähnliche Weise Zeitschichten. Um die unter den gemalten Schichten verborgenen „Geheimnisse" aufzudecken, ziehen die Forscher in Dunhuang manchmal die oberen Schichten der Malereien in bestimmten Ecken von Wänden ab, die mit mehreren Schichten von Wandmalereien geschmückt sind, sodass der Betrachter die darunter liegenden Werke sehen kann. Einige Wandmalereien weisen sogar drei oder mehr Schichten von Malereien auf. So ermöglicht beispielsweise in der Ostwand der Höhle 220 in den Mogao-Höhlen eine quadratische Öffnung in der oberen linken Ecke dem Betrachter, florale Muster aus der westlichen Xia- und frühen Tang-Zeit unter der Darstellung der Tausend Buddhas aus der Song-Dynastie zu sehen. Die Schichten unter Tan Pings „grauen Malereien" sind weitaus zahlreicher als die in den Dunhuang-Wandmalereien, doch sie haben auch ähnlich aufschlussreiche „Ecken". Hier können aufmerksame Betrachter Details unter den grauen Oberflächen erkennen – darunter verborgene helle Farbschichten, die Interesse und Kontemplation wecken.

Was genau ist also die „Überlagerung", die durch die „Zeit" geformt wird? Mit anderen Worten, was ist das spezifische „Konzept" hinter Tan Pings Kunst? In den Beispielen der archäologischen „Kulturschichten" und der geschichteten Wandmalereien von Dunhuang symbolisiert der Lauf der Zeit die menschliche „Geschichte" und zeugt von Zivilisationen. Im Gegensatz dazu repräsentiert die Schichtung der Zeit in Tan Pings „grauen Gemälden" zutiefst persönliche Erfahrungen, die zusammen „Leben" bilden. Ein Menschenleben dauert nur wenige Jahrzehnte, und die Schaffung eines Kunstwerks dauert nur wenige Stunden oder Dutzende von Stunden. Im Vergleich zu den Millionen Jahre alten archäologischen Schichten oder den tausend Jahre alten Wandmalereien von Dunhuang ist es so flüchtig wie ein Wimpernschlag. Doch dieser flüchtige Moment wird im Gemälde und im Akt des Malens intensiv real. Das Konzept materialisiert sich – es ist da, Schicht für Schicht. Während des kreativen Prozesses legt Tan Ping großen Wert auf den „Zusammenprall der Gefühle, ihr harmonisches Zusammenleben und sogar die Stille der Ruhe". Diese flüchtigen „Erfahrungen" können nicht simuliert oder reproduziert werden; sie sind die „Wahrheit" unter der grauen Oberfläche. Jeder Strich, jede Linie und jede Farbschicht ist einzigartig, nicht im Hinblick auf das „Bild" des Gemäldes oder das „Konzept" der Kunst, sondern in Bezug auf die eigene Subjektivität des Künstlers. Tan Ping sagt: „Die Welt verändert sich ständig, ist voller Drama und Ungewissheit. Jeder Tag und jeder Moment ist unersetzlich und nicht wiederholbar. Angesammelte Fragmente und sich überschneidende Momente können jedoch eine unsichere, aber dennoch lebendige Realität schaffen." Tan Pings „Überlagerung" ist ein fortlaufender Prozess. Unter dem monotonen Grau liegen Geschichte, Leben und Existenz.

Sheng Wei

Chefredakteur des Fine Arts Magazine, Professor an der Tsinghua-Universität

The White Wall Project:
From Blank to Blank

The White Wall Project is an art initiative that I
completed with Swiss artist Luciano Castelli in
2016 at the Shanghai Oil Painting and Sculpture
Institute Art Museum. Using work on site as our
method, we spent 5 days covering nearly 2,000
square meters with our work. After the exhibition
concluded, I spent an additional 2 days using white
paint to return the museum to its original, blank wall
state.

Tan Ping

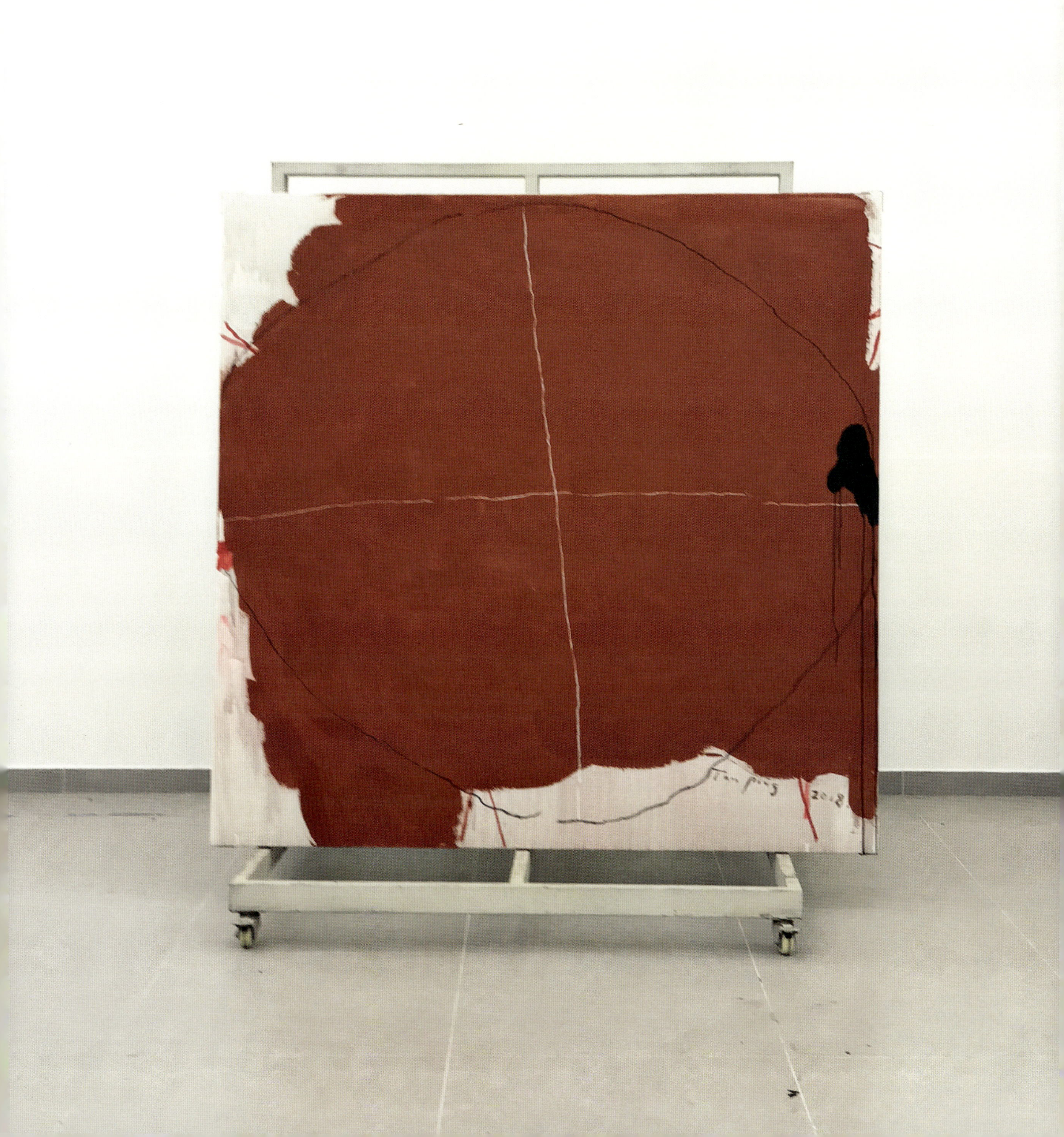

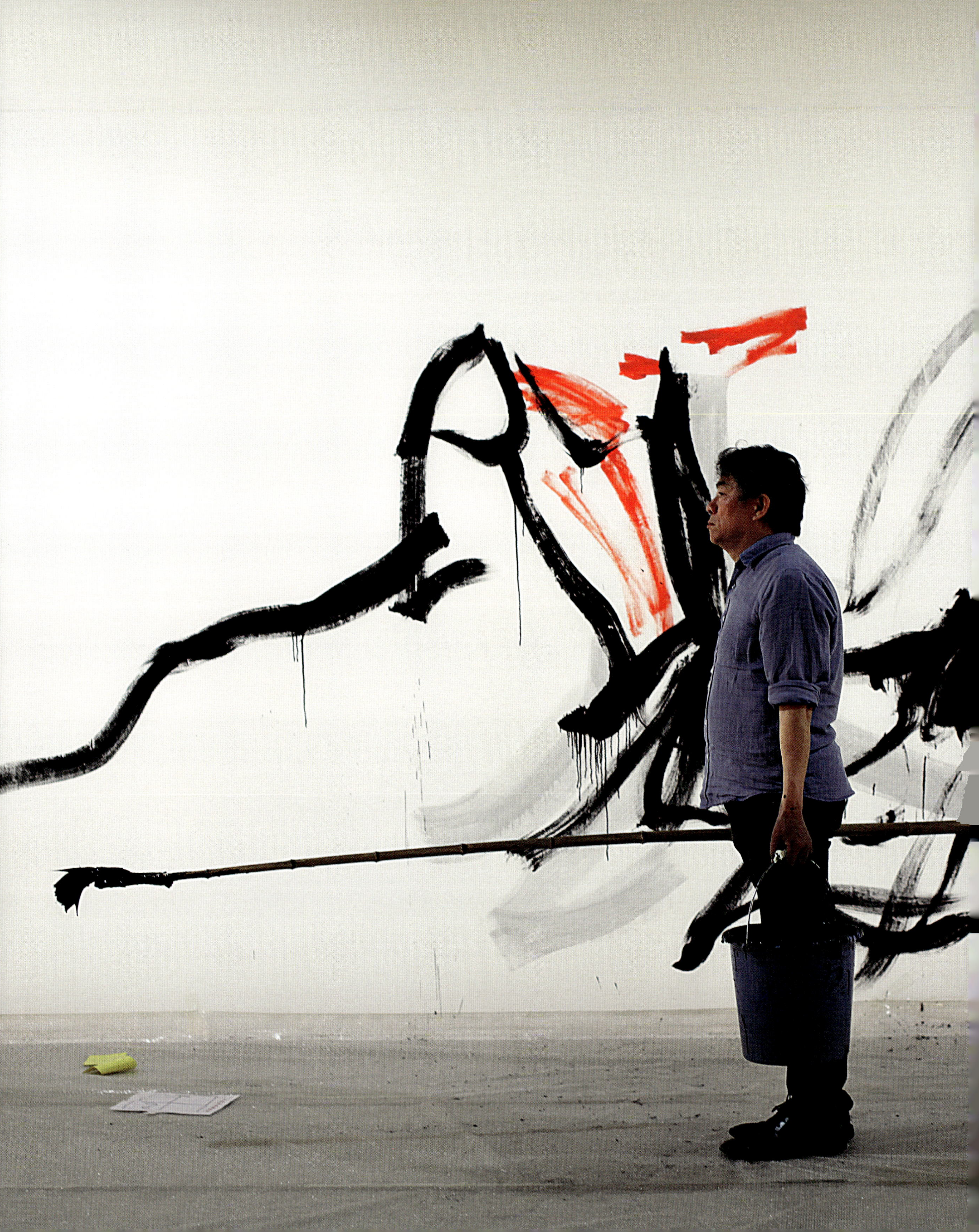

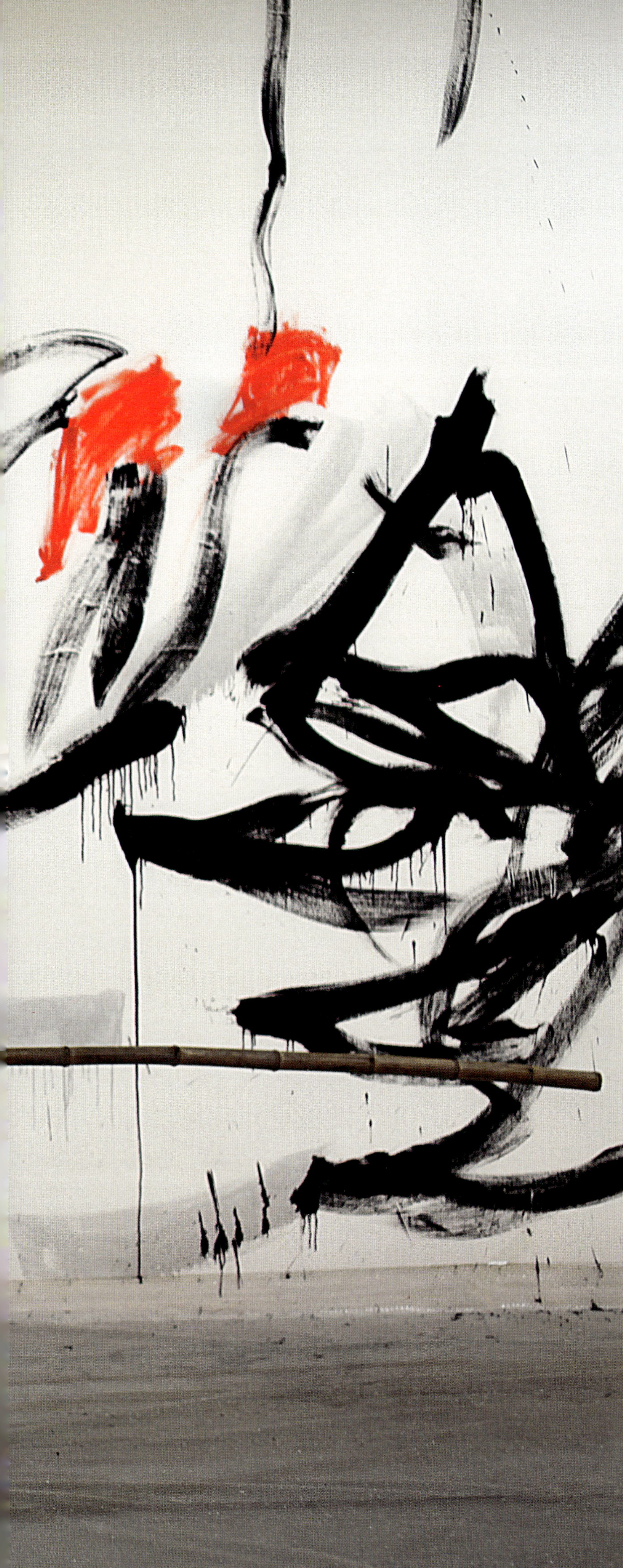

Das Projekt Weiße Wand:
Von Blank zu Blank

Das „White Wall Project" ist eine Kunstinitiative, die ich 2016 zusammen mit dem Schweizer Künstler Luciano Castelli im Shanghai Oil Painting and Sculpture Institute Art Museum durchgeführt habe. Indem wir vor Ort arbeiteten, verbrachten wir 5 Tage damit, fast 2.000 Quadratmeter mit unserer Arbeit zu bedecken. Nach dem Ende der Ausstellung verbrachte ich weitere 2 Tage damit, das Museum mit weißer Farbe wieder in seinen ursprünglichen, leeren Zustand zu versetzen.

Tan Ping

Punkt, Linie, Ebene

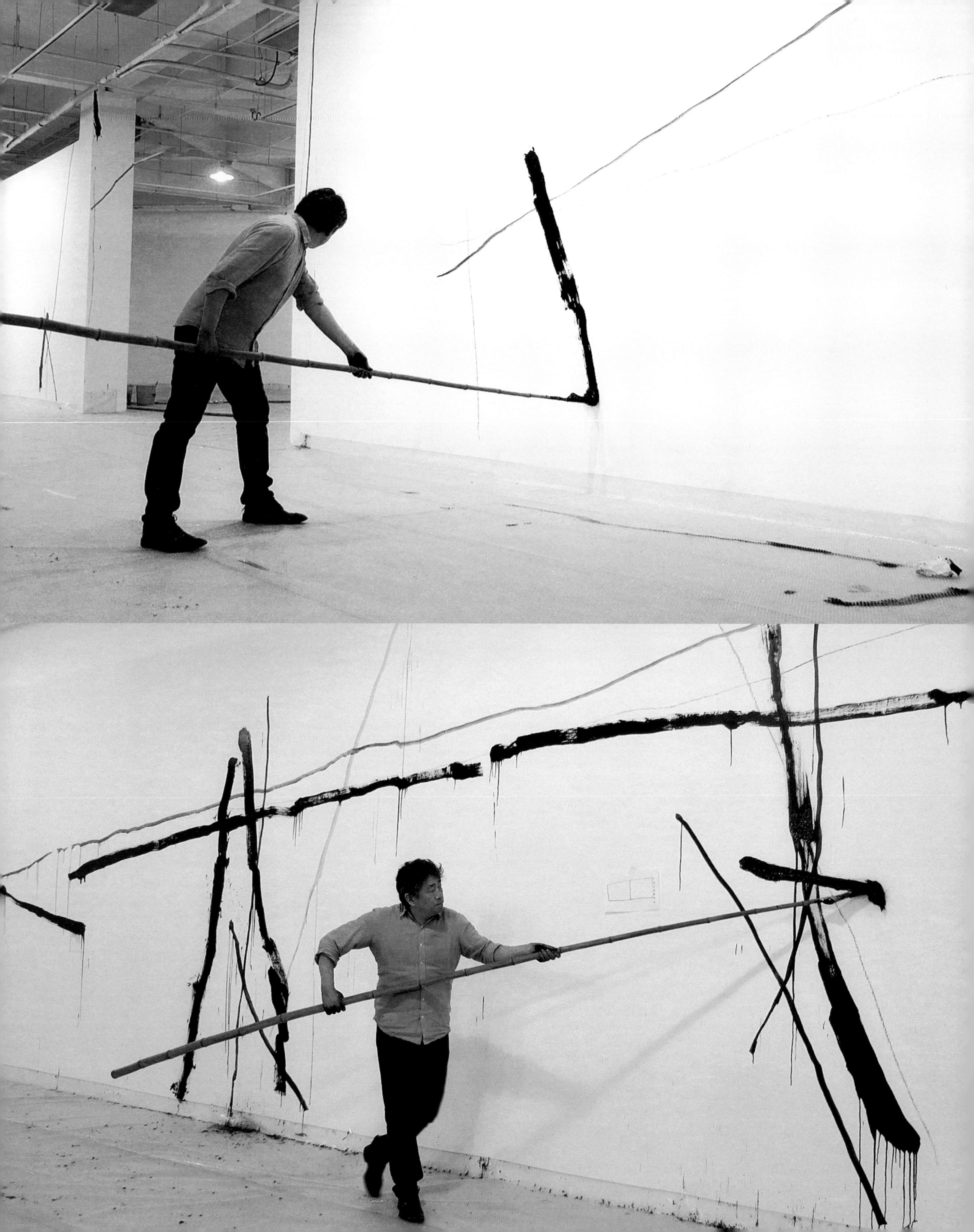

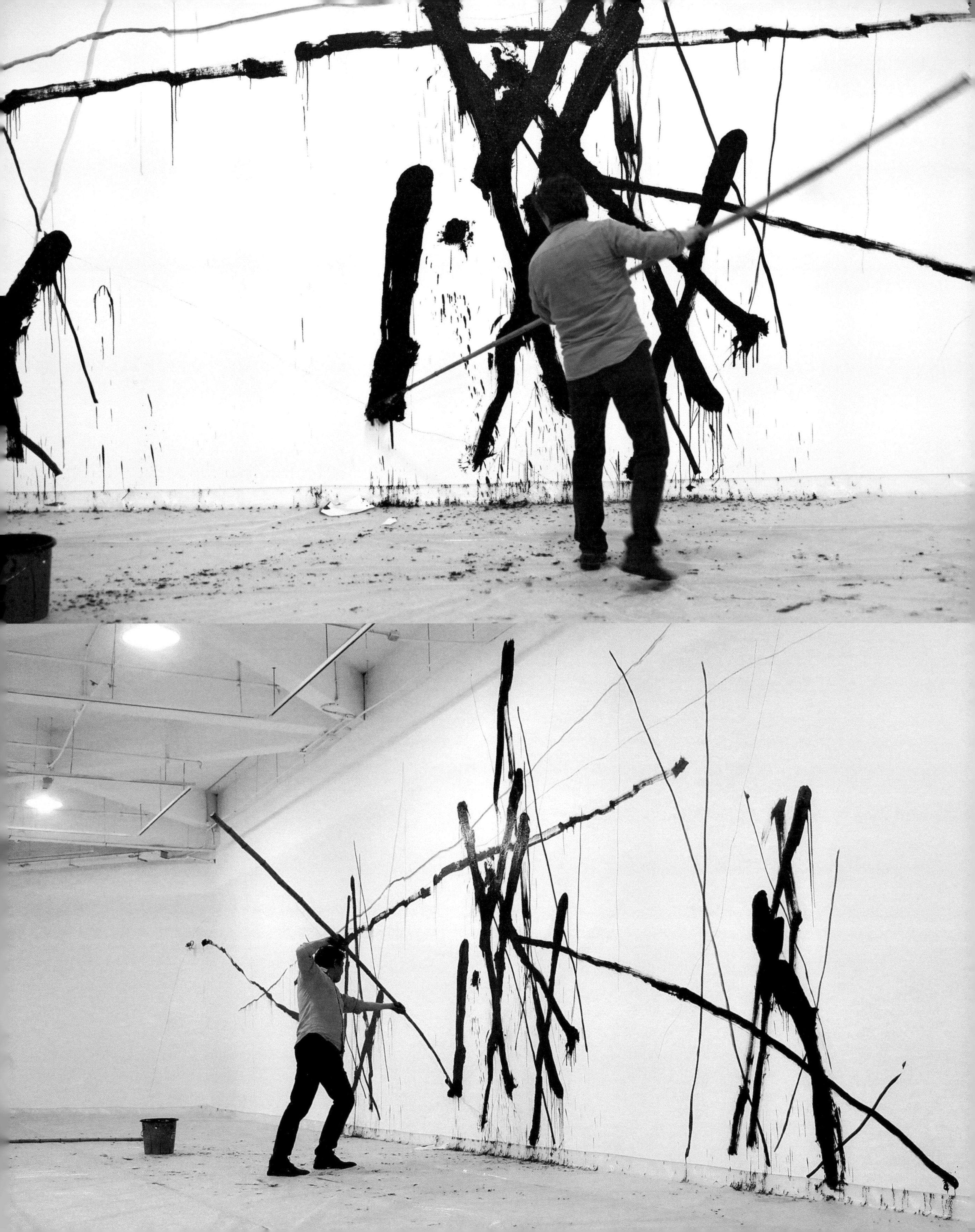

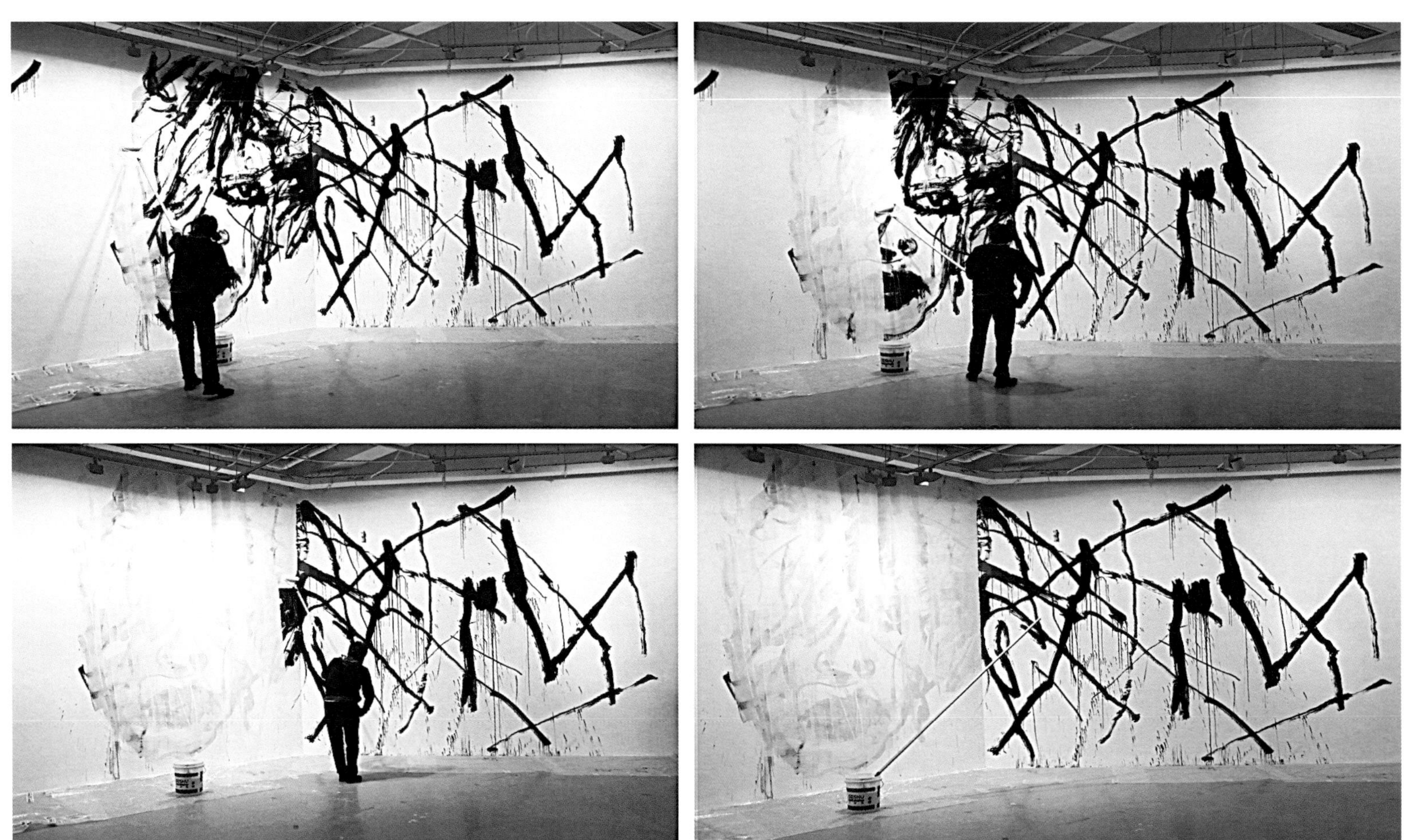

The White Wall Project,
2016
work on site / **Arbeit vor Ort**
Shanghai Oil Painting
and Sculpture Institute,
Shanghai, China

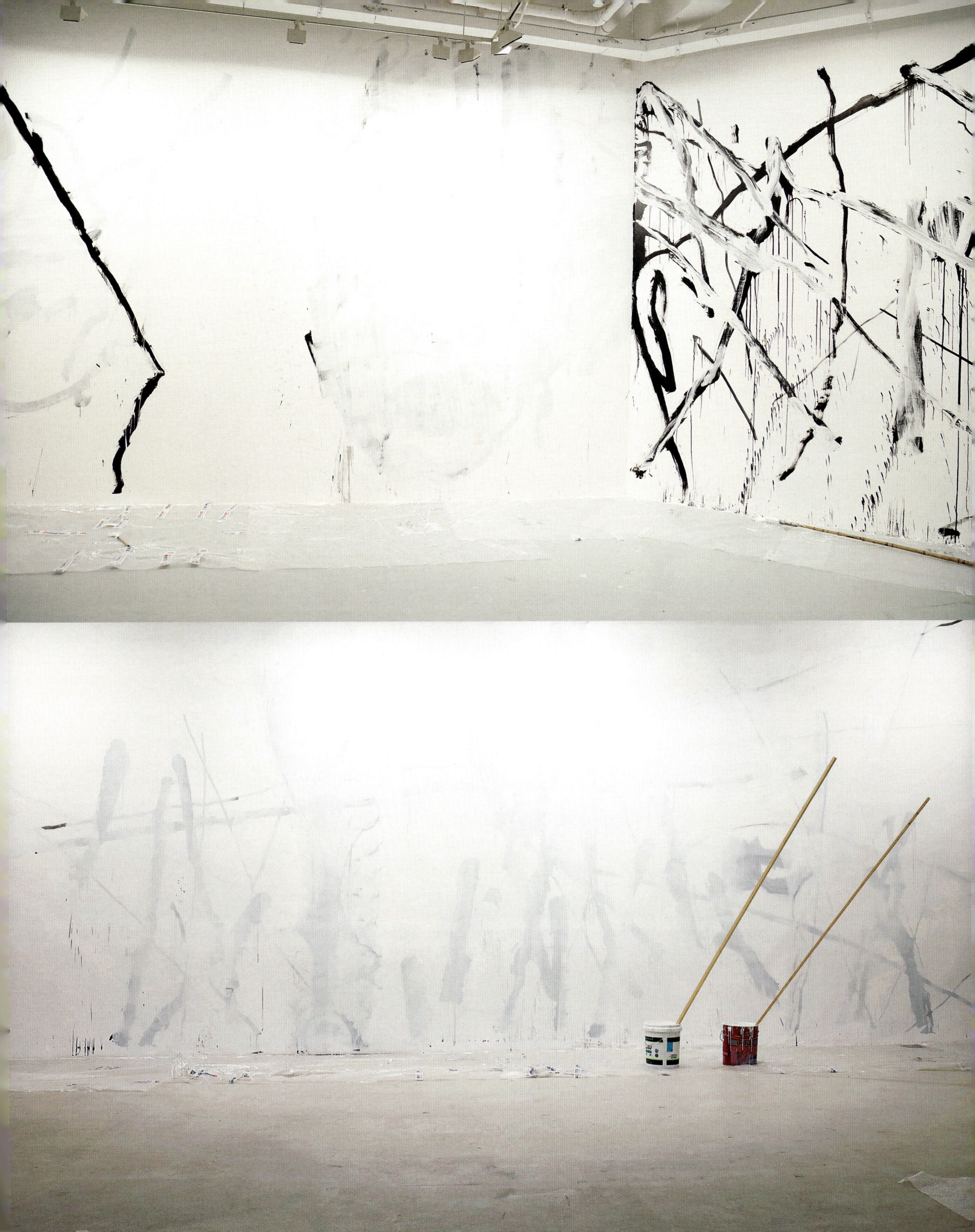

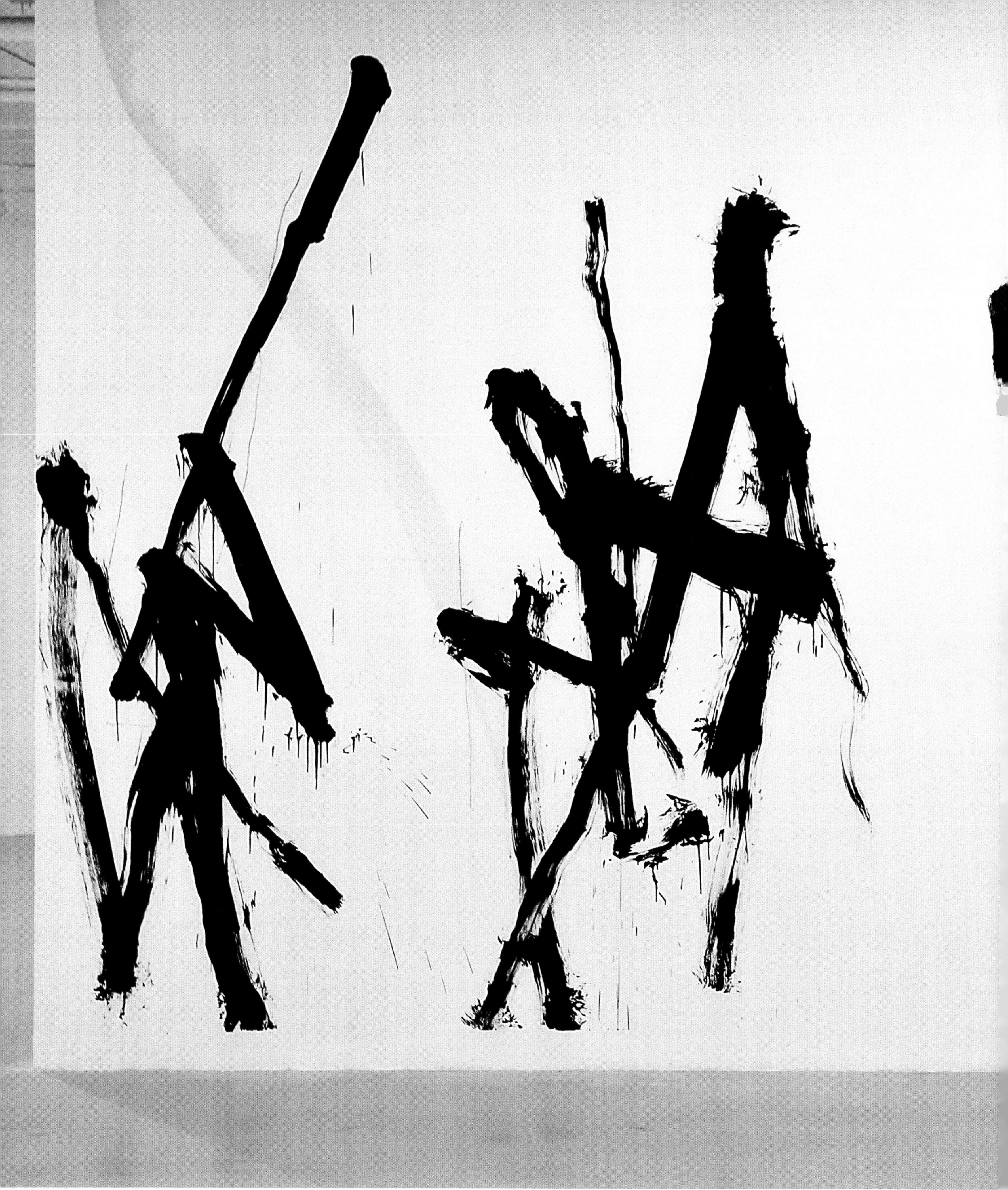

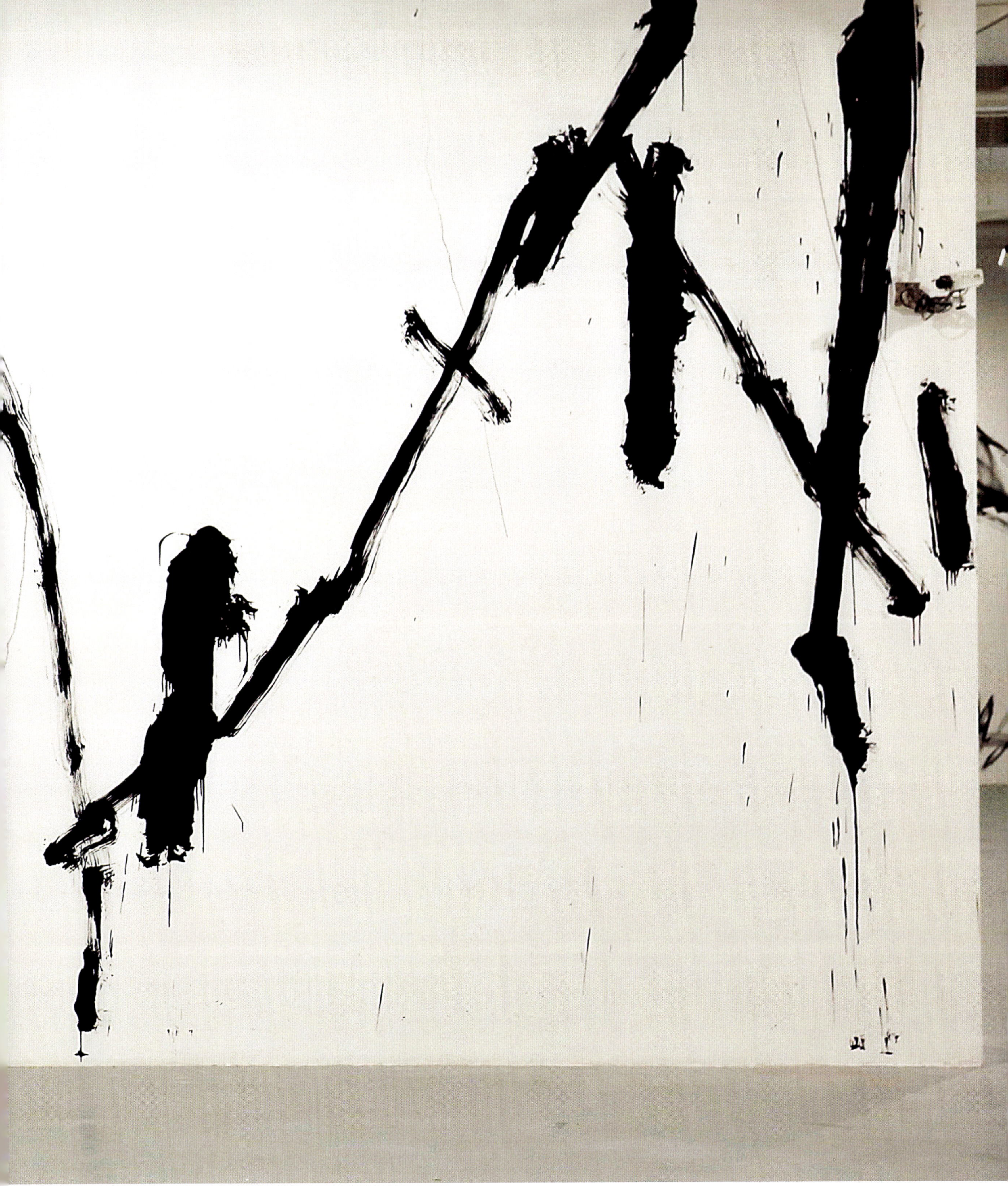

Punkt, Linie, Ebene

The White Wall Project,
2016
work on site / **Arbeit vor Ort**
Shanghai Oil Painting
and Sculpture Institute,
Shanghai, China

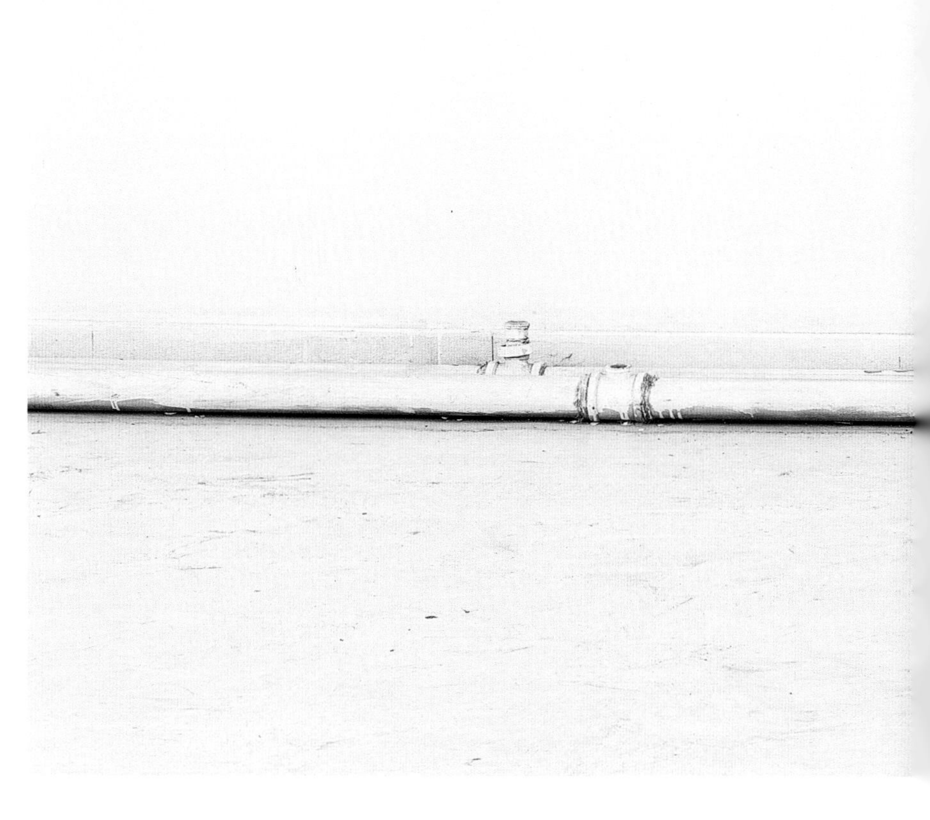

Punkt, Linie, Ebene

Limited Freedom

Internal Cycle

A line on a floor plan. In reality, it captures a fleeting moment of my existence within the turmoil of time and space.

Tan Ping

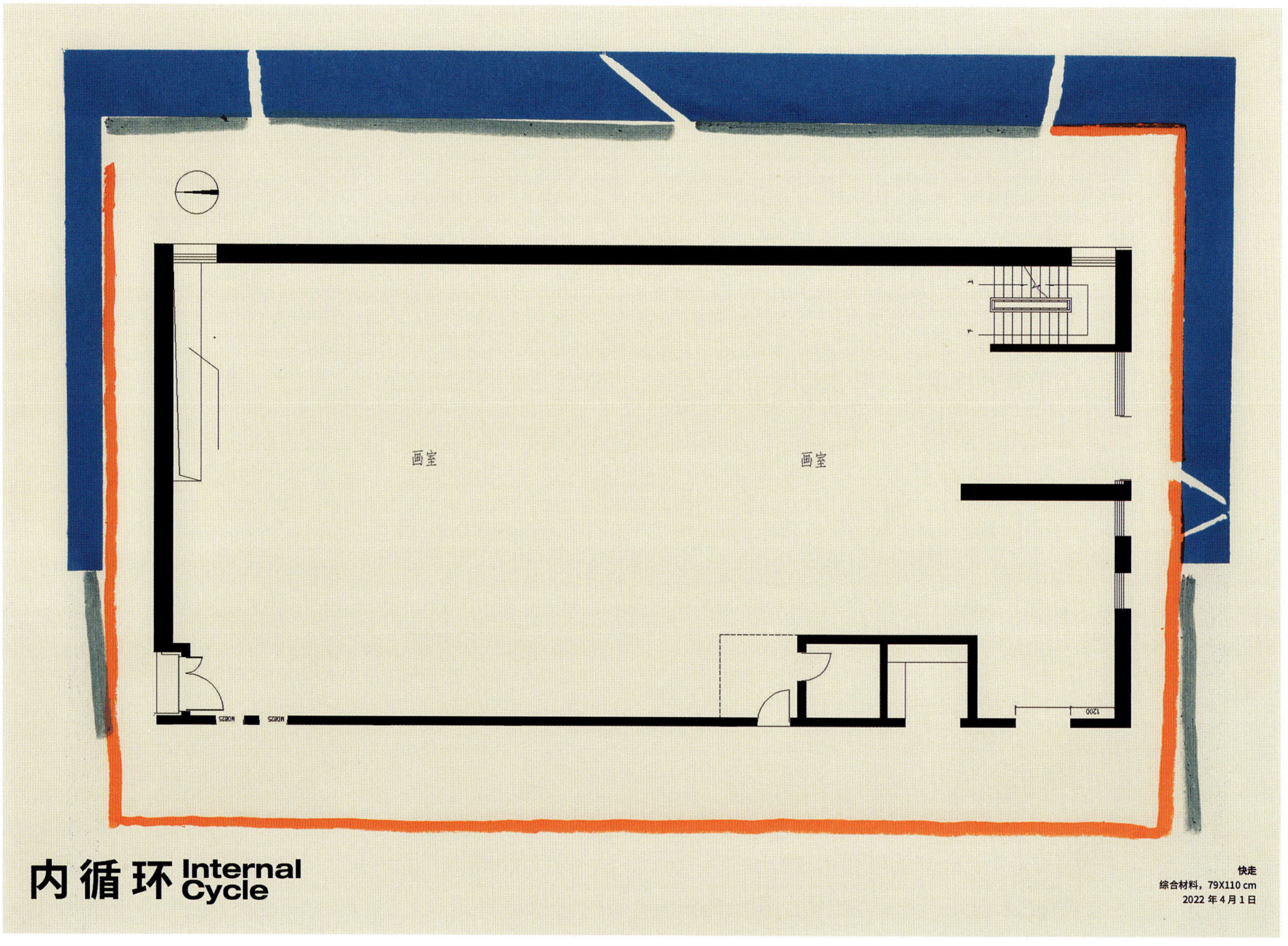

Eingeschränkte Freiheit

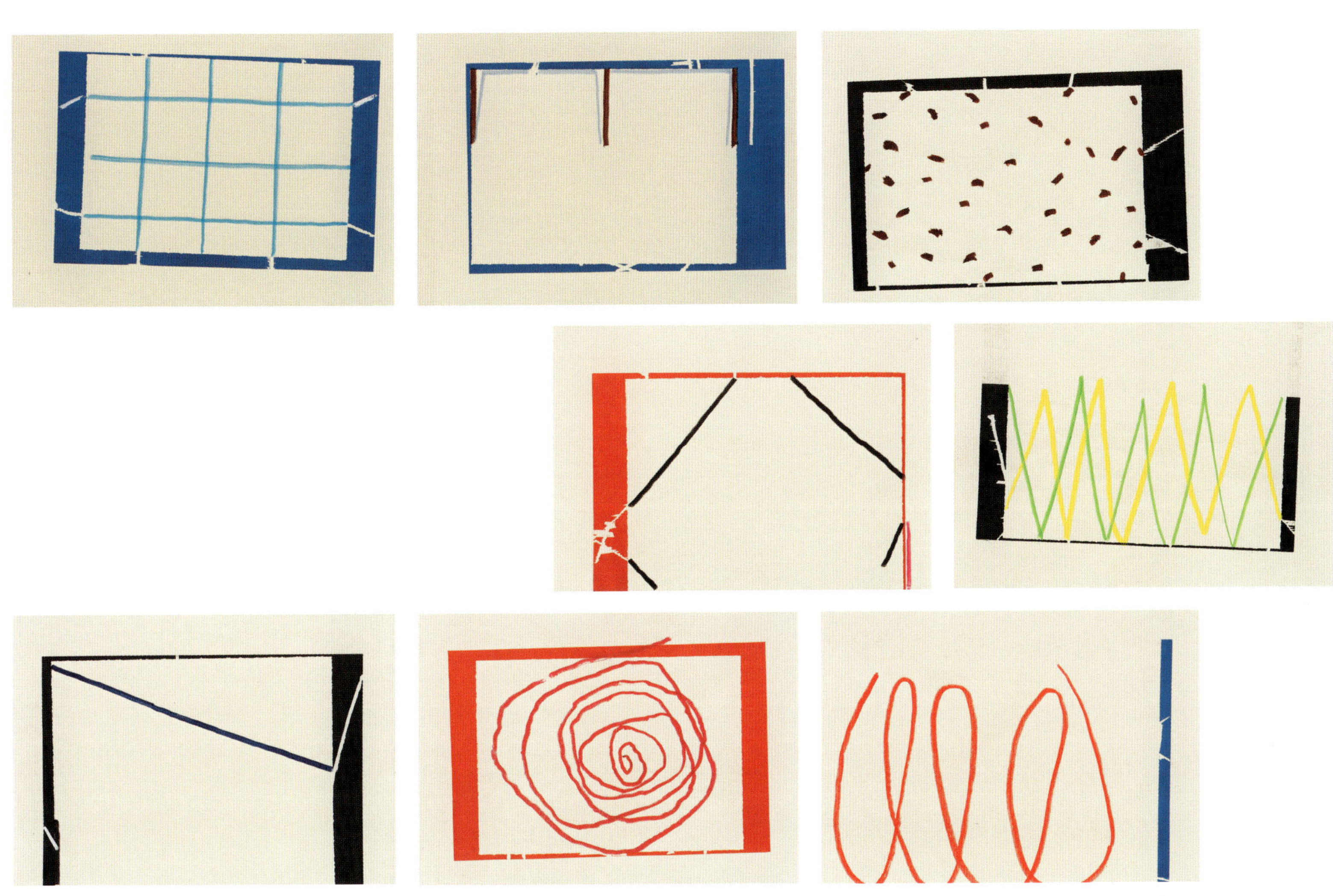

Interner Zyklus

"Internal Cycle" series, 2022
mixed media on paper /
Mischtechnik auf Papier,
79 × 110cm,
Beijing, China

Eine Linie auf einem Grundriss. In Wirklichkeit
fängt sie einen flüchtigen Moment meiner
Existenz im Getümmel von Zeit und Raum ein.

Tan Ping

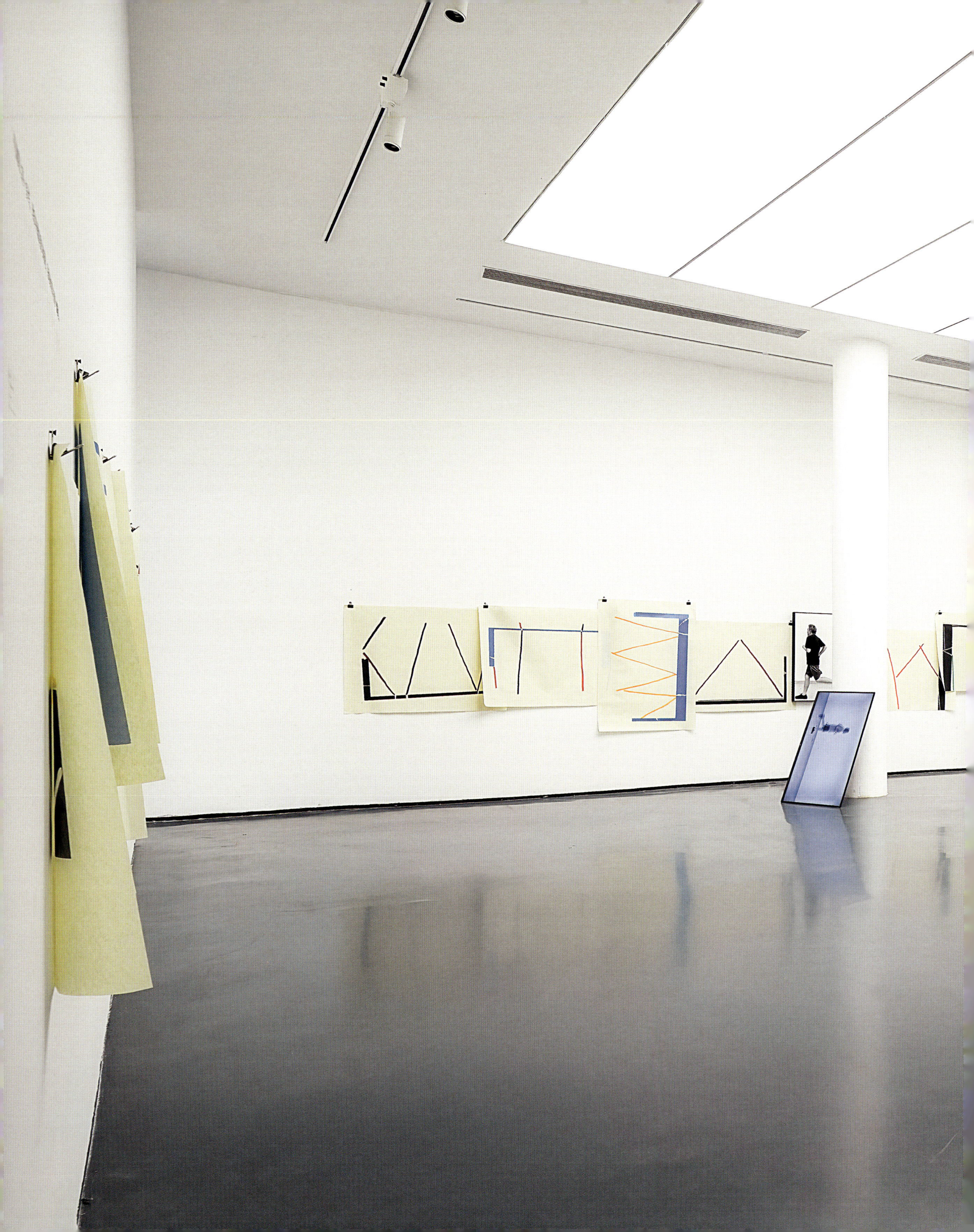

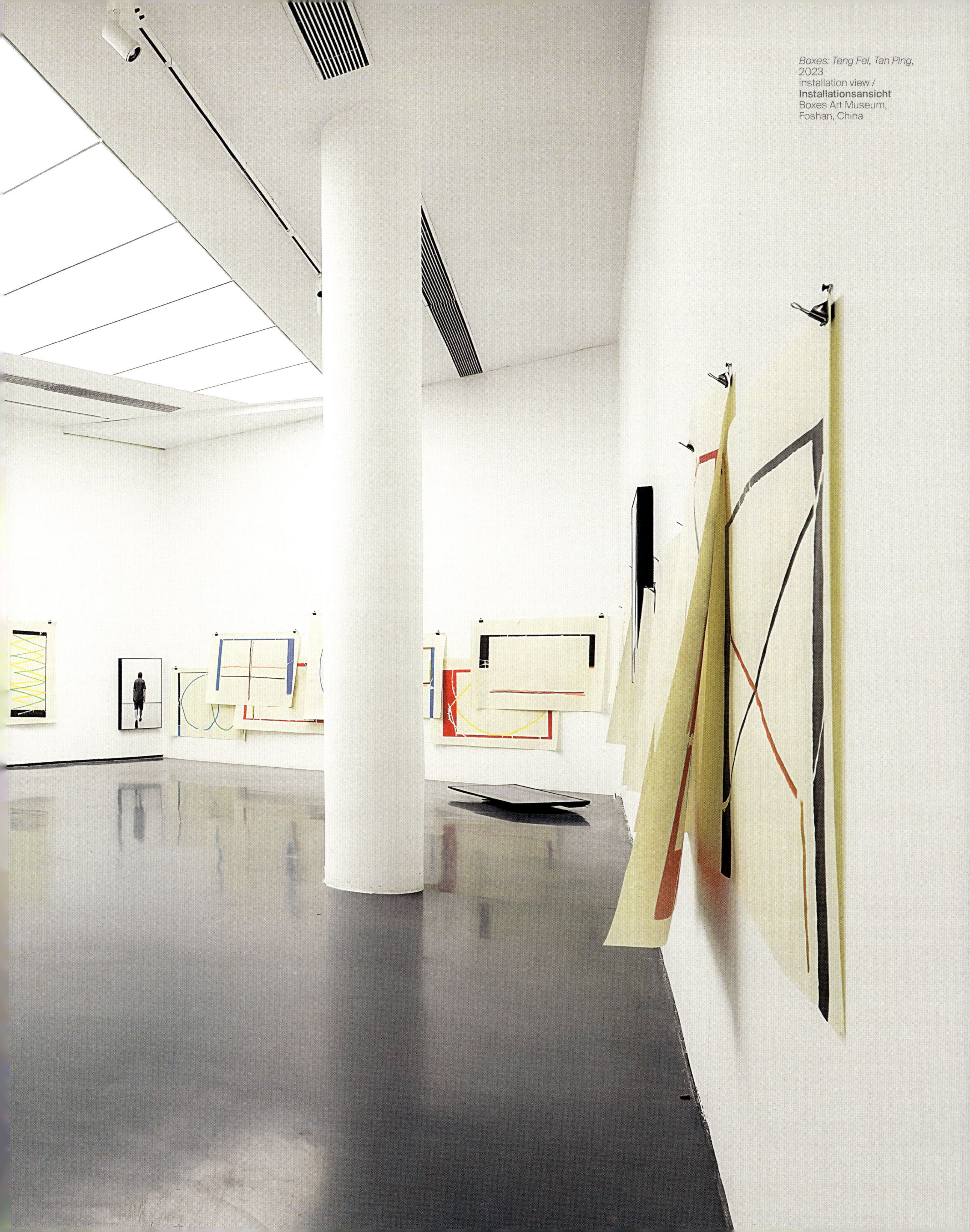

Boxes: Teng Fei, Tan Ping,
2023
installation view /
Installationsansicht
Boxes Art Museum,
Foshan, China

Boxes: Teng Fei, Tan Ping,
2023
installation view /
Installationsansicht
Boxes Art Museum,
Foshan, China

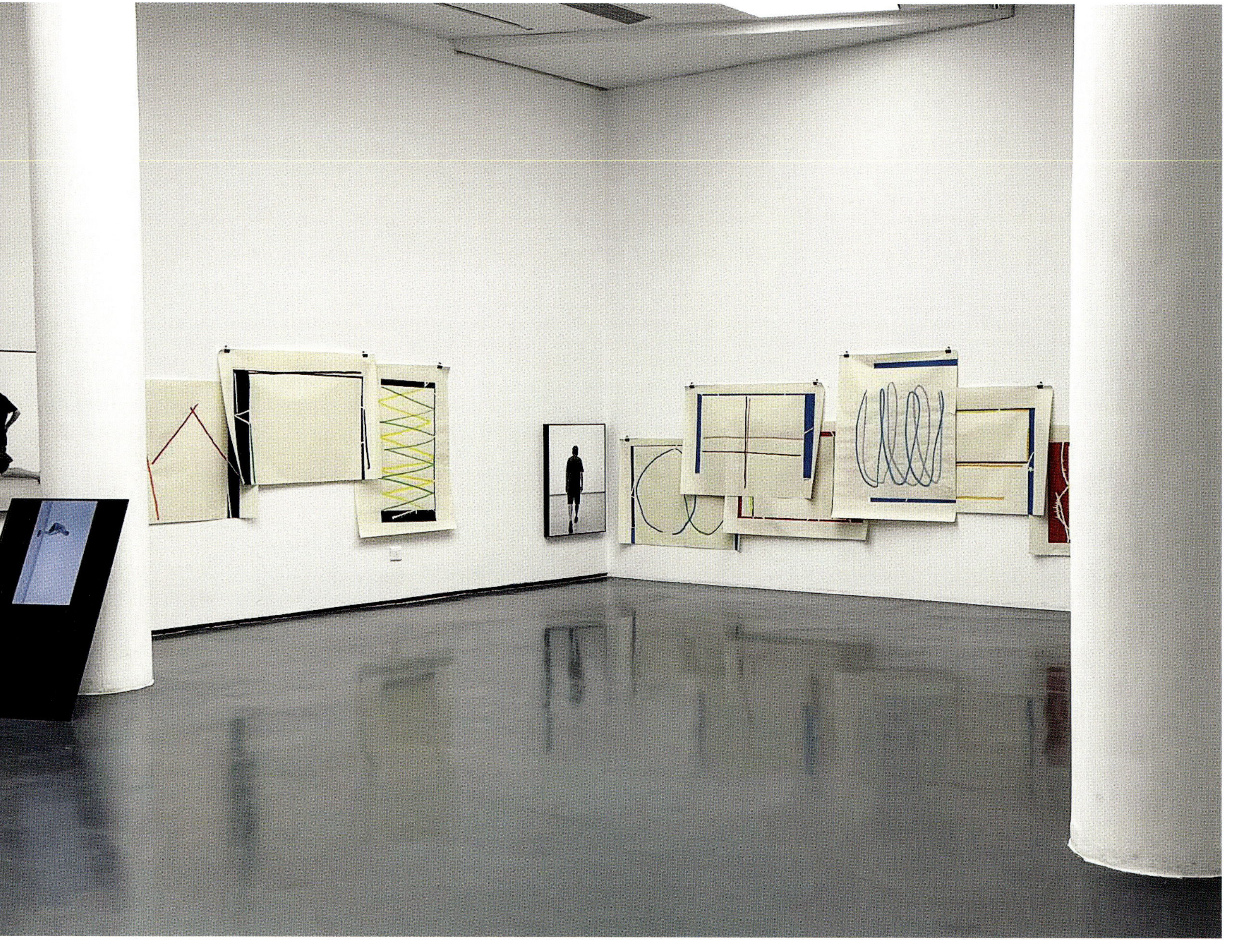

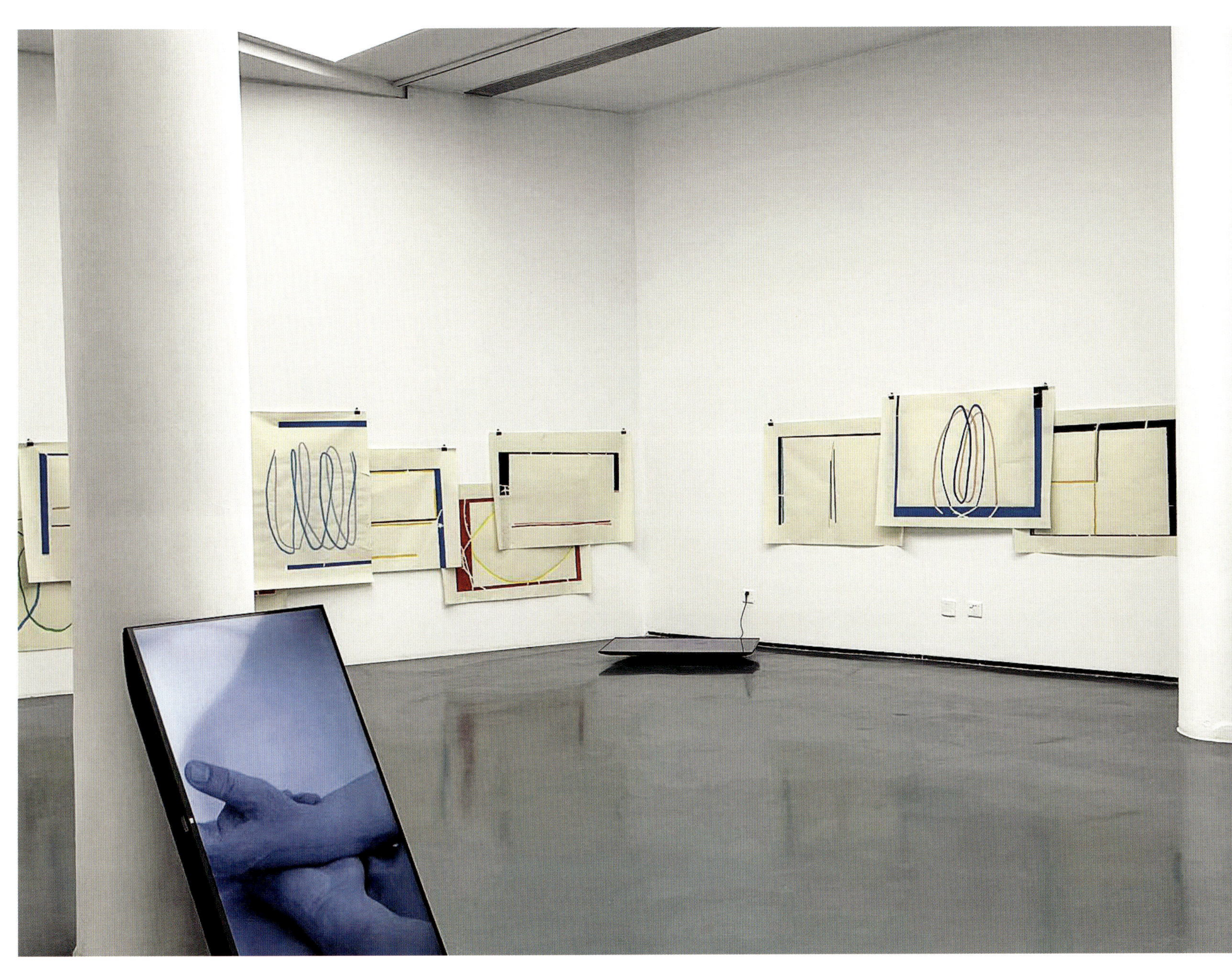

Eingeschränkte Freiheit

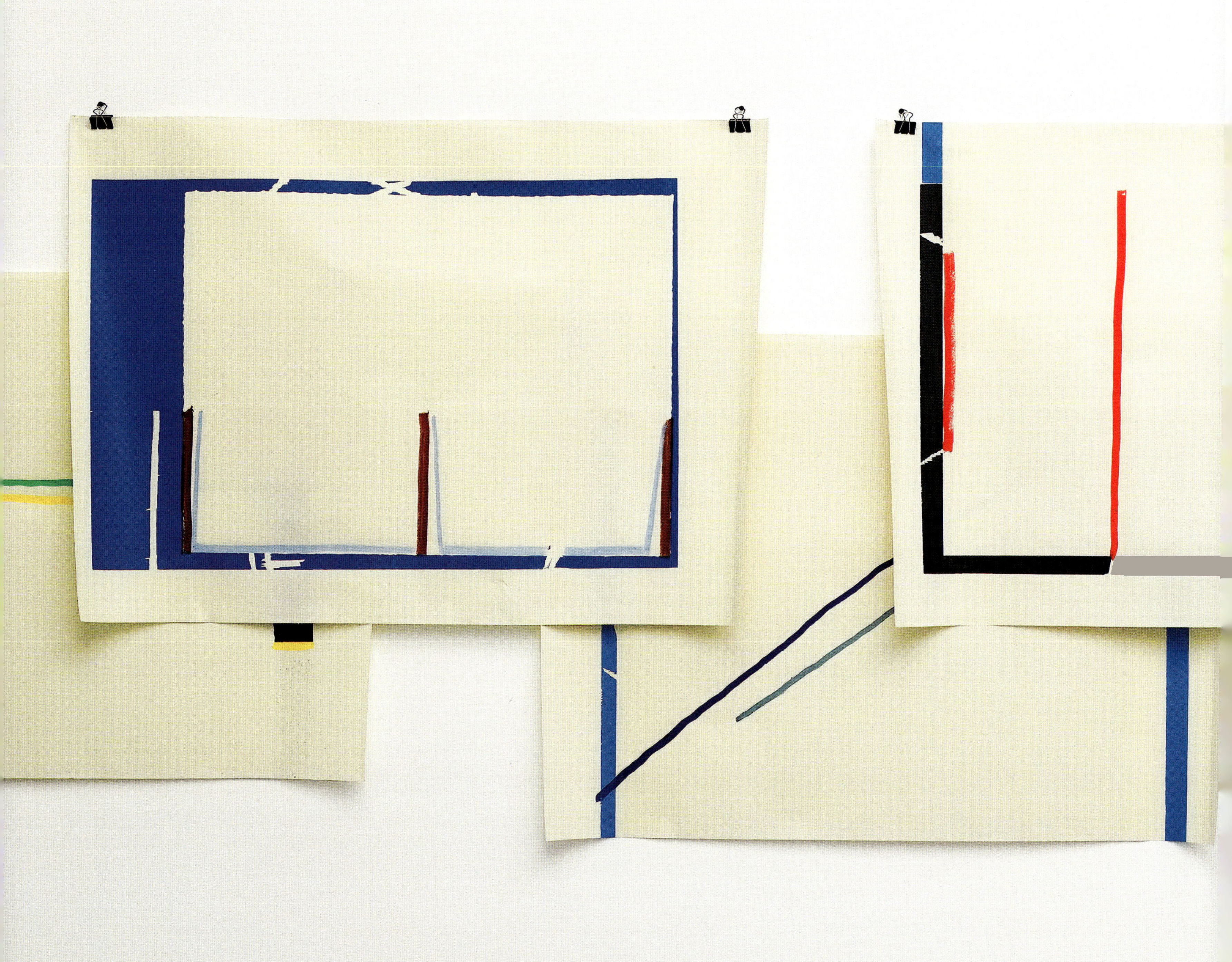

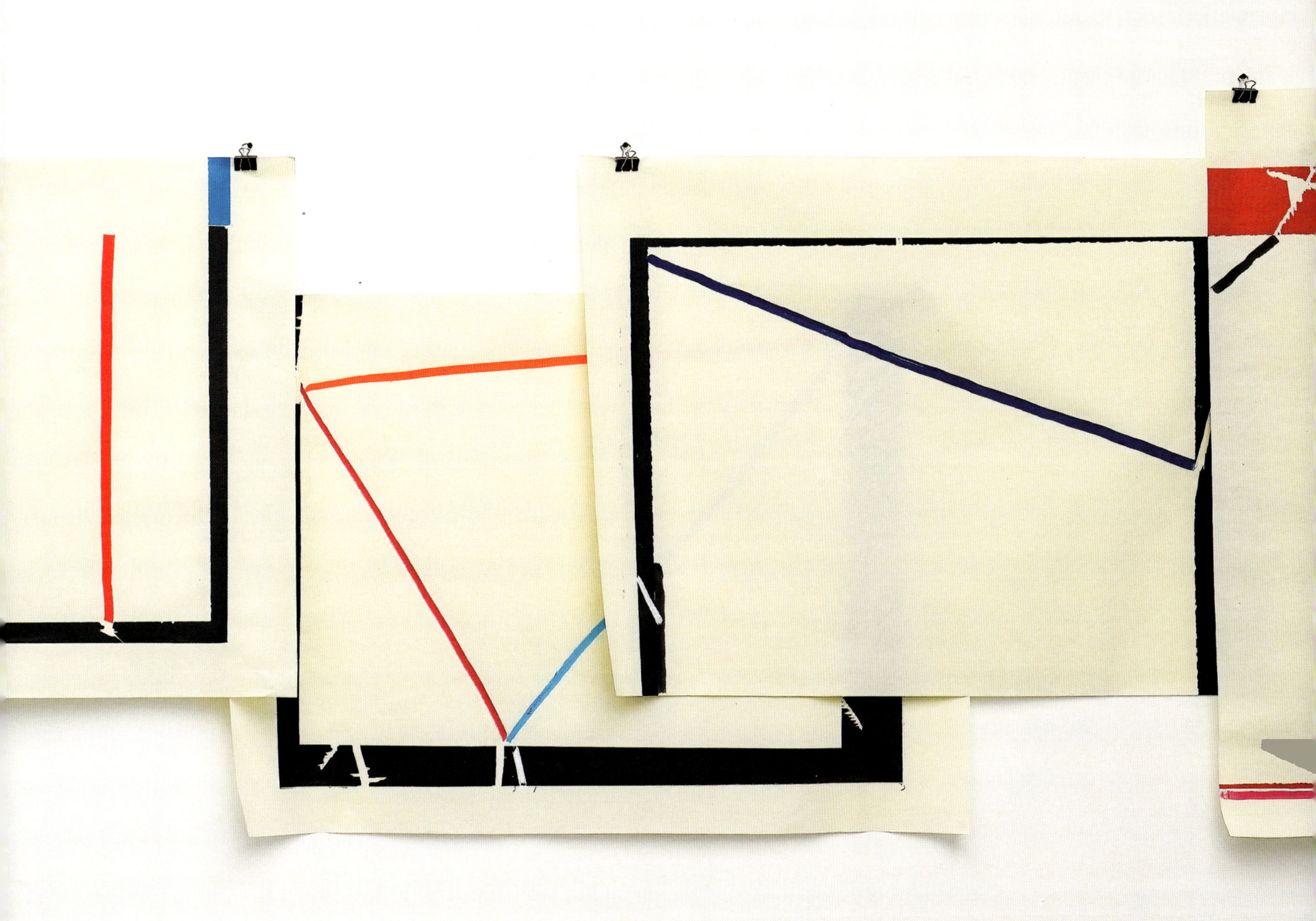

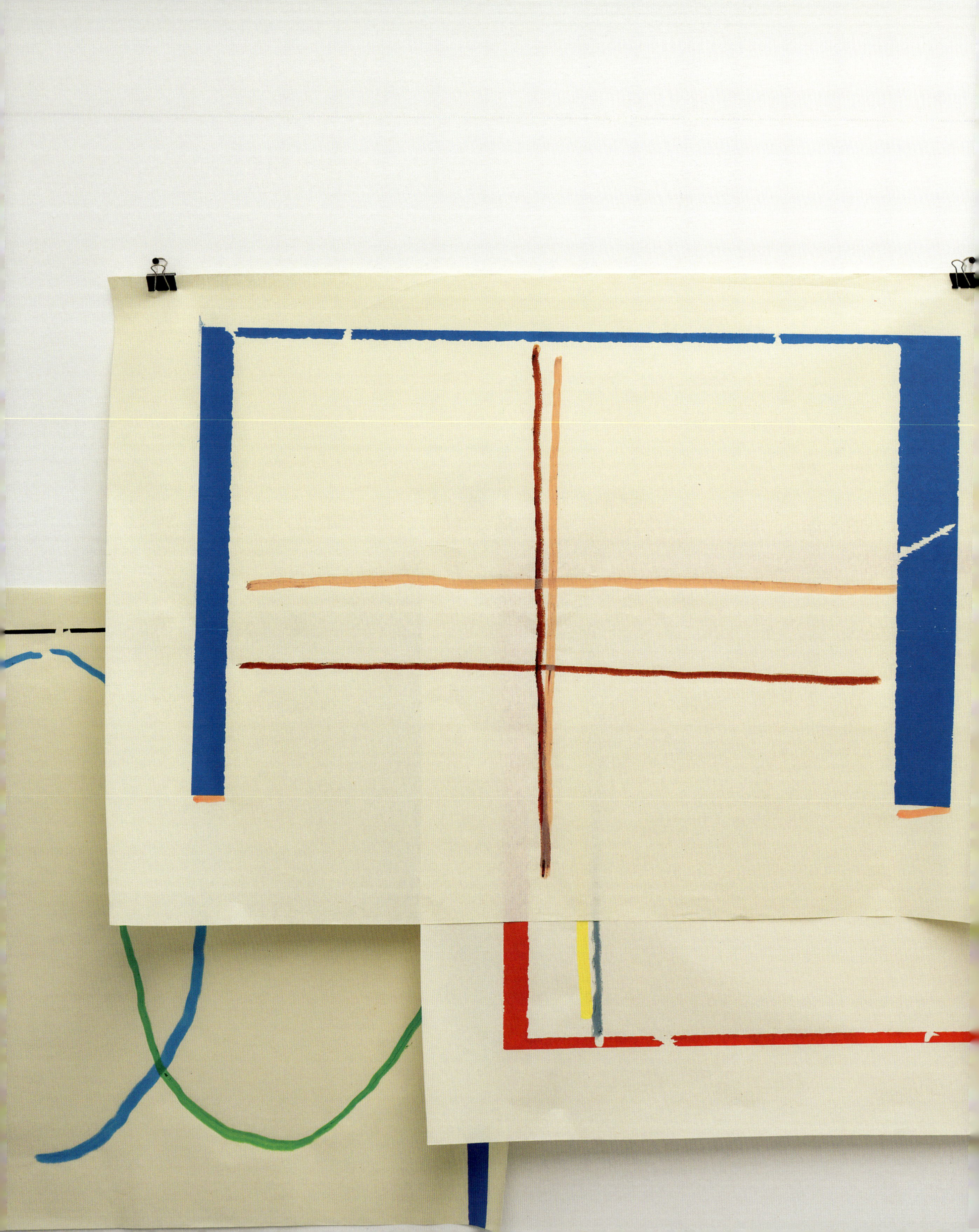

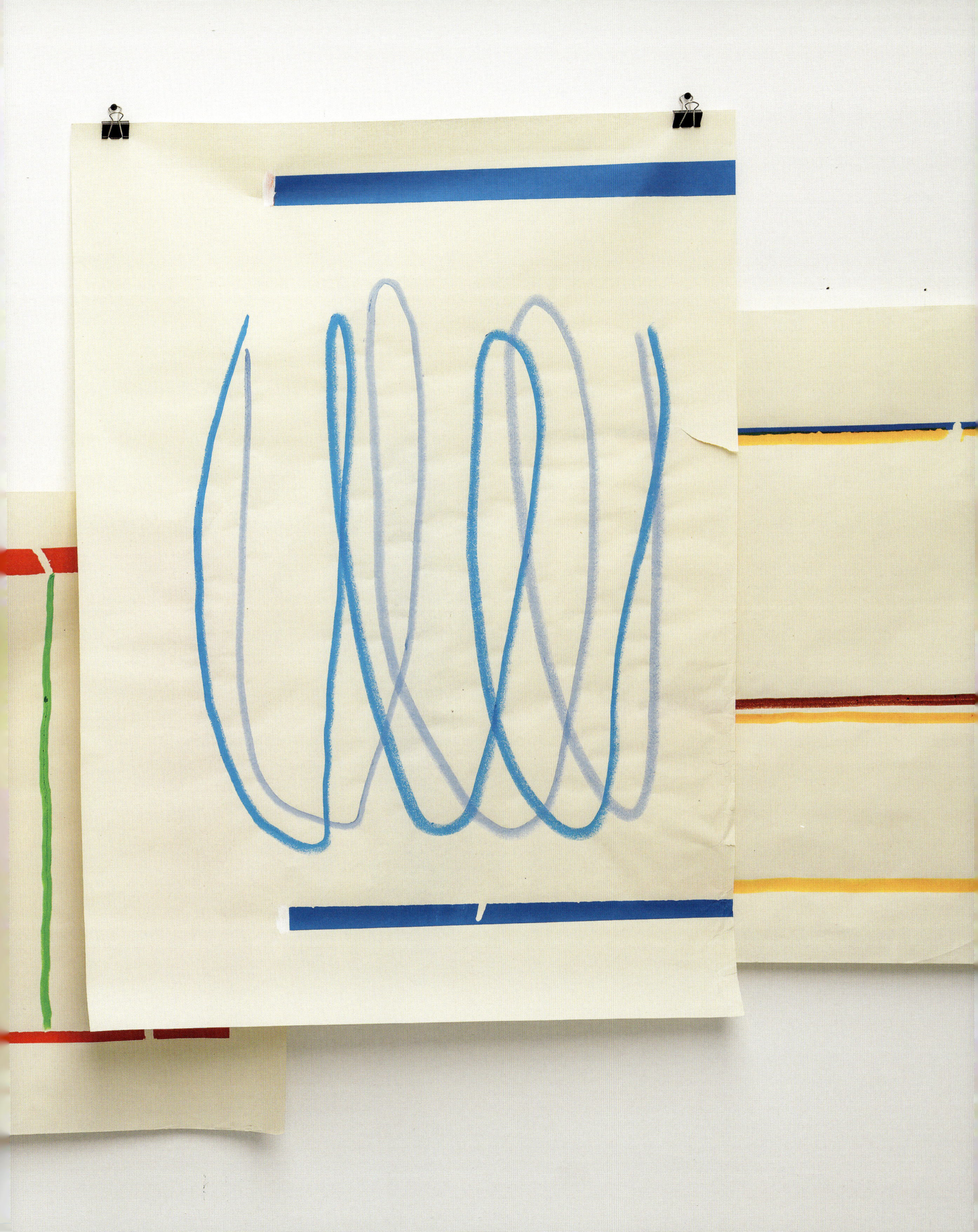

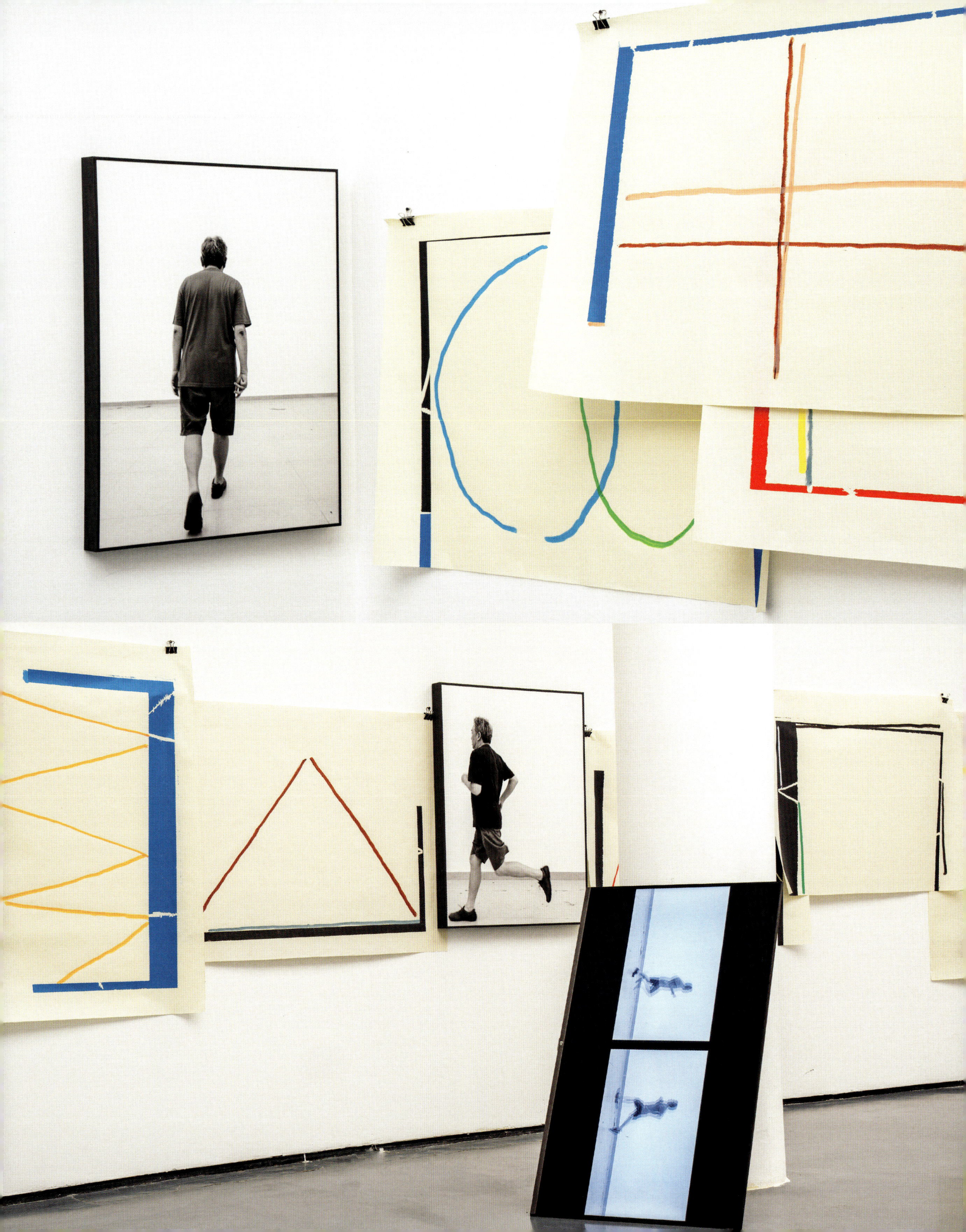

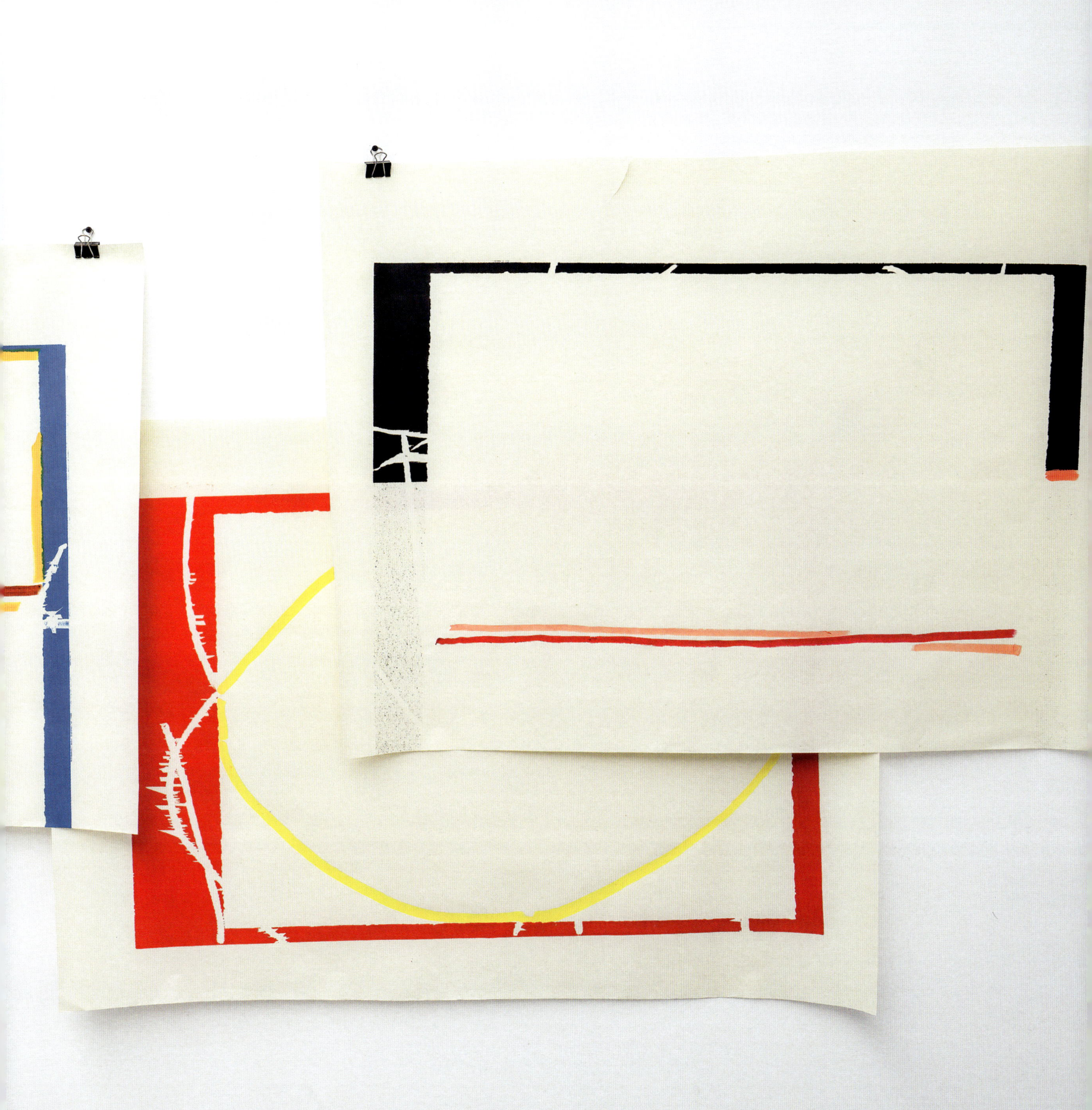

The exhibition title "Internal Cycle" is drawn from a series of new works I created in April 2022. This series includes 28 paper drawings, organized in sets of seven, each representing a day of the week, and a 3-minute video.

Due to the COVID-19 pandemic, I was isolated in my 240-square-meter studio. Each day, I set a different route for myself within the studio—walking, brisk walking, or jumping—to alleviate both physical and mental stress and to exercise. The daily route was influenced by my mood, varying from calm to restless, which affected the route and the type of movement. Occasionally, I would wander aimlessly, run, or jump unpredictably.

This process was exhilarating, as I experimented with various changes. It seemed that when confined to a limited space, my imagination was at its most vibrant. Through these daily activities, I transcended the constraints of space and time, finding stimulation and humor to conceal the unavoidable anxieties. I sought personal calm amidst the circumstances I had to accept, gaining both mental and physical strength. The visual results extracted from these daily actions also exude a sense of "being in time" during this unique period.

"Internal Cycle" is not just an economic concept but also points to an individual's inward gaze.

Tan Ping

"Internal Cycle" series,
2022
video clip

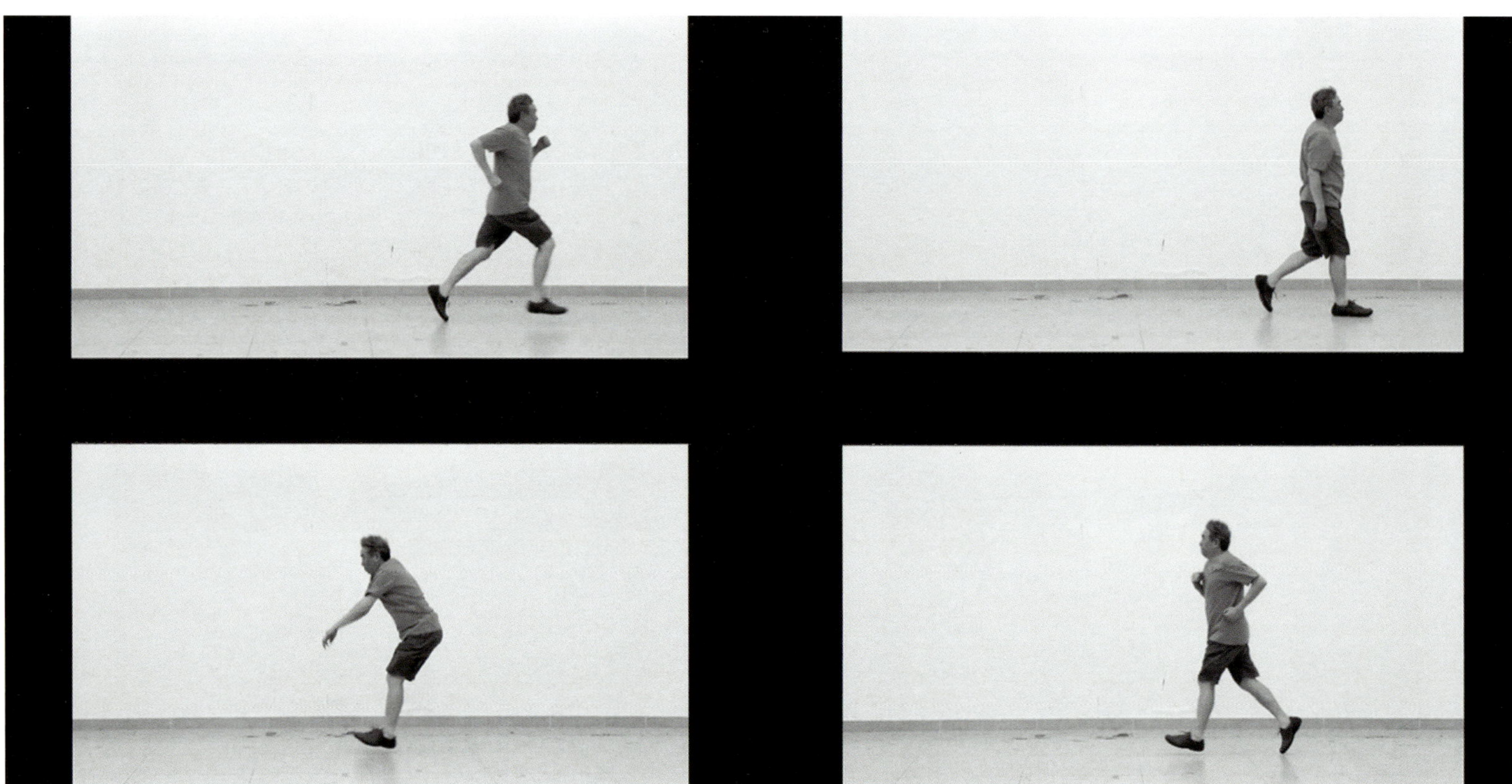

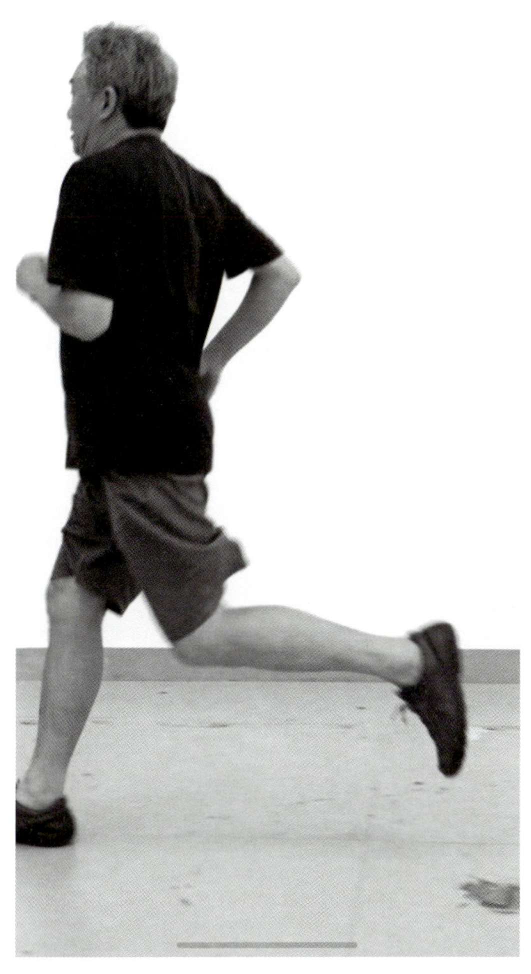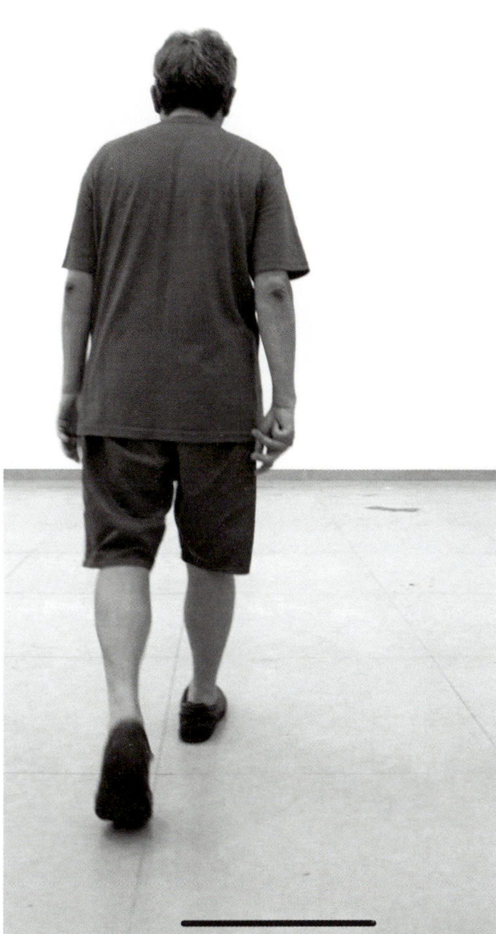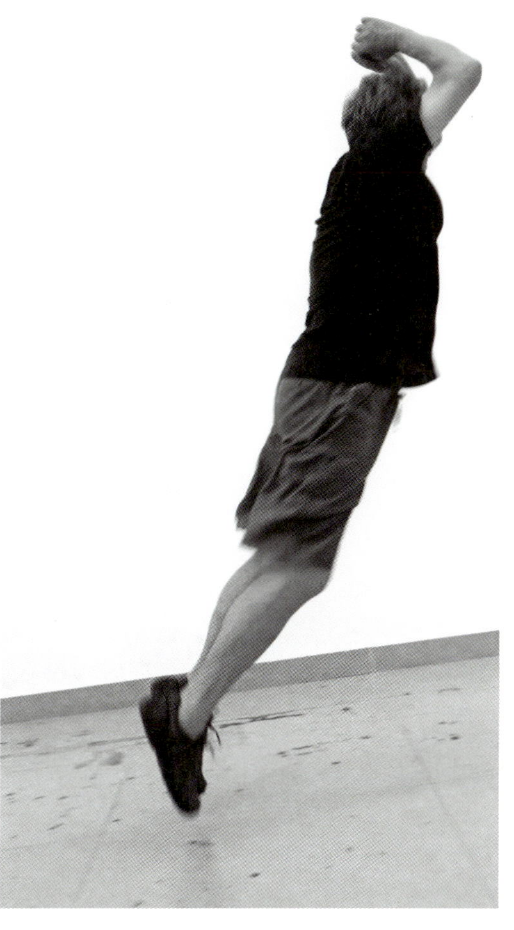

Der Ausstellungstitel „Interner Zyklus" bezieht sich auf eine Serie neuer Werke, die ich im April 2022 geschaffen habe. Diese Serie umfasst 28 Papierzeichnungen, die in Siebener-Sets organisiert sind und jeweils einen Wochentag darstellen, sowie ein 3-minütiges Video.

Aufgrund der COVID-19-Pandemie war ich in meinem 240 Quadratmeter großen Studio isoliert. Jeden Tag legte ich eine andere Route innerhalb des Studios fest – Gehen, zügiges Gehen oder Springen –, um sowohl körperlichen als auch geistigen Stress abzubauen und mich zu bewegen. Die tägliche Route wurde von meiner Stimmung beeinflusst, die von ruhig bis unruhig reichte, was sich auf die Route und die Art der Bewegung auswirkte. Gelegentlich wanderte ich ziellos umher, rannte oder sprang unvorhersehbar.

Dieser Prozess war sehr aufregend, denn ich experimentierte mit verschiedenen Veränderungen. Es schien, dass meine Fantasie in einem begrenzten Raum am lebhaftesten war. Durch diese täglichen Aktivitäten überwand ich die Zwänge von Raum und Zeit, fand Anregung und Humor, um die unvermeidlichen Ängste zu verbergen. Ich suchte persönliche Ruhe inmitten der Umstände, die ich akzeptieren musste, und gewann sowohl geistige als auch körperliche Kraft. Die visuellen Ergebnisse dieser täglichen Handlungen vermitteln auch ein Gefühl des „In der Zeit seins" während dieser einzigartigen Zeit.

„Interner Zyklus" ist nicht nur ein wirtschaftliches Konzept, sondern verweist auch auf den Blick des Einzelnen nach innen.

Tan Ping

Shan Shui Jing
(Between Mountains and Rivers)

TAN PING & HOU YING CROSSBORDER
COLLABORATION 2023, XIAMEN MUSEUM
OF CONTEMPORARY ART, CHINA
HOU YING, DANCER

History is constantly evolving; today's landscapes
are no longer the same as those from a thousand
years ago.

The split scroll of "A Thousand Miles of Rivers and
Mountains" here symbolizes the fragmented reality
of the post-pandemic world. "Tear" represents
the action, while "split" signifies the result. The
images painted on the long wall scroll are torn into
two parts: one portion remains blank, representing
rivers, while the remaining ink on the wall
symbolizes mountains, serving as evidence of the
rift between mountains and waters.

Tan Ping

HOU YING & TAN PING,
2023 work on site / **Arbeit
vor Ort**
Topred Center for
Contemporary Art, Xiamen,
China

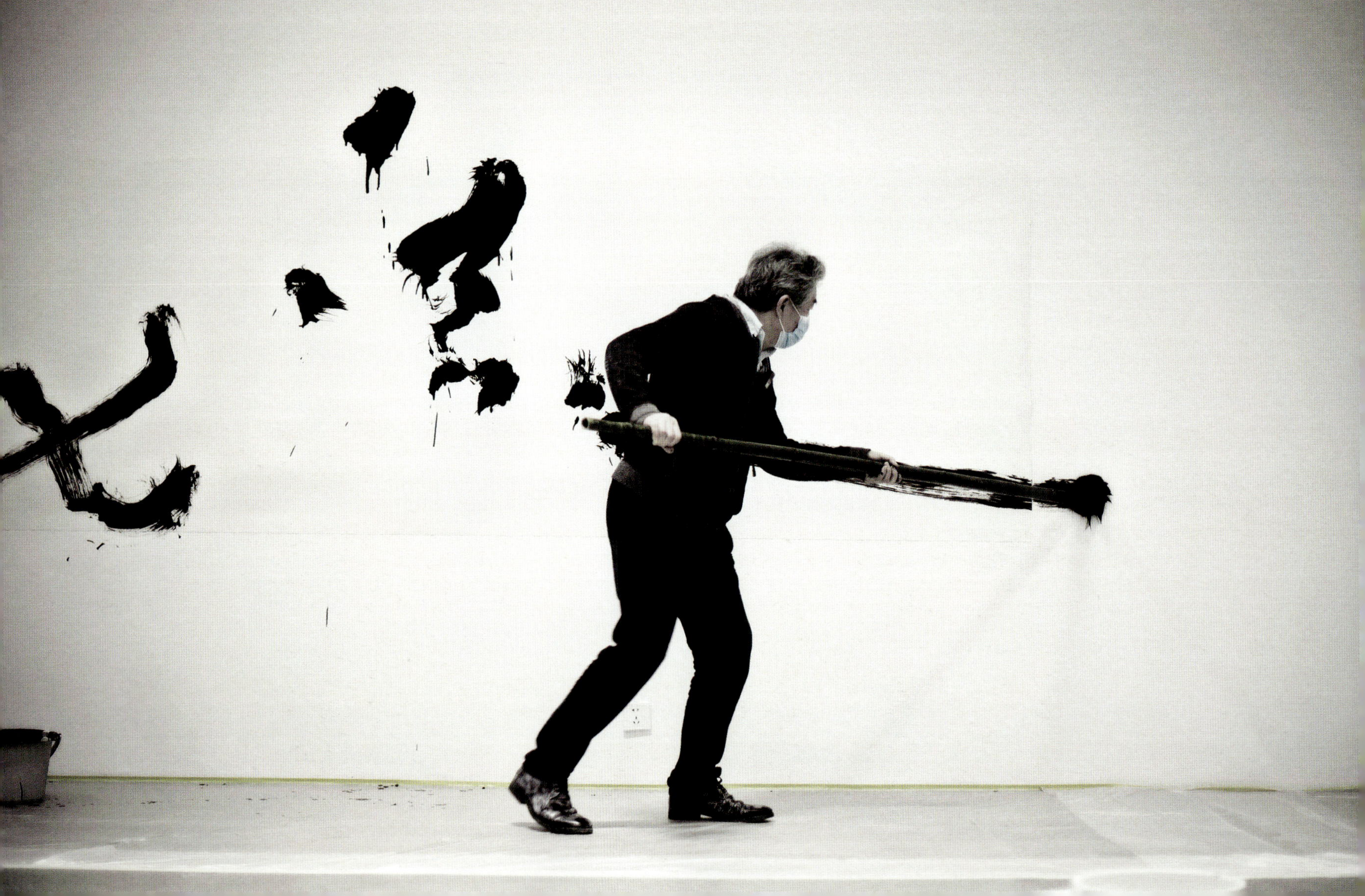

Shan Shui Jing (Zwischen Bergen und Flüssen)

GRENZÜBERSCHREITENDE
ZUSAMMENARBEIT ZWISCHEN TAN PING
UND HOU YING 2023,
XIAMEN MUSEUM OF CONTEMPORARY ART,
CHINA HOU YING, TÄNZERIN

Die Geschichte entwickelt sich ständig weiter;
die heutigen Landschaften sind nicht mehr
dieselben wie vor tausend Jahren.

Die gespaltene Schriftrolle „Tausend Meilen
von Flüssen und Bergen" symbolisiert hier
die fragmentierte Realität der Welt nach der
Pandemie. „Tear" steht für die Handlung,
während „split" das Ergebnis bezeichnet. Die
auf die lange Wandrolle gemalten Bilder sind in
zwei Teile gerissen: Ein Teil bleibt leer und stellt
Flüsse dar, während die verbleibende Tinte an
der Wand Berge symbolisiert und als Beweis für
die Kluft zwischen Bergen und Gewässern dient.

Tan Ping

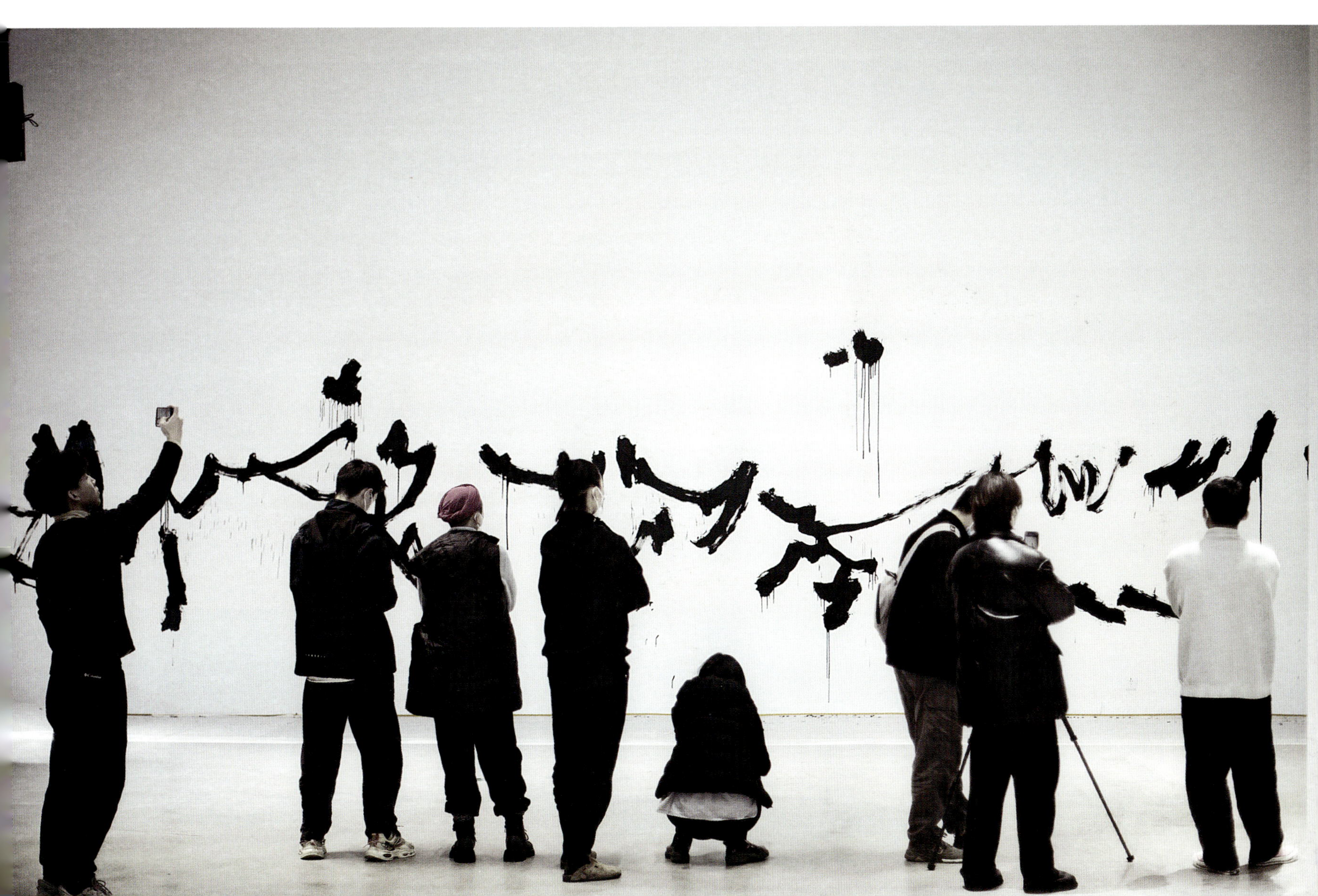

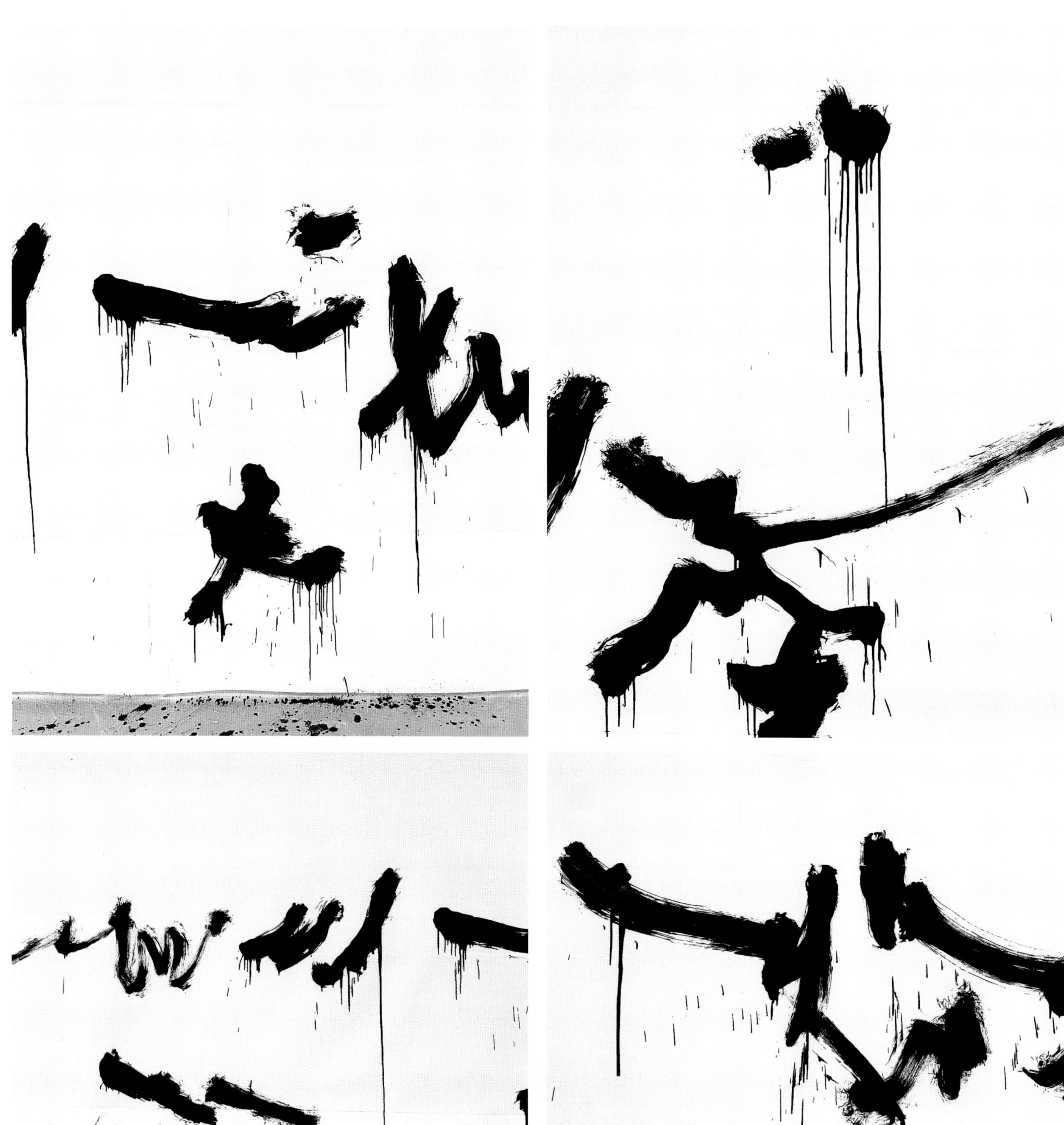

HOU YING & TAN PING,
2023
work on site / **Arbeit vor Ort**
Topred Center for
Contemporary Art, Xiamen,
China

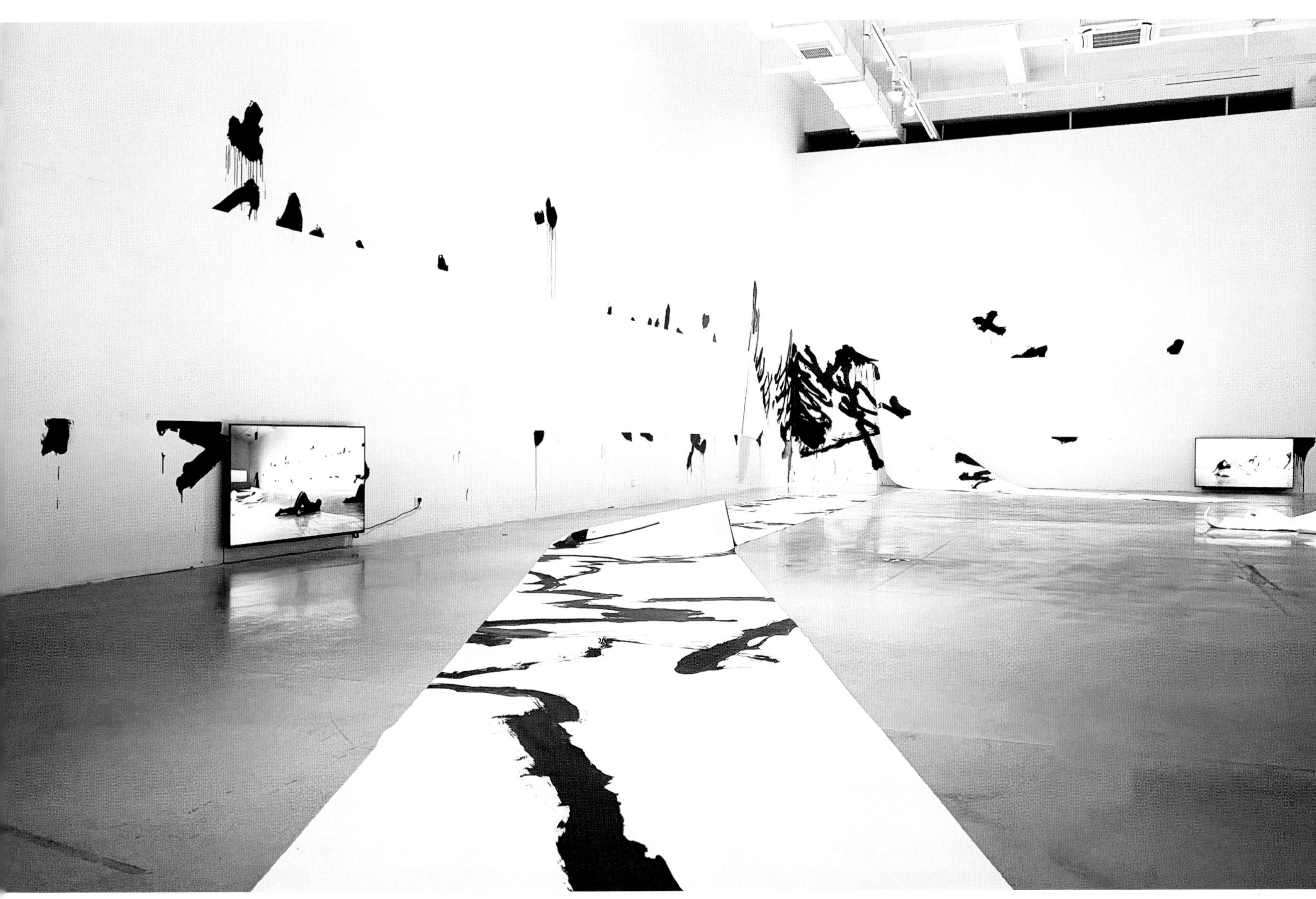

Eingeschränkte Freiheit

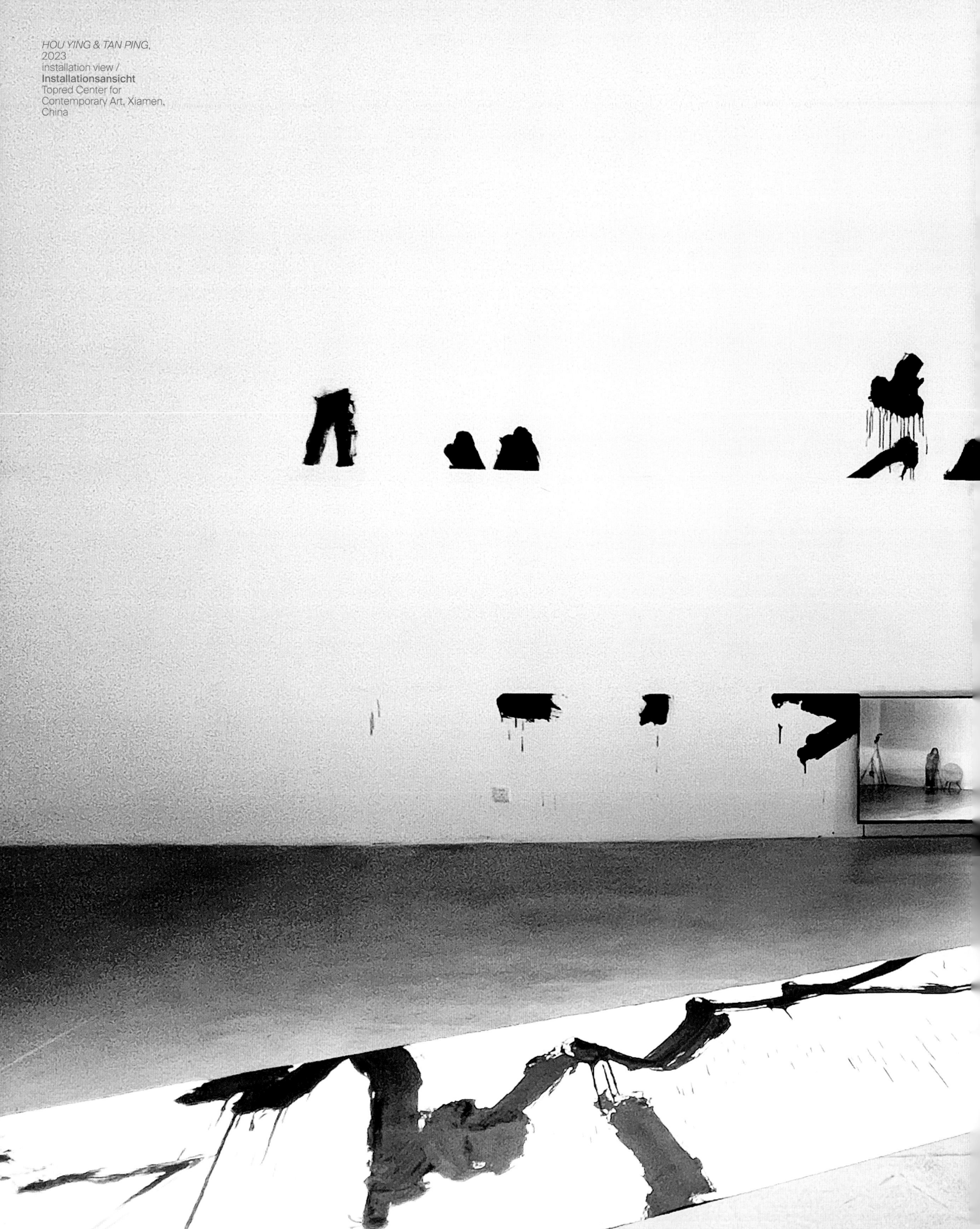

HOU YING & TAN PING,
2023
installation view /
Installationsansicht
Topred Center for
Contemporary Art, Xiamen,
China

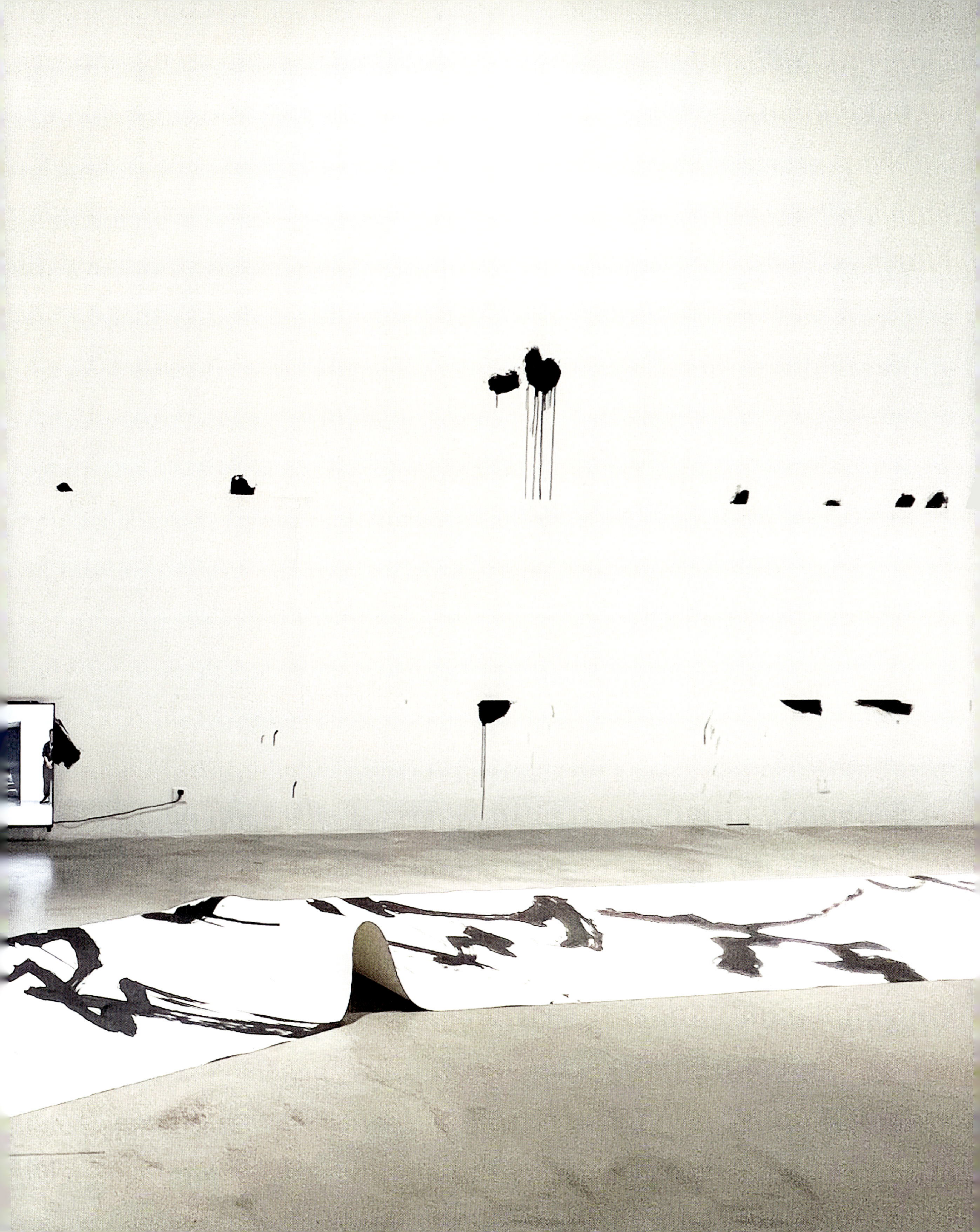

HOU YING & TAN PING,
2023
work on site / **Arbeit vor Ort**
Topred Center for
Contemporary Art, Xiamen,
China

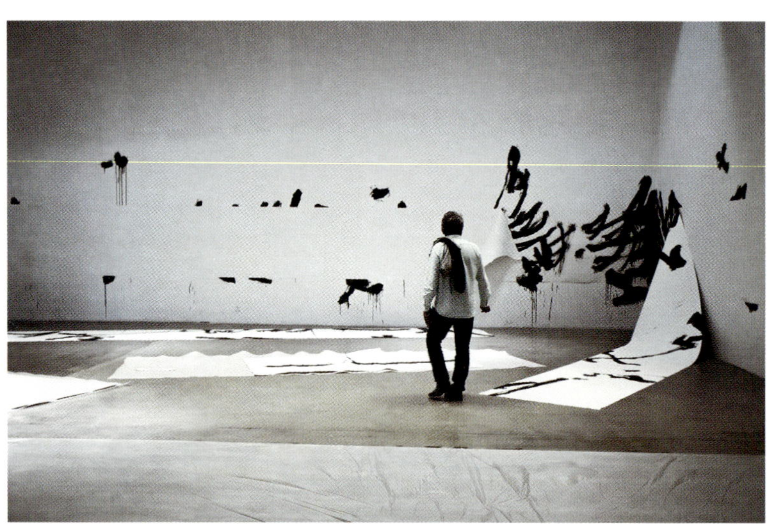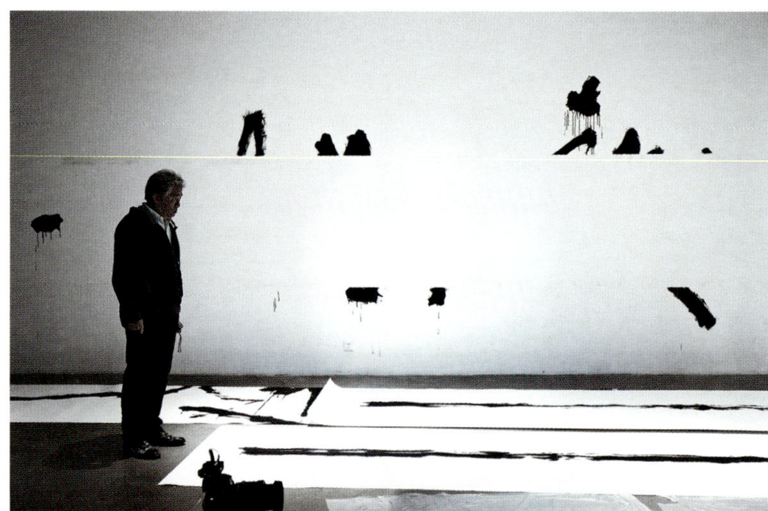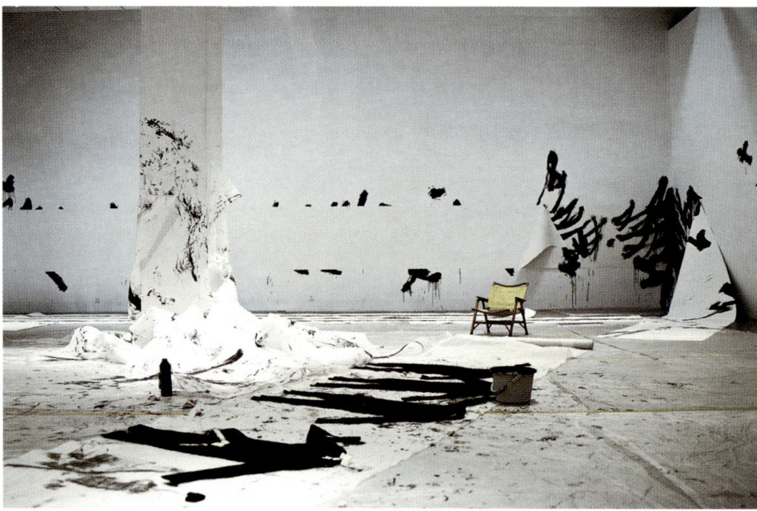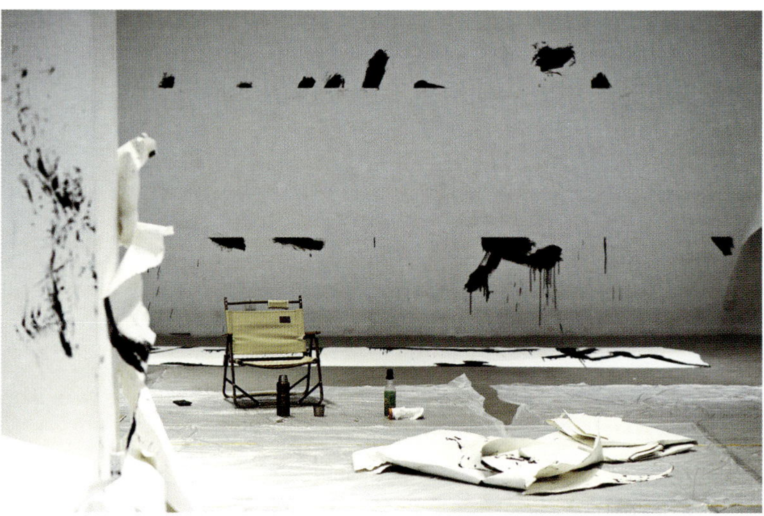

HOU YING & TAN PING,
2023
installation view /
Installationsansicht
Topred Center for
Contemporary Art, Xiamen,
China

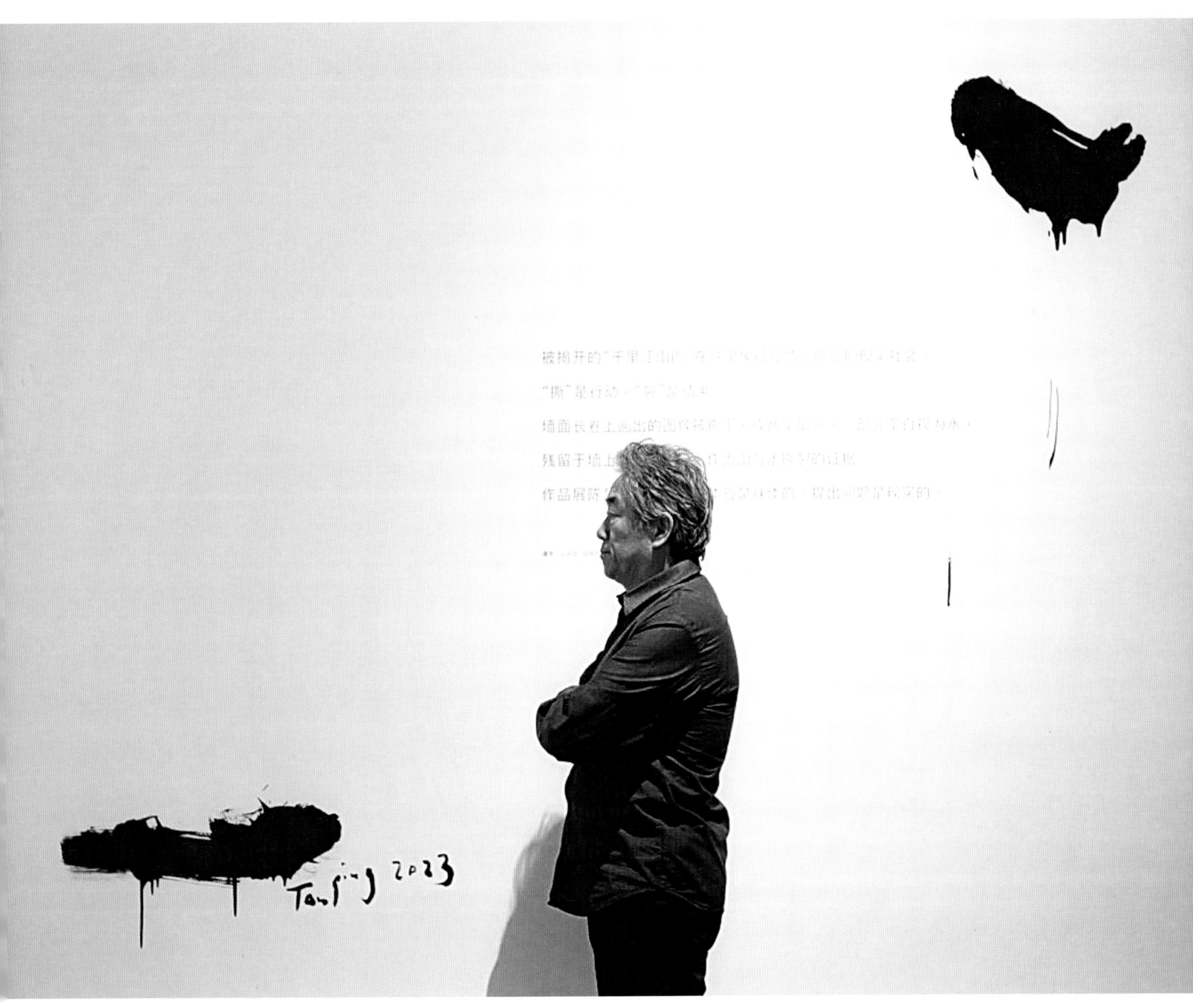

TAN PING & HOU YING, DANCER, CROSSBORDER COLLABORATION, 2023

Tan Ping's huge on-site scroll, "— I", unfolds before the viewer like an expansive landscape, reminiscent of the classic scroll of A Thousand Miles of Rivers and Mountains.

As the music begins, the dancer's presence becomes elusive, yet they are drawn to the blank scroll on the wall. Hidden behind it, the dancers remain out of sight while Tan Ping, brush in hand, inadvertently draws a horizontal line on the scroll. This line continues to evolve, at times clear and profound, and at other times, bewilderingly deep. Are the thousand miles of rivers and mountains a picturesque landscape or a chasm? Under Tan Ping's hand, a single line consistently emerges, as if it represents another river or mountain within the artist's heart. A horizontal line becomes water, a vertical one, a mountain. At this moment, a dancer seeks to deconstruct traditional landscapes with their body, rebuilding a new one. Hidden behind the paper, the dancer stands still, as the "horizontal" line traces history. It feels as if the concealed scroll of history is suddenly torn apart, fragmented. The dancer twists and struggles forward, like the "foolish old man moving mountains," embodying a spirit unmoved by history, standing like a sculpture amidst mountains and rivers, eventually disintegrating into pieces.

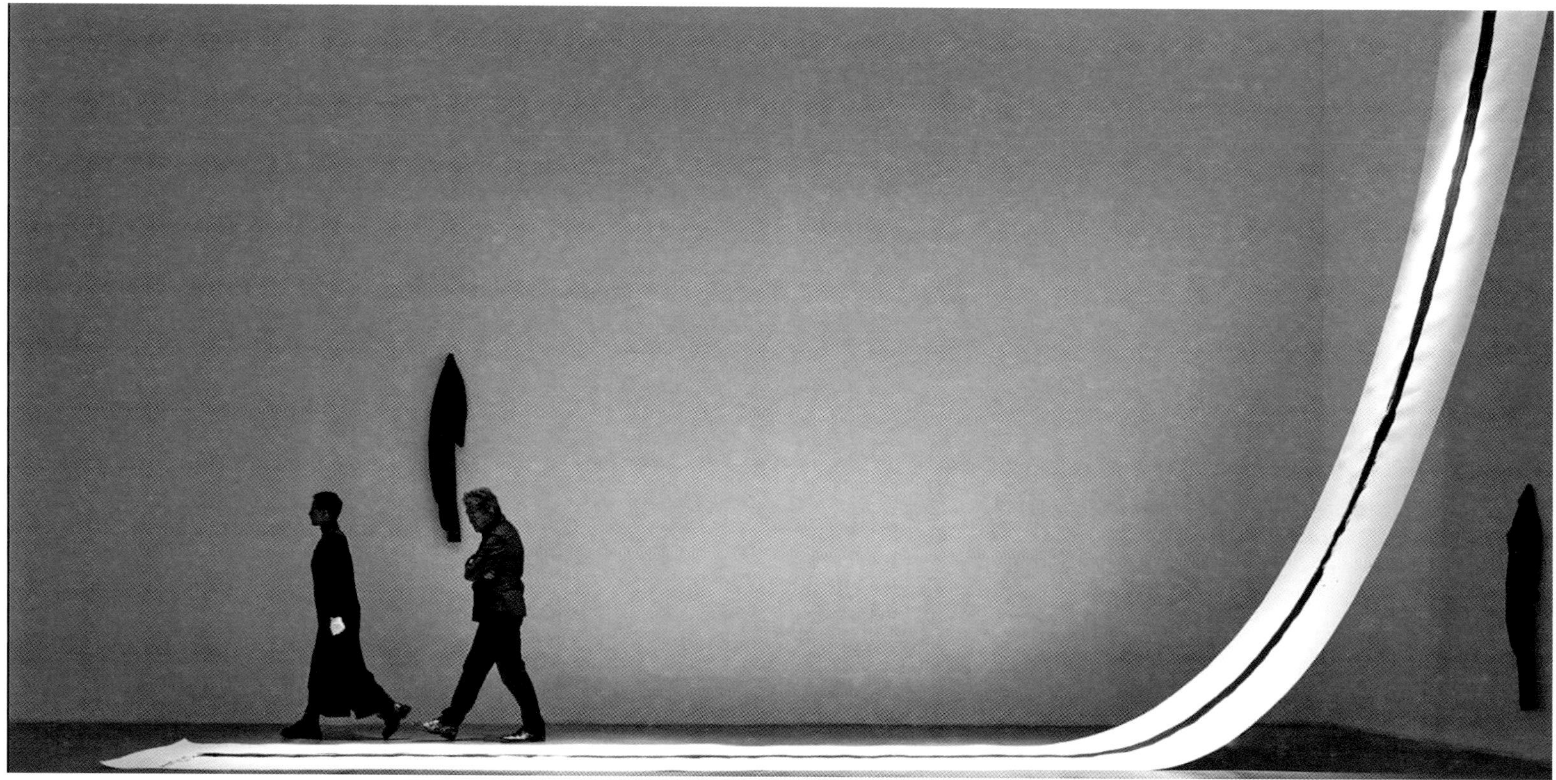

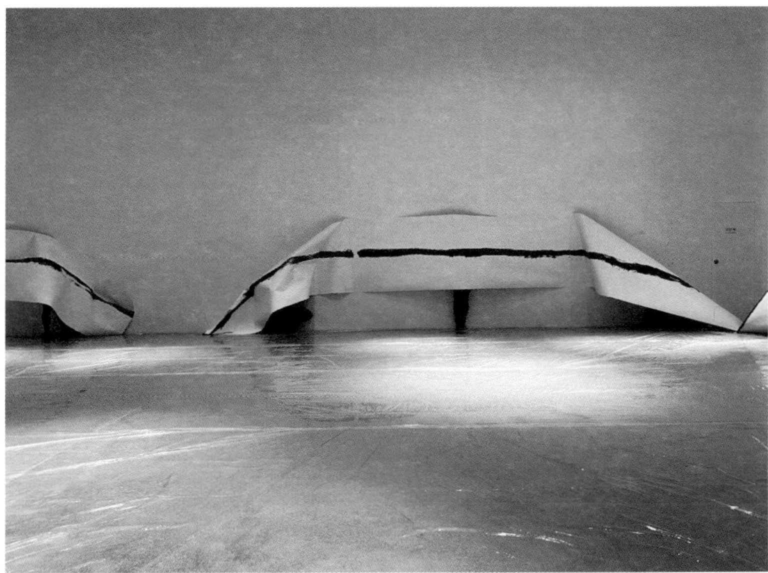
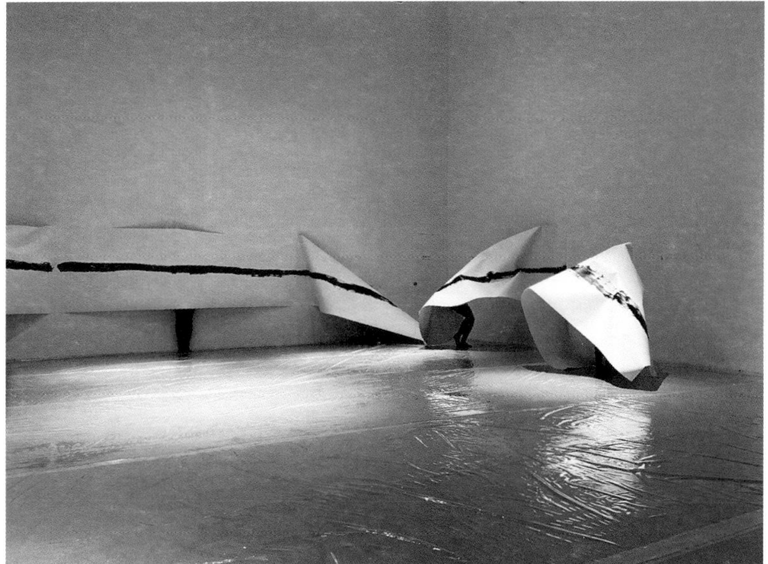
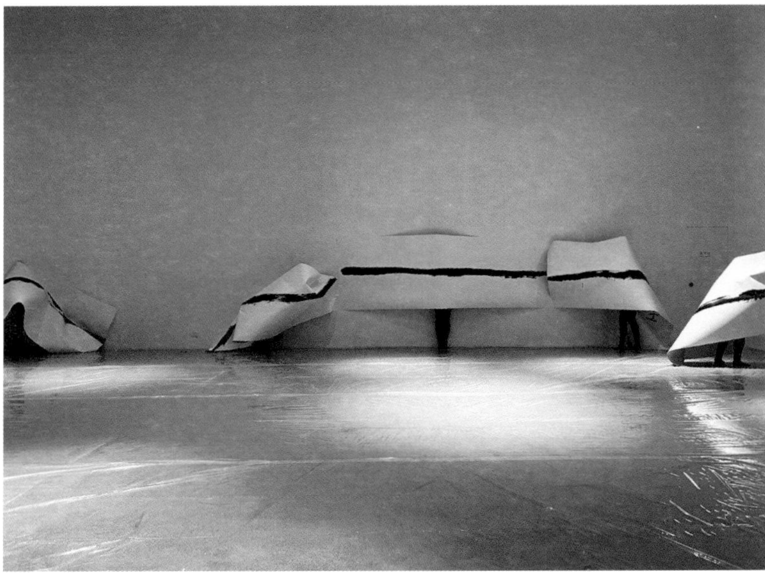

Als die Musik einsetzt, verschwindet die Präsenz der Tänzer, doch sie werden von der leeren Schriftrolle an der Wand angezogen. Dahinter verborgen bleiben die Tänzer außer Sicht, während Tan Ping mit dem Pinsel in der Hand versehentlich eine horizontale Linie auf die Schriftrolle zeichnet.

Diese Linie entwickelt sich weiter, manchmal klar und tiefgründig, manchmal verwirrend tief. Sind die tausend Meilen von Flüssen und Bergen eine malerische Landschaft oder ein Abgrund? Unter Tan Pings Hand entsteht konsequent eine einzelne Linie, als ob sie einen anderen Fluss oder Berg im Herzen des Künstlers darstellen würde. Eine horizontale Linie wird zu Wasser, eine vertikale zu einem Berg. In diesem Moment versucht ein Tänzer, traditionelle Landschaften mit seinem Körper zu dekonstruieren und eine neue wieder aufzubauen. Versteckt hinter dem Papier steht der Tänzer still, während die „horizontale" Linie die Geschichte nachzeichnet. Es fühlt sich an, als ob die verborgene Schriftrolle der Geschichte plötzlich auseinandergerissen und zersplittert wird. Der Tänzer windet sich und kämpft sich vorwärts, wie der „törichte alte Mann, der Berge versetzt", und verkörpert einen Geist, der von der Geschichte unberührt bleibt. Er steht wie eine Skulptur inmitten von Bergen und Flüssen und zerfällt schließlich in Stücke.

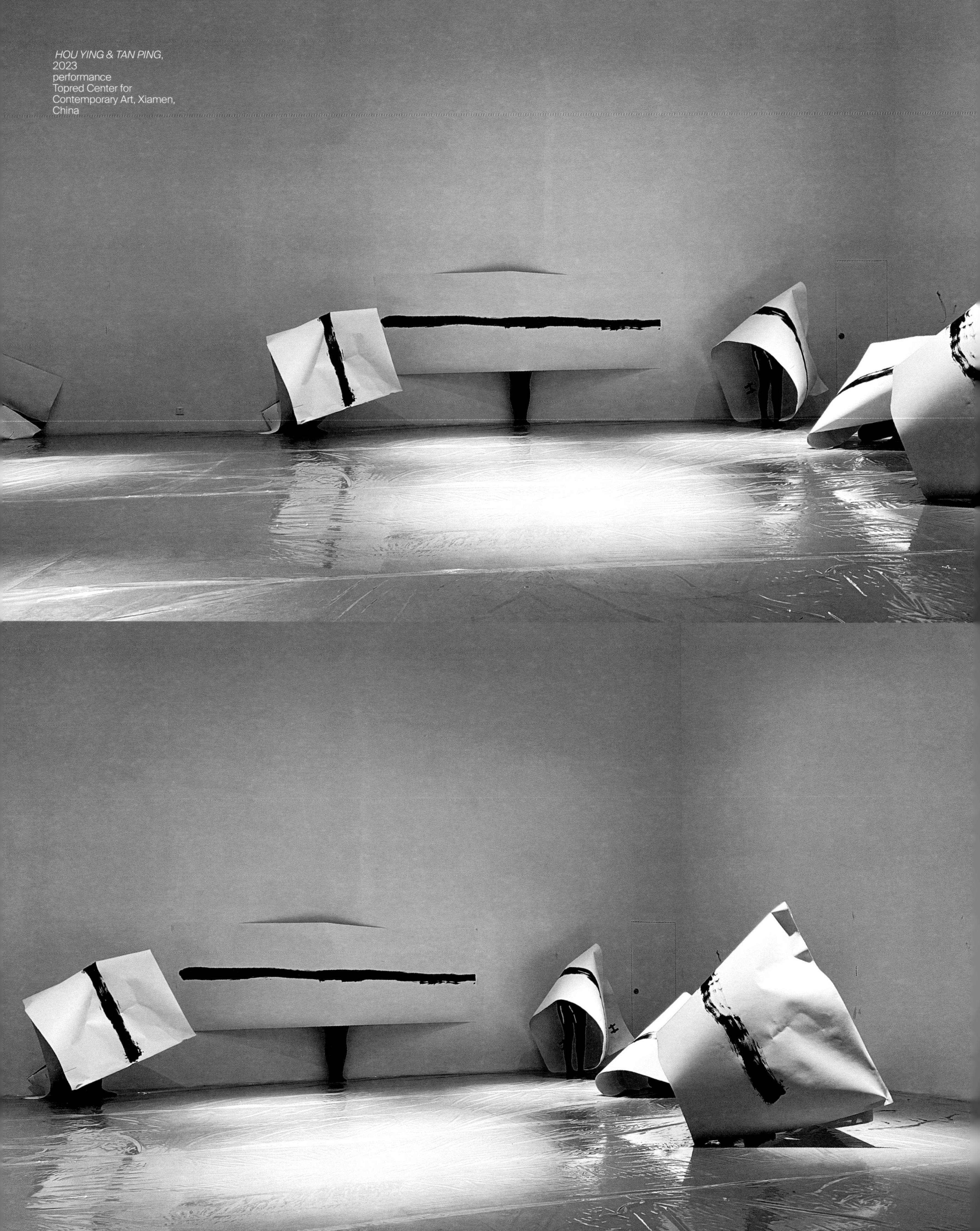

HOU YING & TAN PING,
2023
performance
Topred Center for
Contemporary Art, Xiamen,
China

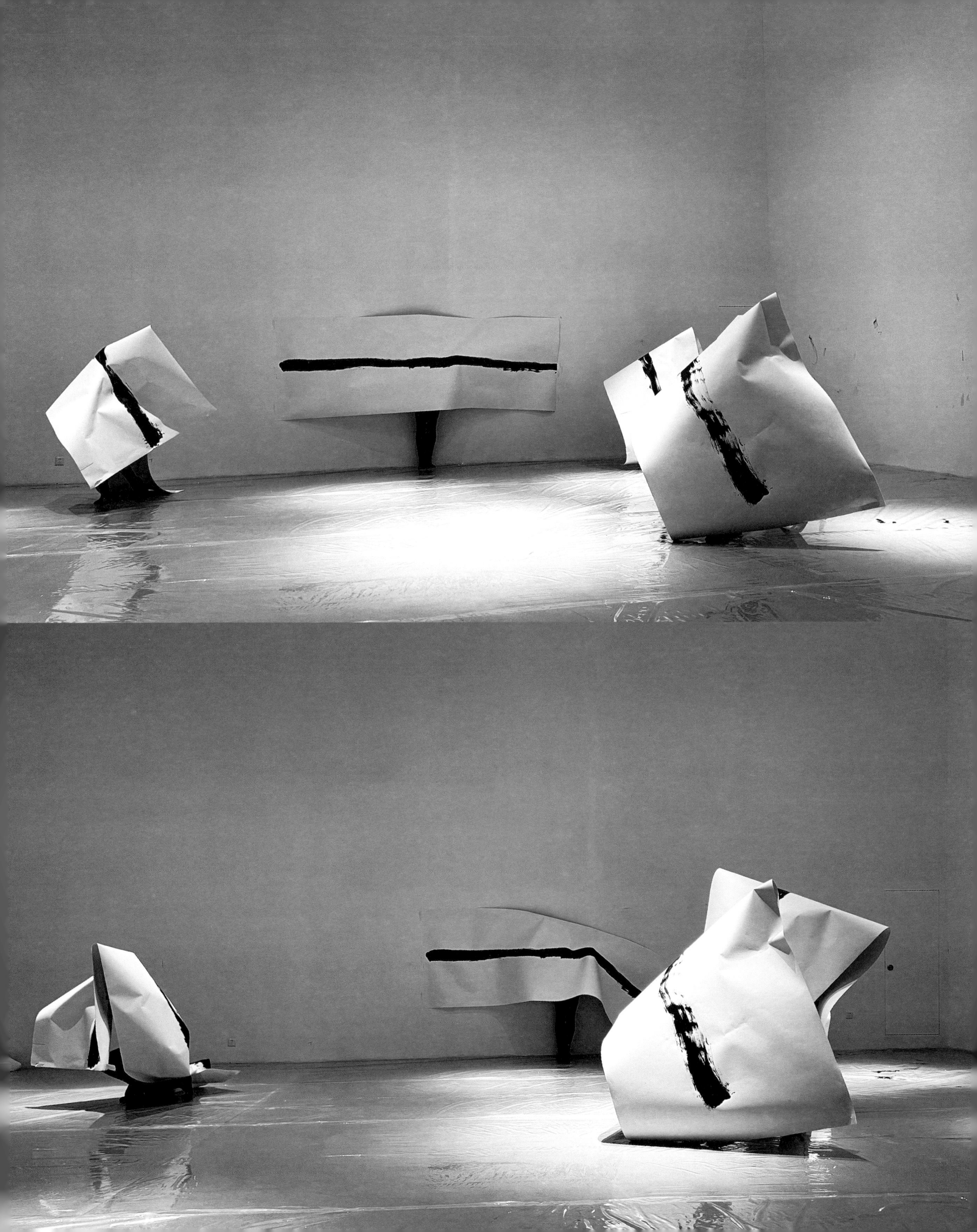

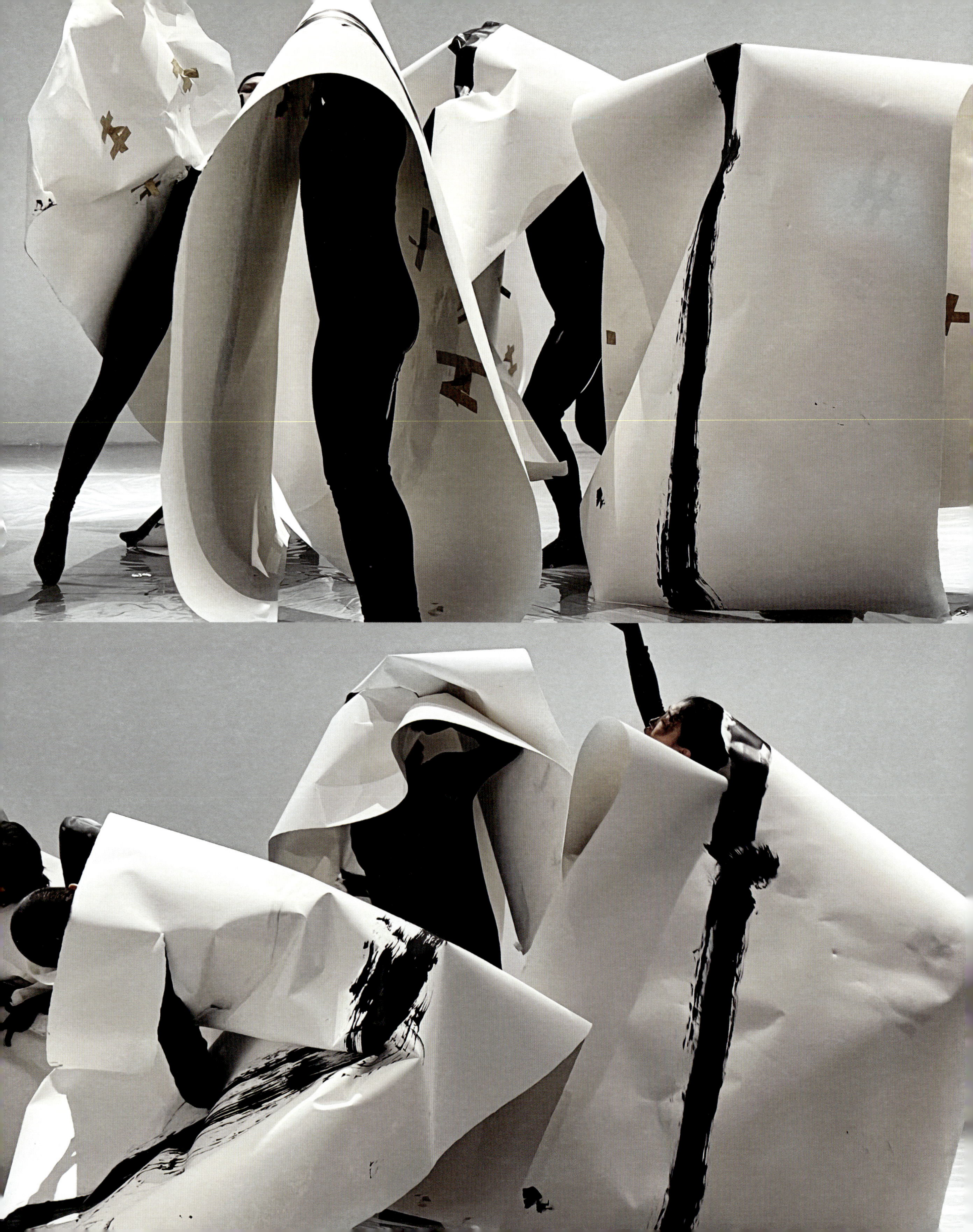

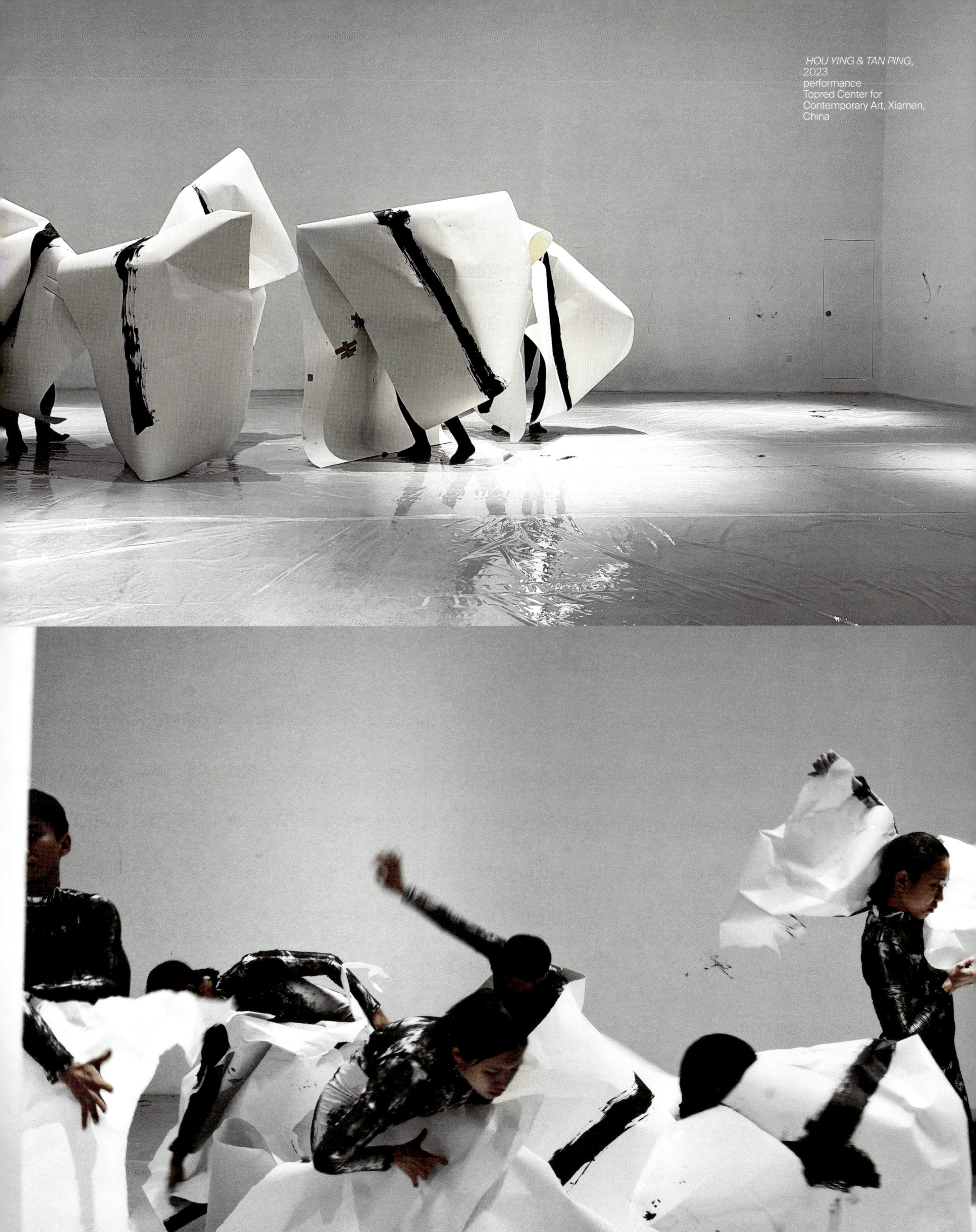

HOU YING & TAN PING,
2023
performance
Topred Center for
Contemporary Art, Xiamen,
China

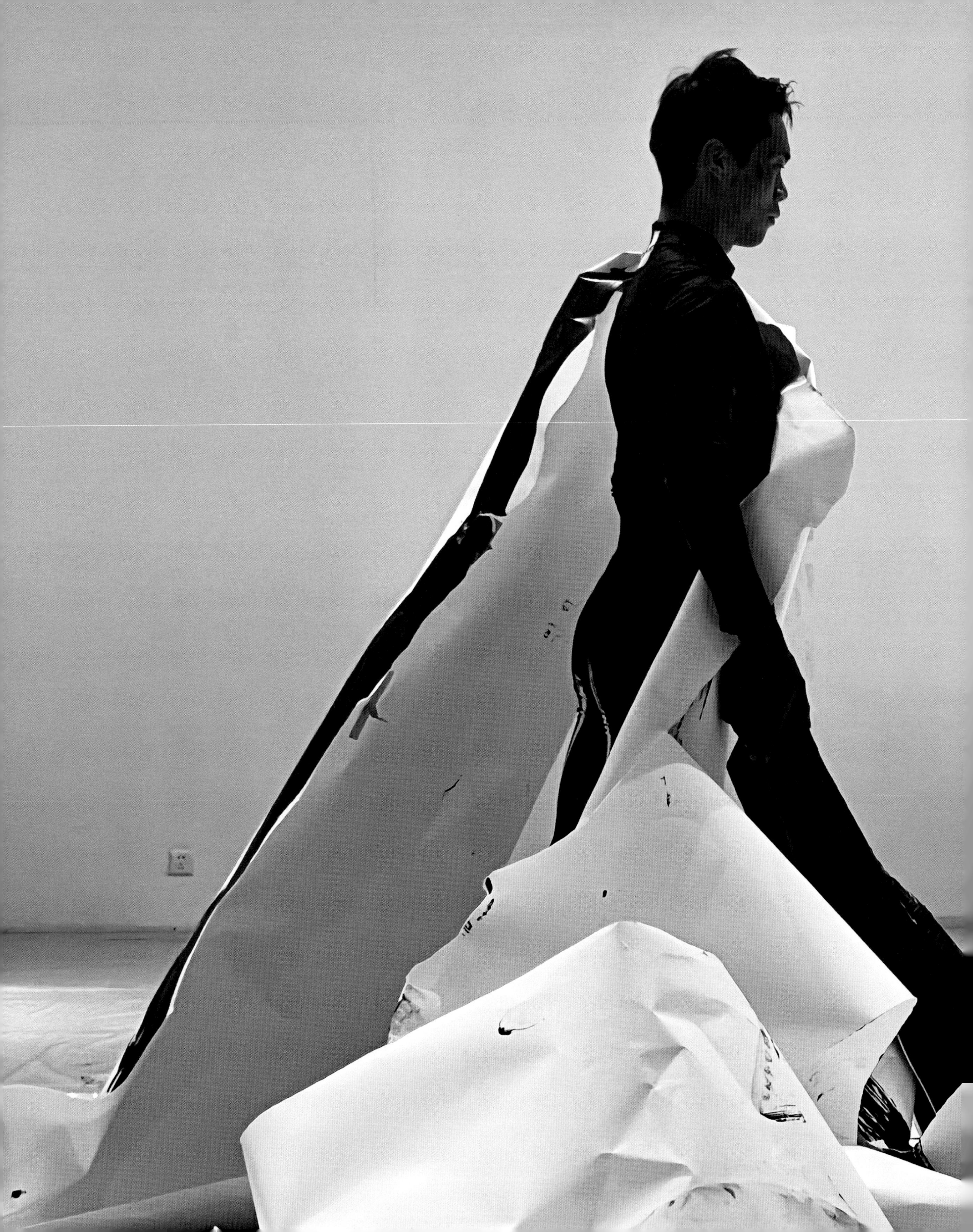

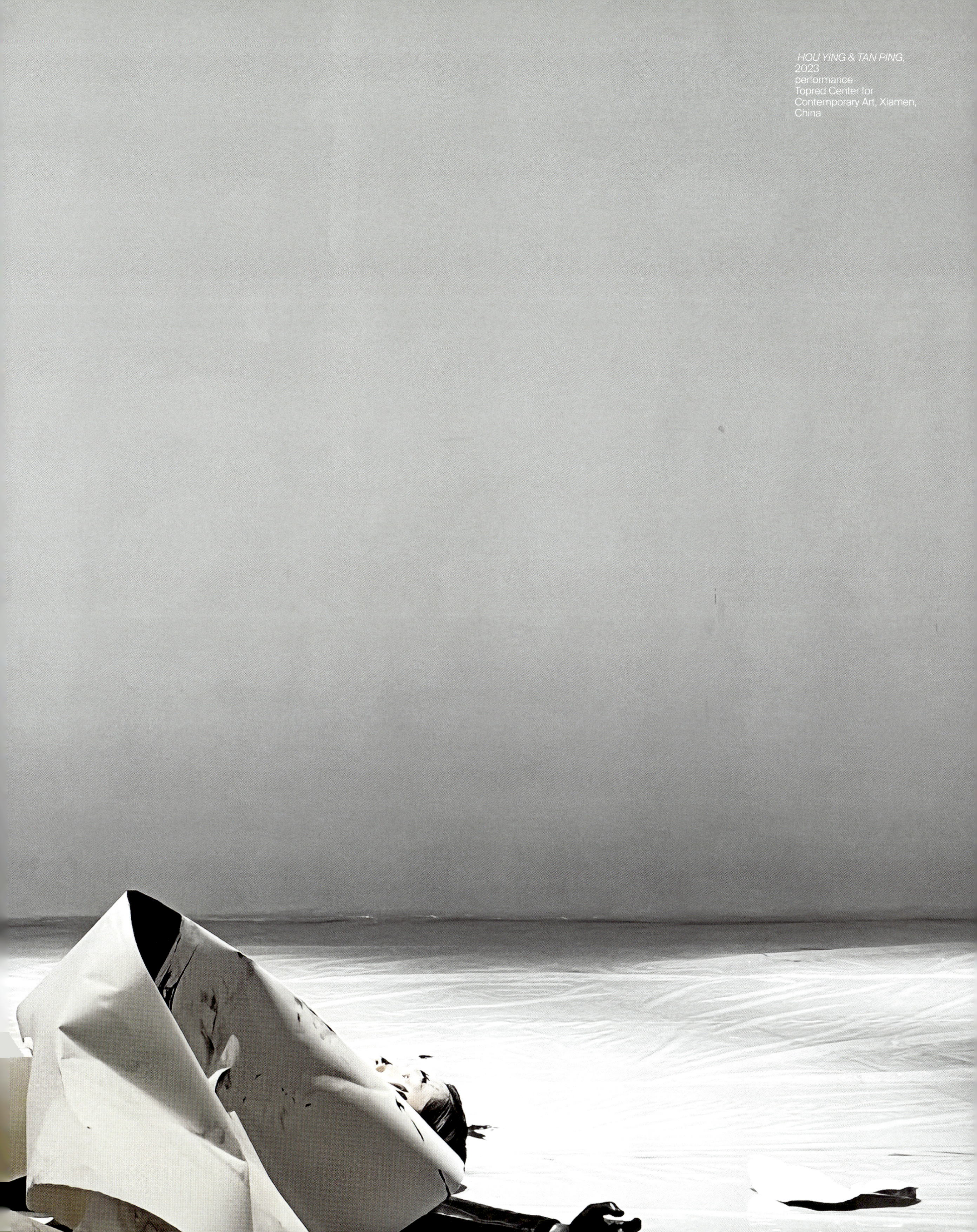

HOU YING & TAN PING,
2023
performance
Topred Center for
Contemporary Art, Xiamen,
China

Overflow and Suture

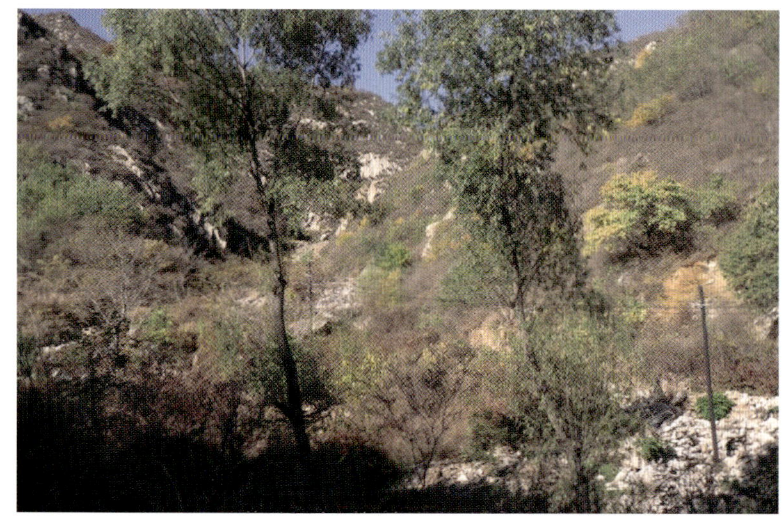

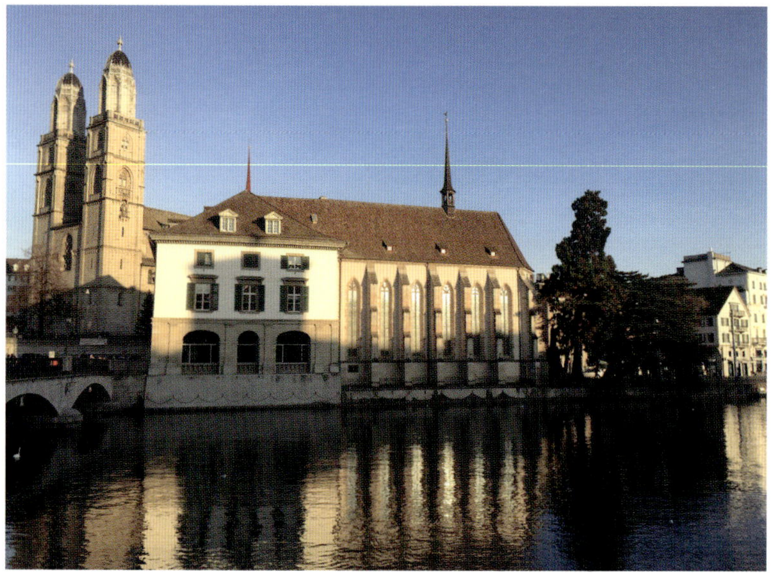

Mountainous area of
Beijing / **Bergregion von
Peking**
photo by Tan Ping, 2023

Zurich / **Zürich**, photo by
Tan Ping, 2016

Zurich: Beyond Every Mountain
Is Another Mountain

In 2016, Tan Ping again challenged the logic of
traditional methods by painting on site over five,
2x3 meter, blank canvases for ten days at the first
floor of Helmhaus Zurich, Switzerland. Tan Ping
created this piece while experiencing the multi-
perspective of frame, wall, and space that form
the creative environment. The display consists of
abstract elements mixed with definitive work-on-
site style.

Überlauf und Naht

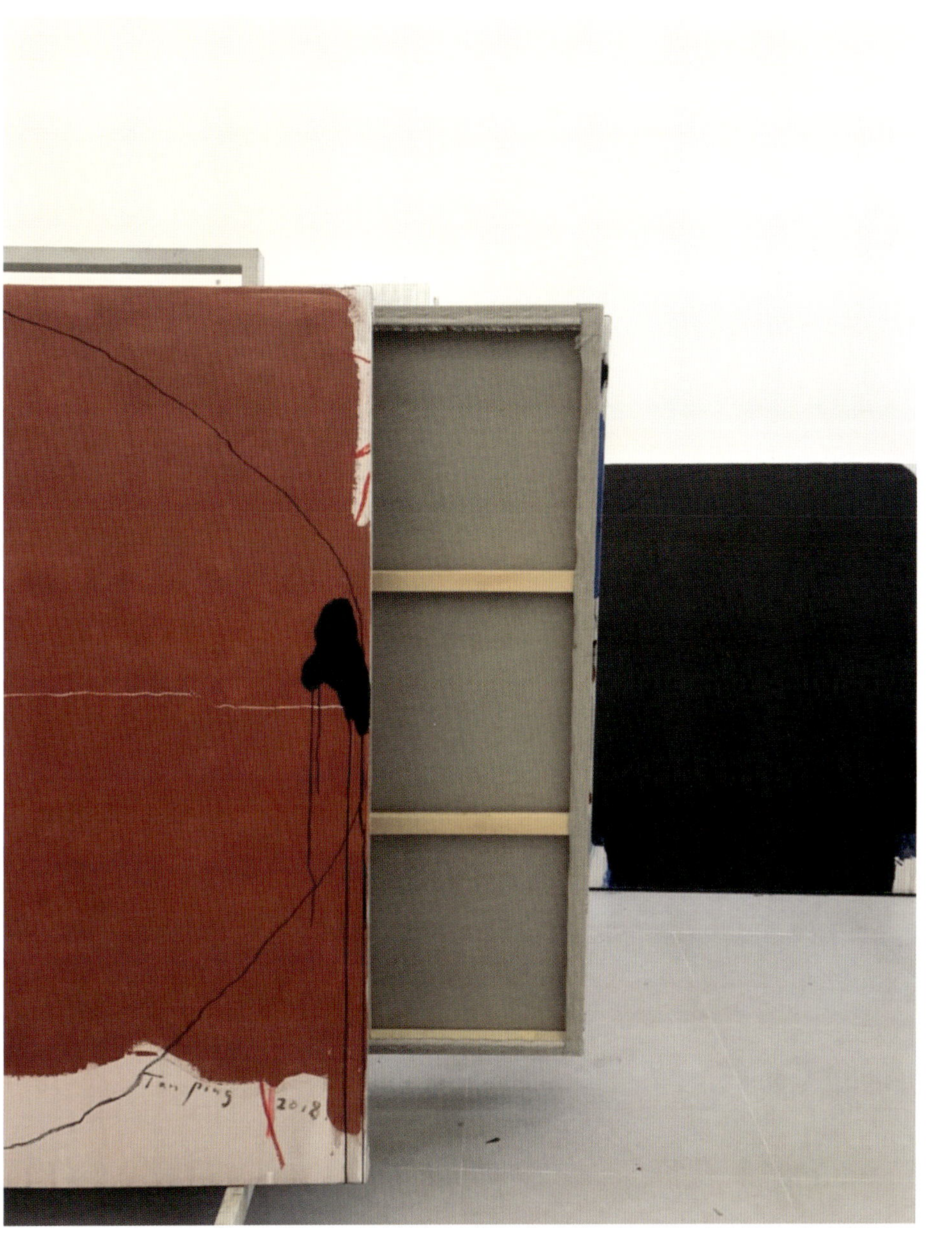

Zürich: Hinter jedem Berg liegt ein weiterer Berg

2016 stellte Tan Ping die Logik traditioneller Methoden erneut in Frage, indem er zehn Tage lang im ersten Stock des Helmhaus Zürich in der Schweiz auf fünf 2 x 3 Meter große, leere Leinwände malte. Tan Ping schuf dieses Werk, während er die Multiperspektive von Rahmen, Wand und Raum erlebte, die die kreative Umgebung bilden. Die Ausstellung besteht aus abstrakten Elementen, gemischt mit einem definitiven Stil der Arbeit vor Ort.

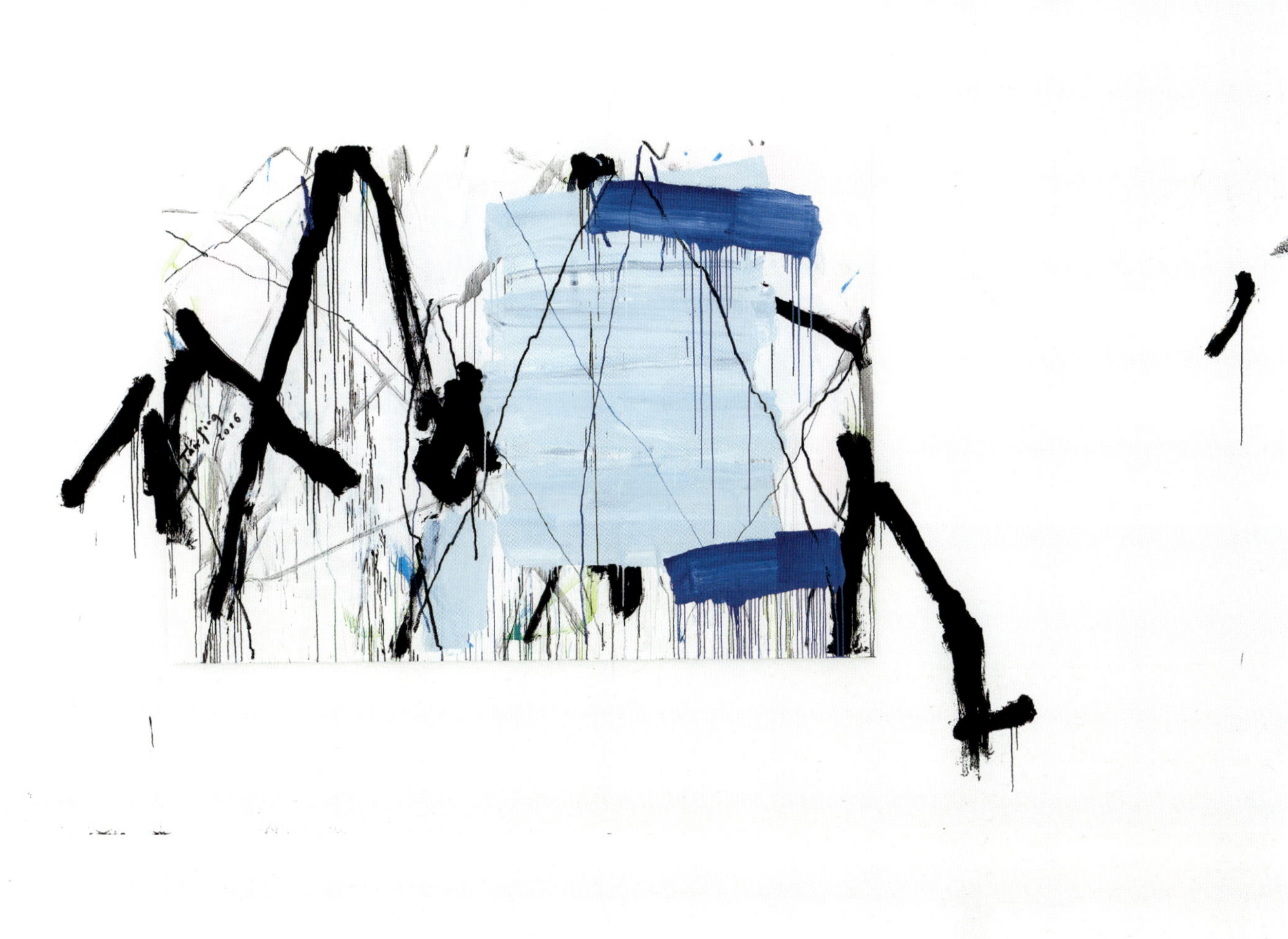

Überlauf und Naht

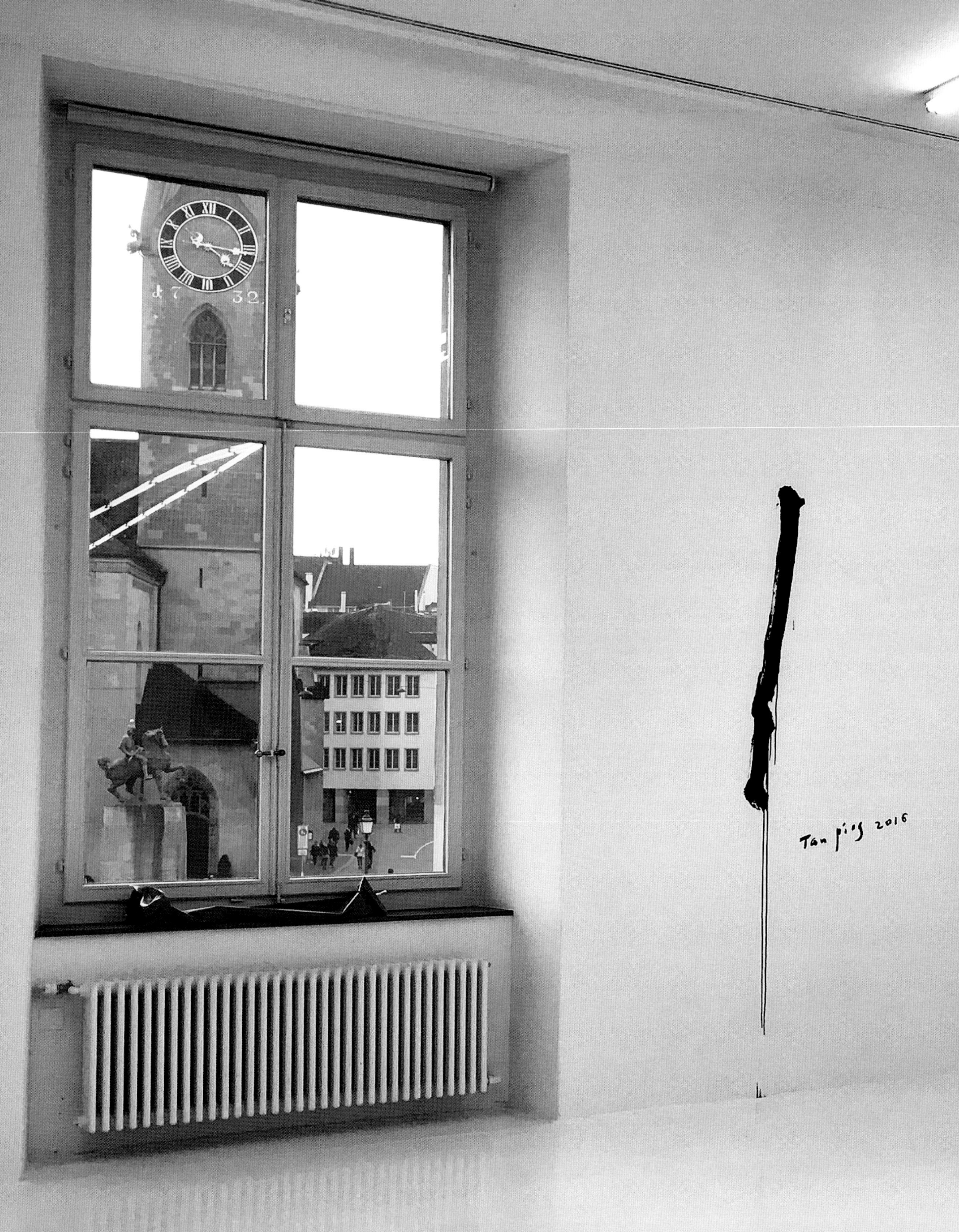

Tàpies 2016

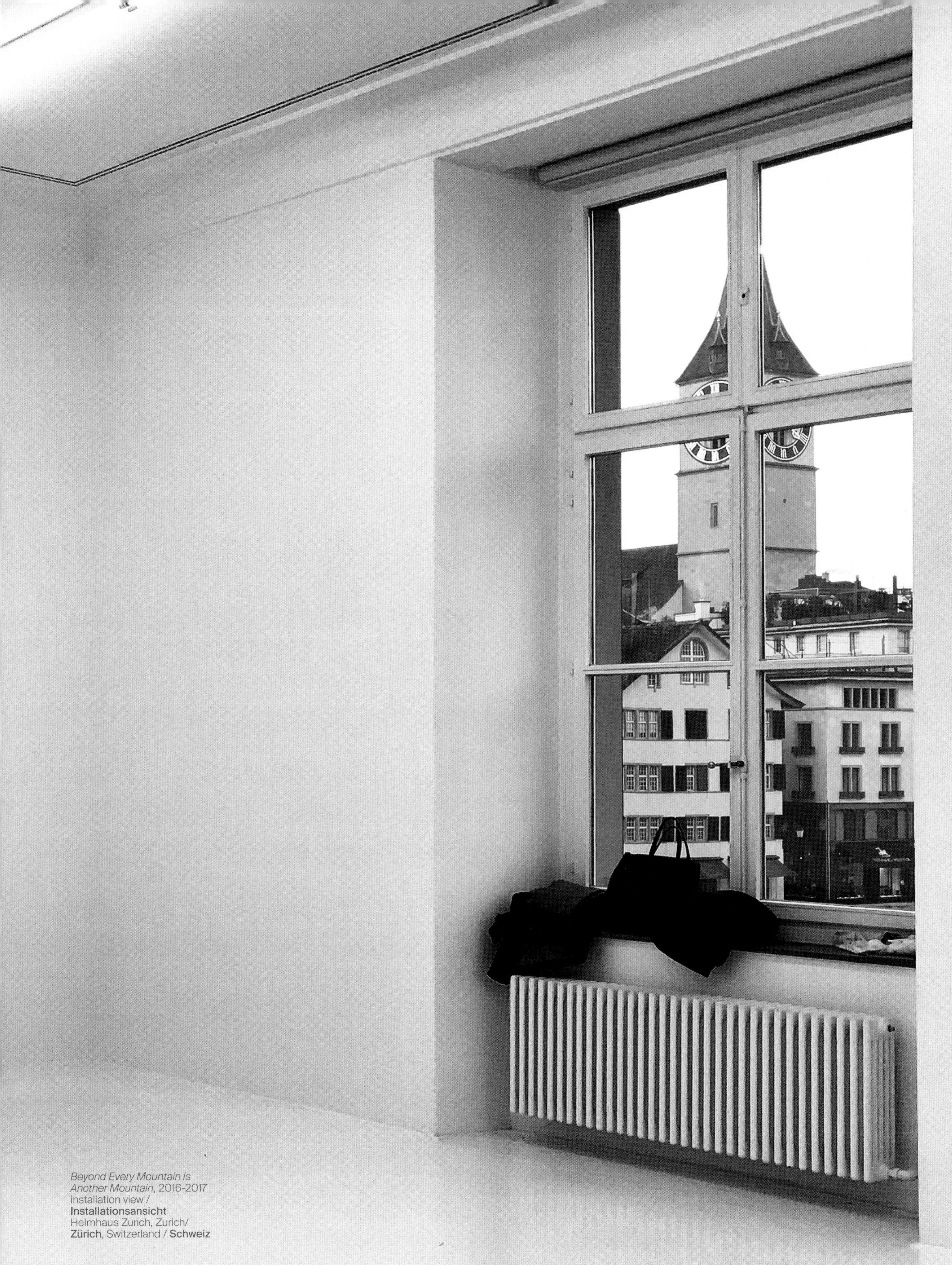

*Beyond Every Mountain Is
Another Mountain*, 2016-2017
installation view /
Installationsansicht
Helmhaus Zurich, Zurich/
Zürich, Switzerland / **Schweiz**

Tan Ping: What is Painting?,
2021
installation view /
Installationsansicht
Tang Contemporary Art
Center, Beijing, China

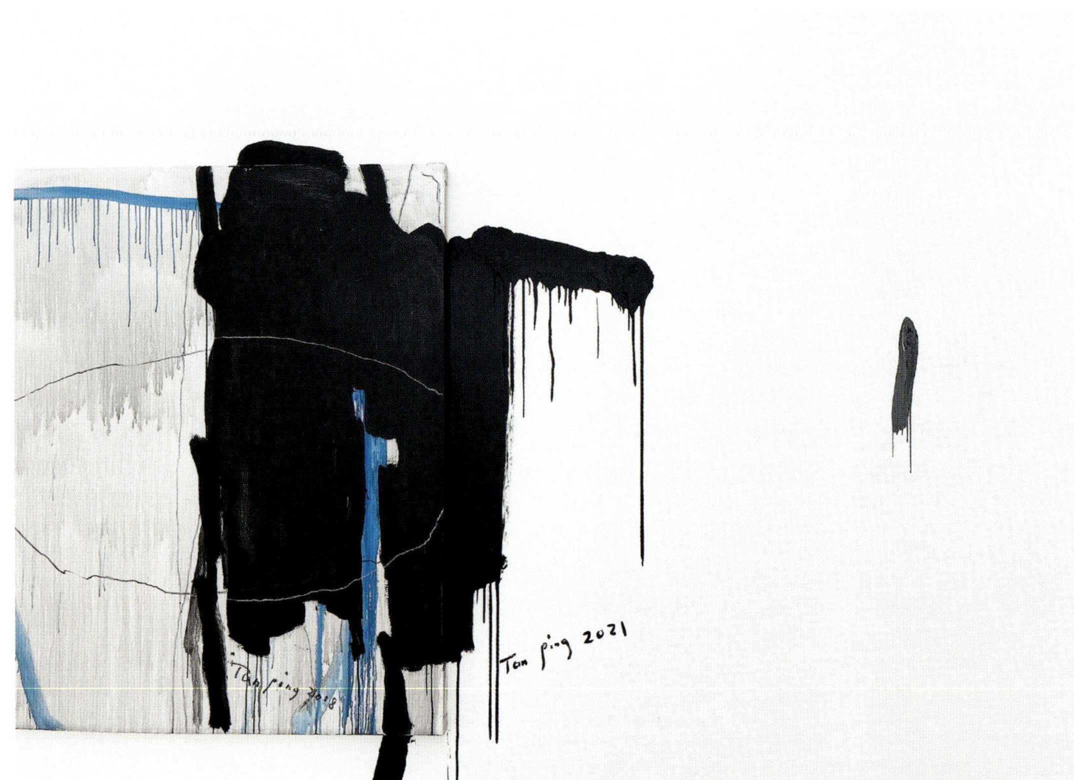

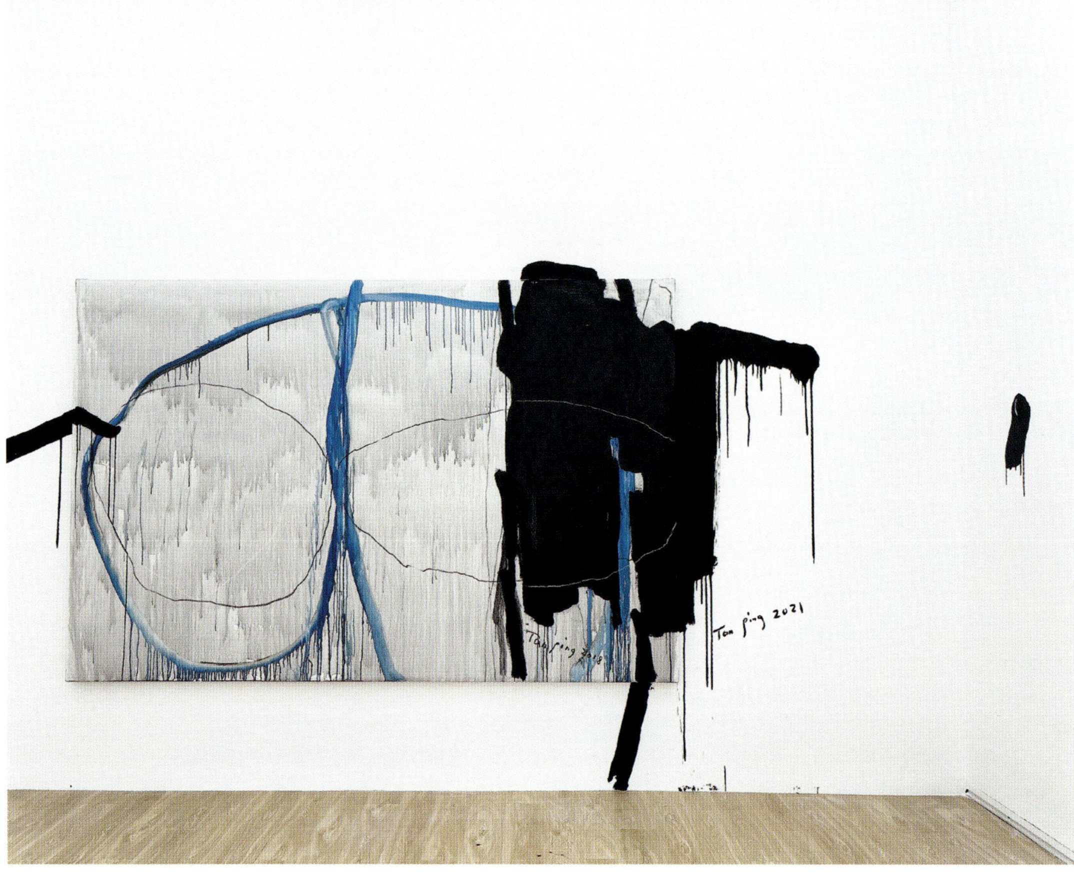

Beijing: Overflow

An unfinished piece hanging on the wall uses
"overflowing" as its impetus for completion, defined
by the specific space in which it is placed.

Tan Ping

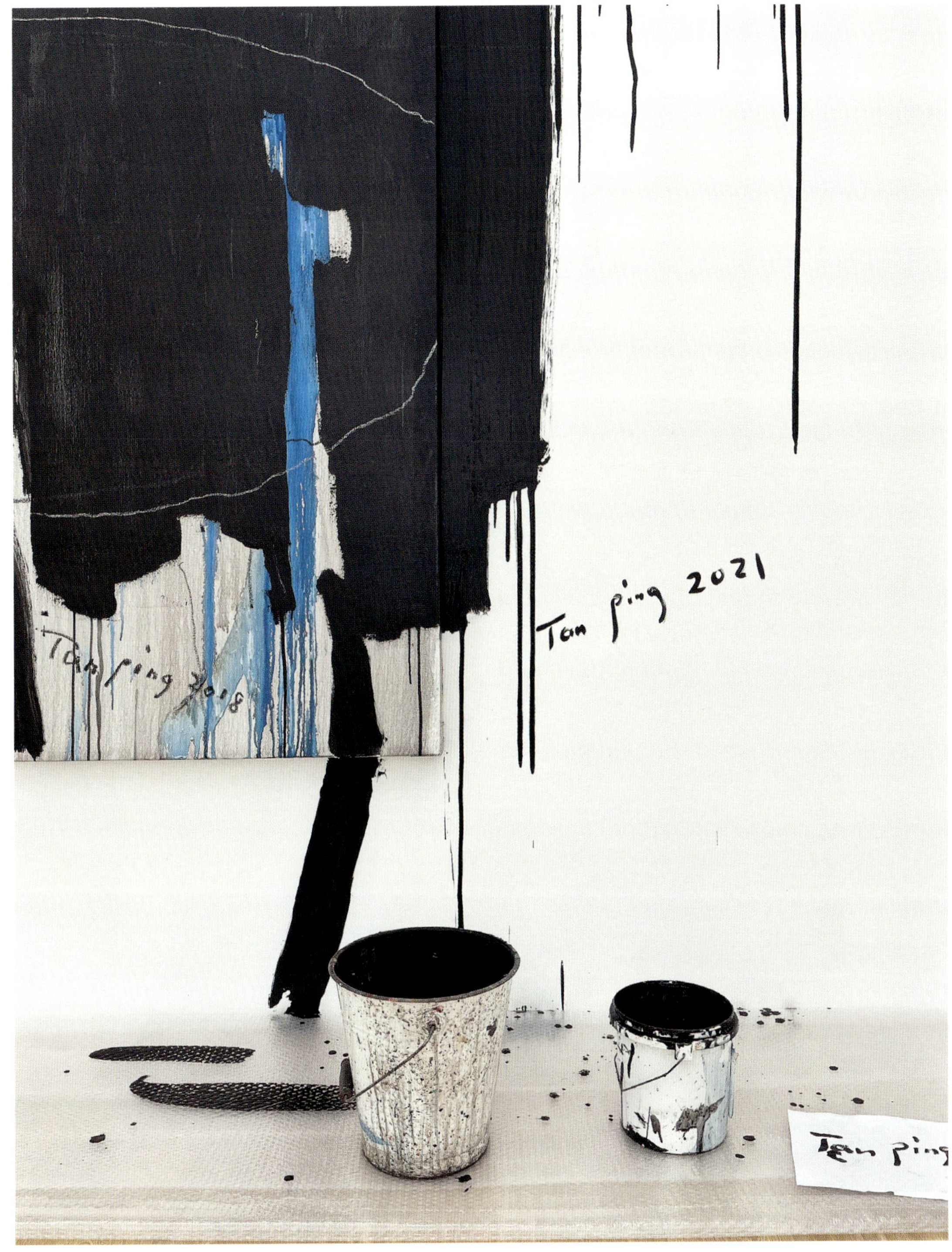

Peking: Überlauf

Ein unvollendetes Stück, das an der Wand hängt,
nutzt „Überfließen" als Impuls zur Vollendung,
definiert durch den spezifischen Raum, in dem
es platziert ist.

Tan Ping

Beijing: Hidden Narratives

A set of 23 unfinished works is combined into different series based on various themes and spaces. I have always focused on the relationship between the artwork and the exhibition space. Finding the connection between a set of "paintings" and their specific setting is central to my creation.

Tan Ping

Hidden Narratives, 2019
installation view /
Installationsansicht
Today Art Museum, Beijing,
China

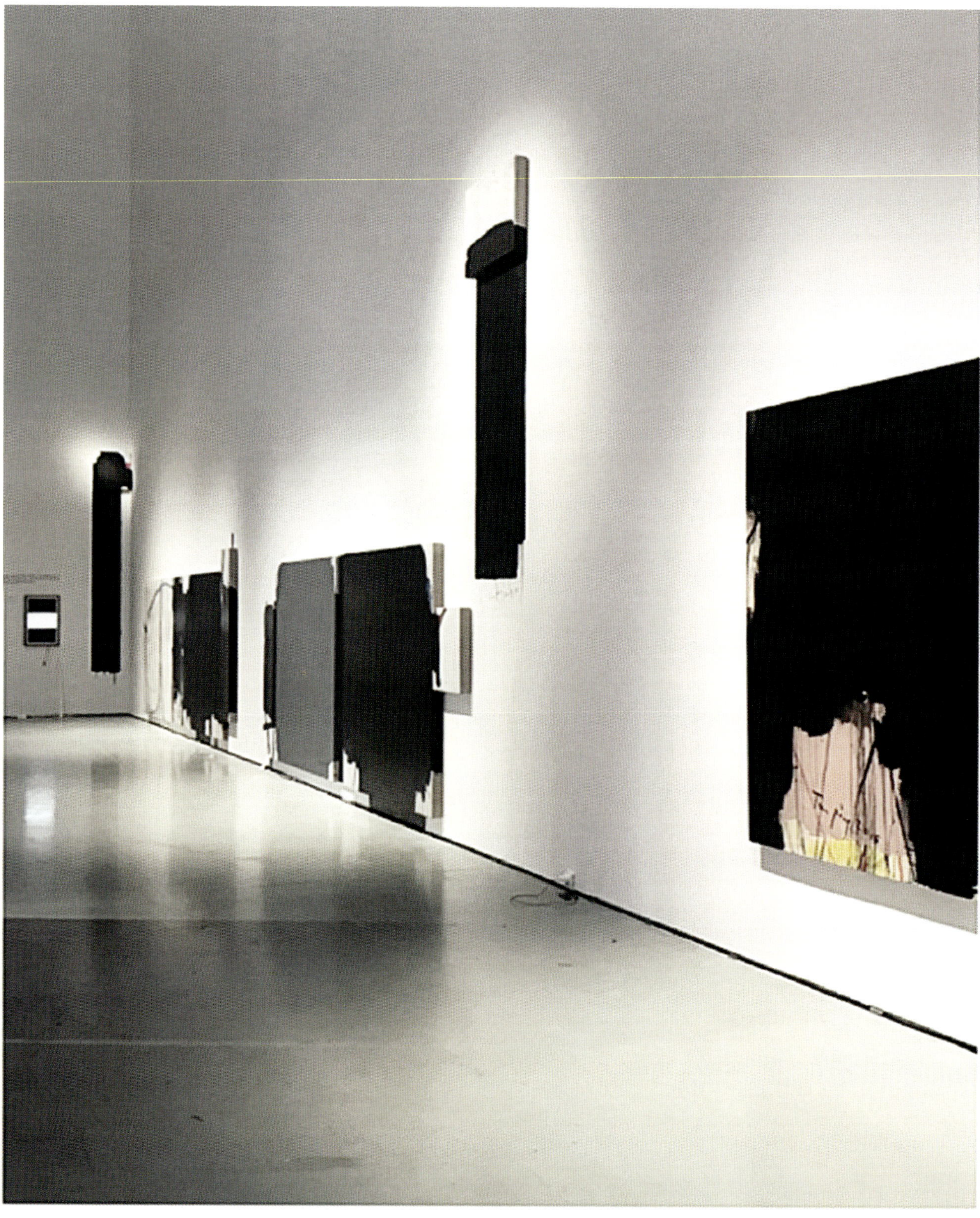

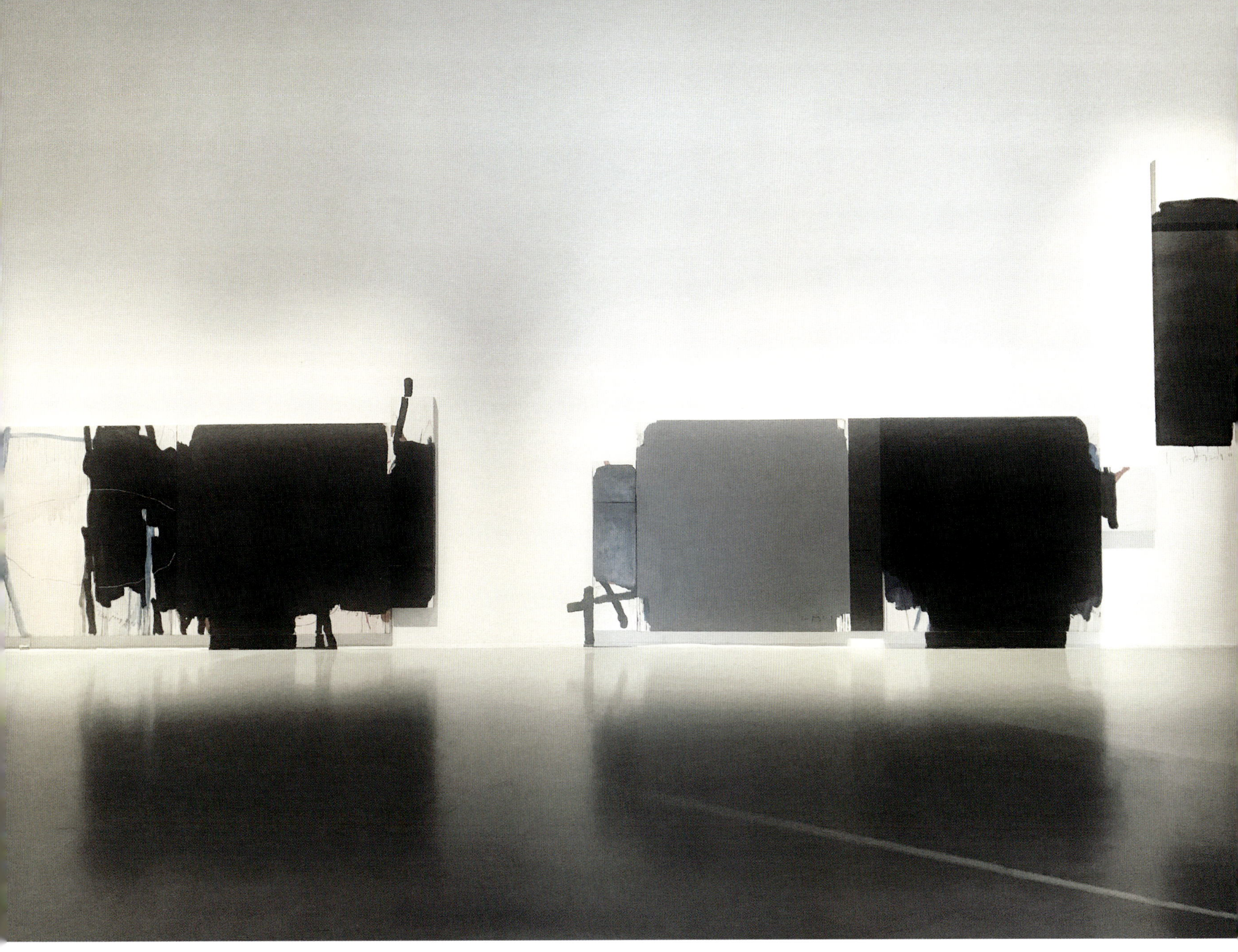

Peking: Verborgene Narrative

Eine Reihe von 23 unvollendeten Werken
wird zu verschiedenen Serien kombiniert,
die auf verschiedenen Themen und Räumen
basieren. Ich habe mich immer auf die
Beziehung zwischen dem Kunstwerk und dem
Ausstellungsraum konzentriert. Die Verbindung
zwischen einer Reihe von „Gemälden" und ihrer
spezifischen Umgebung zu finden, ist für mein
Schaffen von zentraler Bedeutung.

Tan Ping

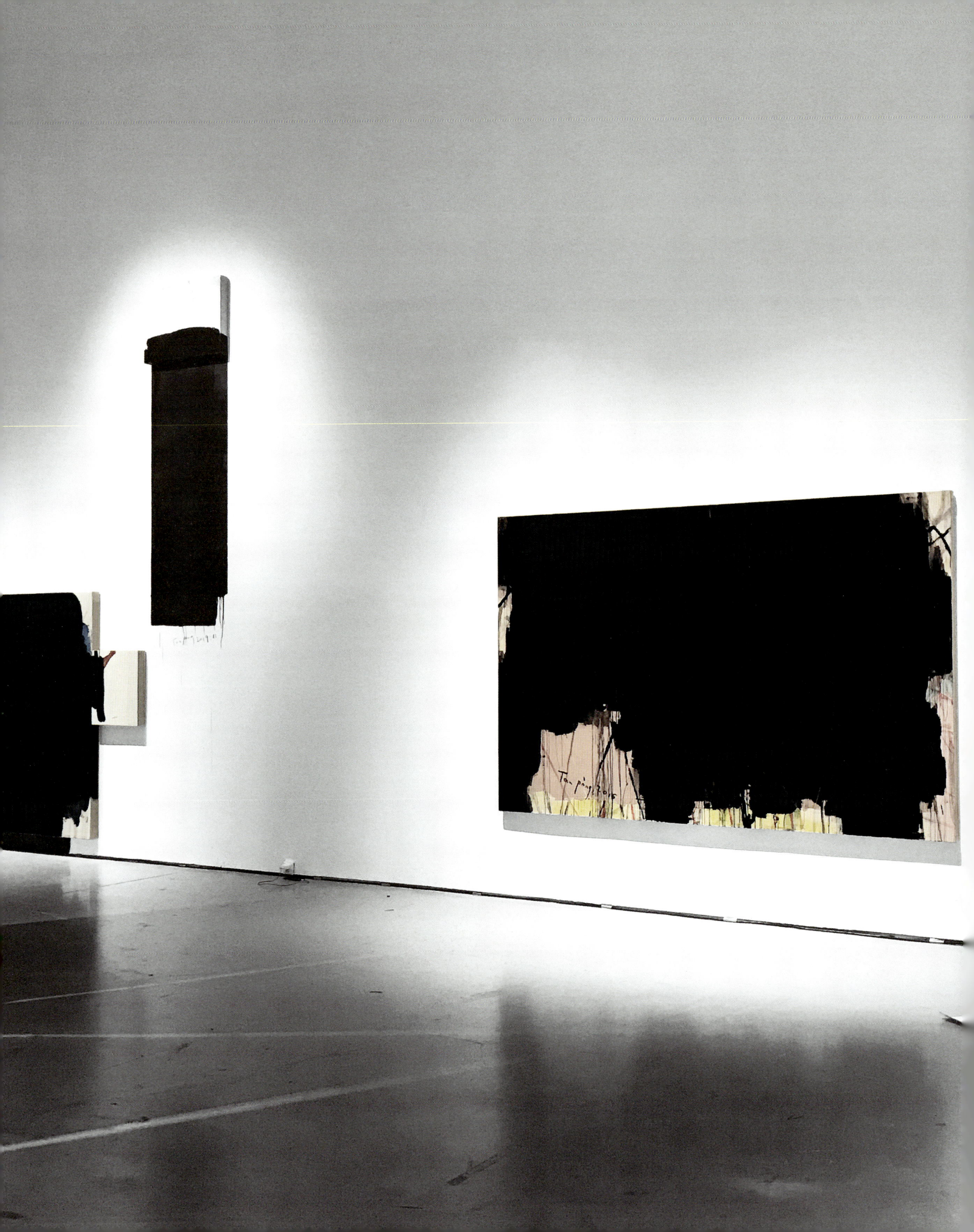

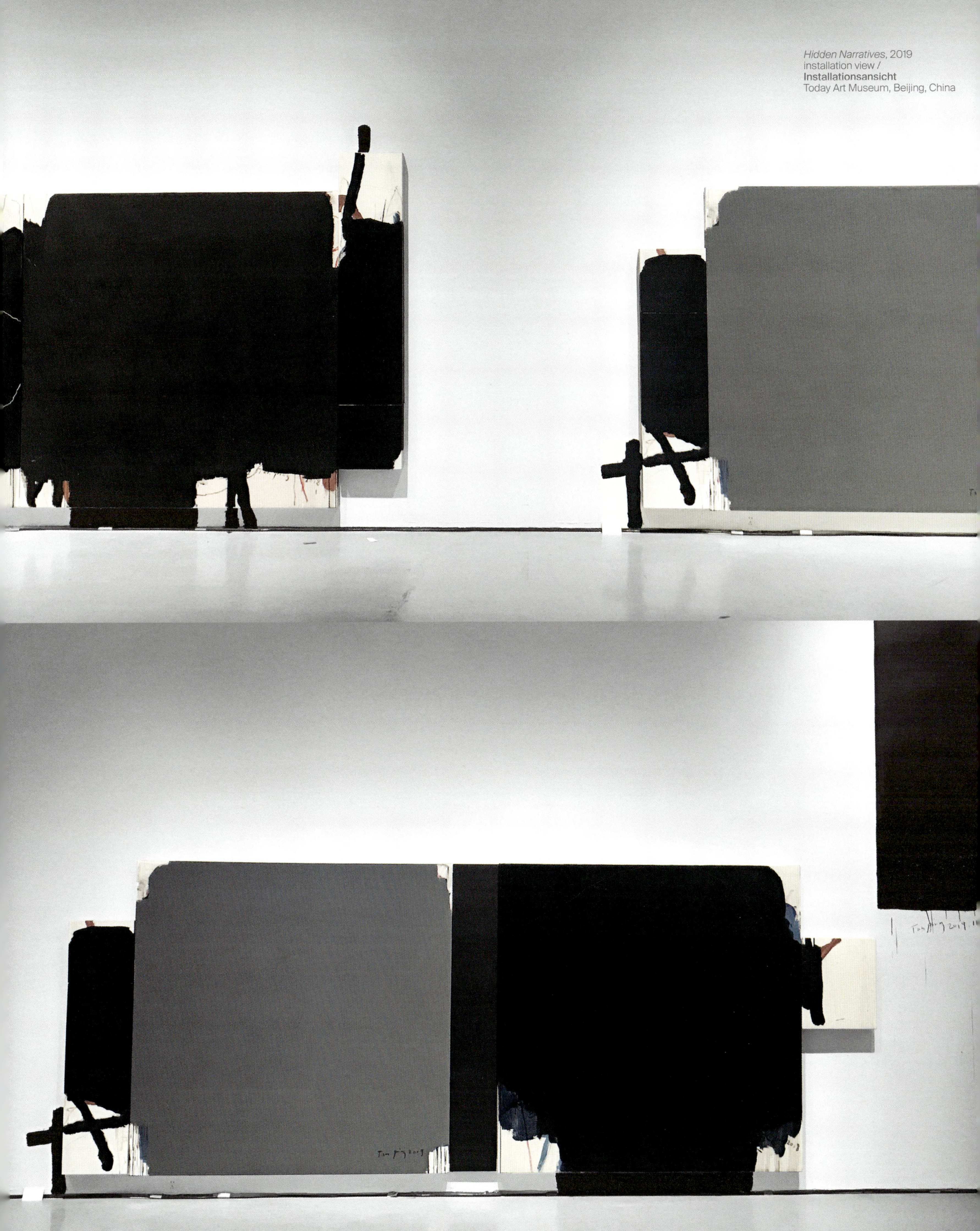

Hidden Narratives, 2019
installation view /
Installationsansicht
Today Art Museum, Beijing, China

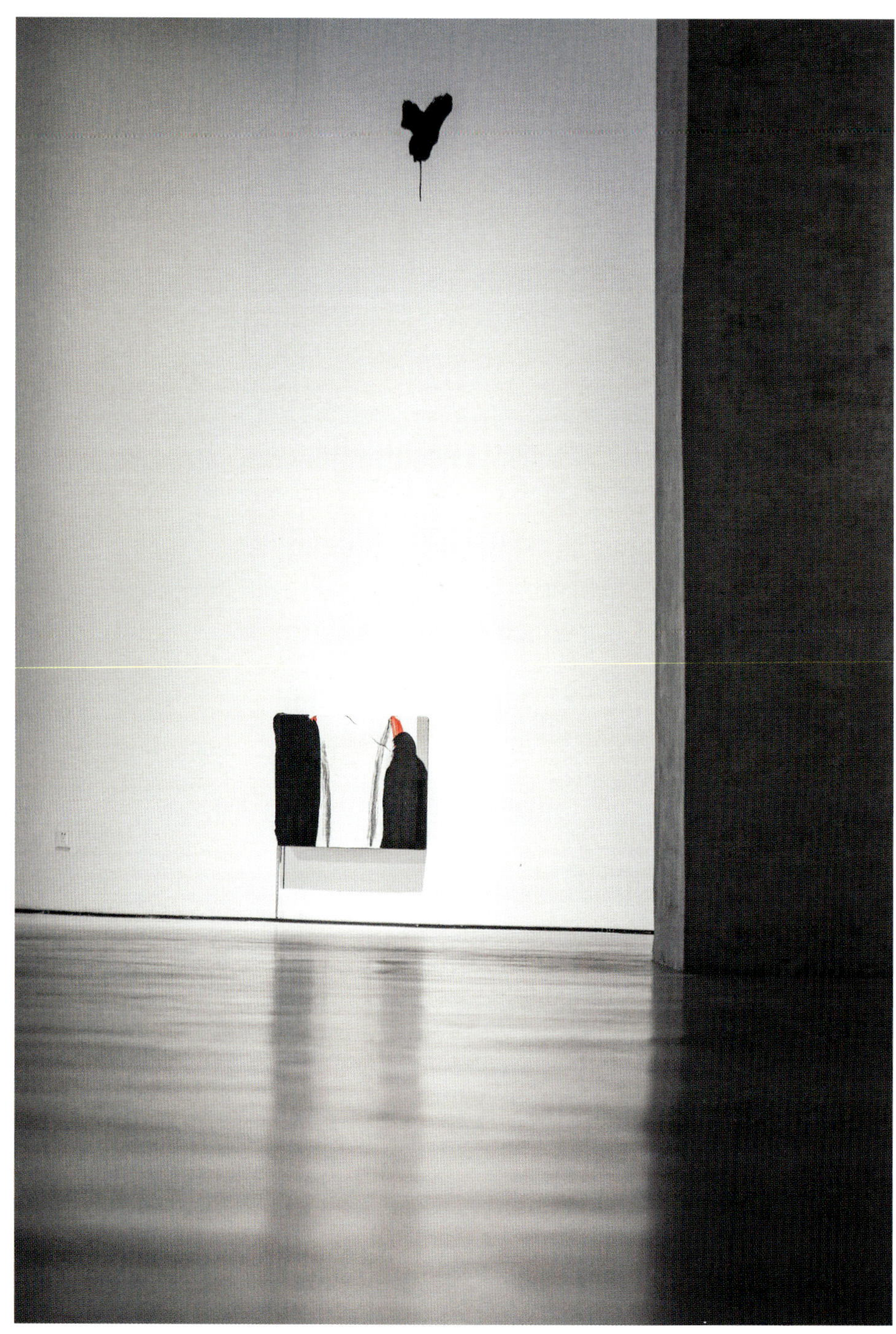

Shenzhen: Commemorating 2020

In 2020, a profoundly significant historical moment unfolded with the outbreak of the COVID-19 pandemic. The fear of the virus and the anxiety about the unknown led each of us to a deeper awareness of the sudden approach of death. I am revisiting an unfinished body of work, similar to the "Hidden Narratives" series, in a museum setting during these exceptional moments. In this act of commemoration, I am seeking to reassemble and find a fleeting inner peace in order to achieve a form of spiritual transcendence.

Tan Ping

*2020: Tan Ping
Site-Specific*, 2020
installation view /
Installationsansicht
Artron Art Center,
Shenzhen, China

Shenzhen: Gedenken an 2020

Im Jahr 2020 ereignete sich mit dem
Ausbruch der COVID-19-Pandemie ein
zutiefst bedeutsamer historischer Moment.
Die Angst vor dem Virus und die Angst vor
dem Unbekannten führten dazu, dass sich
jeder von uns des plötzlichen Herannahens
des Todes stärker bewusst wurde. In diesen
außergewöhnlichen Momenten schaue ich
mir ein unvollendetes Werk, ähnlich der Serie
„Hidden Narratives", in einem Museumsumfeld
noch einmal an. In diesem Akt des Gedenkens
versuche ich, einen flüchtigen inneren Frieden
wieder zusammenzusetzen und zu finden,
um eine Form spiritueller Transzendenz zu
erreichen.

Tan Ping

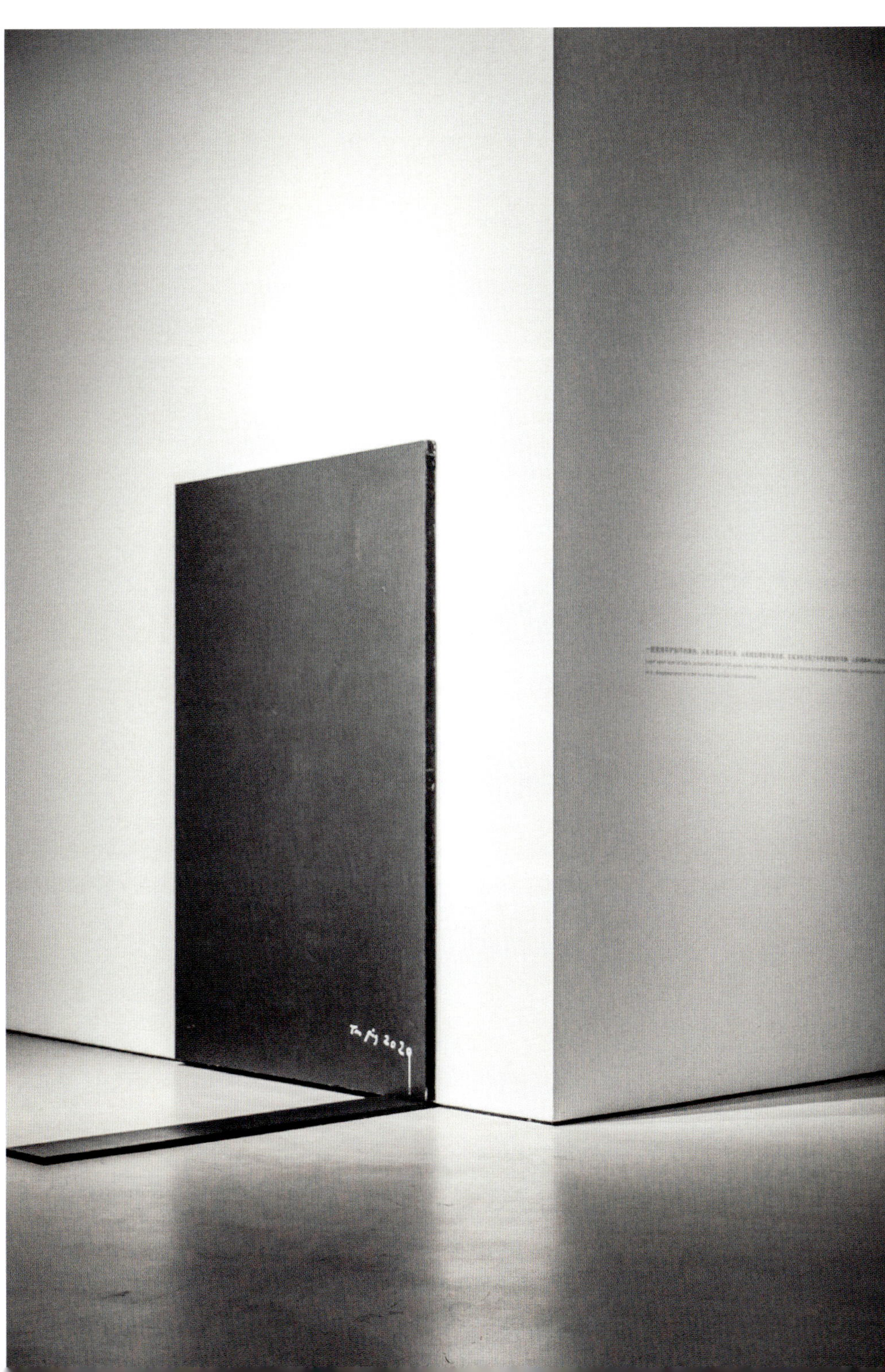

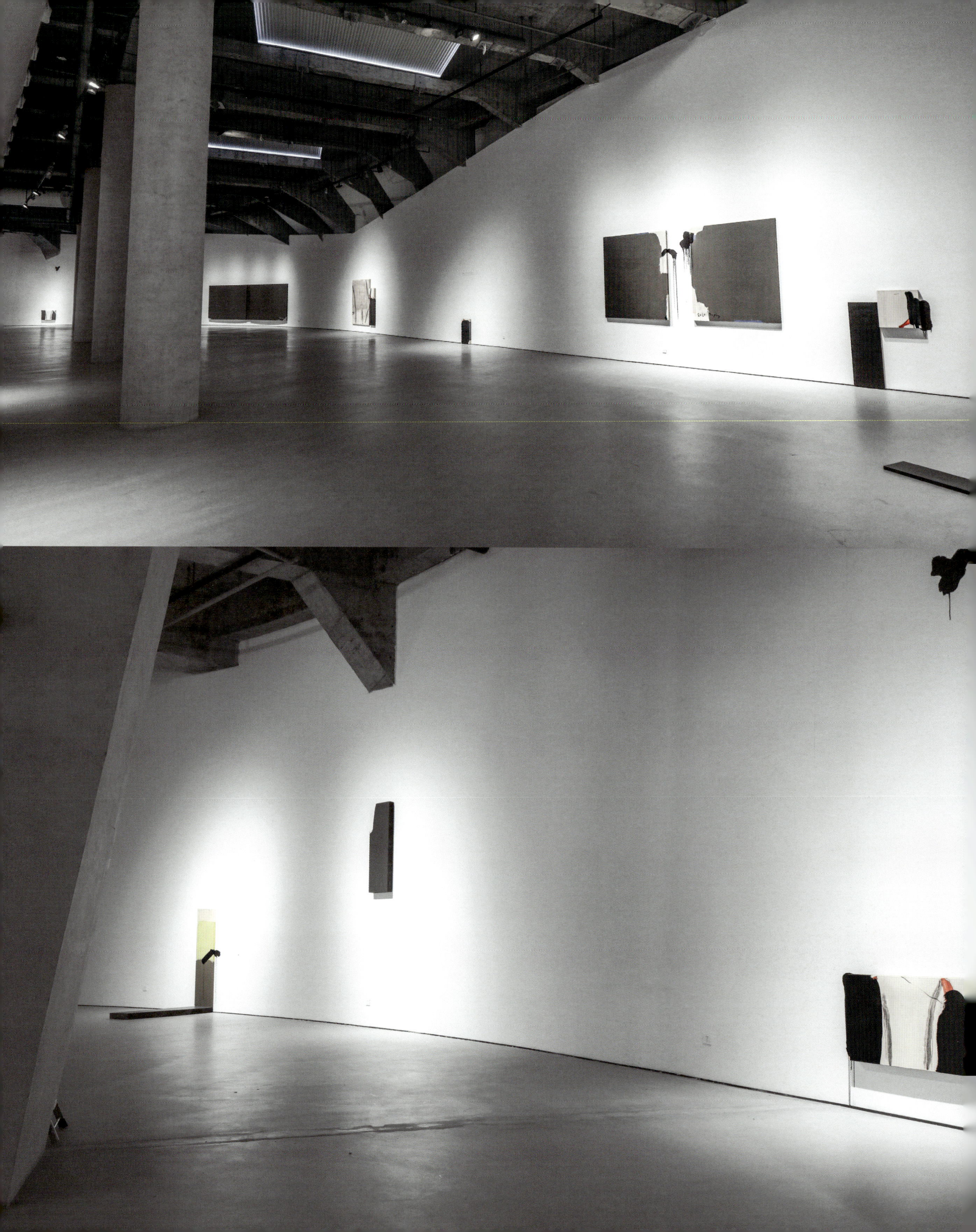

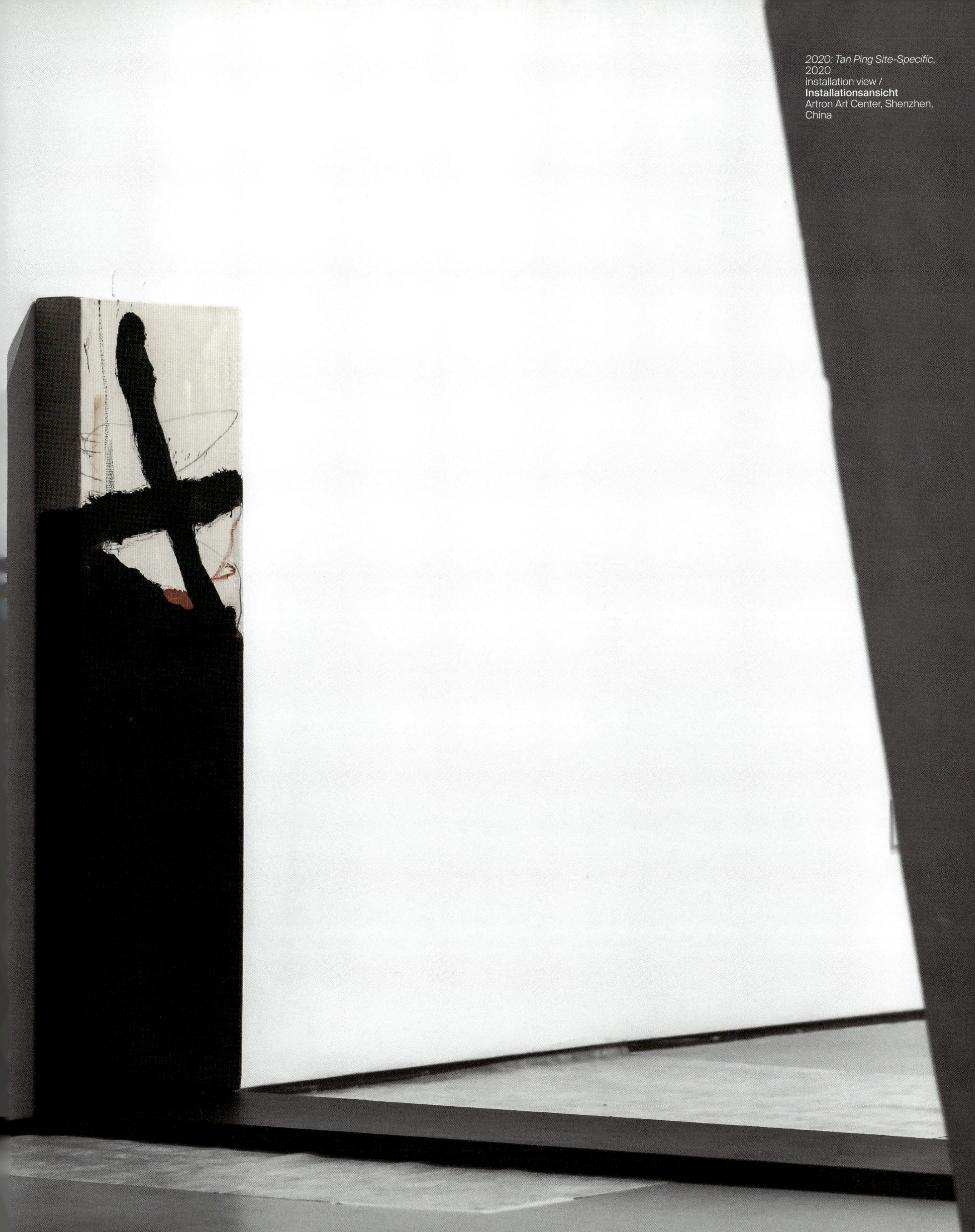

2020: Tan Ping Site-Specific,
2020
installation view /
Installationsansicht
Artron Art Center, Shenzhen,
China

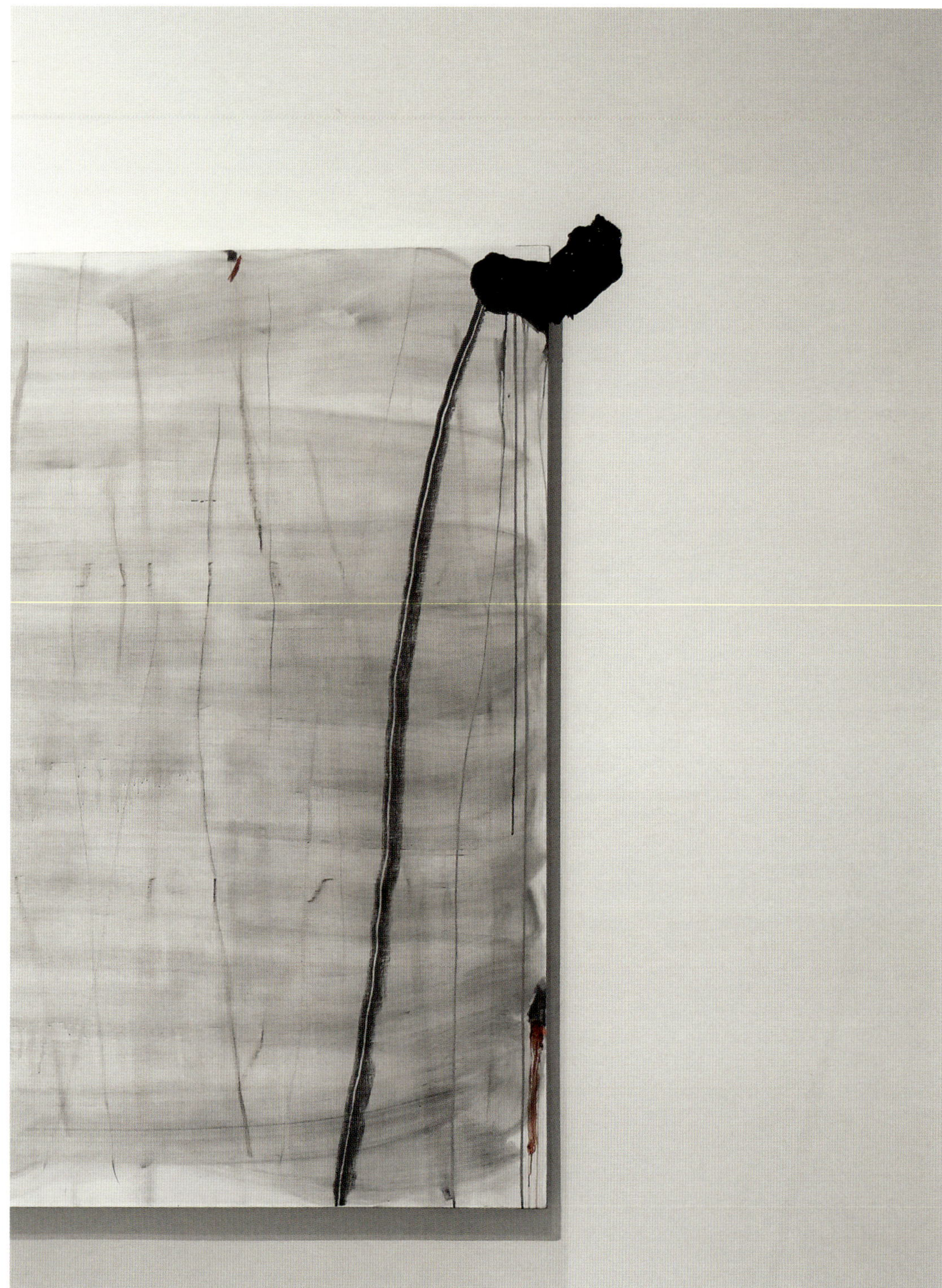

Beijing: Farewell 2022

The series "Farewell 2022", exhibited at Yuan Art
Museum, is a continuation of "Commemorating
2020". The gallery resembles a square box, where
standing inside feels like being in a square well.
This time, I hung the same set of works at the top
of the 7-meter-high walls. As you look up, a sense
of losing the future naturally arises.

Tan Ping

Peking: Abschied 2022

Die im Yuan Art Museum ausgestellte Serie „Lebewohl 2022" ist eine Fortsetzung von „Gedenktag 2020". Die Galerie ähnelt einer quadratischen Box, in der man sich wie in einem quadratischen Brunnen fühlt. Dieses Mal habe ich die gleiche Reihe von Werken oben an den 7 Meter hohen Wänden aufgehängt. Wenn man nach oben blickt, entsteht natürlich ein Gefühl, die Zukunft zu verlieren.

Tan Ping

2020: Tan Ping Site-Specific, 2020
installation view /
Installationsansicht
Artron Art Center, Shenzhen, China

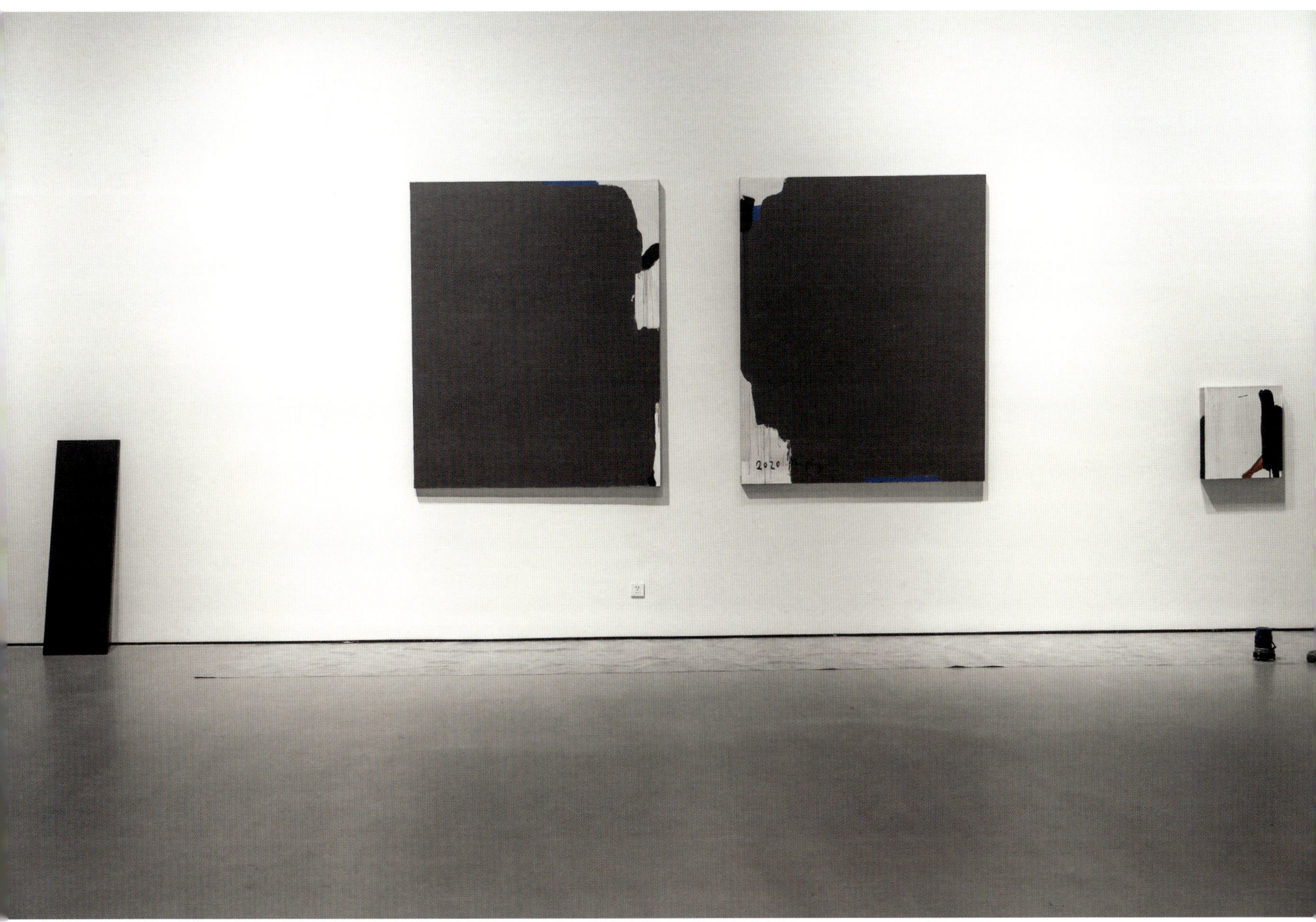

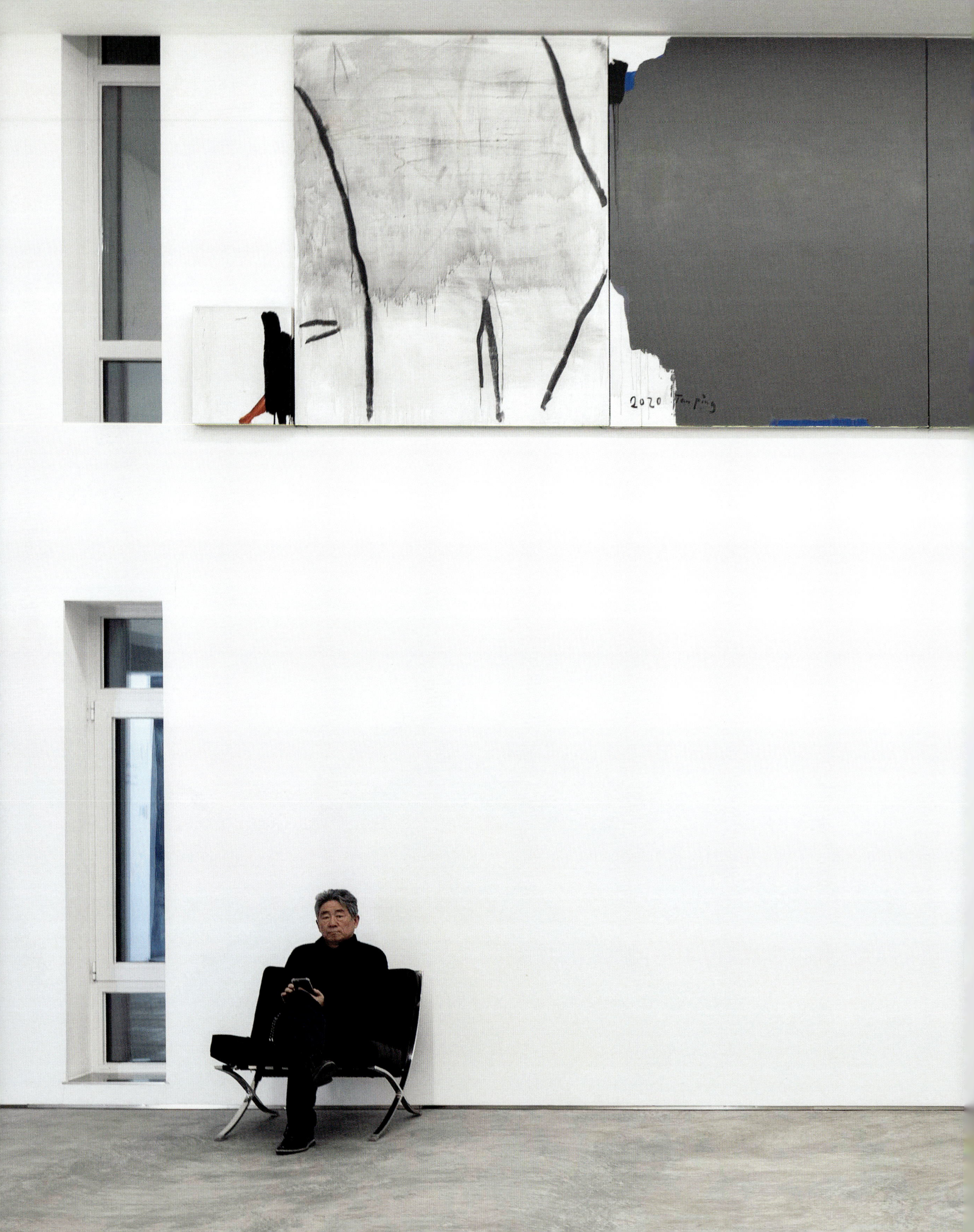
2020 Tan ping

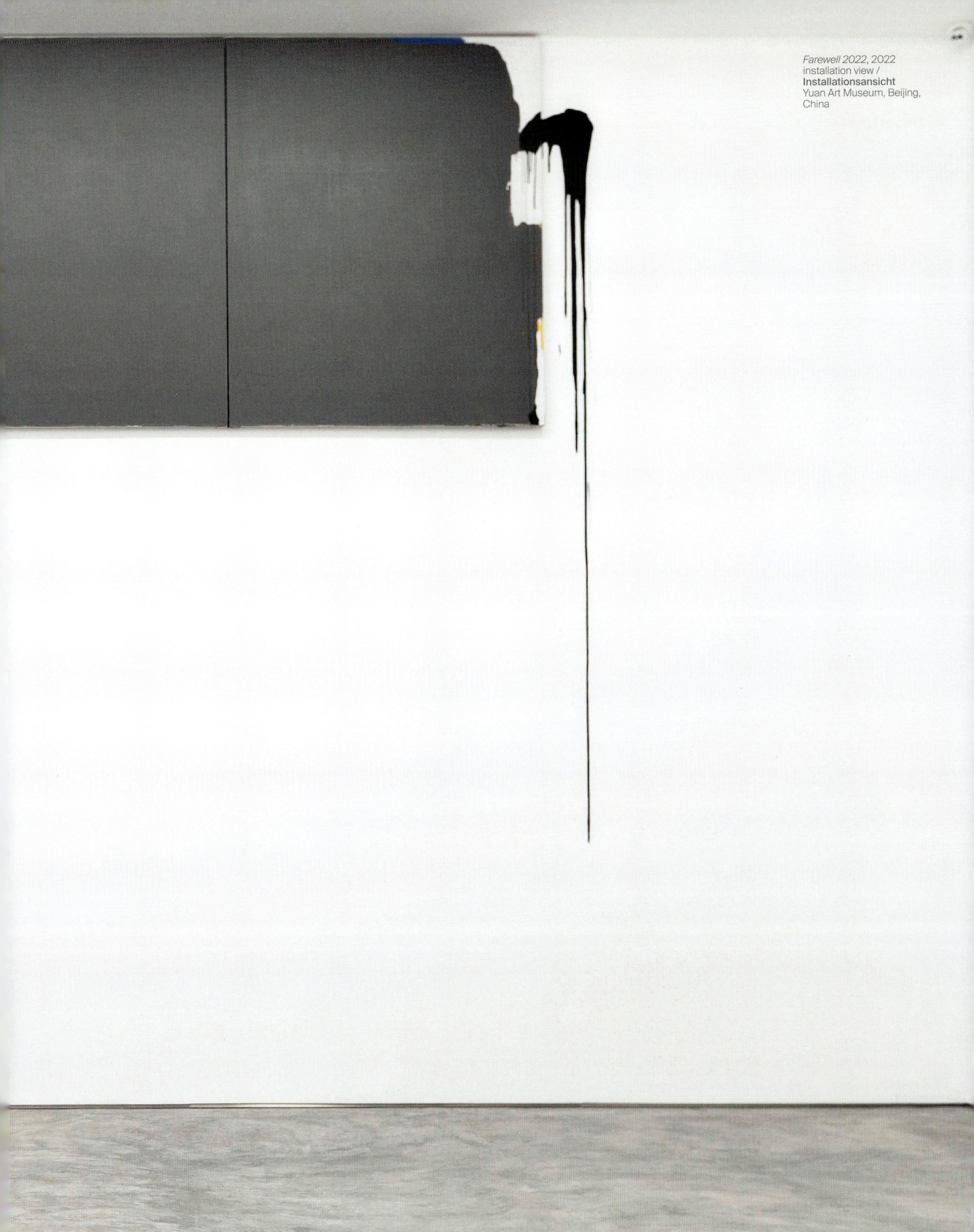

Farewell 2022, 2022
installation view /
Installationsansicht
Yuan Art Museum, Beijing,
China

Farewell 2022, 2022
installation view /
Installationsansicht
Yuan Art Museum, Beijing,
China

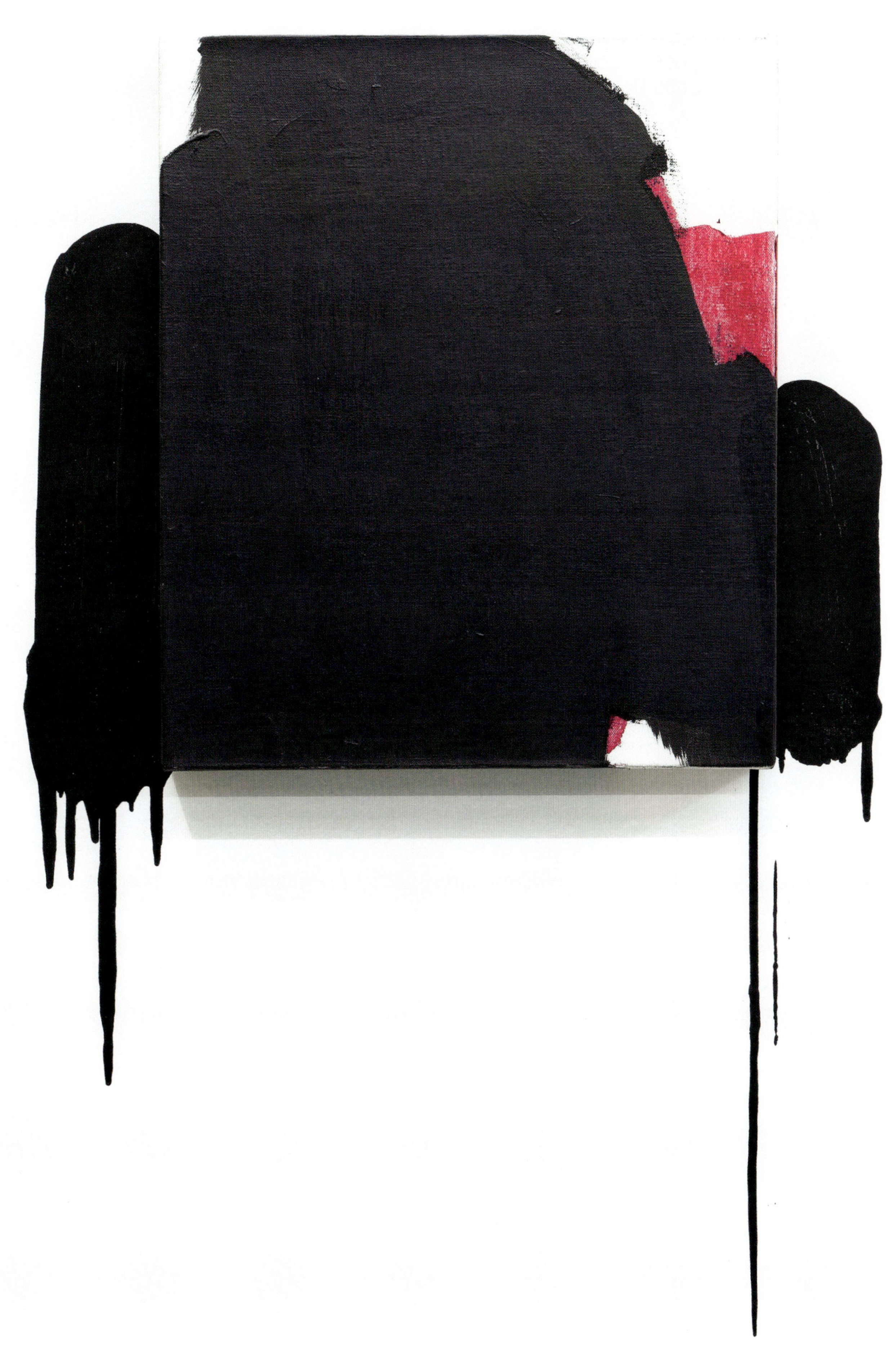

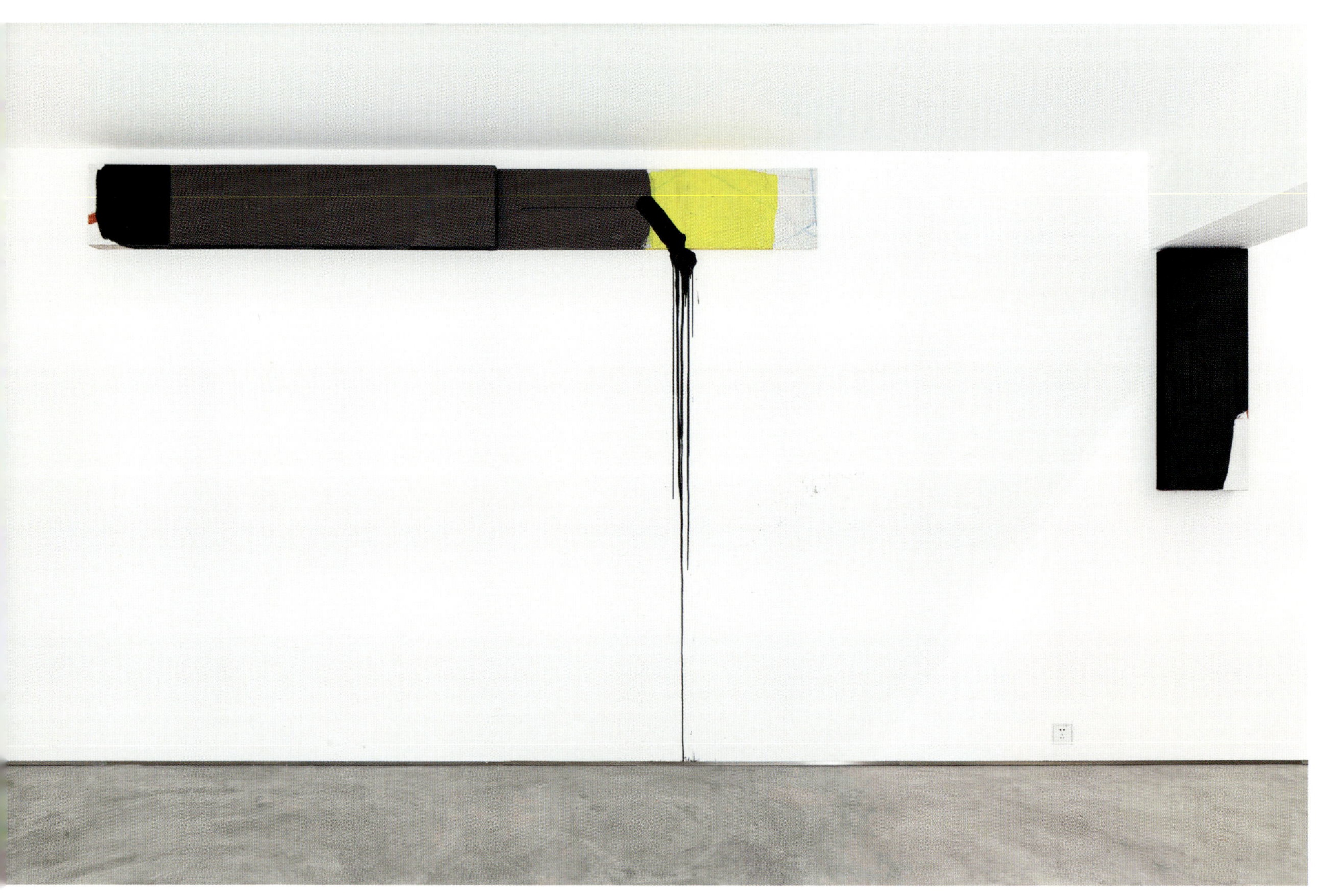

Farewell 2022, 2022
installation view /
Installationsansicht
Yuan Art Museum, Beijing,
China

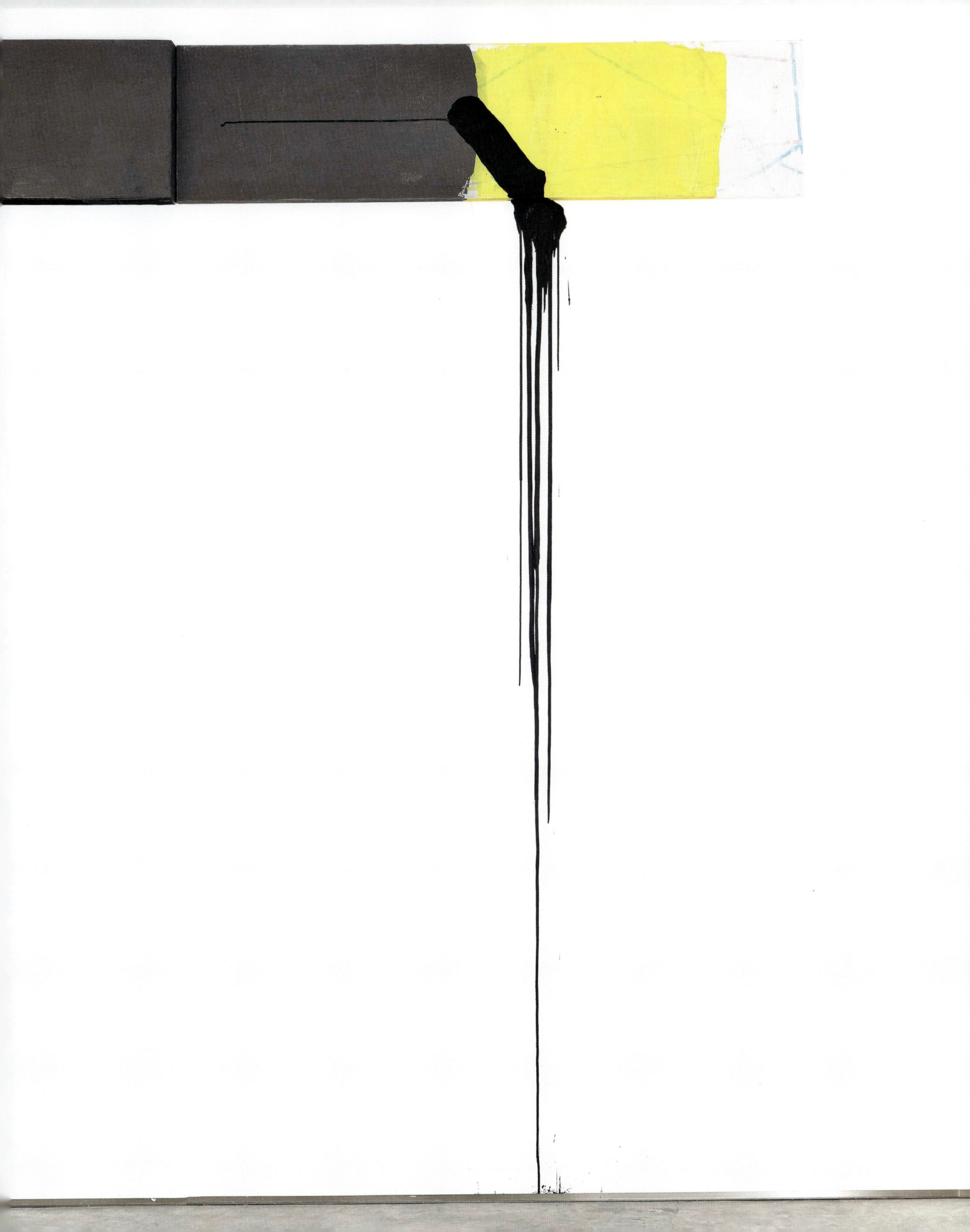

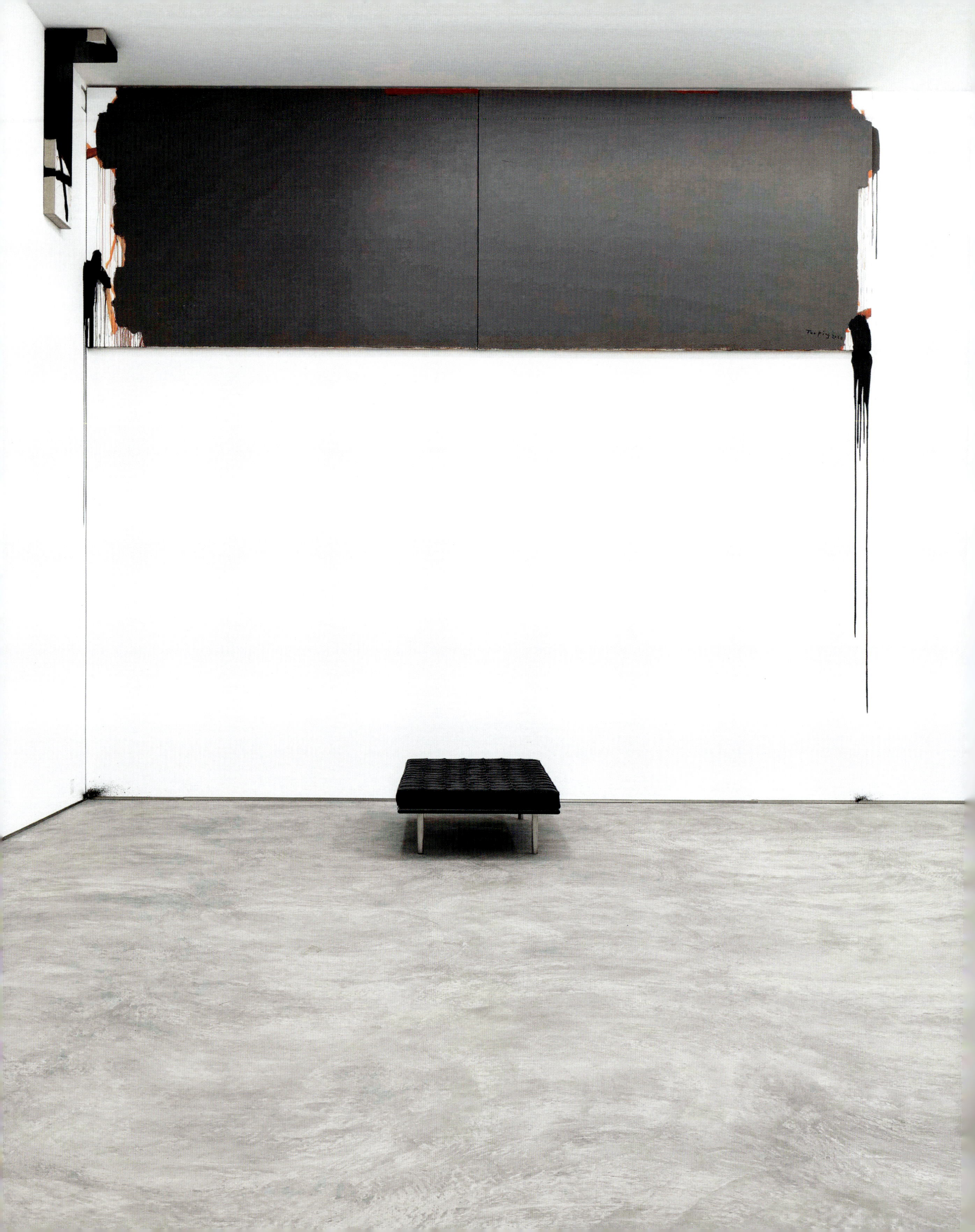

Farewell 2022, 2022
installation view /
Installationsansicht
Yuan Art Museum, Beijing,
China

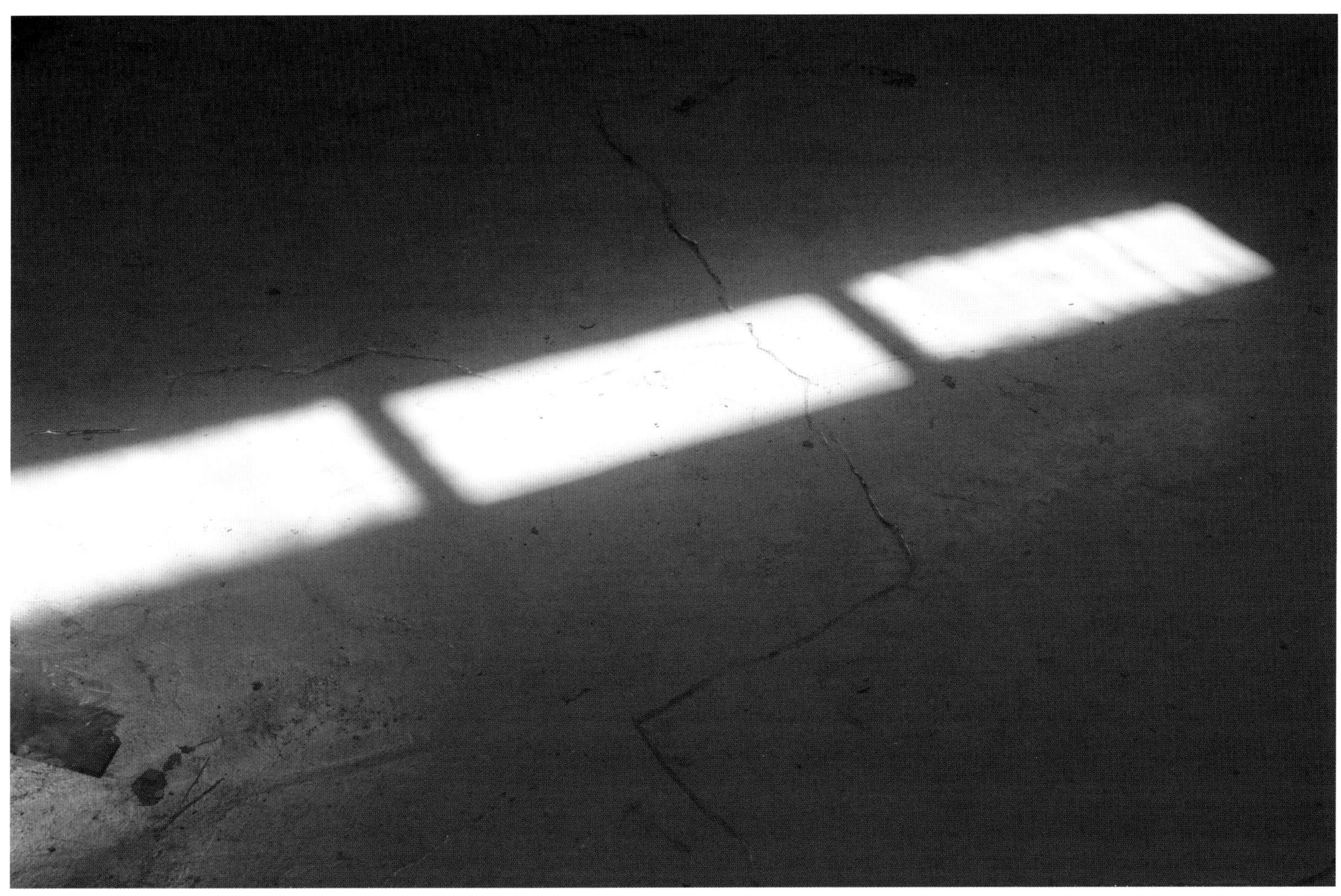

Überlauf und Naht

Painting as Inner Action

Simplicity means granting painting the potential for unspoken possibilities—a chance for it to continually unleash its own power. Tan Ping consistently channels his energy into his work, painting relentlessly, with painting and non-painting materials continuously interacting and alternating without pause. It is well known that art constantly progresses, and painting cannot remain fixed in a set procedure. This is the core element of the ever-evolving nature of Tan Ping's art, reflected in his many works from different periods.

Driven by a truly romantic élan, gesture in informal art aimed to recreate a whole vision of the world through the problematic experience of the fragment: if the world escaped a global outlook, nevertheless the action painter's vigorous gesture has tried to put together reality's broken pieces in some sort of exciting and reassuring connection.

Tan Ping has passed through many stages of contemporary art research. His production is profuse and unconstrained; the points he reaches are never beautifully frozen results, rather an unceasing process of overcoming each artwork for the next. His idea of errance in painting is explained by his open and round movements always kept within the field of signs and color, constantly aiming to push against the skin of the painting, right to its stretching point: this is the place where the image becomes irreversible appearance. In this image nothing exists but the unreachable deep content of the unconscious that can only emerge as signs and colors on the canvas' surface.

Tan Ping is not at all interested in art as conquest: for him art is a transit place, since movement does not allow stable property. He rather believes in a mobile possession, in a non-violent use of the means, thus getting nearer to the new international painters' generation. If there is an acceptable distance between art and life, there's also a connection between the two: they're both ruled by the same unrestrained stream and no other destiny is possible for contemporary artists but facing up to mutability. Tan Ping chooses to split up the pictorial matter in order to handle this mutability and mobility, making it similar to music, so that images are filled with inner content, yet light and suitable for representing links between eastern philosophy and western linguistic abstractions.

All in all, intensity and surprise can be declared as strategic aspects in Tan Ping's view, which is based on a global vision of different cultural references combining in the idea of art as something organic, maybe the very breath of humanity, which is necessarily filtered through stylistic exactitude and sensibility.

Achille Bonito Oliva

Art Critic, Art Historian

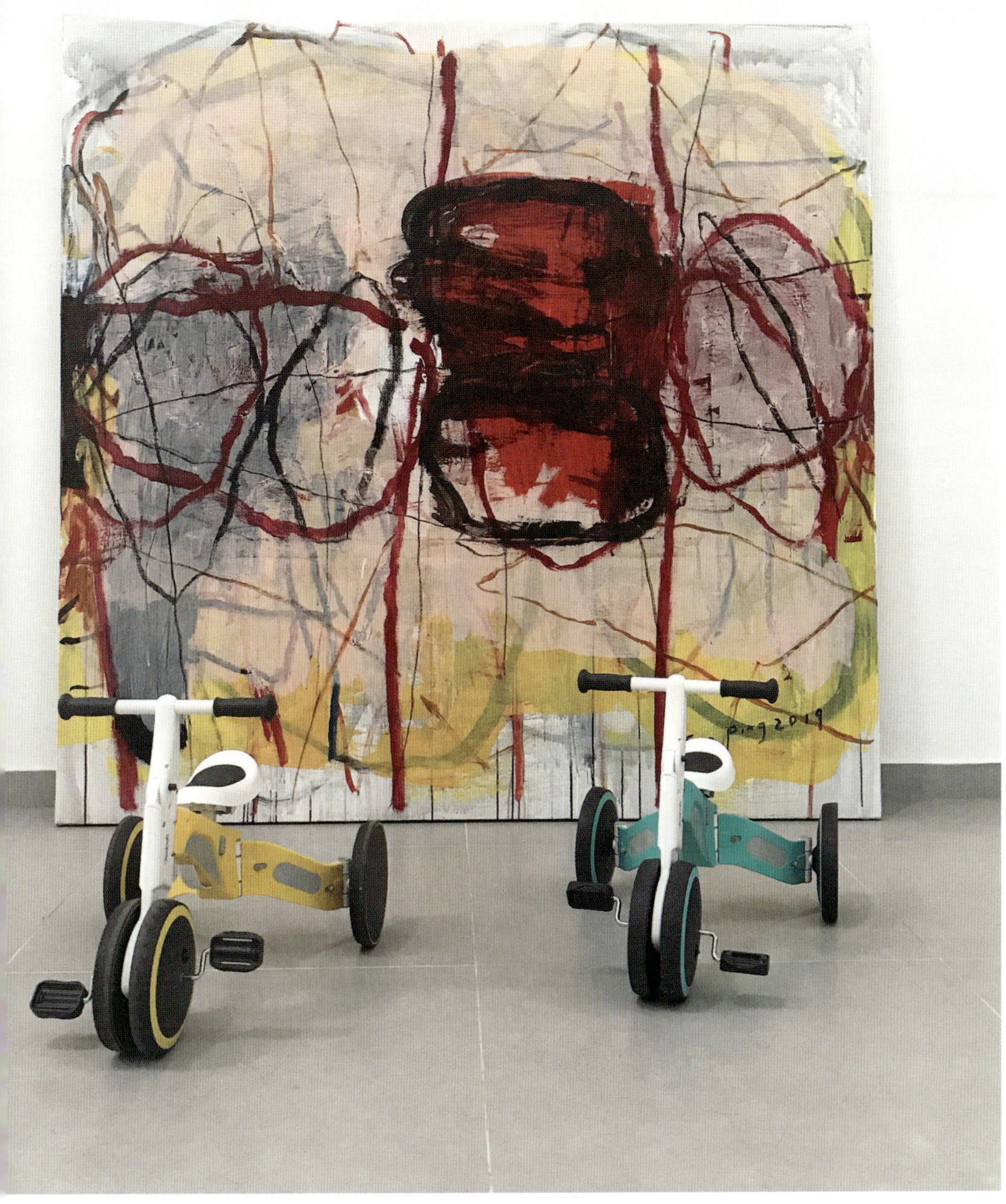

Malen als innere Handlung

Einfachheit bedeutet, der Malerei das Potenzial unausgesprochener Möglichkeiten zu geben – eine Chance, ihre eigene Kraft kontinuierlich zu entfesseln. Tan Ping kanalisiert seine Energie konsequent in seiner Arbeit, malt unermüdlich, wobei malerische und nicht-malerische Materialien kontinuierlich interagieren und sich ohne Pause abwechseln. Es ist bekannt, dass sich die Kunst ständig weiterentwickelt und die Malerei nicht in einem festgelegten Verfahren verharren kann. Dies ist das Kernelement der sich ständig weiterentwickelnden Natur von Tan Pings Kunst, die sich in seinen vielen Werken aus verschiedenen Epochen widerspiegelt. Angetrieben von einem wahrhaft romantischen Elan zielte die Geste der informellen Kunst darauf ab, durch die problematische Erfahrung des Fragments eine Gesamtvision der Welt wiederherzustellen: Auch wenn die Welt einer globalen Sichtweise entging, versuchte die energische Geste des Action-Malers dennoch, die zerbrochenen Teile der Realität in einer Art aufregender und beruhigender Verbindung zusammenzusetzen. Tan Ping hat viele Stadien der zeitgenössischen Kunstforschung durchlaufen. Seine Produktion ist üppig und ungezwungen; die Punkte, die er erreicht, sind nie schön eingefrorene Ergebnisse, sondern eher ein unaufhörlicher Prozess der Überwindung jedes Kunstwerks für das nächste.

Seine Idee des Irrtums in der Malerei erklärt sich aus seinen offenen und runden Bewegungen, die immer im Feld der Zeichen und Farben bleiben und ständig darauf abzielen, gegen die Haut des Gemäldes zu drücken, bis zu seinem Dehnungspunkt: Dies ist der Ort, an dem das Bild zu einer irreversiblen Erscheinung wird. In diesem Bild existiert nichts als der unerreichbare tiefe Inhalt des Unterbewusstseins, der nur als Zeichen und Farben auf der Oberfläche der Leinwand erscheinen kann. Tan Ping ist überhaupt nicht an Kunst als Eroberung interessiert: Für ihn ist Kunst ein Transitort, da Bewegung kein stabiles Eigentum zulässt. Er glaubt eher an einen mobilen Besitz, an einen gewaltlosen Einsatz der Mittel und nähert sich so der neuen internationalen Malergeneration. Wenn es eine akzeptable Distanz zwischen Kunst und Leben gibt, gibt es auch eine Verbindung zwischen den beiden: Sie werden beide vom selben ungezügelten Strom beherrscht und für zeitgenössische Künstler ist kein anderes Schicksal möglich, als sich der Veränderlichkeit zu stellen. Um diese Veränderlichkeit und Mobilität zu verarbeiten, wählt Tan Ping eine Aufspaltung des Bildmaterials, die es der Musik ähnlich macht, sodass die Bilder mit innerem Inhalt gefüllt, aber dennoch leicht sind und sich zur Darstellung von Verbindungen zwischen östlicher Philosophie und westlichen sprachlichen Abstraktionen eignen. Insgesamt können Intensität und Überraschung als strategische Aspekte in Tan Pings Sichtweise bezeichnet werden, die auf einer globalen Vision verschiedener kultureller Referenzen basiert, die sich in der Idee der Kunst als etwas Organisches vereinen, vielleicht als der Atem der Menschheit selbst, der notwendigerweise durch stilistische Genauigkeit und Sensibilität gefiltert wird.

Achille Bonito Oliva
Kunstkritiker, Kunsthistoriker

Überlauf und Naht

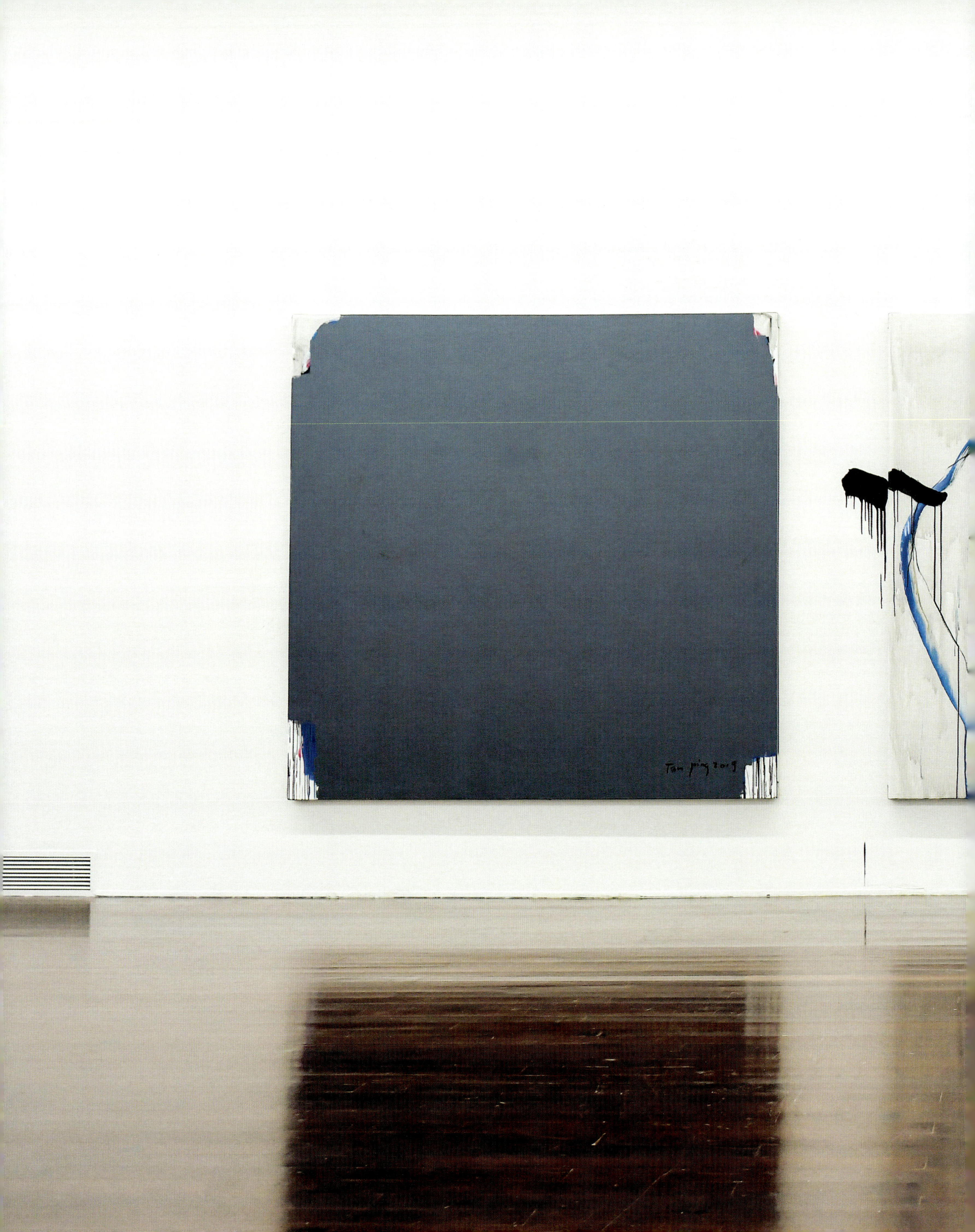

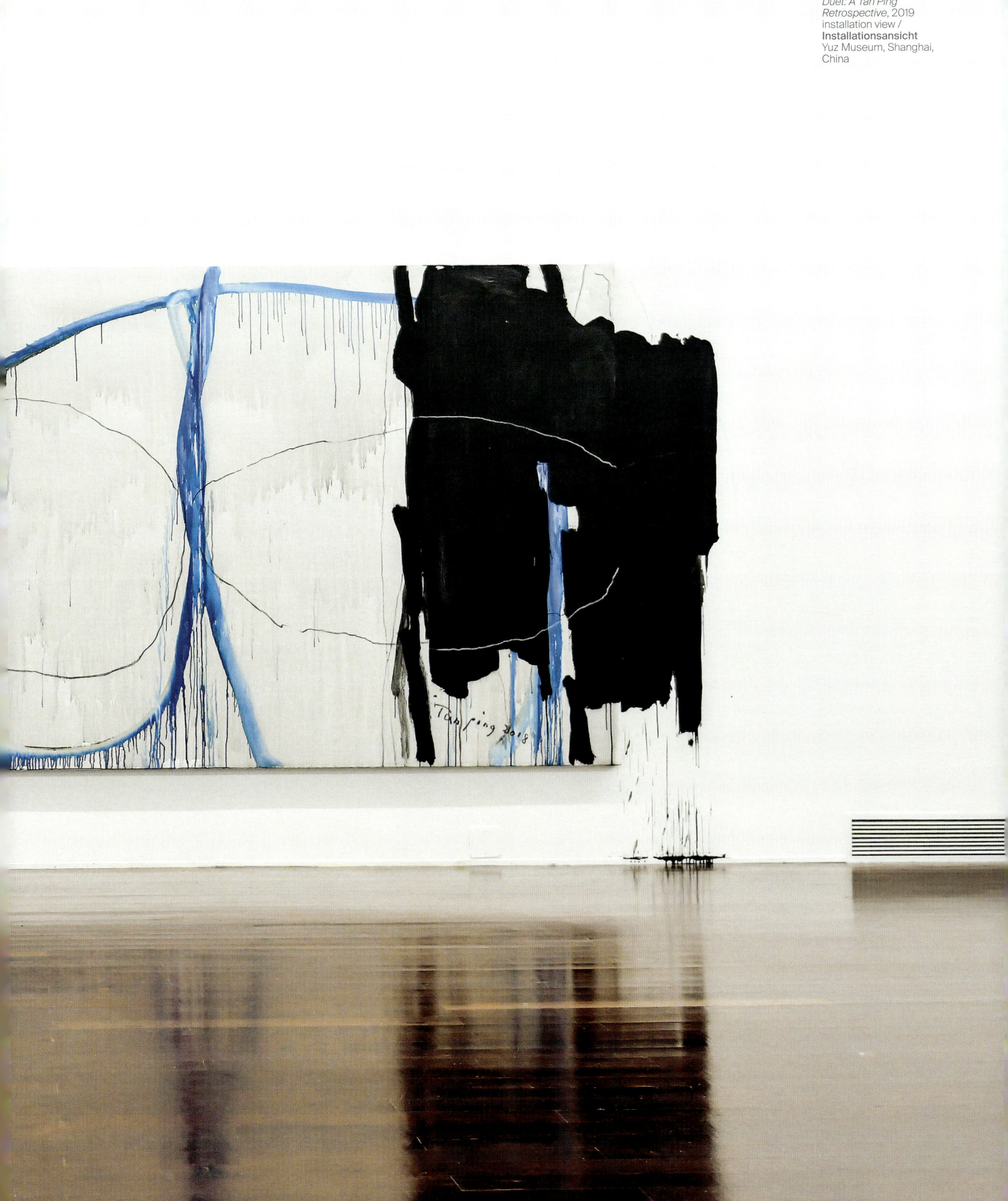

Duet: A Tan Ping
Retrospective, 2019
installation view /
Installationsansicht
Yuz Museum, Shanghai,
China

Chronology
Chronologie

1960

Born in Chengde, Hebei Province, China, Tan Ping spent his childhood in Yantai, Shandong, before returning to Chengde to be with his parents at the age of six. His mother, a gynecologist at Chengde Medical College, was highly talented in painting. In an era with limited medical resources, she took on the task of creating illustrative charts for the college's gynecology teaching. Tan Ping's early passion for painting is closely linked to his mother's influence.

Tan Ping wurde in Chengde in der chinesischen Provinz Hebei geboren und verbrachte seine Kindheit in Yantai in Shandong, bevor er im Alter von sechs Jahren nach Chengde zurückkehrte, um bei seinen Eltern zu sein. Seine Mutter, eine Gynäkologin am Chengde Medical College, war sehr talentiert in der Malerei. In einer Zeit mit begrenzten medizinischen Ressourcen übernahm sie die Aufgabe, illustrative Diagramme für den Gynäkologieunterricht des Colleges zu erstellen. Tan Pings frühe Leidenschaft für die Malerei ist eng mit dem Einfluss seiner Mutter verbunden.

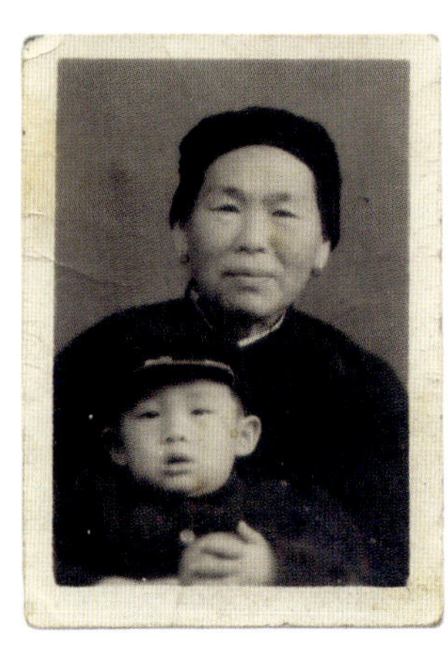

1

1973

Tan Ping's mother became conscious in developing his artistic talents. At the age of 13, Tan Ping started formal instruction in drawing under a mentor.

Tan Pings Mutter wurde sich der Förderung seines künstlerischen Talents bewusst. Im Alter von 13 Jahren begann Tan Ping mit dem formellen Zeichenunterricht bei einem Mentor.

1975

At the age of 15, Tan Ping was selected as a key member of the Youth Creation Group at the Chengde Cultural Center, where he used his spare time for thematic artistic creation. It was during this period that he completed his first work, a watercolor painting titled Double Bridges are Easy

Im Alter von 15 Jahren wurde Tan Ping als wichtiges Mitglied der Jugendkreationsgruppe am Chengde Cultural Center ausgewählt, wo er seine Freizeit für thematische künstlerische Kreationen nutzte. In dieser Zeit vollendete er sein erstes Werk, ein Aquarell mit dem Titel

Fig. / **Abb**. 1. Family photo / **Familienfoto**, 1963

Fig. / **Abb**. 2. Tan Ping at the / **am** Central Academy of Fine Arts in Beijing, 1980

Fig. / **Abb**. 3. "Tibetan" series, 1984

to Cross, but the Single Log is Difficult. In 1978, his work When I Grow Up, I Will Also Build Tall Buildings won third place in the National Youth Art Exhibition.

„Doppelte Brücken sind leicht zu überqueren, aber der einzelne Baumstamm ist schwer". 1978 gewann sein Werk „Wenn ich groß bin, werde ich auch hohe Gebäude bauen" den dritten Platz bei der Nationalen Jugendkunstausstellung.

1977

The college entrance exams were reinstated, and the Central Academy of Fine Arts in Beijing began to accept new students. Tan Ping prepared for the entrance exams.

Die Aufnahmeprüfungen für das College wurden wieder eingeführt und die Zentralakademie der Schönen Künste in Peking begann, neue Studenten aufzunehmen. Tan Ping bereitete sich auf die Aufnahmeprüfungen vor.

1980

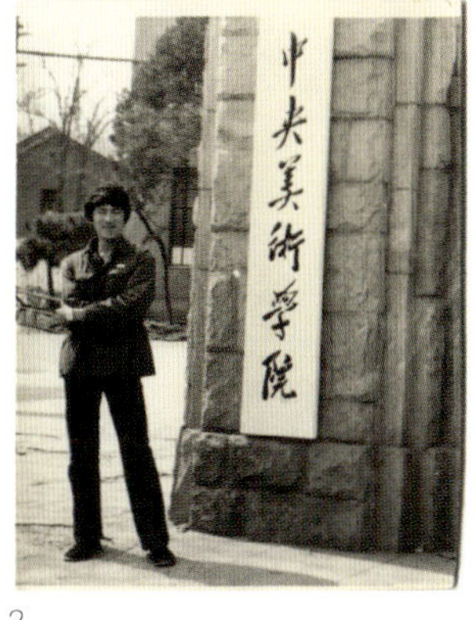

2

Tan Ping achieved the highest scores of 95 in both drawing and color courses, gaining admission to the Printmaking Department of the Central Academy of Fine Arts. Starting his studies in 1980, Tan Ping was not interested in the prevailing realist art style of the time. Instead, he devoted himself to experimenting with and exploring visual forms and languages.

Tan Ping erreichte die Höchstpunktzahl von 95 in den Zeichen- und Malkursen und wurde in die Druckgrafikabteilung der Zentralakademie der Schönen Künste aufgenommen. Als Tan Ping 1980 sein Studium begann, interessierte er sich nicht für den damals vorherrschenden realistischen Kunststil. Stattdessen widmete er sich dem Experimentieren und Erforschen visueller Formen und Sprachen.

1982

In his second year of the academy, after joining the etching studio, Tan Ping spent more time focusing on oil painting, which offered a more direct expression and greater creative freedom.

In seinem zweiten Jahr an der Akademie, nachdem er in das Radierstudio eingetreten war, konzentrierte sich Tan Ping mehr auf die Ölmalerei, die einen direkteren Ausdruck und größere kreative Freiheit bot.

1983

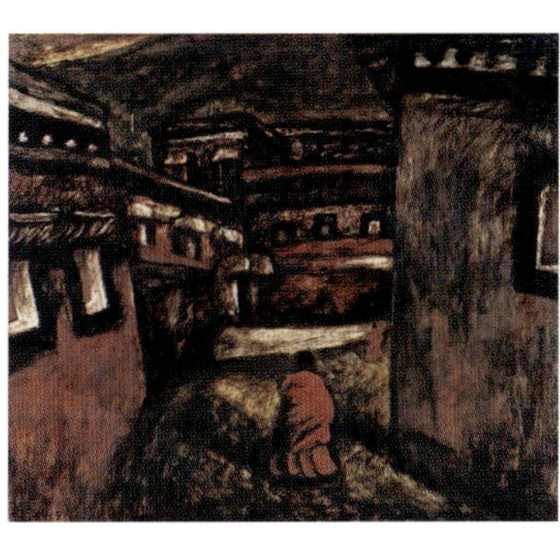

3

Tan Ping began preparing his graduation project, a series of copperplate engravings titled "Miner" series. Influenced by the work of German printmaker Käthe Kollwitz, Tan Ping focused on conveying solid forms and a strong sense of "light" in his copperplate creations. He intentionally removed themes and narratives, using stark black-and-white contrasts and the depiction of miners' various postures to express the desire for life and the fear of death he experienced in the mines. In another set of his graduation works, "Tibetan" series, Tan Ping depicted the intense twilight of the plateau and the heavy red walls of temples, highlighting the primitive vitality of life in Tibet as he had inwardly experienced.

Tan Ping begann mit der Vorbereitung seines Abschlussprojekts, einer Reihe von Kupferstichen mit dem Titel „Bergmann". Beeinflusst von der Arbeit der deutschen Druckgrafikerin Käthe Kollwitz konzentrierte sich Tan Ping in seinen Kupferstichen auf die Vermittlung fester Formen und eines starken „Licht"-Gefühls. Er entfernte absichtlich Themen und Erzählungen und verwendete starke Schwarz-Weiß-Kontraste und die Darstellung verschiedener Körperhaltungen der Bergleute, um den Lebensdrang und die Todesangst auszudrücken, die er in den Minen erlebte. In einer anderen Reihe seiner Abschlussarbeiten, der „Tibetischen"-Serie, stellte Tan Ping die intensive Dämmerung des Plateaus und die schweren roten Wände der Tempel dar und betonte damit die primitive Vitalität des Lebens in Tibet, wie er es innerlich erlebt hatte.

1984

Tan Ping's graduation work, "Miner" series, received acclaim for its strong formal qualities Following graduation, he stayed on at the university as a faculty member.

Tan Pings Abschlussarbeit, die „Bergmann"-Serie, erhielt Anerkennung für ihre starken formalen Qualitäten. Nach seinem Abschluss blieb er als Fakultätsmitglied an der Universität.

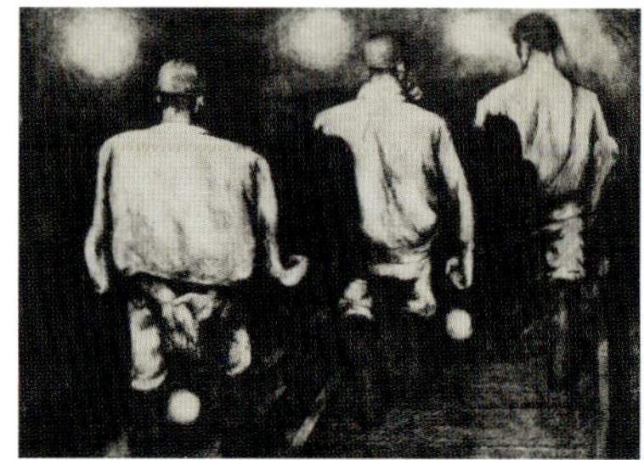
4

1986

Tan Ping created the "Black Sea" series, the "Great Wall" series, and the urban-themed work "View from the Back." These creations, which do not have explicit thematic references, reflect Tan Ping's genuine emotions and his pursuit of new artistic directions. Great Wall was featured as the cover image in the June issue of Fine Arts magazine.

Tan Ping schuf die Serien „Schwarzes Meer", „Große Mauer" und das urbane Werk „Ansicht von hinten". Diese Werke, die keine expliziten thematischen Bezüge aufweisen, spiegeln Tan Pings wahre Emotionen und sein Streben nach neuen künstlerischen Richtungen wider. „Große Mauer" war das Titelbild der Juni-Ausgabe des Fine Arts-Magazins.

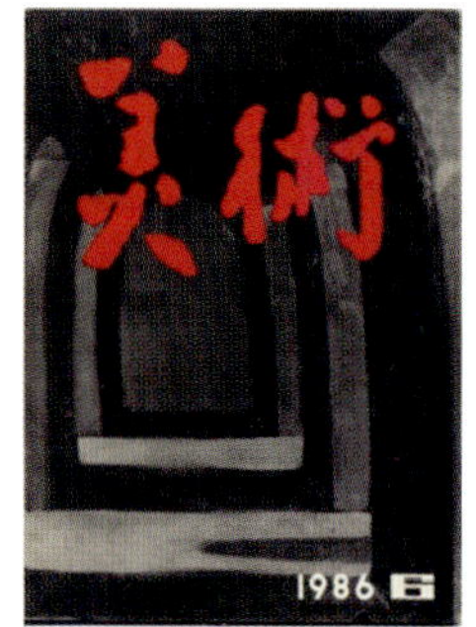
5

1987

Tan Ping married Teng Fei, who also graduated from the Printmaking Department of the Central Academy of Fine Arts.
He began working with etching. It was an etched copperplate, damaged by being left too long in the acid bath, that marked the beginning of Tan Ping's initial exploration into "abstract" language. That same year, he created a series of etchings titled "Abstract."

Tan Ping heiratete Teng Fei, die ebenfalls die Abteilung für Druckgrafik der Central Academy of Fine Arts absolvierte.
Er begann mit dem Ätzen. Es war eine geätzte Kupferplatte, die durch zu langes Liegen im Säurebad beschädigt wurde, die den Beginn von Tan Pings anfänglicher Erforschung der „abstrakten" Sprache markierte. Im selben Jahr schuf er eine Reihe von Radierungen mit dem Titel „Abstrakt".

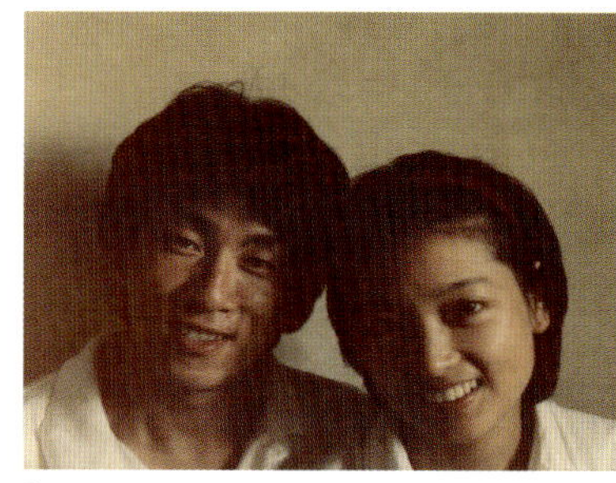
6

1988

At the Central Academy of Fine Arts faculty drawing exhibition held at the National Art Museum of China, Tan Ping presented his "Net" series of works, created using pencil rubbings. In contrast to the realistic sketches of his colleagues, Tan Ping's works offered a conceptual exploration of drawing. That same year, he began studying German at a foreign language institute in preparation for studying abroad. His son, Tan Tian, was born.

Auf der Zeichenausstellung der Fakultät der Central Academy of Fine Arts im National Art Museum of China präsentierte Tan Ping seine Werkreihe „Net", die mit Bleistiftabreibungen erstellt wurde. Im Gegensatz zu den realistischen Skizzen seiner Kollegen boten Tan Pings Werke eine konzeptuelle Erforschung des Zeichnens. Im selben Jahr begann er, an einem Fremdspracheninstitut Deutsch zu studieren, um sich auf ein Auslandsstudium vorzubereiten. Sein Sohn Tan Tian wurde geboren.

1989

Tan Ping received the DAAD (German Academic Exchange Service) Cultural and Arts Scholarship and went to study at the Free Painting Department of the Berlin University of the Arts. He was mentored by German Neo-Expressionist master H.K. Hödicke and Professor Klaus Fussmann. In 1989, Tan Ping witnessed the fall of the Berlin Wall and the reunification of Germany firsthand.

Tan Ping erhielt ein Kultur- und Kunststipendium des DAAD (Deutscher Akademischer Austauschdienst) und studierte an der Fakultät für Freie Malerei der Universität der Künste Berlin. Er wurde von dem deutschen Meister des Neoexpressionismus H.K. Hödicke und von Professor Klaus Fussmann betreut. 1989 erlebte Tan Ping den Fall der Berliner Mauer und die Wiedervereinigung Deutschlands aus erster Hand.

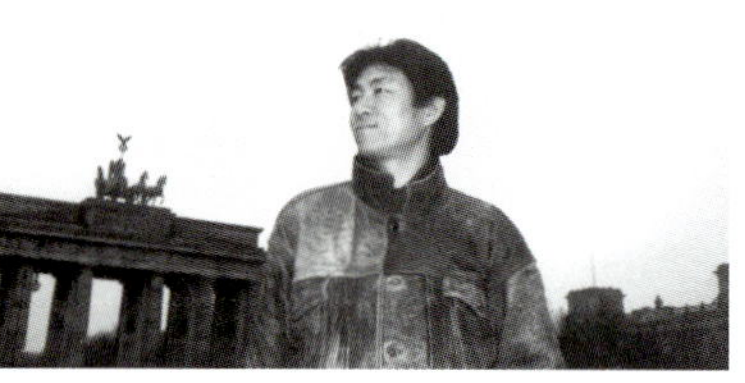
7

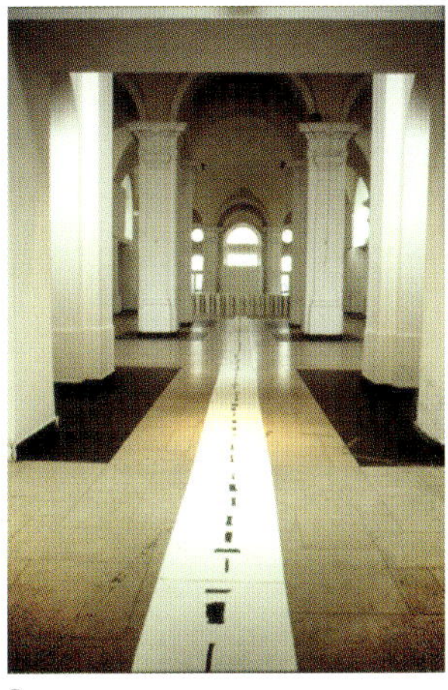

8

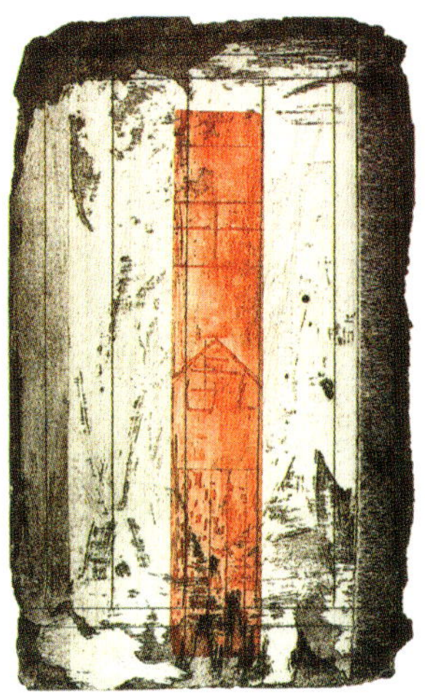

9

1991~1992

Tan Ping's solo exhibitions of printmaking were held successively at the Moench Gallery in Berlin, Germany. In 1994, his paintings were also featured in an exhibition at the Christof Weber Gallery in Berlin. His five years of study in Germany provided him with an opportunity to view his work from a new perspective. From the omnipresent red stamps in his early works to the widely discussed "Time" series created for his graduation at the Berlin University of the Arts, Tan Ping completed a journey from imitating forms to establishing a personal artistic identity.

Tan Pings Einzelausstellungen mit Druckgrafik fanden nacheinander in der Galerie Mönch in Berlin statt. 1994 wurden seine Gemälde auch in einer Ausstellung in der Galerie Christof Weber in Berlin gezeigt. Sein fünfjähriges Studium in Deutschland bot ihm die Gelegenheit, seine Arbeit aus einer neuen Perspektive zu betrachten. Von den allgegenwärtigen roten Stempeln in seinen frühen Werken bis hin zu der viel diskutierten „Time"-Serie, die er für seinen Abschluss an der Universität der Künste Berlin schuf, hat Tan Ping eine Reise von der Nachahmung von Formen zur Entwicklung einer persönlichen künstlerischen Identität hinter sich.

1994

Tan Ping graduated from the Berlin University of the Arts with a master's degree and a Meisterschule diploma. That autumn, he chose to return to the Central Academy of Fine Arts to continue teaching in the Printmaking Department.
Tan Ping held his first exhibition in China at the Beijing Contemporary Art Museum, showcasing the printmaking works he created in Berlin. These prints, which were based on visual experimentation and conceptual approaches, had a significant impact on the printmaking community at the time.

Tan Ping schloss sein Studium an der Universität der Künste Berlin mit einem Master und einem Meisterschülerdiplom ab. Im Herbst desselben Jahres beschloss er, an die Central Academy of Fine Arts zurückzukehren, um dort weiter in der Abteilung für Druckgrafik zu unterrichten.
Tan Ping veranstaltete seine erste Ausstellung in China im Beijing Contemporary Art Museum, wo er die Druckgrafiken zeigte, die er in Berlin geschaffen hatte. Diese Druckgrafiken, die auf visuellen Experimenten und konzeptuellen Ansätzen basierten, hatten damals einen erheblichen Einfluss auf die Druckgrafik-Community.

1995

Tan Ping experienced another pivotal moment in his life as he participated in the establishment of the Design Department of the Central Academy of Fine Arts. The challenge of creating a new design education system became one of his primary concerns and significantly influenced his subsequent artistic trajectory.

Tan Ping erlebte einen weiteren Wendepunkt in seinem Leben, als er an der Gründung der Designabteilung der Central Academy of Fine Arts teilnahm. Die Herausforderung, ein neues Design-Ausbildungssystem zu schaffen, wurde zu einem seiner Hauptanliegen und beeinflusste seine spätere künstlerische Laufbahn erheblich.

1997

Tan Ping created the "Modular Series" of etchings, incorporating principles from architecture and design into his printmaking. That same year, he, along with printmakers Su Xinping, Wang Huaxiang, and Zhou Jirong, founded the Sifang Studio, which focused on printmaking as its primary research and creative direction.

Tan Ping schuf die „Modular Series" von Radierungen, bei denen er Prinzipien aus Architektur und Design in seine Druckgrafik einfließen ließ. Im selben Jahr gründete er zusammen mit den Grafikern Su Xinping, Wang Huaxiang und Zhou Jirong das Sifang Studio, dessen Forschungs- und Kreativschwerpunkte die Grafik waren.

1999~2000

The group exhibitions of Sifang Studio were held successively at the Shanghai Art Museum and the Adenauer Foundation in Bonn, Germany. In 2000, Tan Ping's printmaking exhibition took place at the Berlin Art Loft. During this period, Tan Ping focused more on the "materiality" of his work. The "Calligraphy" series emerged, featuring minimalist works created using paper pulp and iron plates as materials.

Die Gruppenausstellungen des Sifang Studios fanden nacheinander im Shanghai Art Museum und in der Adenauer-Stiftung in Bonn statt. Im Jahr 2000 fand Tan Pings Grafikausstellung im Berliner Art Loft statt. In dieser Zeit konzentrierte sich Tan Ping mehr auf die „Materialität" seiner Arbeit. Die „Kalligraphie"-Serie entstand, die minimalistische Arbeiten umfasste, die aus Papierbrei und Eisenplatten als Materialien hergestellt wurden.

10

2002

The School of Design at the Central Academy of Fine Arts was officially established, and Tan Ping was appointed as its Dean.

Die School of Design an der Central Academy of Fine Arts wurde offiziell gegründet und Tan Ping wurde zu ihrem Dekan ernannt.

2003

Tan Ping began serving as the Vice President of the Central Academy of Fine Arts, overseeing teaching affairs. During this period, he created a series of woodblock prints featuring circular symbols.

Tan Ping wurde Vizepräsident der Central Academy of Fine Arts und war für die Lehrangelegenheiten zuständig. Während dieser Zeit schuf er eine Reihe von Holzschnitten mit kreisförmigen Symbolen.

2004

Tan Ping's father was diagnosed with cancer and underwent surgery to remove a tumor. The presence of cancer cells stimulated Tan Ping's artistic instincts. The "cells" began to gradually replace his earlier symbols of "circles". In 2005, this "Cell" series, which appeared highly abstract to viewers but particularly concrete to Tan Ping himself, was exhibited in a solo show at the National Art Museum of China.

Krebs wurde bei Tan Pings Vater diagnostiziert und er unterzog sich einer Operation zur Entfernung eines Tumors. Die Anwesenheit von Krebszellen stimulierte Tan Pings künstlerischen Instinkt. Die „Zellen" begannen allmählich seine früheren „Kreise"-Symbole zu ersetzen. 2005 wurde diese „Zellen"-Serie, die den Betrachtern sehr abstrakt, Tan Ping selbst jedoch besonders konkret erschien, in einer Einzelausstellung im National Art Museum of China gezeigt.

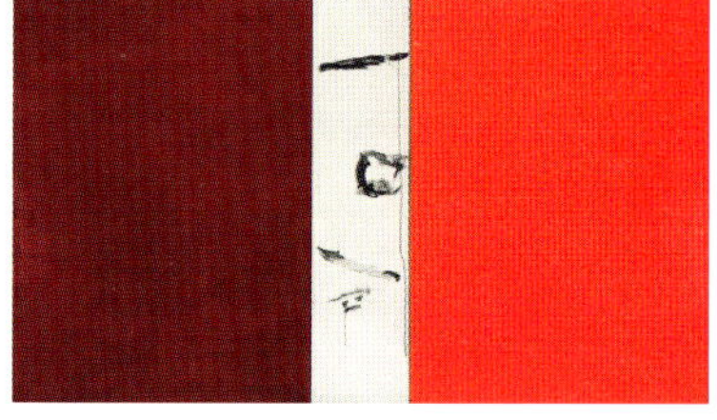
11

2006

"Ruins—Tan Ping and Zhu Jinshi Paintings" exhibition was held at the Today Art   Museum in China. The works featured in this exhibition were among the largest and most symbolic pieces in Tan Ping's painting during that period, establishing his position and influence in the field of abstract art in China.

Die Ausstellung „Ruinen – Gemälde von Tan Ping und Zhu Jinshi" fand im Today Art Museum in China statt. Die in dieser Ausstellung gezeigten Werke gehörten zu den größten und symbolträchtigsten Werken Tan Pings aus dieser Zeit und begründeten seine Stellung und seinen Einfluss auf dem Gebiet der abstrakten Kunst in China.

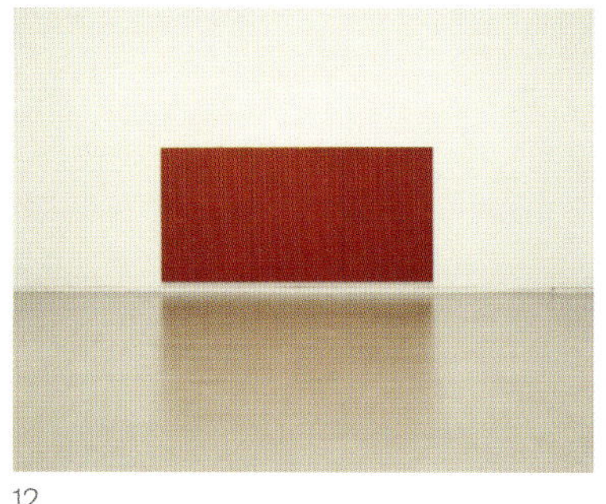
12

2008

In November, Tan Ping's painting exhibition "Sting and Sooth" opened at Today Art Museum, Beijing, showcasing works from the past five years. It was followed by a solo exhibition at the Shenzhen Art Museum. That same year, Tan Ping participated in

Im November wurde im Today Art Museum in Peking Tan Pings Gemäldeausstellung „Sting and Sooth" eröffnet, in der Werke der letzten fünf Jahre gezeigt wurden. Darauf folgte eine Einzelausstellung im Shenzhen Art Museum.

the "Yi School" exhibition, curated by Gao Minglu, which was held at Caixa-Forum Madrid, Spain. This exhibition highlighted thirty years of Chinese abstract art.

Im selben Jahr nahm Tan Ping an der von Gao Minglu kuratierten Ausstellung „Yi School" teil, die im Caixa-Forum Madrid in Spanien stattfand. Diese Ausstellung beleuchtete dreißig Jahre chinesischer abstrakter Kunst.

2010

Tan Ping's "60x60" series, which represents a further advancement in his conceptual approach to printmaking, was exhibited at various venues including the Central Academy of Fine Arts Art Museum and the Yuan Art Museum. That same year, Tan Ping participated in the group exhibition "The Great Celestial Abstraction - Chinese Art in 21st Century" curated by Italian curator Achille Bonito Oliva and held at the National Art Museum of China, which featured Chinese abstract artists.

Tan Pings „60x60"-Serie, die eine Weiterentwicklung seines konzeptuellen Ansatzes in der Druckgrafik darstellt, wurde an verschiedenen Orten ausgestellt, darunter im Central Academy of Fine Arts Art Museum und im Yuan Art Museum. Im selben Jahr nahm Tan Ping an der Gruppenausstellung „Die große himmlische Abstraktion – Chinesische Kunst im 21. Jahrhundert" teil, die vom italienischen Kurator Achille Bonito Oliva kuratiert und im Nationalen Kunstmuseum Chinas abgehalten wurde und chinesische abstrakte Künstler präsentierte.

2012

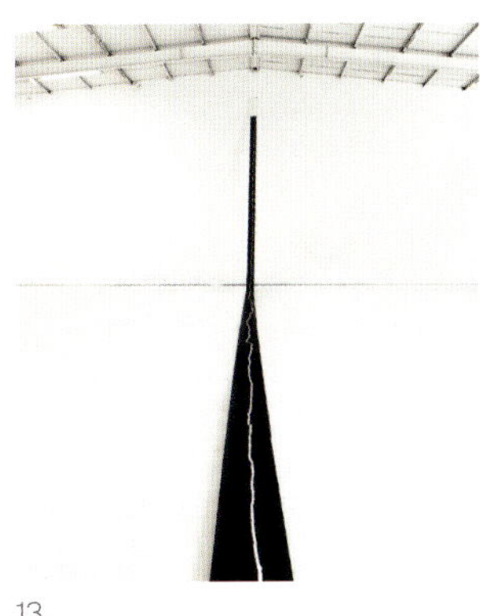

13

At his major solo exhibition at the National Art Museum of China, Tan Ping showcased the 40-meter-long woodblock print titled *+40m* in the museum's Round Hall. Other works from his forty-year artistic career were displayed in the two adjacent side halls as a backdrop to this piece. As the first solo exhibition of a Chinese abstract artist held in the Round Hall, it sparked widespread discussion within the art community. The display of this 40-meter-long piece in the Round Hall at the National Art Museum of China was unprecedented.

Bei seiner großen Einzelausstellung im National Art Museum of China zeigte Tan Ping den 40 Meter langen Holzschnitt mit dem Titel *+40m* in der Rundhalle des Museums. Andere Werke aus seiner vierzigjährigen künstlerischen Karriere wurden in den beiden angrenzenden Seitenhallen als Hintergrund zu diesem Werk ausgestellt. Als erste Einzelausstellung eines chinesischen abstrakten Künstlers in der Rundhalle löste sie innerhalb der Kunstszene weitreichende Diskussionen aus. Die Ausstellung dieses 40 Meter langen Werks in der Rundhalle des National Art Museum of China war beispiellos.

2013

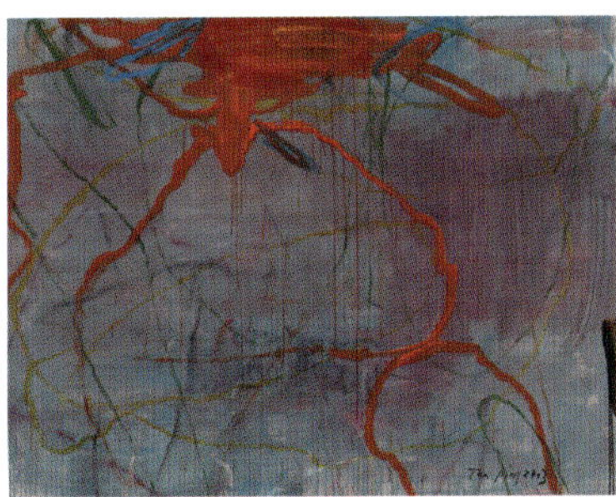

14

Tan Ping began working on the "Overlay" series. The creative process of a painting titled Overlay No. 2 was documented in its entirety on video. This documentary, as another aspect of Tan Ping's work, reveals discussions on various issues related to "action," "motivation," and other aspects of his painting process.

Tan Ping begann mit der Arbeit an der „Overlay"-Serie. Der kreative Prozess eines Gemäldes mit dem Titel Overlay Nr. 2 wurde vollständig auf Video dokumentiert. Diese Dokumentation, als ein weiterer Aspekt von Tan Pings Arbeit, enthüllt Diskussionen zu verschiedenen Themen im Zusammenhang mit „Handlung", „Motivation" und anderen Aspekten seines Malprozesses.

2014

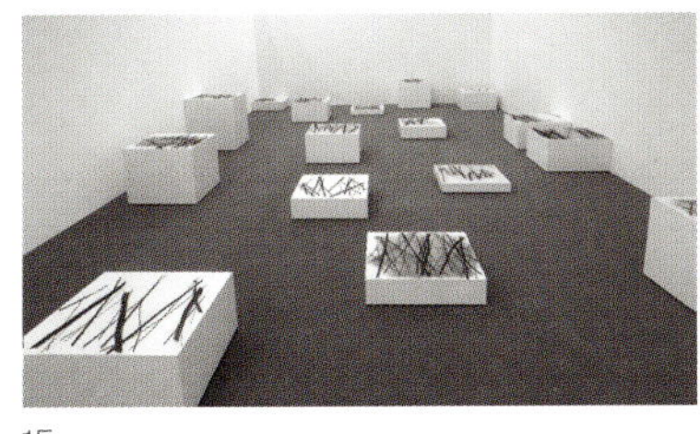

15

Tan Ping was appointed as the Vice President of the Chinese National Academy of Arts. During this period, he produced a large number of sketches, which, much like a diary, recorded the fluctuations of his emotions. In September, an exhibition titled "Follow My Line," featuring primarily these sketches, was held at the PIFO New Art Gallery in Beijing.

Tan Ping wurde zum Vizepräsidenten der Chinesischen Nationalen Kunstakademie ernannt. Während dieser Zeit fertigte er eine große Anzahl von Skizzen an, die wie ein Tagebuch die Schwankungen seiner Gefühle festhielten. Im September fand in der PIFO New Art Gallery in Peking eine Ausstellung mit dem Titel „Follow My Line" statt, in der hauptsächlich diese Skizzen gezeigt wurden.

2015

An exceptionally busy year for Tan Ping. At the start of the year, his exhibition "Follow My Line" moved to the Arizona State University Art Museum in the United States. In May, "Oriental Abstraction VS Western Figuration: A Dialogue between Tan Ping and Luciano Castelli" in collaboration with Swiss artist Luciano Castelli, was held at the National Art Museum of China. In June, following his 2013 painting exhibition "Monologue", the exhibition "Drawing: The Art of Tan Ping," which presented his 2014-2015 creations, opened at the Jinge Art Center. In October, a duo exhibition with Liu Qinghe titled "Divergence" was launched at the Meilun Art Museum in Shangsha. Alongside this, the exhibition catalog Tan Ping was published, providing a comprehensive review of the various directions and threads in Tan Ping's artistic journey.

Ein außergewöhnlich arbeitsreiches Jahr für Tan Ping. Zu Beginn des Jahres zog seine Ausstellung „Follow My Line" in das Arizona State University Art Museum in den USA. Im Mai fand im National Art Museum of China die Ausstellung „Oriental Abstraction VS Western Figuration: A Dialogue between Tan Ping and Luciano Castelli" in Zusammenarbeit mit dem Schweizer Künstler Luciano Castelli statt. Im Juni wurde im Jinge Art Center nach seiner Gemäldeausstellung „Monologue" aus dem Jahr 2013 die Ausstellung „Drawing: The Art of Tan Ping" eröffnet, in der seine Kreationen aus den Jahren 2014-2015 präsentiert wurden. Im Oktober wurde im Meilun Art Museum in Shangsha eine Doppelausstellung mit Liu Qinghe mit dem Titel „Divergence" eröffnet. Parallel dazu wurde der Ausstellungskatalog Tan Ping veröffentlicht, der einen umfassenden Überblick über die verschiedenen Richtungen und Stränge von Tan Pings künstlerischer Reise bietet.

2016

At the Shanghai Oil Painting and Sculpture Institute Art Museum, Tan Ping and Swiss artist Luciano Castelli jointly completed China's first museum "White Wall Project." The two artists treated the 1,500-square-meter exhibition space as a site for creative interaction. Tan Ping used an approach of shifting perspectives, responding with abstract and gestural lines to Castelli's relatively figurative and perspectival images.
In late December, Tan Ping was invited to Helmhaus Zurich, Switzerland, for a ten-day on-site creation. For the first time, he broke the boundary between the canvas and the exhibition space, allowing large areas of black on the canvas to spill over onto the walls. This marked a new milestone in Tan Ping's painting, as it ventured into spatial expression. The exhibition, titled "Beyond Every Mountain is Another Mountain," initiated a dialogue between Tan Ping and Swiss audiences.

Im Shanghai Oil Painting and Sculpture Institute Art Museum stellten Tan Ping und der Schweizer Künstler Luciano Castelli gemeinsam Chinas erstes Museum „White Wall Project" fertig. Die beiden Künstler betrachteten die 1.500 Quadratmeter große Ausstellungsfläche als Ort kreativer Interaktion. Tan Ping verwendete einen Ansatz wechselnder Perspektiven und reagierte mit abstrakten und gestischen Linien auf Castellis relativ figurative und perspektivische Bilder. Ende Dezember wurde Tan Ping für eine zehntägige Kreation vor Ort ins Helmhaus Zürich in der Schweiz eingeladen. Zum ersten Mal durchbrach er die Grenze zwischen Leinwand und Ausstellungsraum und ließ große schwarze Bereiche der Leinwand auf die Wände überlaufen. Dies markierte einen neuen Meilenstein in Tan Pings Malerei, da sie sich in den räumlichen Ausdruck wagte. Die Ausstellung mit dem Titel „Hinter jedem Berg liegt ein anderer Berg" initiierte einen Dialog zwischen Tan Ping und dem Schweizer Publikum.

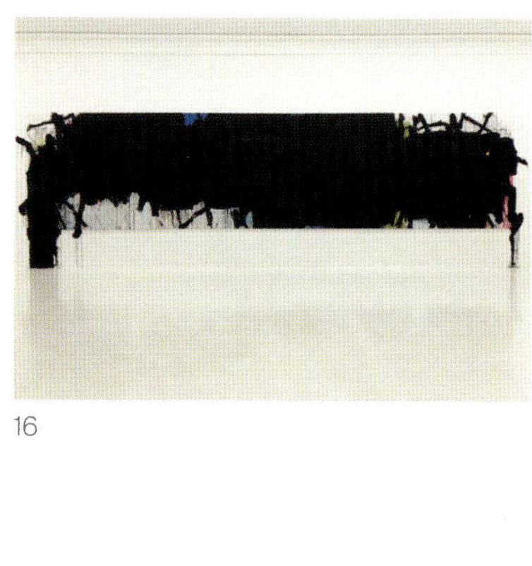

16

Fig. / **Abb**. 16. Tan Ping, *Beyond Every Mountain Is Another Mountain*, 2016-2017 installation view / **Installationsansicht** Helmhaus Zurich, Switzerland

Fig. / **Abb**. 17. *Duet: A Tan Ping Retrospective*, 2019 installation view / **Installationsansicht** Yuz Museum, Shanghai, China

Fig. / **Abb**. 18. *Duet: A Tan Ping Retrospective*, 2019 installation view / **Installationsansicht** Yuz Museum, Shanghai, China

2017

In February, Tan Ping held his first solo exhibition in Hong Kong, titled "Certainty in Uncertainty", curated by Huang Du at the Leo Gallery. Tan Ping brought the large-scale paintings he had previously created at Helmhaus Zurich into the gallery space, reworking them through an uncertain process to redefine the concept of "presence." This once again broke the traditional logic of painting, presenting an exhibition that blended "abstract"

Im Februar veranstaltete Tan Ping seine erste Einzelausstellung in Hongkong mit dem Titel „Certainty in Uncertainty", kuratiert von Huang Du in der Leo Gallery. Tan Ping brachte die großformatigen Gemälde, die er zuvor im Helmhaus Zürich geschaffen hatte, in die Galerieräume und überarbeitete sie in einem unsicheren Prozess, um das Konzept der „Präsenz" neu zu definieren. Dies brach erneut

elements with "live action" for the audience.
In April, Tan Ping held a solo exhibition at Yuan Art Museum in Beijing, titled "…", where no painting elements were presented. Instead, carefully arranged "light tubes" along the turns of the walls became the main creative feature. The "empty" exhibition hall, along with all actions on-site, became the work itself. This challenged conventional perceptions of exhibitions, allowing for open-ended personal participation, experience, and interpretation.
In September, the solo exhibition "Tan Ping" was held at the Horsens Museum of Modern Art, one of Denmark's most important contemporary art museums. Over 20 large-scale paintings created in recent years were presented to the Western art world for the first time. Additionally, he created a site-specific work Fairy Tale, a painting over ten meters long, in the homeland of Hans Christian Andersen.

mit der traditionellen Logik der Malerei und präsentierte dem Publikum eine Ausstellung, die „abstrakte" Elemente mit „Live-Action" vermischte. Im April veranstaltete Tan Ping eine Einzelausstellung im Yuan Art Museum in Peking mit dem Titel „…", in der keine Malereielemente präsentiert wurden. Stattdessen wurden sorgfältig angeordnete „Lichtröhren" entlang der Wandkurven zum wichtigsten kreativen Element. Die „leere" Ausstellungshalle wurde zusammen mit allen Aktionen vor Ort zum Werk selbst. Dies stellte konventionelle Wahrnehmungen von Ausstellungen in Frage und ermöglichte eine offene persönliche Teilnahme, Erfahrung und Interpretation. Im September fand die Einzelausstellung „Tan Ping" im Horsens Museum of Modern Art statt, einem der wichtigsten Museen für zeitgenössische Kunst in Dänemark. Über 20 großformatige Gemälde, die in den letzten Jahren entstanden sind, wurden der westlichen Kunstwelt erstmals präsentiert. Darüber hinaus schuf er ein ortsspezifisches Werk namens Fairy Tale, ein über zehn Meter langes Gemälde in der Heimat von Hans Christian Andersen.

2018

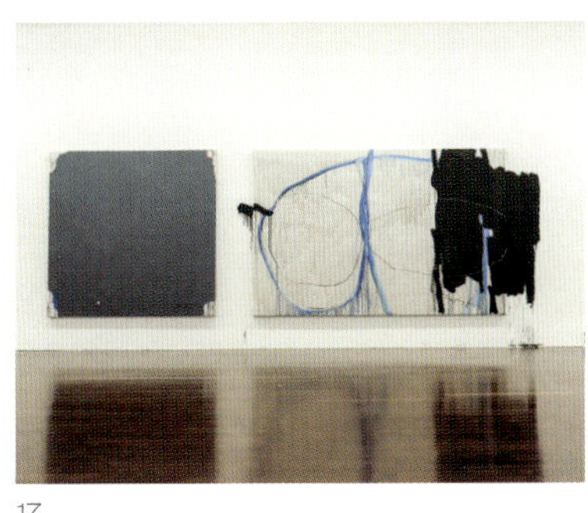
17

Tan Ping's solo exhibition at Platform China, titled "Tan Ping 1993: The Beginning of Two Modules", was curated by Cui Cancan.
In December, Tan Ping participated in the exhibition "Minimalism: Space. Light. Object", co-organized by the National Gallery Singapore and the ArtScience Museum, featuring two of his works: +40m and 60×60. Curated by Adrian George, this large-scale exhibition was considered to be the first museum exhibition in Southeast Asia dedicated to Minimalism. Tan Ping's works were exhibited alongside those of Donald Judd, one of the Minimalist Greats.

Tan Pings Einzelausstellung bei Platform China mit dem Titel „Tan Ping 1993: Der Beginn zweier Module" wurde von Cui Cancan kuratiert. Im Dezember nahm Tan Ping an der Ausstellung „Minimalismus: Raum. Licht. Objekt" teil, die von der National Gallery Singapore und dem ArtScience Museum gemeinsam organisiert wurde und zwei seiner Werke zeigte: +40m und 60×60. Diese groß angelegte Ausstellung, kuratiert von Adrian George, galt als die erste Museumsausstellung in Südostasien, die sich dem Minimalismus widmete. Tan Pings Werke wurden neben denen von Donald Judd, einem der wichtigsten Minimalisten, ausgestellt.

2019

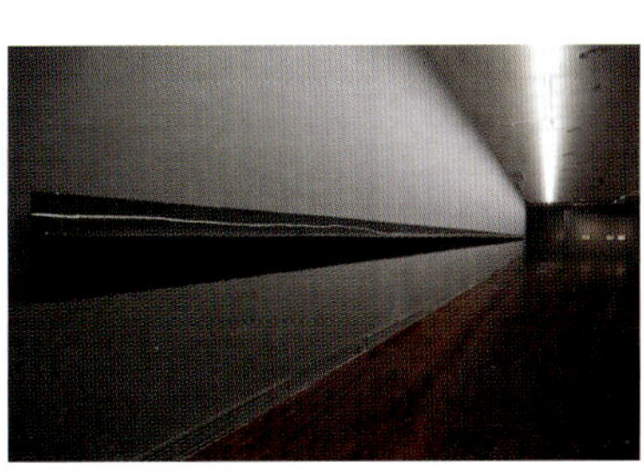
18

From June to September, the exhibition "Duet: A Tan Ping Retrospective" was held at the Yuz Museum in Shanghai, curated by Wu Hung. The exhibition featured over 40 works, including paintings, prints, site-specific paintings, and videos, tracing the artist's growth, life, and reflections. It provided a view into Tan Ping's 35-year artistic evolution, observed through the lens of personal experience and perspective.

Von Juni bis September fand im Yuz Museum in Shanghai die Ausstellung „Duett: Eine Tan Ping-Retrospektive" statt, kuratiert von Wu Hung. Die Ausstellung zeigte über 40 Werke, darunter Gemälde, Drucke, ortsspezifische Gemälde und Videos, die das Wachstum, das Leben und die Reflexionen des Künstlers nachzeichneten. Sie bot einen Einblick in Tan Pings 35-jährige künstlerische Entwicklung, betrachtet durch die Linse persönlicher Erfahrung und Perspektive.

2020

Tan Ping retired from the Chinese National Academy of Arts.
On October 31st, the exhibition "2020:Tan Ping Site-Specific" opened at Artron Art Center in Shenzhen. Addressing the theme "2020", in an 815-square-meter exhibition space, Tan Ping created a thought-provoking and sacred environment, leading viewers into a profound, contemplative memorial of the soul. In the exhibition's preface, Tan Ping wrote: "2020—the sudden onset of the COVID-19 pandemic made each of us feel the nearness of death. In the darkest moments, art became the light squeezed out in the face of death."

Tan Ping schied aus der Chinesischen Nationalen Kunstakademie aus. Am 31. Oktober wurde die Ausstellung „2020: Tan Ping ortsspezifisch" im Artron Art Center in Shenzhen eröffnet. Unter dem Thema „2020" schuf Tan Ping in einem 815 Quadratmeter großen Ausstellungsraum eine zum Nachdenken anregende und heilige Umgebung, die die Betrachter in eine tiefgründige, kontemplative Gedenkstätte der Seele führte. Im Vorwort der Ausstellung schrieb Tan Ping: „2020 – der plötzliche Ausbruch der COVID-19-Pandemie ließ jeden von uns die Nähe des Todes spüren. In den dunkelsten Momenten wurde die Kunst zum Licht, das angesichts des Todes ausgequetscht wurde."

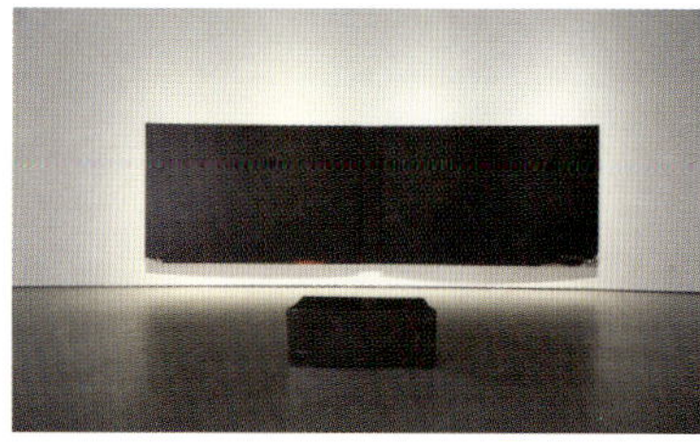

19

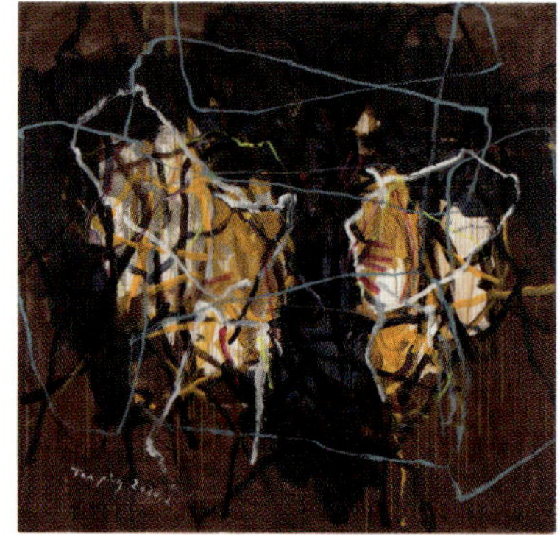

20

2021

Curated by Cui Cancan, the solo exhibition "What is Painting—Tan Ping 1984-2021", which systematically explores Tan Ping's artistic trajectory, opened on May 15 at Tang Contemporary Art Center, Beijing. The exhibition title, both a definitive statement and a question, mirrors the artist's own inquiry—a continuous search for the essence of art, even in times of stagnation.

Die von Cui Cancan kuratierte Einzelausstellung „Was ist Malerei – Tan Ping 1984-2021", die Tan Pings künstlerische Laufbahn systematisch untersucht, wurde am 15. Mai im Tang Contemporary Art Center, Beijing, eröffnet. Der Ausstellungstitel, sowohl eine definitive Aussage als auch eine Frage, spiegelt die eigene Untersuchung des Künstlers wider – eine kontinuierliche Suche nach dem Wesen der Kunst, selbst in Zeiten der Stagnation.

2022

"Farewell 2022", exhibited at Yuan Art Museum, Beijing, is a continuation of "Commemorating 2020". In this piece, Tan Ping reflects on a historically significant moment that profoundly impacted human survival and development. The outbreak of the COVID-19 pandemic brought with it a fear of the virus, anxiety about the unknown, and a deeper understanding of the sudden nearness of death for each of us. As an individual artist confronting the uncertainty of the year 2022, Tan Ping chose a gesture of "farewell"—seeking temporary peace through introspection, as a way to attain spiritual transcendence.

„Farewell 2022", ausgestellt im Yuan Art Museum, Beijing, ist eine Fortsetzung von „Commemorating 2020". In diesem Werk reflektiert Tan Ping über einen historisch bedeutsamen Moment, der das Überleben und die Entwicklung der Menschheit tiefgreifend beeinflusst hat. Der Ausbruch der COVID-19-Pandemie brachte Angst vor dem Virus, Angst vor dem Unbekannten und ein tieferes Verständnis für die plötzliche Nähe des Todes für jeden von uns mit sich. Als individueller Künstler, der mit der Ungewissheit des Jahres 2022 konfrontiert war, wählte Tan Ping eine Geste des „Abschieds" – die Suche nach vorübergehendem Frieden durch Selbstbeobachtung als Weg zur Erlangung spiritueller Transzendenz.

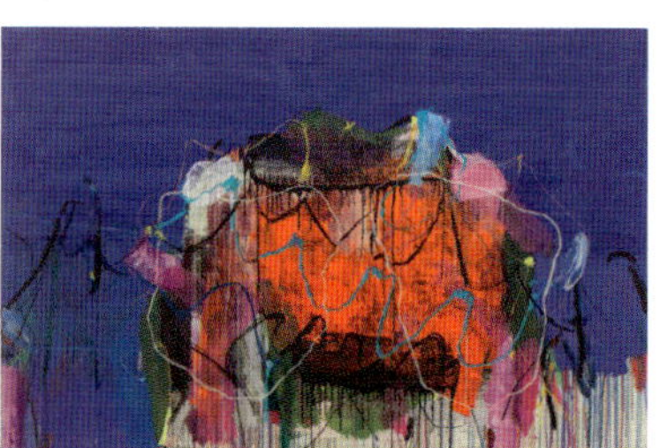

21

Fig. / **Abb**. 19. *2020: Tan Ping Site-Specific*, 2020 installation view / **Installationsansicht** Artron Art Center, Shenzhen, China

Fig. / **Abb**. 20. Tan Ping, *Fear*, 2020

Fig. / **Abb**. 21. Tan Ping, *Cut to the chase*, 2020

Fig. / **Abb**. 22. *Back and Forth The Art of Tan Ping*, 2024, exhibition / **Ausstellung**, Rothko Museum, Daugavpils, Latvia

2023

The exhibition "Internal Cycle" was showcased at ZiWU Beijing, humorously addressing the absurd quarantine policies during the COVID-19 pandemic. Another significant exhibition, "Ask Again: Tan Ping Painting 2020-2023", which was delayed due to the pandemic, was held at the Guangdong

Die Ausstellung „Internal Cycle" wurde im ZiWU Beijing gezeigt und thematisierte auf humorvolle Weise die absurden Quarantänerichtlinien während der COVID-19-Pandemie. Eine weitere bedeutende Ausstellung, „Ask Again: Tan Ping Painting 2020-2023", die aufgrund

Museum of Art. Curated by Cui Cancan, the exhibition featured nearly 40 of Tan Ping's works from the past three years. It explored how painting regained its vitality, feeding back into stories and experiences that shape us in the present. This marked a new starting point for Tan Ping, moving away from "purified formal exploration" to embracing the complexities, ambiguities, and multi-faceted nature of the times reflected in his recent works.

der Pandemie verschoben wurde, fand im Guangdong Museum of Art statt. Die von Cui Cancan kuratierte Ausstellung zeigte fast 40 von Tan Pings Werken aus den letzten drei Jahren. Sie untersuchte, wie die Malerei ihre Vitalität wiedererlangte und auf Geschichten und Erfahrungen zurückgriff, die uns in der Gegenwart prägen. Dies markierte einen neuen Ausgangspunkt für Tan Ping, der sich von der „reinen formalen Erforschung" abwandte und die Komplexität, Mehrdeutigkeit und Vielschichtigkeit der Zeit annahm, die sich in seinen jüngsten Werken widerspiegelt.

2024

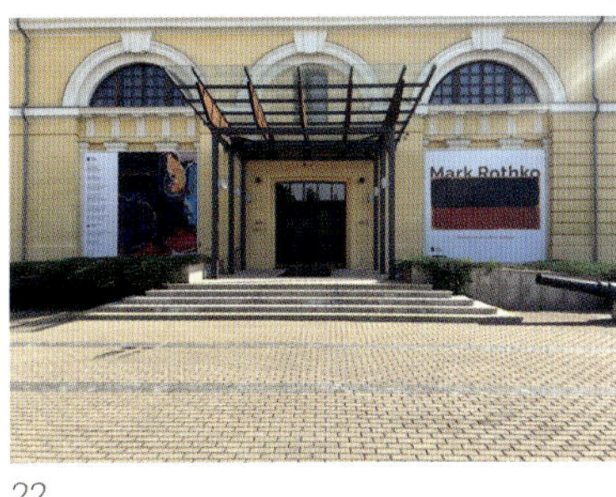

22

As a prominent figure in contemporary abstract art in China, Tan Ping's major exhibition, "Back and Forth: The Art of Tan Ping," officially opened at the Rothko Museum in Latvia, Europe. Curated by Philip Dodd, the exhibition showcases Tan Ping's multifaceted identity as an artist and educator, reflecting his rich life experiences. It also pays tribute to the profound influence that Mark Rothko's works have had on his artistic career.
The exhibition "Tan Ping. Body of Abstraction" is opened at the Ludwig Museum in Koblenz, Germany. This exhibition serves as a retrospective of Tan Ping's artistic journey, marking the 30th anniversary of his graduation from the Berlin University of the Arts in 1994. It highlights the profound influence that studying in Germany has had on his art, as well as how three decades of social changes in both the world and China have shaped his evolving artistic style, resulting in a distinctive artistic voice. This exhibition offers European audiences an opportunity to look into the artistic journey of an Eastern artist who studied in Germany and returned to China during a transformative era marked by China's reform and the fall of the Berlin Wall, providing a unique case study on the relationship between individuals, their times, and art.

Als prominente Figur der zeitgenössischen abstrakten Kunst in China wurde Tan Pings große Ausstellung „Back and Forth: The Art of Tan Ping" offiziell im Rothko-Museum in Lettland, Europa, eröffnet. Die von Philip Dodd kuratierte Ausstellung zeigt Tan Pings facettenreiche Identität als Künstler und Pädagoge und spiegelt seine reichen Lebenserfahrungen wider. Sie würdigt auch den tiefgreifenden Einfluss, den Mark Rothkos Werke auf seine künstlerische Karriere hatten. Die Ausstellung „Tan Ping. Body of Abstraction" wird im Ludwig Museum in Koblenz, Deutschland, eröffnet. Diese Ausstellung ist eine Retrospektive von Tan Pings künstlerischer Reise und markiert den 30. Jahrestag seines Abschlusses an der Universität der Künste Berlin im Jahr 1994. Sie zeigt den tiefgreifenden Einfluss, den sein Studium in Deutschland auf seine Kunst hatte, und zeigt, wie drei Jahrzehnte sozialer Veränderungen sowohl in der Welt als auch in China seinen sich entwickelnden künstlerischen Stil geprägt und ihm eine unverwechselbare künstlerische Stimme verliehen haben. Diese Ausstellung bietet dem europäischen Publikum die Möglichkeit, einen Blick auf die künstlerische Reise eines östlichen Künstlers zu werfen, der in Deutschland studierte und in einer transformativen Ära, die von Chinas Reformen und dem Fall der Berliner Mauer geprägt war, nach China zurückkehrte. Sie bietet eine einzigartige Fallstudie über die Beziehung zwischen Individuen, ihrer Zeit und der Kunst.

Exhibitions
Ausstellungen

Solo Exhibitions
Einzelausstellungen

1991
Tan Ping Prints Exhibition, Gallery Moench, Berlin, Germany

1992
"Calling from the Distance" – Tan Ping Works Exhibition, Gallery Germering, Munich, Germany

1994
Tan Ping Works Exhibition, Gallery Christof Weber, Berlin, Germany

"Beijing – Berlin" Tan Ping Prints Exhibition, Museum of Contemporary Art, Beijing, China

1995
Tan Ping Works Exhibition, Red Gate Gallery, Beijing, China

1999
Tan Ping Works Exhibition, Red Gate Gallery, Beijing, China

2000
Tan Ping Prints Exhibition, Berlin Art Loft, Berlin, Germany

2002
Tan Ping Works Exhibition, Red Gate Gallery, Beijing, China

2003
Tan Ping Works Exhibition, Red Gate Gallery, Beijing, China

2004
Tan Ping Prints Exhibition, Gallery Alexander Ochs, Berlin, Germany

2005
Tan Ping Works Exhibition, National Art Museum of China, Beijing, China

Tan Ping Prints Exhibition, Red Gate Gallery, Beijing, China

2007
Tan Ping Prints Exhibition, Studio Rouge, Shanghai, China

2008
Tan Ping Works Exhibition, Shenzhen Art Museum, Shenzhen, China

"A Metaphor of the Painful" – Tan Ping Works Exhibition, Today Art Museum, Beijing, China

2009
Tan Ping Prints Exhibition, Yun Gallery, Beijing, China

2010
"Tan Ping at Fifty", Red Gallery, Beijing, China

2011
Tan Ping Prints Exhibition, German Embassy, Beijing, China

Tan Ping New Works Exhibition, Yun Gallery, Beijing, China

2012
"A Line", Tan Ping Solo Exhibition, National Art Museum of China, Beijing, China

2013
"Murmurs", Tan Ping Solo Exhibition, Meilidao International Art Institution, Beijing, China

2014
"Follow My Line", Tan Ping Solo Exhibition, PIFO Gallery, Beijing, China

2015
"Tan Ping: Follow My Line", ASU Art Museum, Tempe, USA

"Drawing: The Art of Tan Ping", Ginkgo Space, Beijing, China

2017
"The Certainty of Uncertainty", Leo Gallery, Hong Kong, China

"......", Yuan Art Museum, Beijing, China

"FORM-FORCES", Leo Gallery, Shanghai, China

"TAN PING", Horsens Museum of Modern Art, Horsens, Denmark

2018
"Tan Ping 1993: The Beginning of Two Modules", Platform China, Beijing, China

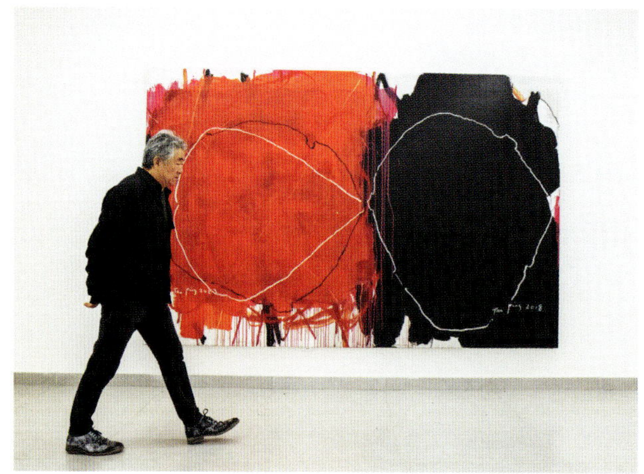

Photo by Zhou Sailan, 2024

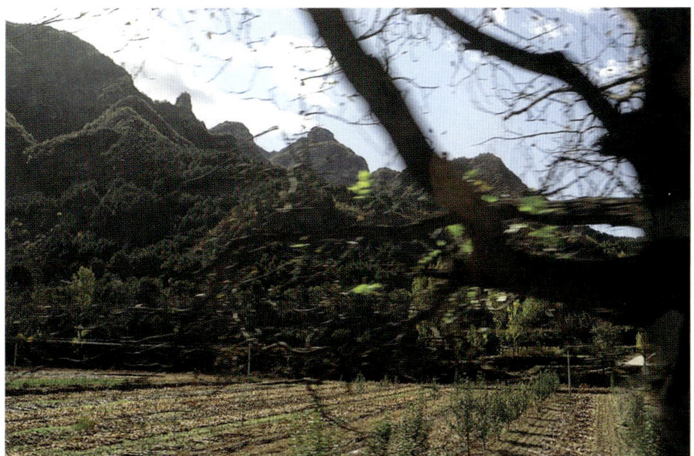

1988
Chinese Artists Works Exhibition, European & Asian Cultural and Art Centre, Paris, France

1995
China – Austria Artists Joint Exhibition, Meridian Gallery, Melbourne, Australia

1998
Chinese Printmaking Exhibition, International Art Palace, Beijing, China

1999
Square Studio Works Exhibition, Shanghai Art Museum, Shanghai, China

2000
Square Studio Works Exhibition, Konrad Adenauer Foundation, Bonn, Germany

2002
Eight Artists' Printmaking, Red Gate Gallery, Beijing, China

2004
The Works of Artists, Square Studio, Beijing, China

2006
"Ruins" Tan Ping and Zhu Jin Shi Works Exhibition, Today Art Museum, Beijing, China

2007
"Friends" China – Denmark Artists Joint Exhibition, Susanne Ottesen Gallery, Copenhagen, Denmark

China – Germany Artists Joint Exhibition, Schreier Von Metternich Gallery, Dusseldorf, Germany

The Works of Artists, Marianne Newman Gallery, Melbourne, Australia

2008
"Grinding the Stone" China – Sweden Artists Joint Exhibition, National Art Museum of China, Beijing, China

China - Sweden Artists Joint Exhibition, Museum of Far Eastern Antiquities, Stockholm, Sweden

"Yipai – 30 Years of Chinese Abstract Art", Caixa Forum, Madrid, Spain

"Dialogue" China – Germany Artists Dual Exhibition, Alexander Ochs Gallery, Berlin, Germany

2010
"The Great Celestial Abstract – Chinese Abstract Art in 21st century", National Art Museum of China, Beijing, China

2011
"The Will of China" Chinese Art Invitation Exhibition, MOCA Beijing, Beijing, China

"Tao of Nature" Chinese Abstract Art Exhibition, MOCA Shanghai, Shanghai, China

2012
"The Unseen" Guangzhou Triennial, Guangdong Art Museum, Guangzhou, China

2013
"ChiFra Art Exhibition", Champs Elysees, Paris France

2014
"In the Absence of Avant - Garde Reading", 798 Art Factory, Beijing, China

"vibrARTion Switzerland 2014", Forms of the Formless: Exhibition of Chinese Abstract Art, art-st-urban, Luzern Switzerland

---

2019
"Duet: A Tan Ping Retrospective", YUZ MUSEUM, Shanghai, China

2020
"2020: Tan Ping Site-specific", Artron Art Center, Shenzhen, China

2021
"Tan Ping: What is Painting 1984-2021", Tang Contemporary Art, Beijing, China

2022
"Boundless", Amanda Wei Gallery, Hong Kong, China

"Farewell 2022", Yuan Art Museum, Beijing, China

"Tan Ping: Internal Cycle", ZiWU, Beijing, China

"Ask Again: Tan Ping Painting 2020-2022", Guangdong Art Museum, Guangzhou, China

2023
"On Paper · Tan Ping's work exhibition", CAN Art Center, Beijing, China

"Intruder", TAG Art Museum, Qingdao China

"Pingo, ergo sum", Tang Contemporary Art, Seoul, Korea

2024
"Back and Forth: The Art of Tan Ping", Rothko Museum, Daugavpils, Latvia

"Tan Ping - Body of Abstraction", Ludwig Museum, Koblenz, Germany

2015

"Oriental Abstraction VS Western Figuration: A Dialogue between Tan Ping and Luciano Castelli" National Art Museum of China, Beijing, China
"Follow My Line" & "Traffic Controls" Tan Ping and Liu Qinghe, Meilun Art Museum, Changsha, China

"The Exhibition of Annual of Contemporary Art of China 2014", Beijing Mingsheng Art Museum, Beijing, China

"The Third Abstraction", Chambers Fine Art, Beijing, China

"Calligraphic Time and Space - Abstract Art in China", Shanghai Contemporary Art Museum, Shanghai, China

"Nonfigurative", Shanghai 21st Century Minsheng Art Museum, Shanghai, China

2016

"The Research Exhibition of Abstract Art in China", Today Art Museum, Beijing, China

"2016 Happy Chinese New Year, Fantastic Art China", Javits Convention Center, New York, USA

"Oriental Abstraction VS Western Figuration: A Dialogue between Tan Ping and Luciano Castelli", SPSI Art Museum of Shanghai, Shanghai, China

"Beyond Every Mountain Is Another Mountain - A Meeting of Contemporary Art From China and Switzerland", Helmhaus Museum, Zurich, Switzerland

2017

"Graffiti and Calligraphy:6 Abstract Artists in China", Arario Gallery, Shanghai, China

"Mutual Supplementary and Wedge", Liu Haisu Art Museum, Shanghai, China

"Unbounded" Casa del Mantegna, Italy, Mantua

"China Dialogue Transmission", Ludwig Museum Koblenz

2018 "

Beijing Abstract", PARKVIEW ART Hong Kong, Hong Kong, China

"ABSTRACTION AS PAINTERLY RHETORIC. A CASE STUDY BETWEEN GERMANY AND CHINA", PIFO Gallery, Beijing, China

"MINIMALISM: SPACE. LIGHT. OBJECT.", ArtScience Museum, Singapore, Singapore

2019

"Painting and Existence", Tang Contemporary Art, Hong Kong, China

"The Gaze of History – Contemporary Chinese Art Revisited", Jupiter Museum of Art, Shenzhen, China

"Latent Paradigm – Research on the Status and Ecology of Chinese Contemporary Art 2019", Today Art Museum, Beijing, China

2020

"Ways of Working: Artists' Time, Space and Body", One Art Museum, Beijing, China

"In Thinking – the Intellectual History and Methodologies of Chinese Contemporary Art", Guangdong Museum of Art, Guangdong, China

"Eingedunkelt" Karl Horst Hödicke, Tan Ping, Leo Gallery, Shanghai, China

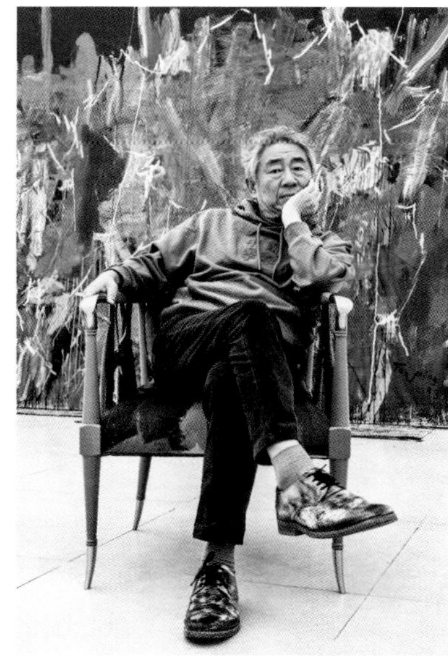

Photo by Zhou Sailan, 2024

2021

"Between and Beyond – A Contemporary Art Quartet", Shandong Art Museum, Jinan, China

2022

"Song of Soul", SOUL Art Center, Beijing, China
2023 "HOU YING & TAN PING" Two-Person Exhibition, Topped Center for Contemporary Art, Xiamen, China

2023

"Boxes: Teng Fei, Tan Ping", OCT Boxes Art Museum, Foshan, China

"MO·SE: Tan Ping & Chen Qi", TAICANG Art Museum, Taicang, China

"The Wild Theatre", Artron Art Center, Shenzhen, China

Collections
Sammlungen

Artron Art Museum, Beijing, China
ASU Art Museum, Tempe, USA
CAFA Art Museum, Beijing, China
Can Art Center, Beijing, China
Chatham Maison Archive Centre, Hongkong, China
Eurasian Art Center, Paris, France
Guangdong Art Museum, Guangzhou, China
Guangzhou Baiyun International Convention Center, Guangzhou, China
He Art Museum, Shunde, China
Hebei Art Museum, Shijiazhuang, China
Hubei Museum of Art, Wuhan, China
Ludwig Museum, Aachen, Germany
Ludwig Museum, Koblenz, Germany
Museum for Modern Visual arts, Kolding, Denmark
National Art of China, Beijing, China
National Centre for the Performing Arts, Beijing, China
PIFO Gallery, Beijing, China
Portland Art Museum, Portland, USA
Qingdao Art Museum, Qingdao, China
Rothko Museum, Daugavpils, Latvia
Shanghai Art Museum, Shanghai, China
Shenzhen Art Museum, Shenzhen, China
SPSI Art Museum of Shanghai, Shanghai, China
TAICANG Art Museum, Taicang, China
Today Art Museum, Beijing, China
Topped Center for Contemporary Art, Xiamen, China
University of Sydney, Sydney, Australia
USC Pacific Asia Museum, Los Angeles, USA
Yuan Art Museum, Beijing, China

Acknowledgements
Dank

Our thanks go first and foremost to Tan Ping, whose great commitment to this exhibition can hardly be adequately recognised. Thanks to his long friendship and excellent collaboration, this unique exhibition project has been realised on the occasion of his graduation from the UDK in Berlin in 1994. In times of global shifts and new focal points in social dialogue, it seems particularly important to us to explore the profound influences of mutual cultural exchange. Tan Ping is an outstanding representative of an innovation in artistic practice in China; as an artist and as a teacher, he contributes to opening up new, experimental forms and courageously breaking new ground for art. The lively art scene in Germany initially had a decisive influence here.

We would like to thank Wei Gallery in Hong Kong for their outstanding support in coordinating the exhibition and the intensive editing of the catalogue. Our thanks also go to all the supporters and sponsors of this exhibition, without whom such a project would hardly have been conceivable.

Last but not least, we would like to thank the team at the publishing house Silvana Editoriale for their profound work on the catalogue and Barbara Leers and Susana Leu, Ludwig Museum, for their editing.

Unser Dank gilt in erster Linie Tan Ping, dessen großes Engagement für diese Ausstellung kaum hinreichend gewürdigt werden kann. Durch die lange Freundschaft und die ausgezeichnete Zusammenarbeit ist dieses besondere Ausstellungsvorhaben, anläßlich seines Abschlusses 1994 an der UDK in Berlin, zustande gekommen. In Zeiten globaler Verschiebungen und neuer Schwerpunkte im gesellschaftlichen Dialog, erscheint es uns besonders wichtig, die tiefgreifenden Einflüsse eines wechselseitigen kulturellen Austausches zu erforschen. Tan Ping ist ein herausragender Vertreter einer Neuerung in der künstlerischen Praxis in China, als Künstler und als Lehrender trägt er dazu bei, neue, experimentelle Formen zu erschließen und mutig Neuland für die Kunst zu betreten. Die vitale Kunstszene in Deutschland hat hier anfänglich maßgeblichen Einfluss gehabt.

Wir danken der Wei Gallery in Hongkong für die hervorragende Unterstützung bei der Koordination der Ausstellung und der intensiven Katalogredaktion. Unser Dank richtet sich ebenso an alle Unterstützer und Sponsoren dieser Ausstellung, ohne die ein solches Projekt kaum denkbar gewesen wäre.

Nicht zuletzt sei dem Team im Verlag Silvana Editoriale für die profunde Arbeit an dem Katalog sowie Barbara Leers und Susana Leu, Ludwig Museum, für die Redaktion gedankt.

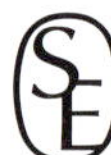

Silvana Editoriale

Director General / *Vorstandsvorsitzender*
Michele Pizzi

Editorial Director / *Verlagsleiter*
Sergio Di Stefano

Art Director
Giacomo Merli

Editorial Coordinator / *Redaktionskoordinator*
Maria Chiara Tulli

Copy Editing / *Redaktion*
Cristina Pradella

Layout
Mirco Ameglio

Production Coordinator / *Produktionskoordination*
Antonio Micelli

Editorial Assistant / *Redaktionsassistentin*
Giulia Mercanti

Photo Editor
Silvia Sala

Press Office / *Pressestelle*
Alessandra Olivari, press@silvanaeditoriale.it

ISBN 978-88-366-5995-1

Available through ARTBOOK | D.A.P.
155 Sixth Avenue, 2nd Floor,
New York, N.Y. 10013
Tel: (212) 627-1999
Fax: (212) 627-9484

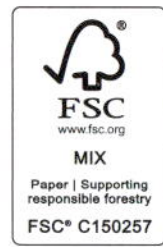

Silvana Editoriale S.p.A.
via dei Lavoratori, 78
20092 Cinisello Balsamo, Milano
tel. 02 453 951 01
fax 02 453 951 51
www.silvanaeditoriale.it

Reproductions, printing and binding in Italy
Reproduktionen, Druck und Einbindung
wurden in Italien ausgeführt

Printed by / Gedruckt von
Esperia Srl, Lavis, Trento, Italy
Fertig gedruckt im November 2024 /
Printed in November 2024

This catalogue is published on the occasion of the exhibition
Dieser Katalog erscheint anlässlich der Ausstellung

Tan Ping. Body of Abstraction

Ludwig Museum im Deutschherrenhaus
December 1st, 2024 to February 23th, 2025
1. Dezember 2024 bis 23. Februar 2025

Editor / Herausgeber
Beate Reifenscheid

Curator / Kurator
Beate Reifenscheid

Editing and Copy editing / Redaktion und Lektorat
Barbara Leers, Ludwig Museum, Koblenz
Suzana Leu, Ludwig Museum, Koblenz

Texts / Texte
Beate Reifenscheid, Lao Zhu (Zhu Qingsheng), Tan Ping, Shan Shui
Jing, He Guiyan, Zhang Jing, Wu Hung, Jiang Jiehong, Peng Feng,
Tony Brown, Achille Bonito Oliva

Photo Credits / Bildnachweise
© Tan Ping, for the reproduction of works by /
für alle abgebildeten von Tan Ping
S. / p. 24: Photo © Stefano Baldini / Bridgeman Images
for / für Hans Hartung: *Rayonnement*, 1962
S./ p. 27: © Christie's Images / Bridgeman Images
for / für Lee Ufan, *From Line*, 1979

Translations / Übersetzungen
Liang Xingyi

1. S./ pp. 58-59: Textauszug von / Text excerpt from He Guiyan: „Time
and Time", 时间"与《时间》, 2015, ISBN 978-7-5356-7420-3, 412 Seiten/
pages.

2. S./ pp. 84-87: Textauszug von / Text excerpt from Peng Feng: „Center
and Periphery: A Philosophical Reading of Tan Ping's Art", 《一划》中
心与边缘：谭平艺术的哲学解读》, 2012, ISBN 978-7-5060-5916-9, 116
Seiten/ pages.

3. S./ pp. 96-97: Textauszug von / Text excerpt from Tony Brown
„Following the Line: Tan Ping's Drawing", 《彳亍：循迹而行：谭平的绘
画》 2014, unanhängiger Verleger / independent publisher, 142 Seiten/
pages.

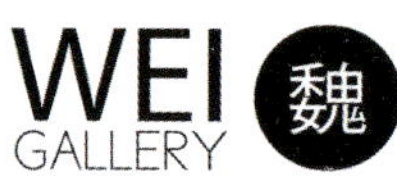
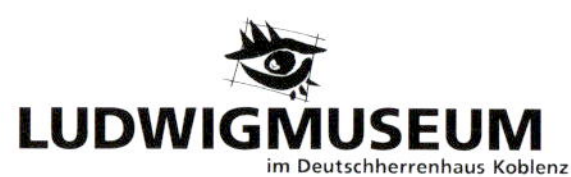
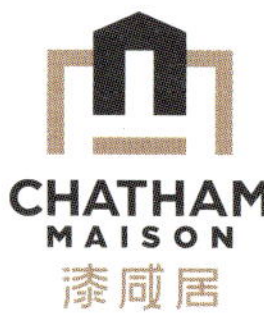
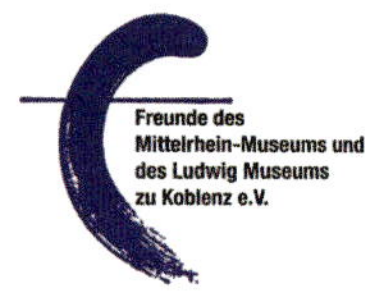
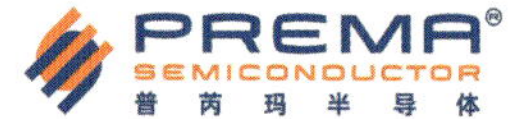
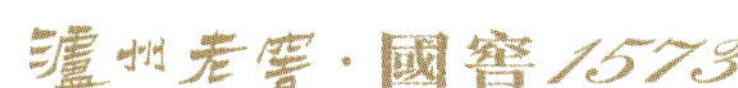